D1368525

Trade Theory and
Economic Reform:
North, South, and East

Trade Theory and Economic Reform: North, South, and East

Essays in Honor of Béla Balassa

edited by

Jaime de Melo
and
André Sapir

Basil Blackwell

June 18, 1991

To Jakob —
who is also
dedicated to
excellence in all
that he endeavors.

Carol
Mark, Gabor

First published 1991

Basil Blackwell, Inc.
3 Cambridge Center
Cambridge, Massachusetts 02142, USA

Basil Blackwell Ltd
108 Cowley Road, Oxford, OX4 1JF, UK

British Library of Congress Cataloguing in Publication Data
Trade theory and economic reform—North, South, and East: essays in
   honor of Béla Balassa / edited by Jaime de Melo and André Sapir.
         p.   cm.
      Includes bibliographical references and index.
      ISBN 1–55786–256–7
      1. International trade—Congresses.   2. Economic development—
Congresses.   3. Balassa, Bela A.—Congresses.   I. Balassa, Bela A.
II. De Melo, Jaime.   III. Sapir, André.
HF1372.T75   1991   90–19642
382—dc20   CIP

British Library Cataloguing in Publication Data
A CIP catalogue record for this book is available from the British Library.

Typeset in 10pt Times roman by the World Bank
Printed in Great Britain by the University Press, Cambridge

Contents

Contributors

Irma Adelman, *University of California, Berkeley*
Robert E. Baldwin, *University of Wisconsin, Madison*
Peter Berck, *University of California, Berkeley*
Jean-Marc Burniaux, *Organization for Economic Cooperation and Development*
William Byrd, *World Bank*
Hollis Chenery, *Harvard Institute for International Development*
W. Max Corden, *Paul Nitze School of Advanced International Studies, Johns Hopkins University*
Henrik Dahl, *Vollmond Securities, Copenhagen*
Paul De Grauwe, *University of Leuven*
Rudiger Dornbusch, *Massachusetts Institute of Technology*
J. Michael Finger, *World Bank*
Stanley Fischer, *World Bank*
Alan Gelb, *World Bank*
Tatsuo Hatta, *Osaka University and Yale University*
Gottfried Haberler, *American Enterprise Institute*
Alexis Jacquemin, *Université Catholique de Louvain*
Charles P. Kindleberger, *Massachusetts Institute of Technology.*
János Kornai, *Harvard University*
Miroljub Labus, *University of Belgrade*
Marie Lavigne, *University of Paris I*
Edmond Malinvaud, *Collège de France*
Jaime de Melo, *World Bank*
Pradeep K. Mitra, *World Bank*
Mieko Nishimizu, *World Bank*
Marcus Noland, *Institute for International Economics*
John M. Page, Jr., *World Bank*
David Roland-Holst, *Mills College*
André Sapir, *Université Libre de Bruxelles*
T.N. Srinivasan, *Yale University*
Ernest Stern, *World Bank*
Wendy E. Takacs, *University of Maryland, Baltimore*
Dominique Van der Mensbrugghe, *University of California, Berkeley*
Timothy Vogelsang, *Princeton University*
Dušan Vujovic, *University of Belgrade*
Jean Waelbroeck, *Université Libre de Bruxelles*

Preface

We had long had the idea of preparing a festschrift in honor of Béla Balassa and had planned to present him with a volume on his sixty-fifth birthday. His recent illness, however, demanded an immediate gesture of moral support. In July 1989, we started to contact friends, colleagues, and students of Béla for contributions to the volume. As the list of contributors testifies, the response was overwhelming despite the tight schedule we imposed. The volume was complete by March 1990 and was presented to Béla at a conference in his honor. Most of the contributors as well as many other friends and colleagues gathered at the conference to pay tribute to Béla's long and productive career.

A great deal of advance organization was required to prepare the festschrift and the conference. We would like to thank Maria Ameal, Karla Cabana, and Rebecca Sugui for their unfailing logistical support. This volume could not have been produced without Meta de Coquereaumont's cheerful and dedicated editorial work. We also enjoyed planning the project with Carol Balassa, Norma Campbell, and Jean Waelbroeck, who provided many useful ideas. Special thanks are also due to Andras Inotai for his valuable help. Finally, we are grateful to the World Bank for generous support under RPO 675-37. To all these friends and colleagues, we extend our appreciation.

To Béla

Polyglot and world traveler, Béla Balassa is the international economist *par excellence*. No topic has escaped his prolific pen, from Hungarian economic planning to Japan's trade policies. It is no wonder he is one of the most cited economists. But Béla also has a lighter side in his writing, well represented by an anthology of French poetry and a primer in culinary economics.

Béla began his professional life as a factory manager. Only several years later did he return to academic pursuits. This unorthodox path led the way to an unusual career characterized throughout by a strong desire to link empirical observations with theory, to derive practical methods, and to give policy advice.

Much of Béla's writing reflects two powerful influences. One, the work of John Stuart Mill on liberal economic philosophy, was the subject of his maiden paper in English. Reading Mill gave Béla a life-long faith in the superiority of markets over central planning. The other strong influence was his life in Hungary as a young man, living under a regime that suppressed both political and economic freedom. His political background led him to internal exile for two years and, eventually, forced him out of the country after the dramatic events of November 1956.

Although he became a U.S. citizen, Hungary has remained his country. Every few years, he evaluates Hungarian economic policies. Long before perestroika, he advocated reform of the economy from central planning to a market-oriented system.

Next to his deep ties to Hungary, Béla keeps up a life-long French connection. His attachment to France, where he and his family spend their summers, is still an enigma to his colleagues. Is it the culinary delights or the local brand of planning that attracts him? His culinary guide, although never officially issued by the World Bank travel office, is at the top of the list of "required documents" for Bank staff going on mission via Paris. Between restaurant samplings, Béla found time to check on the French proclivity toward *dirigisme*. As early as 1965, he foresaw that local indicative planning would become inconsistent with European integration.

The establishment of the European Common Market in the late 1950s heightened interest in economic integration. And to quote Fritz Machlup, "the flow of [Béla's] untiring theoretical as well as empirical research in this field has been virtually unrivaled." On the theoretical front, he produced a classic text that considered all facets of economic integration. In particular, along with Tibor Scitovsky, Béla saw that economic integration could create the conditions for exploitation of scale economies and for more effective competition, themes that have resurfaced in the current debate on the completion of the European internal market. At the same time, on the empirical front, he produced and directed assessments of the Common Market indicating its net trade-creating effect.

In his acclaimed 1964 paper on the purchasing power parity doctrine, Béla gave a theoretical justification for the observed relationship between purchasing power parities and exchange rates. The explanation rested on intercountry differences in productivity levels between traded and nontraded activities and on the tendency for the prices of traded goods to be equalized across countries. Under these conditions, relatively high-productivity (or high-income) countries would tend to exhibit relatively high prices of nontraded goods. In turn, income comparisons based on exchange rates would result in an overstatement of real incomes in rich countries.

Béla's great interest in practical methods is apparent throughout his contributions to the international trade literature. In the mid-1960s he published, in rapid succession, papers offering measures that have become indispensable tools in the kit of applied international economics. The index of revealed comparative advantage (RCA) is a practical measure of a country's trade pattern. The index of intraindustry trade (IIT), subsequently elaborated by Herbert Grubel and Peter Lloyd, enables the distinction between inter- and intraindustry patterns of specialization. Measurements based on the IIT revealed the importance of intraindustry trade which in turn provided the motivation for the modern theory of international trade. Finally, the effective rate of protection (ERP), jointly developed with Max Corden and Harry Johnson, is now routinely used to assess the restrictiveness of a country's trade policies.

Béla never overlooks the policy implications of his empirical work on international trade. Applications of the IIT showed that trade liberalization within the European Common Market led primarily to intraindustry specialization rather than to interindustry specialization. So Béla, along with others, argued that the adjustment costs associated with European trade liberalization would be relatively small. Likewise, in his work on the determinants of the pattern of trade, he advocated that countries' trade policies be made consistent with the pattern of comparative advantage dictated by their evolving factor endowments.

In the mid-1960s, when Béla entered the development field, it was dominated by towering figures — Arthur Lewis, Gunnar Myrdal, Raul Prebisch. For the previous two decades, the profession, under their leadership, had advocated an inward-looking development strategy based on export pessimism. Within that context, pride of place was given to planning rather than to the market. There were, however, a few rebels like Gottfried Haberler and Jacob Viner. Béla naturally sided with them. Not only did he, along with a few others, refute the arguments of the export pessimists, but he went well beyond. To him, there are boundless export opportunities for countries that can seize them. Export-oriented policies are the key to growth for developing countries.

Without ever advocating free trade, Béla recommended a system of incentives that did not discriminate between sales for domestic markets and sales for foreign markets. The rationale for this position came from his strongly held view that the small size of domestic markets in developing countries prevents the establishment of an efficient manufacturing sector. Although Béla supported the principle of economic integration to overcome the limitation imposed by domestic market size, he fought actual experiments in integration among developing countries because they were usually established under excessively high external protection.

With equal determination, Béla strove to establish empirically the superiority of export orientation over inward orientation. From his multicountry studies on the structure of protection, he showed that countries with more uniform protection levels between domestic and export sales had higher export growth. In turn, he emphasized a positive correlation between export performance and economic growth. Following the oil shocks, Béla also developed a practical methodology for studying the adjustment experience of developing countries to an adverse external environment. He showed that outward-oriented countries, thanks to their added flexibility, fared better than inward-oriented ones.

At the beginning of the 1990s, looking back at Béla's contributions up to this point, one is struck by his consistency and perseverance in the advocacy of economic liberalism. What a satisfaction it must be for Béla to observe the changes toward market orientation in so many countries, not the least those in Eastern Europe. Even if the achievements are still fragile, one can hardly imagine a greater satisfaction for a policy-oriented economist.

It is with great pleasure and pride that we present you, our teacher, adviser, and colleague, with this volume in recognition of your contributions.

Brussels, December 1989
Jaime de Melo   *André Sapir*

A Tribute to Béla

Gottfried Haberler

I met Béla Balassa for the first time in Vienna in 1956, the year Russian tanks put down the Hungarian revolution. Béla was one of the Freedom Fighters who fought the Russians and were driven into Austria. He was then twenty-eight years old and had already made a remarkable career in Budapest, both in academia and in the business world. On the academic side, Béla was awarded a degree, corresponding to the B.A. of an American business school, from the Academy for Foreign Trade of Budapest in 1948. At the University of Budapest he earned a *doctor juris rerumque politicarum* (doctor of law and political sciences, including economics) and did some teaching. To mention just two of his various non-academic activities, in 1951-52 he was head of finances at an alcohol factory, and in 1953-56 he was a planner and later head of the price and cost department, Construction Trust, Hungary.

From Vienna, Béla went to the United States, where over the next ten years he had a most impressive career and was fortunate to have the guidance of his great compatriot, the late professor William Fellner. In 1957-59 he took his M.A. and Ph.D. in economics at Yale University; from 1959 to 1961, he was an assistant professor at Yale; in 1961-62, a visiting assistant professor at the University of California, Berkeley; in 1962-67, an associate professor at Yale; and in 1963-64, a visiting associate professor at Columbia University.

In 1966, ten years after he had left Hungary, he was appointed professor of political economy, Johns Hopkins University, and was a consultant for the World Bank. From these prestigious and strategic positions he has been operating ever since, teaching at the university and supervising the work of his students, and organizing research at the World Bank and visiting developing countries to advise them on economic policy. Many of his reports have been published by the Bank (see his bibliography at the end of this volume).

Béla's favorite foreign country is France. He has frequently lectured at the University of Paris and at provincial universities. Béla has always been a great gourmet, managing on his trips to seek out and discover good food and then to write about it in a culinary guide for his friends.

In 1987 he was struck by cancer of the larynx and esophagus and had to undergo several operations. His voice was reduced to a whisper, and he cannot eat or drink through his mouth. These are formidable handicaps, but with the loving care of his wife Carol and the support of his daughter Mara (nineteen years old) and his son Gabor (seventeen years old), Béla recovered sufficiently to resume work at the World Bank. Although the loss of his voice makes oral communication very difficult for him, he has conducted some seminars with his students in the university. In 1989 he even managed to make two trips abroad, one to Hungary and the other to his beloved Paris, where he was awarded an honorary degree from the Sorbonne.

In this short note, I cannot discuss any of Béla's many important contributions to economics. The reader will find all that in the papers in this volume. I will confine myself to saying that Béla Balassa is undoubtedly one of the great economists of his generation. That has been widely recognized. In addition to the honorary doctorate from the Sorbonne, he was awarded the much coveted Bernhard-Harms prize by the prestigious Institute for World Economics in Kiel, West Germany. In 1986, Béla delivered the V.K. Ramaswami Memorial Lecture in New Delhi, India, and in 1987 he delivered the Böhm-Bawerk Memorial Lecture in Innsbruck, Austria.

Béla at the World Bank

Hollis Chenery

When I arrived at the World Bank in 1970, Béla Balassa was already a consultant there. He soon became one of my advisers. His wide-ranging interests and disciplined energy have enabled him to carry two nearly full-time jobs: teaching at Johns Hopkins University and doing research and advising at the World Bank. As organized by Béla, the two endeavors are mutually reinforcing.

In retrospect, it appears that the World Bank and Béla Balassa were made for each other. The Bank's orientation is comparative, as is Béla's in most of his work. Béla ranges widely over the fields of international economics, trade, development, and country studies. In his quarter century as a consultant at the World Bank, Béla has developed an analytical style that leads to easy communication with the Bank's country economists as well as its researchers, and which makes him both a good team leader for Bank missions and an effective adviser to country officials.

Like most of us, Béla also has the defects of his qualities. He is known to some as a rather dogmatic advocate of neoclassical economics and outward-oriented trade policies. Yet while my views occasionally differ from his, I have never found that the differences get in the way of empirically based discussions of development policy. On the contrary, Béla's participation in a discussion or seminar tends to raise its quality to a higher level.

One of my first assignments from Robert McNamara at the World Bank was to draw up a research program for the Bank. I asked Béla for help, and he quickly became a strong supporter of this venture. He was a principal contributor to the Bank's first research program in 1972 and continued to provide guidance throughout its formative years, as the program evolved into what is now a very substantial enterprise. One of its main features has been its equal treatment of proposals from researchers in advanced and developing countries. A typical research project also combines scholars from inside and outside the Bank to ensure an inflow of new ideas and to challenge the preconceptions that may exist on either side.

Over the years, Béla has developed a form of policy-oriented research that has struck a responsive chord among those in the operating departments of the Bank as well as its researchers. Because of the expansive geographic range of his work — he has conducted country studies in virtually all parts of the world — he can readily adapt and apply his conclusions to many different political and institutional settings. Béla's work on semi-industrial countries and on comparative advantage in manufacturing are notable examples of his broad-ranging interests.

As is true of any institution, the World Bank depends not only on the formal structure that is reflected in job descriptions and the chain of command, but also on informal networks based on intellectual leadership and friendly criticism. Béla is a master of the informal network. Whether it be the hiring of an economist, the setting up of a committee, or the evaluation of a manuscript, Béla is likely to be consulted. This role is strengthened by the fact that he has no organizational axe to grind in the Bank.

Béla's talents as tutor, critic, and professional guide are apparent throughout the contributions to this book. These are the skills of the university rather than the bureaucracy, and they constitute a form of external economy that contributes inestimably to the research environment. Making room for people with these kinds of skills is important for any organization that aspires to scholarly functions.

In this age of specialization, the perspective and contributions of a broader approach tend to be underestimated. Béla has chosen an intermediate position that combines the best qualities of the specialist and the generalist. In my view, Béla Balassa's principal contribution to development research — at the World Bank and outside it — has been his ability to blend theory and policy issues and to place every study in the broad framework of policy analysis that has been put together over the years.

Béla Balassa: An Appreciation[*]

Ernest Stern

It is a great honor to join many others in paying tribute to our colleague of many years, Béla Balassa.

Béla's accomplishments are numerous, and the scope of his interests is very broad. I think this is very well represented in the range of topics that have been chosen with great difficulty for the festschrift. I do not want to preempt the discussions or to dwell on the diversity of Béla's interests for this audience. Rather, I want to comment briefly by way of introduction on the centrality of his advice.

In 1990, it is quite easy to believe that the operations of a market system, the freedom for relative price movements, and a relatively open trading system have been commonplace features of development strategy and advice. But we know that while it might be very comforting to believe that that has been the case, it is wide of the mark. Not only was there a pervasive pessimism about the ability of developing countries to compete in export markets, but there was also a basic belief that somehow developing countries ought to have a more benign set of economic rules facing them than did the rest of the world. Now this very compassionate concern with the ability of developing countries to compete in domestic markets and externally, this concern with their ability to manage conditions of uncertainty, soon turned this desire into operational objectives that affected trade regimes adversely, tended to bloat governments, distorted markets and prices, and had all the other undesirable effects with which we are now all too familiar.

Within the development economics community, there was a widespread, although perhaps somewhat implicit, view that there was a third way, somewhere between the forces of a market economy and the rigidities of a planned system. It was clear that central planning was too rigid, and yet market systems seemed too rigorous. Consequently, many development economists and certainly many development economics practitioners focused on the marginal changes (in prices, interest rates, subsidies) that would tend to reduce the more obvious inefficiencies.

Today, looking back, we realize that much of the economic advice to developing countries would have been more beneficial had it been more clearly focused

---

[*]The remarks reproduced here were made at the conference in honor of Béla Balassa held at the World Bank on March 23, 1990.

on the fundamentals. Béla has been one of those who has stayed with the fundamentals since he first came to the World Bank. He has consistently emphasized the importance of effectively functioning markets and of analyses that focus on efficient investment decisions. While he was fully cognizant of the institutional weaknesses in developing countries, he nonetheless stressed time and again the importance of not discriminating between foreign and domestic markets and of the ability of developing countries, given a proper framework and proper support, to compete. He provided us with the tools for assessing the costs of protection and the growth-stimulating effects of export-oriented policies.

The World Bank's economic work in the 1960s and 1970s very much reflected the views that were prevalent in the development community at large. And in those days, too, there was quite a weak link between our economic analysis and our operational strategies. And Béla's contribution must be seen and appreciated at many different levels. His clear, persistent, and elegant analyses contributed to a rethinking of the basic approach to development strategies. He contributed to what we can see today as a great shift in thought. Indeed, at the analytical level, it is fair to say that his work helped us to think less about development economics and more about the economic issues facing developing countries. Béla's contribution was not only that of a superb analyst dedicated to a liberal economic approach but also his clear understanding that analysis alone does not move policymakers. And his abilities as a teacher served him remarkably well in his advisory role to the many developing countries around the world.

Supported by his often path-breaking analysis of the effects of trade regimes in specific countries — and he often did that path-breaking analysis in countries where no data were available, or so it seemed to the rest us — he was able to persuade policymakers to consider the costs of protection, to appreciate the opportunities created by change, and to take the difficult and almost always unpopular steps needed to liberalize their trade regimes. His analytical contributions and his work in individual countries were both precursors of and important contributions to the World Bank's evolving role in macroeconomic and structural adjustment issues. Within the Bank, Béla's blend of creative analysis and persistent attention to the fundamentals and his capacity for practical dissemination gradually made our focus on more equal and lower tariffs and reductions and eventual elimination of quantitative restrictions seem increasingly routine. Trade liberalization has become the centerpiece in virtually all of our adjustment programs.

The World Bank has a very peculiar culture that blends a high level of intellectual capacity and curiosity with strong antibodies to outsiders. And on our operational side, there is a limited tolerance of academics. I realize that it is not going to be rated as one Béla's greatest achievements historically, but seen from the inside it is nonetheless quite remarkable how well he has been able to integrate himself and his work with the rest of the Bank, even though that work cuts across functions, regions, and individual pieces of turf. This success is a testimony to his professional skills, his down-to-earth approach, and his qualities as a human being.

The contributions to this volume pay tribute to Béla as an outstanding professional, a creative analyst, and a persuasive teacher. But they do much more than that. They also honor an outstanding human being who has given much to all of us in the Bank and outside and with whom it has been a pleasure to be associated for so many years.

Béla, on behalf of all my colleagues here in the Bank, I want to say, "thank you."

Béla: The Economist and the Person[*]

Stanley Fischer

It is hard to follow Ernie Stern, Jagdish Bhagwati, Jean Waelbroeck, Irma Adelman, Rudi Dornbusch, and those who have spoken from the floor in discussing Béla's work and Béla the person. I would like to speak first about Béla the professional economist. Béla's main contributions as measured by the Index of Social Science Citations are, in order, *The Structure of Protection in Developing Countries* (1971), "The Purchasing-Power Parity Doctrine: A Reappraisal" (1964), "Tariff Protection in Industrial Countries: An Evaluation" (1965), and *The Theory of Economic Integration* (1961), which was his thesis and which is still referred to regularly. And, of course, his primer on culinary economics has had a very wide readership, and many of us have read his article, "My Life Philosophy."

I do not want to discuss all of those books and articles, but I did go back and look at two of them, which I had read as an undergraduate — "The Purchasing-Power Parity Doctrine" and *The Theory of Economic Integration*. When I was an undergraduate at the London School of Economics, Karl Popper was the dominant influence. He tended to discuss not so much the economics but the methodology by which a particular position had been reached. I remember the discussion of Béla's article on purchasing power parity, which was a subject of several consecutive seminars. We argued about whether Béla really had a theory, whether he was really testing it, or whether it was a tautology. I must say that in rereading the article, I could not understand how we could have spent any time discussing this issue, because it is patently clear that it is a very simple theory, a very persuasive theory, a tested theory, and it has other implications that have been tested subsequently. This is a justifiably famous article, and its point is really very basic, as Rudi Dornbusch recognizes in his contribution to this festschrift, which is about purchasing power parity. When you read Béla's article now, you still appreciate the sophistication of what Béla did some twenty-five years ago. There is nothing much that you would change in that article in the light of modern econometrics or of any other discipline. I think I caught Béla once slipping on the distinction between absolute prices and relative prices, but that was really all I could find to fault in this substantial article. And I, too, was struck in reading it, as Rudi Dornbusch was, by its relevance to one of the key issues regularly discussed at the World Bank, which is how to measure real income.

---

[*]The remarks reproduced here were made at the conference in honor of Béla Balassa held at the World Bank on March 23, 1990.

The other very early work, *The Theory of Economic Integration*, was inspired by the beginnings of the European Common Market and of Latin American regional integration. I think all the important issues are in that book, particularly the emphasis on the dynamic efficiency gains. It also has a good analysis of static efficiency gains. I would say after rereading it that it shows the influence of his continental education in the excessive deference to the literature and to his distinguished predecessors. Also, ideas that I suspect are his own he attributes to several earlier authors, either to render them respectable or out of generosity.

It is also interesting, reading his early work, to recognize so many familiar names, especially in two issues of the *Journal of Political Economy*. The December 1964 issue contains a review of a book on foreign trade and economic development in Africa by Gerry Helleiner, a review by Carl Christ of a book by Henry Rosovsky, a review by Stan Wellisz of a book by Montias on central planning in Poland, and a review by Jagdish Bhagwati of a book by Gerry Meier on international trade and development. Not only that, but Béla's article is followed by articles by two of his contemporaries, Dick Cooper and Paul Samuelson.

The December 1965 issue shows that Béla was already moving toward the World Bank. There were two accompanying articles, one on the "Economics of Usury Regulation," by Rudolph Blitz and Millard Long — and you'll be pleased to know that Millard Long was opposed to usury regulation at the time but did get the issue straight and recognized that some people benefited from it. The other article with a World Bank connection, although it was not a connection at the time, is called "Industrial Conflict in Business Fluctuations: A Comment," by F.S. O'Brien of Williams College and now of the World Bank. So, even then all our friends were around and Béla was among them, as part of a fine company. I guess then, as always, you could judge people by the company they kept.

Béla's contributions within the World Bank have already been noted today by Ernie Stern and by many others. I think if you look at the literature during Béla's association with the Bank, you are impressed by the work on outward orientation, which is far more sophisticated than simple laissez-faire arguments. Béla is very aware of the policies that have to be taken to promote exports and of the role of an active government in the process of developing an outward orientation. When you read that material you are struck by how much is going on beneath the surface, by the far more subtle understanding, particularly of what happened in East Asia, than would be indicated by simple caricatures of that position. I think if you ask what we have learned since then in the Bank, I would say that it is a recognition of the need to go even further and to combine those supportive policies with internal changes, internal deregulation, concerns that have been relatively less emphasized. But the basic emphasis in that work is appropriate.

The other part of Béla's work that is associated with his World Bank period, and a part that in a very satisfying way has come to fruition now, is the work on reform of socialist economies. Throughout his long period of professional work, Béla has retained an interest in the socialist economies not only of Hungary but also of Yugoslavia and the Soviet Union. It is a testimony to his insights that so much of what he has written on socialist economies is visibly apparent in what is now happening in Eastern Europe. There is no question in talking to people in the Bank of the enormous influence that Béla has had and of the enormous respect he has from his colleagues for his professional drive and determination.

I would like also to say something about Béla the person. The first characteristic one notices about Béla is that he is an absolutely prodigious worker — to an extent even greater than Max Corden described to us today. I though Max was going to say that you cannot measure yourself against Harry Johnson, but it is tougher yet in terms of volume of contributions to measure yourself against Béla Balassa. The prodigy of that work was brought home to me in the past two years. The Bank has a Policy, Research, and External Affairs working papers series, of which Béla is the sole reviewer. Every article submitted to that series is reviewed and edited and occasionally rejected by Béla — I think the rate is something like 150 a year. And the review process is extremely thorough. Even when Béla went to the hospital, he demanded that these papers be sent to him, and the reviews kept coming back from the hospital. The amount of work is just astonishing. In fact, Béla himself is a major cause of global warming, just through the number of trees he has caused to be cut to produce the tremendous volume of paper that has one way or another passed through his hands.

And then there is, of course, Béla's judgment, which, in his choice of topics is remarkable. When one reads his work, one sees applied economics at its best. That is, he has a very clear policy question in mind, a very clearly defined issue, and he gets the numbers he wants and applies them. While his choice of topics may be unerring — he has chosen the right and the important ones — he has certain blind spots in his judgment. Rudi Dornbusch mentioned that Béla didn't think that Rudi would succeed in the United States, but of course, he wasn't alone in that judgment: Rudi proudly has hanging on his wall his rejection letter from the MIT graduate program. Béla's other blind spot, I may say, can be seen in his "Life Philosophy," where he reveals that in 1960 he rejected an offer from MIT. This shows again a certain lack of judgment, from which I am sure both he and MIT have suffered.

Nor can one fail to mention Béla the *bon vivant*. I too have used his culinary guide in Paris. The first two of the restaurants he recommended were closed, but the third one was open and it was very good indeed. So again, I must praise Béla's judgment in yet another area. Then there is Béla the family man, and those of us who have had the pleasure of being with Béla's family and talking to them know how lucky he is and how lucky they are in having each other. And finally, of course, there is the sheer courage that Béla has shown, courage on a scale that one is not often privileged to see, courage that we all admire tremendously.

Béla, you honor our profession and I think you honor our Bank with your energy, your devotion, and the intellect you bring to your tasks. You have enriched the lives of millions of people around the world, and we are very proud to have this opportunity to say thank you.

Part I

Trade Theory and Commercial Policy

1

Real Exchange Rates and Purchasing Power Parity

Rudiger Dornbusch and Timothy Vogelsang

Béla Balassa's interest in real exchange rates began with his path-breaking work on purchasing power parity, which formalized and quantified the proposition that relative national price levels over time are determined by differences in productivity growth (Balassa 1964). His interest has focused with even more vigor on the role of real exchange rates in the development strategy. Stable and competitive real exchange rates, in this view, are essential to strong growth performance.

Both strands of Balassa's work have been highly influential. The study of real exchange rates has become a central part of international economics — far more so than was the case in the 1960s when Balassa renewed interest in the topic. And the experience with large fluctuations in the real exchange rate in developed and developing countries has provided fertile ground for developing and testing hypotheses. This essay sketches some of these strands.[1]

Productivity Differentials and Price Discrepancies

Whether relative national price levels are substantially invariant over time, as purchasing power parity doctrine asserts, or whether, to the contrary, they show a trend, continues to be a lively and fruitful topic of research. Balassa (1964) has shown that the relative national price levels of two countries, measured in a common currency, are related systematically to the level of economic development. The real exchange rate or relative price level is expressed as the ratio of price levels, in national currencies, at home (P) and abroad (P^*) times the exchange rate, e (home currency relative to foreign currency):

$$(1) \qquad\qquad R = eP^* \, / \, P.$$

Balassa (1964) found that the country with the more rapid growth experiences an increase in its relative price level. (Figure 1.1 reproduces Balassa's findings.)

This phenomenon is accounted for by differential productivity growth in the traded and nontraded goods sectors of a country and differences in productivity growth across countries. The nontraded goods sectors (haircuts, for example) experience little productivity growth, whereas manufactures, the tradable *par excellence*, is the sector in which it is concentrated. International differentials in

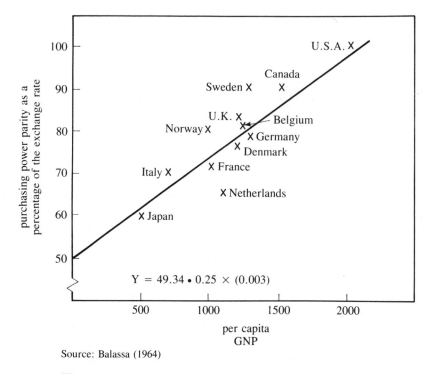

Source: Balassa (1964)

**Figure 1.1   Purchasing Power Parity as a Percentage of the
Exchange Rate and GNP per Capita**

productivity growth will therefore be reflected in traded goods competitiveness. Facing given prices in world trade, countries with higher productivity growth will try to expand production of tradables to take advantage of their favorable cost condition. The expansion raises wages and therefore increases the cost of non-traded goods. So the higher the growth of productivity relative to that of other countries, the higher the increase in the price of nontradables relative to the price of tradables and in the relative price level.

This mechanism helps explain why, under the fixed exchange rates of the 1950s and 1960s, the price level could rise by 140 percent in Japan compared with only 52 percent in the United States and Japan could still get ahead in world trade, having gained rather than lost in competitiveness. The following figures compare the cases of Japan and Korea relative to that of the United States for 1965-88:

	Real GNP	Relative price level
Japan / U.S.	1.9	2.4
Korea / U.S.	4.1	2.1

The index of relative national price levels for these countries (1985 = 100), depicted in figure 1.2, replicates the Balassa finding that the more rapidly growing countries experience a rise in their *trend* relative national price levels.

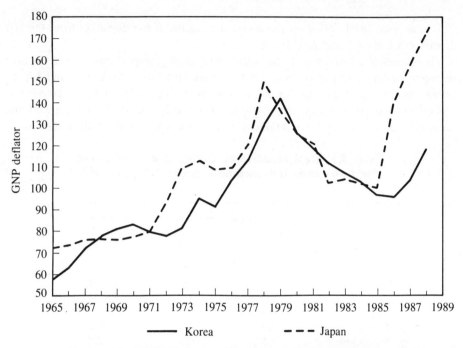

**Figure 1.2   GNP Deflators for Japan and Korea Relative to the
United States, 1965-89 (1985 = 100)**

The Real Income Comparison Project

The trend deviation from purchasing power parity is at the basis of a major research project that is conducting detailed international real income comparisons. In the context of this real income comparison project (RICO), Kravis, Heston, Summers, and Lipsey have constructed a complete analysis of relative national price levels using an absolute price comparison approach.[2] Drawing on a sample of prices, they are constructing matched sets of the prices of individual commodity groups in a particular country relative to prices in a reference country. Thus, for commodity i, the relative price is P_i / P_i^*, where the prices are measured in the respective countries' currencies (an asterisk denotes the reference country). Using an arithmetic average with weights a_i given by final expenditure shares, a purchasing power parity (*PPP*) index is defined:

(2) $$PPP = \sum a_i(P_i / P_i^*).$$

The Kravis real price level of a country (relative to the reference country) is defined as the *PPP* index divided by the actual exchange rate, *e*:

(3)   Kravis real price level = *PPP* / *e*.

This real price level definition represents a measure of the deviation from the law of one price at the aggregate level.

The research allows systematic statements about comparisons of real income between countries and also about relative price structures. As Kravis and Lipsey (1988) report, the systematic finding is that price levels in poor countries are low compared to price levels in rich countries. This finding holds for both traded and nontraded goods. Table 1.1 reproduces a convenient summary of their results.

Table 1.1   Real Income per Capita and Price Levels for Low- and High-Income Country Groups, 1980

| | 15 Countries with | | Relative |
| | Lowest real | Highest real | level |
Item	GDP	GDP	(low / high, %)
Real GDP per capita[a]	$630	$9,903	6.4
Price level for[b]			
GDP	69	119	58.0
Tradables	80	112	71.4
Nontradables	55	129	42.6

a. In international dollars.
b. Base is a sample of sixty countries weighted by their respective GDP.
Source: Kravis and Lipsey (1988, 476).

This massive data effort has had an unusual payoff. Until a decade ago one could make, unchallenged, general statements about what is true of prices in poor countries relative to those of rich countries. But today, with systematic evidence for a large number of countries, some of these statements are being challenged. It is true, as has generally been asserted, that haircuts are cheaper in poor countries, as are nontradables as a group (see table 1.1). But, contrary to received wisdom, luxuries are *not* cheaper in rich countries (Heston and Summers 1988). Similarly, the law of one price was expected to hold for rich countries; it does not, as table 1.1 shows.

The real income project has special relevance now in light of events in Eastern Europe. The immediate interest is to have some way of judging how the level of development in Eastern European countries compares to that in industrial countries or developing market economies. Comparisons of GDP using official exchange rates is useless because the official rates in no way represent market prices.

Reports by the real incomes project on measures of real income in international dollars, however, do provide a basis for making some judgments (see table 1.2). A common reaction to such data is skepticism; for example, is Portugal really poorer than Poland? The real income comparison project answers in the affirmative, and for the time being there is no substantive competing methodology to challenge the finding.

Table 1.2 Real Income per Capita for Selected Eastern and Western European Countries and the Soviet Union, 1985
(in 1980 international dollars)

Region / country	Population (million)	GNP per capita
Eastern Europe		
Bulgaria	9.0	5,113
Czechoslovakia	15.5	7,424
German Democratic Republic	16.6	8,740
Hungary	20.9	5,765
Poland	37.5	4,913
Romania	23.1	4,273
Soviet Union	282.1	6,266
Western Europe		
Federal Republic of Germany	60.9	10,708
Spain	39.1	6,437
Portugal	10.4	3,729

Source: Summers and Heston (1988).

Price Comparisons

International comparisons of prices and earnings are becoming more common. One untapped data source that offers plenty of puzzles for researchers is the Union Bank of Switzerland's *Prices and Earnings Around the Globe* (1988). Consider, for example, a representative basket of household appliances. If we take the dollar cost in Zurich to be a value of 100, the price of the basket is lowest in Rio de Janeiro (34.1) and highest in Caracas (155.7), Nairobi (156.7), and Tokyo (148.4).

What does Tokyo have in common with Nairobi or Caracas? Why is Rio de Janeiro's cost so much lower than Seoul's (92.7)? The research on such questions is only starting. In addition to the systematic effect along the lines of the Ricardo-Harrod-Balassa effect, trade barriers and distribution systems will certainly play a role. The distribution system in particular is becoming a focal point in discussions about the Europe 1992 program and about the openness of Japan to international trade. Balassa and Noland (1988) make the point that the Japanese economy is closed to trade in a manner not readily explained by resource endowments.

Among the possible explanations is inefficiency in the distribution system. Supporting that view is the U.S. Commerce Department report (1989) on direct price comparisons for brand name products which found that 88 of 126 products studied were priced higher in Japan and only 38 in the United States. Moreover, for at least 40 of the products (for example, spark plugs, bed linens, golf clubs, and dental casting machines), Japanese prices were more than 50 percent higher than U.S. prices. Strikingly, a significant number of Japanese goods were higher priced in Japan than in the United States.

Direct price comparisons, when they show significant divergences, easily become a vehicle for policy discussions. They suggest that international prices, far from following the law of one price, exhibit identifiable, major discrepancies due to obstacles in trade or distribution. In the case of the United States-Japan comparison, this finding runs directly counter to the view that by 1989 the yen was overvalued, as McKinnon (1988) has argued. The price comparisons suggest that Japanese prices are high because obstacles to competition, domestic or cross-border, are so pervasive.

Real Exchange Rates in Industrial Countries

Real exchange rates of industrial countries have been far more volatile in the 1970s and 1980s than during the Bretton Woods period of fixed but adjustable rates.[3] Typical is the case of the United States-Germany real exchange rate, whose pattern of quarterly changes is shown in figure 1.3. Virtually the same pattern can be documented for most bilateral real exchange rates involving the United States. The following chart, based on International Monetary Fund data, quantifies the increase in variability as measured by the coefficient of variation of the real exchange rate in quarterly data:

	1958-71	*1973-89*
U.S.-Germany	5.0	20.1
U.S.-France	5.3	18.8
U.S.-Japan	12.1	17.3
Germany-France	5.7	4.9

Of particular interest is the difference in real exchange rate variability between the United States and Europe or the United States and Japan and that between Germany and France. Real exchange rate variability between Germany and France did not increase between 1958-71 and 1973-89 (figure 1.4); however, after the collapse of the Bretton Woods system and before the European Monetary System brought about inflation convergence in the mid-1980s, there was a period of significant fluctuation.

Research on the real exchange rates of developed countries has focused on two issues. First, is the variability of real exchange rates dependent on the exchange

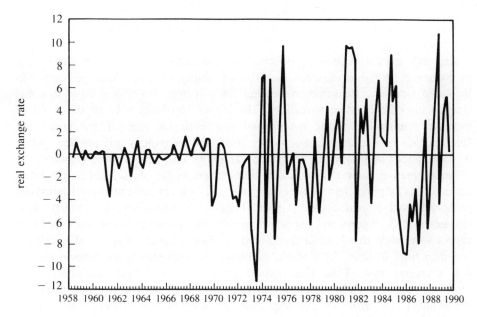

Figure 1.3   United States-Germany Real Exchange Rate, 1958-89
(quarterly percentage change in consumer prices)

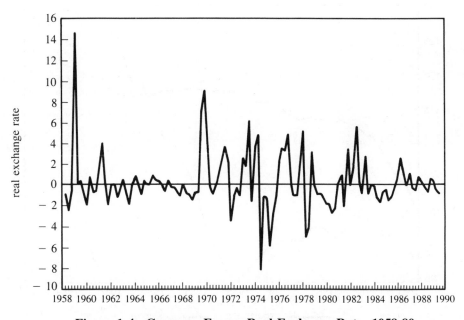

Figure 1.4   Germany-France Real Exchange Rate, 1958-89
(quarterly percentage change in consumer prices)

rate regime? Second, despite the variability, are there any indications that purchasing power parity holds?

Research on the regime dependence of real exchange rates is by and large inconclusive. While it is clear that the variability of real exchange rates has increased since the transition to floating rates, it does not follow from this that floating rates imply more variability. The higher variability may be the result of increased variability in the *equilibrium* real exchange rate. If the underlying fundamentals have changed, specifically tastes and technology and possibly policy or expectations of policy, the increased variability may reflect these changes.

An alternative interpretation is that nominal prices are sticky, and so the interaction of sticky prices and flexible exchange rates causes asset market disturbances to be reflected in real exchange rates. Figure 1.5, which shows quarterly price changes in U.S. exports and imports of nonelectric machinery from 1981 to 1989, supports the view that both in the United States and abroad wages and prices are less than fully flexible. As a result, exchange rate movements are reflected in the real exchange rate. Thus U.S. export prices of nonelectric machinery have increased steadily, while import prices have exhibited more nearly the pattern of the nominal U.S. effective exchange rate. As a result, the export / import price ratio behaves almost exactly as the nominal exchange rate does. From 1980 to 1985, the relative export price rose 30 percent and then declined by 30 percent. There is no indication that the law of one price holds in this particular market.

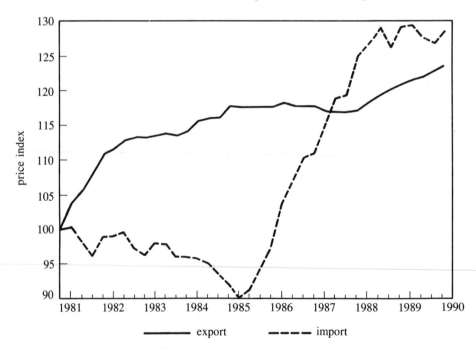

Figure 1.5 U.S. Export and Import Prices of Nonelectric Machinery, 1981-89 (1980, 4th quarter = 100)

Another aspect of this issue remains totally unresolved. Just how efficient are asset markets, and is noise in the real exchange rate magnified by the operation of short-horizon speculation?[4] The possibility that asset market volatility translates into misaligned *real* exchange rates is of considerable interest, particularly when combined with the possibility of hysteresis effects, as explored, for example, by Krugman and Baldwin (1987).

In stark contrast with this latter perspective is the view that real exchange rates basically obey purchasing power parity. According to this view, real exchange rates might deviate for a short period from purchasing power parity patterns, but the deviations would not be persistent. Typical tests of this proposition use a regression of the real exchange rate to determine whether there is significant autoregressive behavior or whether, on the contrary, the real exchange rate was generated by a process that allowed it to "wander off."

(4) $$R_t = a_0 + a_1 R_{t-1}.$$

This kind of research has attracted significant interest and increasing econometric sophistication over the past decade. The critical questions were two: how to test the alternative hypotheses, and how to determine the data requirements for a serious test. The following section offers tests of purchasing power parity for a long time period.

Purchasing Power Parity in Long Historical Series

The preceding discussion has already thrown some cold water on the theory of purchasing power parity. But what does the evidence look like in the long time series? In the past, standard tests of purchasing power parity using two-stage least squares suffered from the presence of unit roots in both nominal exchange rates (under flexible regimes) and national price indices.[5] The nonstationarity of these series renders the standard critical values inappropriate.[6]

Recently, however, unit root theory and cointegration theory have led to tests of purchasing power parity that deal directly with these nonstationarities. Edison (1987) and Frankel (1986) studied the behavior of the United States-United Kingdom real exchange rate over the past century. Enders (1989), using unit root tests and cointegration tests, concluded that purchasing power parity performed fairly well during the U.S. greenback and gold standard periods. For the period after the collapse of the Bretton Woods system, however, Enders (1988) and Corbae and Oularias (1988) found that purchasing power parity could be rejected.

In this section, we develop a unit root test for purchasing power parity similar to that of Enders (1989) and use it to test the validity of purchasing power parity for historical real exchange rates. While some other studies have tested purchasing power parity over relatively short and specific periods, our aim is to test it over the longest time spans for which data are available. Surprisingly, the test shows that purchasing power parity does perform fairly well over these long time spans.

Methodology

In developing a unit root test of purchasing power parity, we consider the following equation:

$$(5) \qquad\qquad e_t P_t^* \ / \ P_t = bw_t,$$

where b is a positive constant and w_t is a positive disturbance term. Since purchasing power parity is rarely considered a theory of exchange rate determination, we can view e_t (the domestic price of foreign currency), P_t (the domestic price level), and P_t^* (the foreign price level) as endogenously determined. We define the left side of equation 5 to be the real exchange rate, R_t, and rewrite it as

$$(6) \qquad\qquad R_t = bw_t \ .$$

By taking the natural logarithm of both sides of equation 6, we arrive at a linear model of the real exchange rate:

$$(7) \qquad\qquad r_t = r + u_t,$$

where r_t is the log of the real exchange rate, r is a constant, and u_t is a disturbance term.

The absolute version of purchasing power parity states that the real exchange rate is equal to one at every point in time. This would imply that $r = 0$ and that $u_t = 0$ in equation 7. The modern view of purchasing power parity, however, qualifies this strict view in several ways. First, since price indices are observed but actual price levels are not, we can only test a relative version of purchasing power parity which states that r must be a constant but places no restriction on its level. Second, since we live in a stochastic world, we would expect deviations from purchasing power parity over time. This would imply that u_t is an error term. If we allow only transitory shocks, then u_t would be restricted to a white noise term. However, since deviations from purchasing power parity are often long and persistent, we could allow u_t to be a more general stationary process with mean zero. It is this version of purchasing power parity that we will test, using unit root theory.

Testing Procedure

Under the null hypotheses that purchasing power parity holds, the only restriction placed on the error term u_t is that it be a stationary process (that is, it has no unit roots). For convenience, we can write the process describing u_t as a general ARMA (p,q)

(8) $$A(L)u_t = B(L)\varepsilon_t \,,$$

where $A(L)$ and $B(L)$ are lag polynomials of degrees p and q, respectively, and ε_t is an i.i.d. process with zero mean. Using equation 8 to rewrite equation 7 yields

(9) $$A(L)r_t = a + B(L)\varepsilon_t \,.$$

Equation 9 describes the log of the real exchange rate as an ARMA (p,q) process. Written in this form, purchasing power parity requires that r_t be a stationary process around some value a. To test purchasing power parity, we must determine whether the ARMA process in equation 9 contains a unit root. Since the order of this ARMA process is unknown, we employ Said and Dickey (1984) techniques.[7]

The ARMA representation of r_t given by equation 9 can be approximated by a long autoregressive process:

(10) $$r_t = \beta_0 + \sum_{i=1}^{k+1} \beta_i r_{t-i} + v_t \,.$$

This can be rewritten to yield the following:

(11) $$r_t = \mu + \alpha_1 r_{t-1} + \sum_{j=1}^{k} \alpha_{j+1} \Delta r_{t-j} + v_t \,,$$

where $\alpha_1 = \sum_{i=1}^{k+1} \beta_i$ and $\alpha_j = -\sum_{j=1}^{k+1} \beta_i$.

Equation 11 is the standard Dickey-Fuller procedure. Under the null hypothesis of a unit root, $\alpha_1 = 1$. Said and Dickey showed that if k increases at an appropriate rate as sample size (T) increases,[8] then the asymptotic distribution of t_a, the standard t-statistic of α_1, has the same distribution as calculated in Fuller (1976). So to test purchasing power parity, we merely estimate equation 11 by ordinary least squares and test the hypothesis that $\alpha_1 = 1$ using the t-statistic.

Results

We constructed long-run real exchange rate series between the United States and the following countries: Canada, Finland, France, Federal Republic of Germany, Japan, Norway, Sweden, and the United Kingdom.[9] We used yearly averages of the respective nominal exchange rates and formed the real series using both consumer price index (CPI) and GDP (or GNP) deflators.[10] The lengths of the series varied according to the availability of data, but most series ranged from the mid-to-late 1800s to the present. Several of the series had to be split because of the large intervals of missing data for the World War II period. Using data from Wagemann (1931), we also constructed real exchange rates based on prices in gold between France, Germany, the United States, and the United Kingdom. These series ran from the early 1800s to 1930.[11]

We implemented the procedure described above by applying the following estimation strategy. We chose an initial value for k according to the sample size.[12]

We then estimated equation 11 using this initial value of k. If the coefficient on Δr_{t-k} was insignificant using a two-tailed 10-percent t-test, we reduced k by one and estimated equation 11 again. We continued this process until we reached a value of k for which the coefficient on Δr_{t-k} was significant. We then conducted F-tests to test the null hypothesis that no additional lags were needed. Once k was determined, we carried out the Dickey-Fuller test.

The results are presented in table 1.3. Included in the table are k,[13] the estimates of α_1, and the t-statistics for α_1. Two results stand out. First, for many of the longer series the null hypothesis of a unit root can be rejected at the 5-percent significance level.[14] For several of these (particularly for Canada and Finland [CPI deflator]), the unit root null hypothesis can be rejected even at the 1-percent level. Second, for many of the shorter series, the null hypothesis of a unit root cannot be rejected at the 10-percent level. Exceptions are postwar France and prewar Norway.

Table 1.3 Results of Dickey-Fuller Tests: Real Exchange Rates

Countries	Period	Deflator	T^a	k	$\hat{\alpha}_1$	t_α
U.S.-Canada	1886-1988	GNP	96	6	0.648	-4.31
U.S.-Finland	1900-1988	CPI	87	1	0.489	-5.74
	1900-1987	GDP	86	9	0.986	-0.20
U.S.-France	1820-1930	gold	110	0	0.763	-3.69
	1860-1940	CPI	74	1	0.838	-2.71
	1946-1988	CPI	41	2	0.639	-3.49
U.S.-Germany	1851-1930	gold	76	3	0.675	-3.74
	1950-1988	CPI	37	1	0.870	-2.03
U.S.-Japan	1885-1943	GNP	57	1	0.888	-2.01
	1950-1987	GNP	33	6	0.992	-0.15
U.S.-Norway	1900-1940	CPI	36	1	0.655	-3.04
	1946-1988	CPI	41	1	0.951	-1.07
	1876-1939	GDP	60	3	0.695	-3.86
	1946-1988	GDP	42	1	0.925	-1.20
U.S.-Sweden	1876-1941	CPI	52	12	0.757	-1.94
	1946-1988	CPI	40	1	0.860	-2.19
	1876-1941	GDP	53	12	0.481	-2.34
	1946-1987	GDP	41	1	0.854	-1.94
U.S.-U.K.	1820-1930	gold	110	0	0.733	-4.08
	1892-1988	CPI	88	4	0.939	-1.59
	1869-1987	GNP	110	8	0.802	-3.23
U.K.-France	1820-1930	gold	104	6	0.658	-3.28
U.K.-Germany	1851-1930	gold	67	11	0.654	-3.18

a. T is the effective number of observations.

The fact that we cannot reject the unit root null hypothesis for the shorter series is not surprising. Simulation experiments of the power of unit root tests (Perron 1989c) indicate that power depends much more on the span of the data than on the number of observations. Put another way, a large span of yearly data is preferable to a short span of monthly data even if the monthly data have more observations. So the fact that we cannot reject the unit root null hypothesis for the short series is mostly a problem of statistical power, and this makes it difficult to draw conclusions about purchasing power parity based on the shorter series.[15] For this reason, we focus our attention on the longer series.

When we consider the real exchange rate series with the longer spans, the unit root tests indicate that purchasing power parity has historically performed fairly well. This result is fairly robust: eight of the eleven series with eighty or more years of data tend to support purchasing power parity. The three exceptions are Finland (GDP), United Kingdom (CPI), and United Kingdom-France (1860-1940). The Finland and United Kingdom cases are of most interest.

It seems odd that while we reject the unit root null hypothesis for the CPI-based United States-Finland real exchange rate, we cannot reject the unit root null hypothesis when GDP deflators are used. Moreover, the two series span the same time period, have the same base year, and generally move together over the entire period as well (see figures 1.6 and 1.7). (The same is generally true for the United Kingdom, but the GNP series is longer; see figures 1.8 and 1.9.) The only difference is that while the mean of the CPI-based United States-Finland real exchange rate series seems to remain fairly constant over the period, the mean of the GDP-based series shows a marked shift around the year 1940. Such a shift also occurred in the CPI-based series for the United Kingdom.

A sudden large shift in the mean of a stationary series will often yield unit root tests that cannot reject the unit root null hypothesis. Perron (1989a, b) has recently developed Dickey-Fuller-type tests that allow for a one-time shift in the mean of a series. These tests treat the shift in mean as an "outlier event."[16] Table 1.4 shows the results of these tests.[17] As in the standard Dickey-Fuller test, we test the null hypothesis that $\alpha_1 = 1$. The distribution of the t-statistic is different from that in Fuller (1976) and can be found in Perron (1989a). As table 1.4 shows, the unit root null hypothesis is rejected at the 1-percent level for the United States-Finland series and at the 5-percent level for the United States-United Kingdom series. Thus, once we have taken into account the shift in mean, we again conclude that purchasing power parity performed fairly well for United States-United Kingdom and United States-Finland regardless of the choice of price index.

The example of a shift in mean highlights the need for caution when using unit root tests to test purchasing power parity. If structural changes in the real exchange rate series occur often, it would be difficult to postulate any meaningful version of purchasing power parity. In that case, unit root tests have little to say.[18] If, however, such structural changes are infrequent, we can still postulate a meaningful "qualified" version of purchasing power parity, that is, purchasing power parity holds except, say, for a one-time shift in the mean level of the real

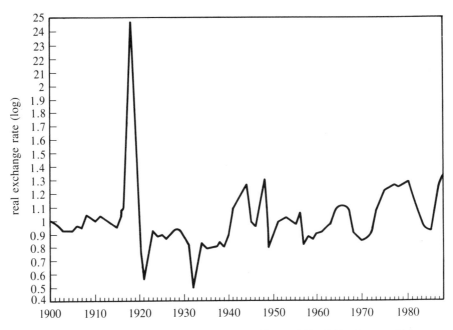

**Figure 1.6   Log of United States-Finland Real Exchange Rate,
1900-88 (CPI deflator)**

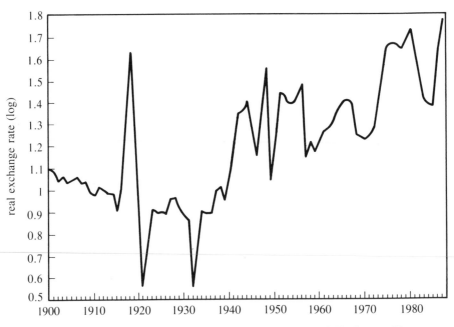

**Figure 1.7   Log of United States-Finland Real Exchange Rate,
1900-88 (GDP deflator)**

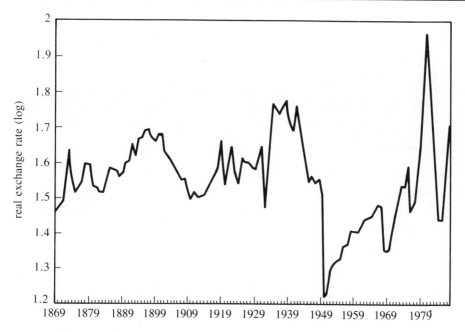

Figure 1.8   Log of United States-United Kingdom Real Exchange Rate, 1869-1988 (GNP deflator)

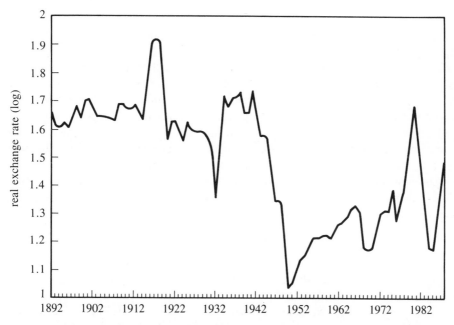

Figure 1.9   Log of United States-United Kingdom Real Exchange Rate, 1892-1988 (CPI deflator)

Table 1.4 Unit Root Tests With Changing Mean

Countries	Period	Price index	λ	k	α	t_α
U.S.-Finland	1900-1987	GDP	0.47	1	0.592	-4.76
U.S.-U.K.	1892-1988	CPI	0.58	8	0.610	-3.73

Note: The years chosen for the shift in the mean were 1940 for Finland and 1947 for the United Kingdom. The value of λ is the proportion of observations occurring before the shift in the mean.

exchange rate. The danger here is that unit root tests that ignore such structural shifts could easily lead to tests that reject purchasing power parity when it does in fact hold outside of the structural shift. Thus, one should be aware of structural shifts in the real exchange rate when considering unit root tests of purchasing power parity.

A final point in this empirical discussion of purchasing power parity concerns the conclusion of Enders (1988) and Corbae and Oularias (1988) that purchasing power parity did not perform well in the period after the breakdown of the Bretton Woods system. Since many of our long series run up to the present and so contain the post-Bretton Woods period, our conclusion that purchasing power parity has performed fairly well contradicts these earlier results. Two explanations for this difference are possible. On the one hand, it may be true that purchasing power parity has held for the post-Bretton Woods period but that the lower power associated with the small span of the period makes it difficult to accept purchasing power parity. On the other hand, it may be that purchasing power parity performed well before 1973 but has broken down in the post-Bretton Woods period — that is, the process describing the real exchange rate has changed. If this were the case, our tests might not pick it up since, for our longer series, the proportion of the sample containing post-1973 data (and hence a unit root) would be quite small. Thus, unit root tests leave unanswered the question of whether purchasing power parity has held since the abandonment of the Bretton Woods system.

Real Exchange Rates in Developing Countries

Successful economic development depends on a trade-oriented development strategy, which itself requires an appropriate exchange rate policy. Balassa's work has given considerable attention to exchange rate policy and real exchange rates in developing countries. In particular, he has shown the implications of exchange rate policy in interpreting growth performance (Balassa 1989a, b).

The experience of Latin America with exchange rate policy brings out at least three lessons in this regard about real exchange rates. First, a policy of overvaluation can be financed for a while, but the strategy becomes very expensive once the financing breaks down and real depreciation becomes inevitable. Overvaluation will contain inflation initially, but in the end the exchange rate inevitably collapses and with it comes major inflation. Second, real exchange rate overvaluation leads to capital flight and so reduces domestic saving and investment. Moreover, capital flight is not easily reversed once an economy has been weakened and once macroeconomic instability undermines credibility in the economy. And third, real depreciation is an essential complement to fiscal correction. The real exchange rate must be allowed to depreciate so as to crowd in demand and maintain full employment. But real depreciation also amounts to a cut in real wages, and thus may be difficult politically. Moreover, the cut in real wages may have to be very large to induce firms to "risk" production rather than to hold working capital and assets abroad.

Argentina, Chile, and Mexico offer examples of these lessons concerning the real exchange rate. Argentina from 1978 to 1981 pursued an exchange rate policy designed to reduce inflationary expectations and that allowed the real exchange rate to appreciate (see figure 1.11).[19] The preannounced rates of depreciation were insufficient to prevent appreciation of the real exchange rate month after month. At the same time, Argentina fully liberalized capital movements. The combination of real appreciation and liberalization of capital movements produced a massive outflow of private capital (see table 1.5). The Argentine government financed the outflow by borrowing in international capital markets. As a result, a large public debt offset the increase in private external assets. Argentina's economic disintegration of the 1980s stems in large part from this extraordinary episode.

Table 1.5 Estimates of Capital Flight from Argentina, Brazil, Mexico, and Venezuela, 1976-82 and 1983-87

(billions of U.S. dollars)

Country	1976-82	1983-87	1976-87	Per capita (US$)
Argentina	22.4	6.7	29.1	924
Brazil	5.8	14.6	20.4	144
Mexico	25.3	35.3	60.6	745
Venezuela	20.7	19.4	40.1	2,195

Note: Estimates are cumulative without imputed interest.
Source: Lessard and Williamson (1987), updated by the authors.

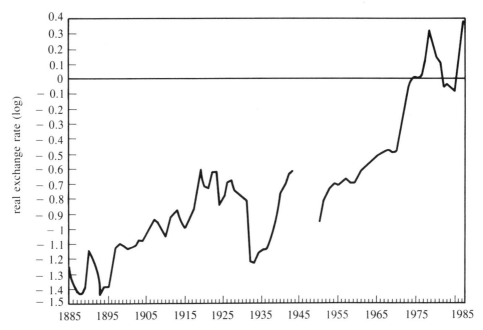

**Figure 1.10   Log of United States-Japan Real Exchange Rate,
1885-1988 (GNP deflator)**

In other Latin American countries, with the exception of Brazil, the situation was much the same. An exchange rate policy focused not on competitiveness but on containing inflation and on overvaluation led to a major increase in external indebtedness. As sources of external financing dried up in the 1980s, the need to service the debt then forced a major real depreciation.

A striking aspect of the behavior of financially distressed economies is the sheer magnitude of the fall in real wages. Mexico's experience amply demonstrates this process (see figure 1.12). The real product wage in manufacturing declined by 60 percent from 1981 to 1988. Manufacturing employment also declined (by 20 percent) despite the sharp drop in real wages. In fact, work by Diaz-Alejandro (1988) suggests that employment declines precisely because of the decline in real wages. On the aggregate demand side, the income effect of lower real wages reduces demand for domestic labor, which dominates the impact of the change in relative prices and the increase in export profitability.

This short-run dominance of the income effect is quite clear to politicians and, together with the disinflation bonus of overvaluation, explains why exchange rates are allowed to become misaligned. But the longer the adoption of realistic exchange rates is postponed, the larger the required adjustment.

More research is needed on the political-economy of exchange rate policy, particularly on situations in which adjustments are postponed until they reach crisis proportions. In this respect the difference between Asia, where adjustments are always timely and large, and Latin America is striking.

Notes

Financial support for the research reported here was provided by grants from the National Science Foundation and the Alfred Sloan Foundation.

1. See, too, Officer (1984) and the survey article on purchasing power parity in Dornbusch (1989).
2. See Kravis, Heston, and Summers (1982) for the methodology; see also Kravis and Lipsey (1983, 1988).
3. Research by Mussa (1986) and Stockman (1983, 1988) has amply demonstrated this finding.
4. On the efficiency question see Frankel and Froot (1987) and Froot and Thaler (1990).
5. For examples of these tests, see Frenkel (1981) and Hakkio (1984).
6. For our purposes here, nonstationarity will refer to a process that contains a unit root. Other types of nonstationarity are not considered.
7. As in Enders (1989), we could have used Box-Jenkins techniques to determine ARMA models of the real exchange rate, but since we are not interested in actually estimating equation 9, we instead use the results of Said and Dickey (1984).
8. Specifically, $k / T^{1/3} \to 0$ as $k,T \to \infty$. However, since this implies that $Ck / T^{1/3} \to 0$ for any constant C, the choice of k becomes somewhat arbitrary in finite samples.
9. A data appendix is available on request.
10. For some countries, only one deflator was available.
11. Details of the data sources and construction of the real exchange rates are available on request.
12. For the larger series $(T > 60)$, we chose an initial k of 15. For the smaller series, we chose an initial k of 7.
13. In picking the final values of k, we had to be sensitive to the robustness of the Dickey-Fuller test. For some series, as k became smaller, the t-statistic on α_1 varied considerably. In a few cases, we found that for a large value of k we could not reject the unit root while for a smaller k we could. The large k could not be flatly ignored because of the significance of the Δr_{t-k} term, but the test suffered from the lower power associated with the larger k. In these cases, we used a liberal F-test to test the null hypothesis that no additional lags were needed beyond the smaller value of k.
14. The critical values are -2.86 at the 5-percent level and -3.43 at the 1-percent level.
15. For example, Sweden (GNP 1876-1940) yields $a_1 = 0.481$, which is not even close to 1, but the t-statistic is -2.34, which implies that the unit root null hypothesis cannot be rejected. The problem here is that k is large, and this severely reduces the effective span, giving low power to the Dickey-Fuller test.
16. For details of the test, see Perron (1989a).
17. The results of this test depend on which year is chosen to represent the shift in the mean. For our purposes, we eyeballed the data to determine the break; however, more formal methods could be used to detect such a break point.
18. For example, consider the United States-Japan real exchange rate series shown in figure 1.10. It is obvious that the real yen has steadily appreciated over time. This can be partly explained by differences in productivity growth in the two countries over time. Since the real exchange rate is trending, we would not expect purchasing power parity

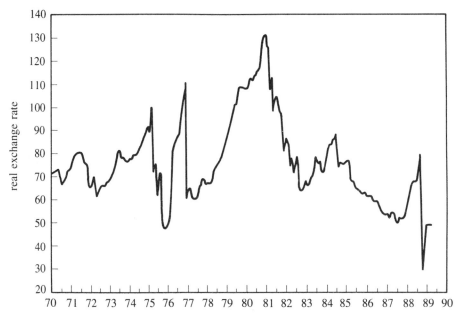

Figure 1.11 Argentina: Real Exchange Rate, 1970-89
(1980-82 = 100)

to hold. That is exactly what the unit root tests indicate (see table 1.3). A more proper unit root test would allow for a time trend, but once we allow for a time trend, we are no longer testing a meaningful version of purchasing power parity.

19. See Dornbusch (1987, 1988) for a discussion of the experience in Argentina, Chile, and Mexico.

References

Balassa, B. 1964. "The Purchasing Power Parity Doctrine: A Reappraisal." *Journal of Political Economy* 72 (December): 584-96.

Balassa, B. 1989a. *Comparative Advantage, Trade Policy and Economic Development.* New York: Harvester Wheatsheaf.

Balassa, B. 1989b. *New Directions in the World Economy.* London: Macmillan.

Balassa, B., and M. Noland. 1988. *Japan in the World Economy.* Washington, D.C.: Institute for International Economics.

Corbae, D., and S. Oularias. 1988. "Cointegration and Tests of Purchasing Power Parity." The Review of Economics and Statistics 70: 508-11.

Diaz-Alejandro, C. 1988. *Trade, Development and the World Economy.* Oxford: Basil Blackwell.

Dickey, D.A., W.R. Bell, and R.B. Miller. "Unit Roots in Time Series Models: Tests and Implications." *The American Statistician* 40: 12-26.

Dickey, D.A., and W.A. Fuller. 1981. "Likelihood Ratio Statistics for Autoregressive Times Series with a Unit Root." *Econometrica* 49: 1057-72.

Dornbusch, R. 1987. *Dollars, Debts and Deficits.* Cambridge, Mass.: MIT Press.

Dornbusch, R. 1988. "Mexico: Stabilization, Debt and Growth." *Economic Policy* 7 (October): 231-83.

Dornbusch, R. 1989. *Exchange Rates and Inflation*. Cambridge, Mass.: MIT Press.

Dornbusch, R., and A. Giovannini. 1990. "Monetary Policy in the Open Economy." In F. Hahn and B. Friedman, eds, *Handbook of Monetary Economics*. Amsterdam: North-Holland.

Dornbusch, R., S. Fischer, and P. Samuelson. 1977, "Comparative Advantage, Trade and Payments in a Ricardian Model with a Continuum of Goods." *American Economic Review* 67 (December): 823-39.

Edison, H. 1987. "Purchasing Power Parity in the Long Run: A Test of the Dollar / Pound Exchange Rate (1890-1978)." *Journal of Money, Credit and Banking* 19 (August): 376-87.

Edwards, S. 1988. *Exchange Rate Misalignment in Developing Countries*. Occasional Paper No. 2 (new series). Washington, D.C.: World Bank.

Edwards, S. 1989. *Real Exchange Rates, Devaluation and Adjustment*. Cambridge, Mass.: MIT Press.

Enders, W. 1988. "ARIMA and Cointegration Tests of Purchasing Power Parity." *Review of Economics and Statistics* 4: 504-08.

Enders, W. 1989. "Unit Roots and the Real Exchange Rate Before World War I: The Case of Britain and the USA." *Journal of International Money and Finance* 8: 59-73.

Frankel, J. 1986. "International Capital Mobility and Crowding Out in the U.S. Economy: Imperfect Integration of Financial Markets or of Goods Markets?" In R. Hafer, ed., *How Open Is the U.S. Economy?* St. Louis, Mo.: Federal Reserve Bank of St. Louis.

Frankel, J., and K. Froot. 1987. "Using Survey Data To Test Standard Propositions Regarding Exchange Rate Expectations." *American Economic Review* 77 (March): 133-53.

Frenkel, J.A. 1981. "The Collapse of Purchasing Power Parities During the 1970's." *European Economic Review* 16: 145-75.

Froot, K., and R. Thaler. 1990. "On the Efficiency of Foreign Exchange Markets." Massachusetts Institute of Technology, Cambridge.

Fuller, W.A. 1976. *Introduction to Statistical Time Series*. New York: John Wiley.

Hakkio, C.S. 1984. "A Re-examination of Purchasing Power Parity: A Multi-Country and Multi-Period Study." *Journal of International Economics* 17: 265-77.

Heston, A., and R. Summers. 1988. "What We Have Learned About Prices and Quantities from International Comparisons: 1987." *American Economic Review* 78 (May): 467-73.

Hsieh, D. 1982. "The Determinants of the Real Exchange Rate." *Journal of International Economics* 12 (May): 355-62.

Kravis, I., A. Heston, and R. Summers. 1978. "Real GDP per Capita for More Than One Hundred Countries." *Economic Journal* 88 (June): 215-42.

Kravis, I., A. Heston, and R. Summers. 1982. *World Product and Income: International Comparisons of Real Gross Product*. Baltimore, Md.: Johns Hopkins University Press.

Kravis, I., and R. Lipsey. 1983. *Toward an Explanation of National Price Levels*. Princeton Studies in International Finance No. 5. Princeton, N.J.: Princeton University Press.

Kravis, I., and R. Lipsey. 1988. "National Price Levels and the Prices of Tradables and Nontradables." *American Economic Review* 78 (May): 474-78.

Krugman, P., and R. Baldwin. 1987. "The Persistence of the U.S. Trade Deficit." Brookings Papers on Economic Activity 1. Washington, D.C.: Brookings Institution.

Lessard, D., and J. Williamson. 1987. *Capital Flight and Third World Debt*. Washington, D.C.: Institute for International Economics.

McKinnon, R. 1988. "Monetary and Exchange Rate Policies for International Financial Stability: A Proposal." *Journal of Economic Perspectives* 2 (winter): 83-103.

Mussa, M. 1986. "Nominal Exchange Rate Regimes and the Behavior of Real Exchange Rates: Evidence and Implications." In K. Brunner and A. Meltzer, eds, *Real Business Cycles, Real Exchange Rates and Actual Policies.* Carnegie-Rochester Conference Series, Vol. 25. Amsterdam: North-Holland.

Officer, L. 1984. *Purchasing Power Parity and Exchange Rates.* Greenwich, Conn.: JAI Press.

Perron, P. 1988. "Trends and Random Walks in Macroeconomic Time Series: Further Evidence from a New Approach." *Journal of Economic Dynamics and Control* 12: 297-332.

Perron, P. 1989a. "Testing for a Unit Root in a Time Series with a Changing Mean." Princeton University, Princeton, N.J.

Perron, P. 1989b. "The Great Crash, the Oil Price Shock and the Unit Root Hypothesis," *Econometrica* 57 (November): 1361-1401.

Perron, P. 1989c. "Testing for a Random Walk: A Simulation Experiment of Power When the Sampling Interval Is Varied." In B. Raj, ed., *Econometrics and Modelling.* Boston, Mass.: Kluwer Academic Publishers.

Said, S.E., and D.A. Dickey. 1984. "Testing for Unit Roots in Autoregressive-Moving Average Models of Unknown Order." *Biometrika* 71: 599-608.

Stockman, A. 1983. "Real Exchange Rates Under Alternative Exchange Rate Regimes." *Journal of International Money and Finance* 2: 147-66.

Stockman, A. 1988. "The Equilibrium Approach to Exchange Rates." Cambridge, Mass.: National Bureau of Economic Research.

Summers, R., and A. Heston. 1988. "A New Set of International Comparisons of Real Product and Prices: Estimates for 130 Countries, 1950-85." *Review of Income and Wealth* 34 (March): 1-25.

Union Bank of Switzerland. 1988. *Prices and Earnings Around the Globe.* Zurich.

U.S. Department of Commerce. 1989. *Department of Commerce / MITI Price Survey Data.* Washington, D.C.

Wagemann, E. 1931. *Struktur und Rhythmus der Weltwirtschaft.* Berlin: Reimar Hobbing.

Figure 1.12   Mexico: Real Wage in Manufacturing, 1970-88
(1980 = 100)

2

Measuring the Effects of Nontariff
Trade-Distorting Policies

Robert E. Baldwin

International trade is distorted by a wide variety of government measures other than tariffs. A study for the World Bank (Olechowski 1987) estimates that in 1984 about 15 percent of the import product categories of the major developed countries, accounting for 18 percent of the value of their imports, were subject to nontariff trade measures. The trade policy actions of these countries during the latter half of the 1980s have very likely increased these percentages.

A concern that these measures may undermine the substantial international benefits achieved from tariff liberalization that began after World War II has recently stimulated interest in measuring the extent and influence of nontariff trade policies by means other than simple measures of product and value coverage.[1] Béla Balassa has long been a leader among international economists in measuring trade-distorting policies. Not only was he a pioneer in developing the concept of the effective rate of protection, but he provided the first comprehensive empirical measures of these rates that included the effects of nontariff policies as well as tariffs (Balassa 1965, 1971). Consistent with Balassa's emphasis on measurement, this study surveys various proposed methods for measuring nontariff policies with the aim of determining which seem most promising for facilitating the process of reducing the trade-distorting effects of nontariff trade measures.[2] The merits and drawbacks of various types of measures are also discussed, followed by conclusions and recommendations.

Measurement of Tariffs and of Nontariff Trade Barriers

When tariffs were the major trade policy instrument, there was general agreement that the most appropriate way of measuring the extent to which government regulation affected international trade was by calculating the rate at which imports were taxed. But both researchers studying patterns of protection and negotiators engaged in tariff-reducing multilateral negotiations realized the imperfect nature of this measure. The tariff rate is only one part of the information needed to assess the impact of reducing an import duty on such key economic variables as the domestic price of the imported good, the volume of imports, the volume of output of the domestic substitute, the change in value added in the domestic industry, and domestic employment.

To determine these effects, it is necessary to know such relationships (and their behavior over time) as the direct and cross-price elasticities of demand for imports and the domestic substitute, the elasticities of supply for imports and the domestic good, and the number of person-years used per unit of output. Furthermore, if a duty cut is part of a general process of tariff reductions in which interactive effects are significant, a general equilibrium model is needed to trace the various indirect price, output, and employment effects.

Despite the limitations of measuring tariff protection as the rate at which imports are taxed, governments have been (and still are) prepared to negotiate reciprocal tariff reductions using changes in this measure as an index of the duty cuts received and granted. For example, participants in the Kennedy Round of multilateral trade negotiations (1962-67) agreed on a 50-percent tariff-cutting formula and regarded equal cuts in tariff rates among countries as achieving an approximate balance of concessions. In effect, trade negotiators were willing to assume that the differences among commodities and countries in such response indicators as demand and supply elasticities tended to even out when tariffs were cut on a wide range of goods.[3]

Nontariff trade measures are expressed in many forms. In one major category, quantitative restrictions, the volume or value of imports or exports is limited, either on a global or a country-selective basis. In another important group, subsidies, the government provides direct financial assistance to producers or factors of production or supplies intermediate goods and services to firms at below their economic cost. In still another category, the government establishes standards and regulations relating to health, safety, packaging, labeling, and so forth that may inadvertently or deliberately discriminate against foreign suppliers. Examples of other trade-distorting measures are government purchasing policies that treat domestic suppliers preferentially, variable import levies, arbitrary customs procedures that restrict imports, and tied-aid programs. Because of the many ways in which nontariff measures are expressed, there is, unlike in the case of tariffs, no one obvious means of comparing nontariff measures.

Price and Quantity Effects of Nontariff Trade Policies

One approach to comparing nontariff trade measures is to focus on the wedges they introduce between the world price of an imported or exported good or service, the prices domestic consumers pay for the imported product and its domestically produced substitute, and the price received by the domestic producers of the good. A quota, for example, like a tariff, introduces a wedge (beyond that associated with any tariff on the product, transportation costs, and other markups) between the price received by foreign producers for the imports they supply and the price charged domestic consumers for these imports.

This similarity between tariffs and quotas is illustrated in figure 2.1, which depicts a country's demand curve for imports (D_M) and the supply curve of imports from foreign countries (S_F) that it faces under perfectly competitive conditions. In the absence of any protection, imports are oq_0 and the domestic and the world prices are both op_0. If an ad valorem tariff is levied on imports, the import supply curve, which indicates the price importers charge consumers after paying their own government the import duty, shifts upward to S_{F+t}, thereby yielding a new equilibrium import quantity and price of oq_1 and op_1, respectively. The tariff creates a wedge between the price consumers pay for imports, op_1, and the foreign price of the import good, op_3. The domestic government collects the difference, p_1LMp_3, as tariff revenue.

A similar wedge is created if a policy is introduced limiting the quantity of imports to oq_1. The foreign supply curve, S_{FQ}, becomes vertical at oq_1 and above op_3, with the price paid by domestic consumers again rising to op_1. If the quota rights are allocated to domestic importers, they will reap the windfall gain of p_1LMp_3 by being able to buy abroad at a price of op_3 and sell at home at a price of op_1. In contrast, if the quota rights are allocated to foreign exporters, as is the case with most voluntary export restraint agreements, these exporters gain this rent.

The price effects of restricting imports by such nontariff means as variable levies or foreign exchange controls can be analyzed in much the same way as for tariffs and quotas. Suppose, for example, that op_1 is the target price below which

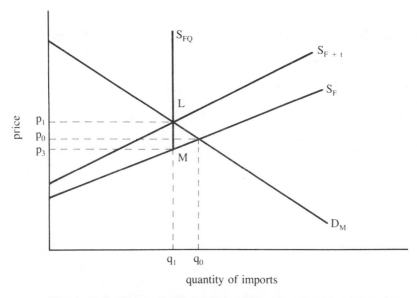

Figure 2.1   Domestic Demand and Foreign Supply of Imports Under Perfect Competition

the government does not want the domestic price to fall. Given the initial domestic demand and foreign import supply curves, an import levy of p_1p_3 per unit accomplishes this goal. If the foreign import supply curve declines, the government will raise the levy, while if the domestic demand curve increases, it will lower the per-unit levy. Unlike the case with quotas, the quantity of imports varies under variable levies while the price remains fixed when domestic demand shifts.

Even the price effects of a discriminatory technical barrier can be analyzed with the aid of figure 2.1. Suppose, for example, that the product supplied by foreigners satisfies in some objective sense the health or safety standards imposed on the product by the importing country, but that this country requires certain costly modifications in the foreign product because technically it is not exactly the same as the domestic substitute. By raising foreign costs, this requirement shifts the foreign import supply curve up to S_{F+t} and produces the same price-raising and import-reducing effects as a tariff.

Officials in the importing country are concerned not only with a trade-restricting policy's price and quantity effects on imports but also with its price and output effects on the domestic product with which imports compete. If imports and domestic products are perfect substitutes, the effects are straightforward. The price of that proportion of output produced domestically rises to the same level as the domestic price of imports, thereby reducing total consumption of the goods but increasing the amount supplied domestically.

In manufacturing, however, many products within a tariff line are similar but not identical. They are differentiated in some way from each other by the firms producing them, making the assumption of perfect substitutability between imports and domestic production inappropriate. In this case, the increase in the price of imports due to the introduction of a trade-restricting policy can be viewed as increasing the demand curve for the domestic variety as domestic consumers substitute the domestic version for higher-priced imports. Given an upward-sloping (but not vertical) domestic supply curve, this shift will, in turn, result in an increase in the price and output level of the domestic substitute.[4]

In contrast to quantitative restrictions and other nontariff policies impinging directly on the domestic price of imports and indirectly on domestic producer prices, trade-distorting government subsidies directly affect the prices domestic producers receive for their products. The impact of a domestic production subsidy on a good that is also imported is shown in figure 2.2. The curve S_D is the domestic supply curve prior to the production subsidy, S_F is the foreign supply curve, and S_T is the horizontal sum of these two curves. The curve D_D is the domestic demand for the home and foreign products, which are assumed to be identical. The equilibrium price and consumption level are op_0 and oq_0, respectively, with oq_1 supplied by domestic producers and q_1q_0 imported.

A fixed subsidy per unit shifts the domestic supply curve to S_{D-s} and the sum of this curve and the foreign supply curve to S_{T-s}. The increased total supply reduces the domestic price to op_1, increases domestic supply to oq_3, and increases consumption to oq_2. Domestic producers now receive op_3 per unit of output they

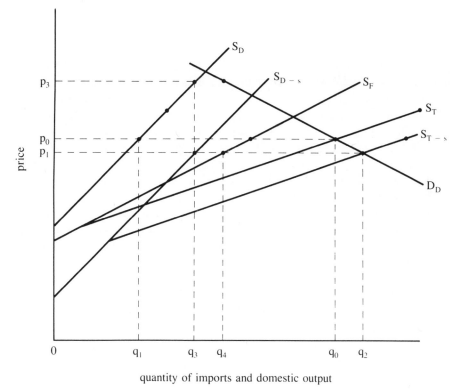

quantity of imports and domestic output

**Figure 2.2   Impact of Domestic Production Subsidy on a Good
That Is Also Imported**

produce; op_1 of this is covered by the price consumers pay for the product, and
p_1p_3 comes from the government as a subsidy. A subsidy that is not tied to
output-producing activities, however, such as a subsidy to existing capital services
(in contrast to a subsidy that is used in acquiring new plant and equipment), has
no effect on output, prices, and trade and is just an income-redistributing policy.

Frequency-Type Measures

As the preceding analysis indicates, nontariff trade policies can be measured by
their price or their quantity effects. Another obvious method, as mentioned in the
introduction, is simply to measure these policies in terms of their numbers and
trade coverage.[5]

Frequency-type measures record the number, form, and trade coverage of nontariff trade policies as determined through surveys, frequency of complaints by
trading partners, and government reports. A well-known effort using this approach
is the joint World Bank-United Nations Conference on Trade and Development
(UNCTAD) study (Nogues, Olechowski, and Winters 1986 and Olechowski 1987)

of commodity-specific border measures affecting the imports of sixteen industrial countries in 1981-84. The data are derived from various official national publications and information supplied by governments to the General Agreement on Tariffs and Trade (GATT). Three indices of the prevalence of selected nontariff trade measures (mainly those with obvious quantity or price effects) are constructed in this study. The first uses a country's own import weights to determine the proportion of imports from its trading partners affected by these policies, and the second employs world import weights. For the third index, the extent of nontariff trade policies is measured simply by the number of commodity trade flows between a country and its trading partners that are affected by these policies.

Since many national governments and other international organizations besides the World Bank and UNCTAD (for example, the International Monetary Fund and the GATT) maintain lists of nontariff measures affecting current trade flows, the trade-coverage approach has the advantage of being relatively easy to implement. Figures cited in the World Bank-UNCTAD study indicating that 18 percent of the imports of the major industrial countries were affected by nontariff border policies in 1984 have also alerted public officials to the pervasiveness of these policies. But there are obvious disadvantages to measuring nontariff policies in this manner. The most serious is the failure to distinguish the degree to which different types of nontariff trade policies or forms of a particular policy affect import prices and quantities and other variables of interest. Another drawback is the sensitivity of frequency-type measures to the degree of country and product-line disaggregation used by the investigator. For these and other reasons, most governments do not accept frequency-type indices as meaningful measures of nontariff policies.

Price-Impact Measures

Given public and private officials' familiarity with measuring tariffs in percentage terms, a strong case can be made for favoring price over quantity measures of nontariff trade-distorting policies. The existence of a wedge between the domestic and foreign prices of imported products, as occurs in the case of a tariff, would also seem to simplify the measurement problem compared to quantity estimates. Most empirical measurement efforts have, in fact, focused mainly on this approach. Three types of price-impact measures are considered in this section: tariff equivalents, subsidy measures, and the effective rate of protection or assistance.

Tariff Equivalents and Their Estimation

The tariff equivalent (t_n) of import-restricting nontariff barriers (also called the implicit rate of protection) is a measure of the rate by which the domestic border price of the imported good (p_m) exceeds the price paid by domestic importers to foreign exporters (p_1), inclusive of transport costs to the importing country and any tariffs levied by this country. Specifically, $t_n = (p_m - p_1) / p_1$.[6] This measure is termed a "tariff equivalent" because under perfectly competitive conditions, an ad valorem tariff at this rate would create the same wedge between the domestic and import prices.

As Moroz (1985) points out, there are two basic methods of estimating tariff equivalents. One is to observe directly the world price of the imported product and the domestic price at which it is sold, taking account of wholesale and retail margins as well as tariffs and transport costs. The other is to use information on the quantity changes resulting from a nontariff measure and data on relevant demand and supply elasticities to estimate the price wedge.

Comparative price analyses. The price-comparison method is clearly the most straightforward way of estimating the tariff equivalent of a nontariff trade measure. This is one of the methods used by the Commission of the European Communities (EC) in estimating the effects of removing existing barriers among EC members by 1992 (Commission of the European Communities 1988). The price data were collected by Eurostat, the Statistical Office of the EC, in cooperation with the statistical services of the member states, as part of its program of calculating purchasing power parities and comparing gross domestic product in real terms between member countries. For 1985, Eurostat obtained price information on household consumption items and equipment goods for 215 basic headings comprising nearly 3,000 products (Eurostat 1988).[7] Other studies relying on the price-comparison approach include Dardis (1967), Roningen and Yeats (1976), Baldwin (1975), and Bhagwati and Srinivasan (1975).

There are numerous data and interpretation problems with the price-comparison method, however. First, there generally is no direct information on the prices that importers pay foreign suppliers,[8] so price data for the identical product must be sought from third-country markets where quality and price are unaffected by the nontariff trade measure.[9] If this effort is successful, the costs of delivering the good to the domestic market, including any import duty, must then be estimated. Finally, if the imported good is resold on an open domestic market and the margins involved in shipping the good from its port of entry to this market can be identified, the price wedge due to nontariff trade-distorting policies can be determined.

The import good usually varies in quality from the domestic substitute with which it competes.[10] Domestic price data usually do not distinguish between domestically produced and imported goods, however. Using the available price series, which typically are an average of the prices of these goods, tends to underestimate the price wedge caused by the trade barrier, especially if imports are a small part of total consumption. As experience with quantitative restrictions on automobiles, footwear, and textiles has demonstrated, quality upgrading also tends to occur when imports are limited by physical quotas in contrast to ad valorem tariffs. Separating the domestic price-increasing effects due to improved quality from those due to a smaller import volume of a given quality requires the use of index numbers (Aw and Roberts 1986), hedonic regression techniques (Feenstra 1984), or estimations of the price elasticities of various qualities of the product (Levinsohn 1988).

It is not easy, furthermore, to separate the various possible causes of the wedge between domestic and foreign prices, once it has been estimated as accurately as possible. The price difference is often due to a number of different nontariff policies, some of which may not be observable. In imperfectly competitive markets, part of the price wedge may also represent producer profit margins that are above those in perfectly competitive markets.

One situation in which price differentials due to a specific nontariff trade barrier can be estimated quite accurately is when export quota rights are sold in an open market with registered prices. Such is the case for quota rights on clothing products in Hong Kong and India and was the case for a short period in Taiwan. Using this information, Hamilton (1986, 1988) has calculated tariff equivalents for the nontariff barriers imposed by various industrial countries against clothing exported by both Hong Kong and Taiwan. Australia and New Zealand also have instituted systems for auctioning quotas for several commodities (see Bergsten et al. 1987). However, if buyers of quota rights have monopsony power, the observed price for these rights will underestimate the tariff equivalent of the quantitative restriction.

When nontariff trade restrictions are applied on a country-specific basis, as in the case for textiles and apparel, the estimated price wedge applies only to imports from a particular country or small group of countries. If an average tariff equivalent for total imports of the product is desired, the tariff equivalent estimated for the restricted exporters must be reduced to take into account the increase in imports from noncontrolled suppliers resulting from the imposition of the country-selective import barrier.[11]

Another problem with measuring the effect of nontariff barriers by comparing foreign and domestic prices is the variability of this measure due to fluctuations in nominal exchange rates. Appreciation of a country's currency, for example, will increase the ad valorem equivalent of a quantitative import restriction as the domestic currency price of the foreign product to importers decreases.[12] The rate of assistance provided by a specific production subsidy (or specific import duty) will also increase as a consequence of the appreciation of a country's currency, whereas the rate of assistance or protection associated with an ad valorem tariff or production subsidy is unaffected by exchange rate changes. Because of the volatility of exchange rates in recent years, participants in OECD discussions on measuring agricultural assistance have suggested that calculations of average rates of assistance cover more than one year in the case of trade-distorting measures that are sensitive to exchange rate changes.

In summary, the price-comparison method of measuring the ad valorem equivalent of nontariff trade barriers is straightforward and logically appealing, but difficult measurement problems are often encountered in estimating and interpreting the differences between foreign and domestic prices. Careful and often costly studies are required to deal with these problems satisfactorily. Nevertheless, as in the EC's study of the effects of removing barriers among member states or the OECD work on quantifying agricultural assistance, the price-comparison method should be an important component of any effort to measure the effects of nontariff trade-distorting policies.

Inferring price changes from quantity changes. Probably the most widely used nontariff trade-distorting measure is quantitative restrictions. A government decides that imports from all or a subgroup of suppliers will be reduced by a specified amount or to a particular market share. The price wedge that would produce this quantitative decline in imports can be calculated, given estimates of the elasticities of import demand and import supply. If imports are imperfect substitutes for domestic production, then estimates of the elasticities of domestic demand and domestic supply as well as of the relevant cross-price elasticities are also needed. Since the tariff equivalents of quantitative restrictions vary as the demand for imports increases over time, an estimate of the rate of growth of import demand is also needed to keep the tariff equivalents up to date. Among the investigators using this approach to estimate tariff and subsidy equivalents are Morici and Megna (1983) and Moroz (1985).

When direct observations of changes in imports are not available, information on the market share of imports prior to the imposition of the nontariff barrier can sometimes be used to estimate quantity reductions. Relevant elasticities can be applied to these quantity changes to infer the price wedge associated with the restriction. Other more elaborate approaches for estimating quantity effects of nontariff policies are also available, such as the use of sector-specific or applied general equilibrium models. (These are discussed in the section on quantity-impact measures.)

While considerable effort is required to obtain good estimates of the parameters needed to measure the tariff equivalents of quantitative trade restrictions, this approach should be used to supplement the information obtained from the price-comparison method.

Surveys. Another estimating method that can complement those already discussed is to survey those who have been affected by nontariff measures. In the Eurostat study (1988), an additional method used to estimate the cost effects of removing trade barriers was to ask firms to estimate the price and quantity impact on them of various technical regulations. Surveying governments and private firms in countries whose exports have been adversely affected by foreign trade restrictions can also yield useful information about the price effects of these measures. In interpreting the results of such surveys, we must, of course, recognize that it may be in the economic interests of some respondents to either exaggerate or minimize the importance of particular nontariff policies.

Subsidy Measures and Their Estimation

Subsidy equivalents. As previously noted, trade-distorting government subsidies, unlike import controls, directly increase the per-unit receipts of domestic producers (p_r) for their output. The most common way of measuring these subsidies is to express them as a percentage of the per-unit sales value of the product (p_c). Specifically, the ad valorem subsidy equivalent, s, can be expressed as follows:

(1) $$s = (p_r - p_c) / p_c.$$

Under this definition, tariff equivalents of nontariff measures (t_n) and subsidy equivalents (s) are not directly comparable; one measure relates to imports and the other to production of the domestic substitute. But if imports and domestic production are perfect substitutes, there is a simple relationship between the two measures on the production side. With perfect substitutes, the domestic price of imports (p_m) will be the same as the consumer price of the domestically produced good (p_c). Ignoring transport costs,

(2) $$p_m = p_1 (1 + t_n) = p_w (1 + t) (1 + t_n),$$

where p_1 is the tariff-inclusive price paid by the domestic importer, p_w is the world price, and t is the ad valorem tariff. Therefore, it follows from the relationship $p_r = p_c (1 + s)$ that

(3) $$p_r = p_w (1 + t) (1 + t_n) (1 + s).$$

Using estimates of elasticities of domestic supply, foreign supply, and domestic demand, it is also possible to determine the tariff equivalent that directly reduces imports by the same quantity that a domestic subsidy does indirectly.

Estimating subsidy equivalents generally is an easier task than estimating tariff equivalents since data on public subsidies are usually published in government budgets. The main problem is identifying the amounts that various industries receive when the subsidy is not industry-specific or the disbursing agency does not have records on the industries receiving the subsidy.

Producer subsidy equivalents. The OECD (1987) and various national governments have undertaken significant work in recent years in measuring the extent of government support of agriculture. For this work, two measurement concepts were developed: the producer subsidy equivalent and the consumer subsidy equivalent. The producer subsidy equivalent is defined as the payment or subsidy required to compensate producers for the removal of government agricultural assistance measures and is usually expressed as a percentage of the total value of output. The consumer subsidy equivalent measures the implicit tax on consumption resulting from agricultural policy measures (the market support element of producer subsidy equivalents) and any subsidies to consumption. Direct price comparisons play an important role in estimating both these measures.

Four elements are included in calculations of producer subsidy equivalents: market price supports, direct income supports, indirect income supports, and other supports. Domestic price support programs, tariffs, and quotas are examples of market price supports, while deficiency and disaster payments illustrate direct income supports. Indirect income supports include capital grants, concessional credit, and input subsidies. In the group of "other supports" are research, advisory, training, and inspection services supplied by the government, as well as taxation and transportation concessions.

Producer and consumer subsidy equivalents have been estimated for all twenty-four members of the OECD. They have been valuable in monitoring trends in agricultural support across countries and have been used in the GATT negotiations on agriculture in the Uruguay Round.

Trade-distortion equivalents. An alternative measure for use in the agricultural sector is the trade-distortion equivalent, which has been proposed by the Canadian government. Like subsidy equivalents, it differs from the producer subsidy equivalent by focusing on the trade-distorting effects of policies rather than on their income-supporting effects. Some agricultural programs such as government research, training, and the provision of market information are assumed to have such an insignificant impact on current production and prices received by producers that they are omitted from these calculations. Some negotiators have proposed that all trade-distorting measures in agriculture, and perhaps in the manufacturing sector as well, be replaced by their equivalent tariffs and that these tariffs then be gradually reduced in successive multilateral trade negotiations.

Production subsidies in agriculture are sometimes tied to a reduction in productive capacity. As Whalley and Wigle (1988) found in analyzing the pre-1985 U.S. wheat program in a general equilibrium framework, eliminating such subsidies and the related capacity-reduction requirement can actually increase output in contrast to what would be expected if the production subsidy alone were considered. Josling and Tangermann (1987) point out that the appropriate calculation for explaining the production effect of such programs is to estimate the production subsidy (or production tax) that would have called forth the actual production in the absence of supply controls. Trade-distortion equivalent estimates attempt to do this by including a corrective factor for reducing calculations of producer subsidy equivalents and subsidy equivalents when subsidies that increase producer prices are tied to supply controls.

The Effective Rate of Assistance or Protection
The effective rate of assistance or protection, a concept refined by Balassa (1965) and Corden (1966), measures the percentage by which the value added in an industry changes due to government protection and subsidization policies compared to its value added under conditions of free trade and an absence of government production-related subsidy programs. Specifically, the effective rate of assistance is defined as $ERA = (VA' - VA) / VA$, where VA' and VA are value added with and without, respectively, trade-distorting government policies. Value added is the difference between the total value of an industry's (or firm's) output and the costs of the intermediate inputs used in producing the final product, for example, raw materials, energy, and transportation. It measures the change in the return to the capital and labor employed directly in an industry or firm.

Calculation of the change in value added is quite straightforward if it is assumed that all inputs and outputs are traded under perfectly competitive conditions, all foreign supply and demand curves are infinitely elastic, imports and domestic production in an industry are perfect substitutes, and intermediate inputs are used in fixed proportions. Under these conditions, tariffs and nontariff measures affecting imports raise the domestic price of imports and of their domestic substitute by the ad valorem equivalents of these trade barriers, while production subsidies raise the price received by producers above the domestic price by the amount of their subsidy equivalents.

Subsidies or import restrictions on intermediate inputs lower or raise input prices to producers by the amount of their subsidy or tariff equivalents. More specifically, *VA'*, the value added resulting because of various government policies, is measured by the existing value added in an industry. The industry's value added under free trade is estimated by deducting from *VA'* the revenue equivalents of the tariff and nontariff barriers affecting the industry's output, the revenue equivalents of production subsidies, and the revenue equivalents of input subsidies and by adding the revenue equivalents of tariff and nontariff barriers affecting intermediate inputs used in production. The difference between *VA'* and *VA* expressed as a percentage of *VA* is the effective rate of assistance. Among the many studies of effective rates of assistance or protection are those by Balassa (1965), Baldwin (1970), Wilkinson and Norrie (1975), and Pitt (1981).

The effective rate of assistance brings out the significance of a product's value added share under free trade in determining the effects of protection. Making the simplified assumptions cited above, contrast the degree of protection on a simply processed good that sells for $1 per unit under free trade conditions, with a cost breakdown of $.90 for traded intermediate inputs and $.10 for value added by primary factors, with that on a more elaborately processed good also selling for $1 but whose cost components consist of $.50 of traded intermediates and $.50 of value added by primary factors. A 5-percent duty on the imports of each good will raise the price of each to $1.05. Since free trade conditions still prevail for the intermediate inputs used in producing both goods, the costs of these inputs remain unchanged. Consequently, the $.05 increase in the domestic value of the final goods will go to the primary factors. This raises by $.05 / $.10 or 50 percent the return to the primary factors used in producing the first good but only by $.05 / $.50 or 10 percent the return to the primary factors used in making the second good. Thus, a low nominal tariff on a simply processed good with a low value added component can yield a high effective rate of assistance or protection.

Modifying the assumptions of the simple model by introducing, for example, less than perfectly elastic supply curves and imperfect substitution between imports and domestic production makes the calculation of effective rates of assistance considerably more difficult — just as it makes the calculation of tariff and subsidy equivalents more difficult. It is a comparatively easy step, however, to calculate effective rates of assistance once tariff and subsidy equivalents have been estimated, especially if a standardized input-output table (or one for developed and another for developing countries) is used to determine the shares of various intermediate inputs used in production.

Quantity Impact Measures

Quantity impact measures focus on changes in the volume of imports and domestic production caused by various nontariff policies. As Jager and Lanjouw (1977) point out, a case can be made that trying to measure quantitative changes in imports and domestic output is more relevant for negotiators and domestic producers than trying to estimate price wedges. Quantitative measures can be aggregated across commodities and compared across countries by expressing the decrease or increase in trade attributable to trade policies as percentages of estimated trade or domestic production in the absence of those policies.

Besides inferring quantity changes from the simple frequency-type methods discussed earlier, as Hufbauer, Berliner, and Elliot (1986) have done, investigators have analyzed the effects of policy changes on particular industries by using both sector-specific and general equilibrium models.

Sector-Specific Models

Instead of attempting to capture all the interrelationships that determine the effects on an industry of changes in nontariff policies, sector-specific models can be used to examine only the most significant of these relationships. Although they require considerable effort to implement, such models are much less time-consuming to build than general equilibrium models, with the additional benefit of not having to rely, as simple methods or applied general equilibrium models often do, on parameter values for elasticities that are based on outdated studies.

Among those who have used this approach to analyze trade policy issues are Grossman (1986), who modeled the U.S. steel industry, Moroz and Salembier (1985), who studied the effects of Canada's footwear import quotas, and Pelzman (1986), who developed a model of the U.S. textile and apparel market. By estimating the reduced-form equation for employment using monthly observations over a ten-year period, Grossman obtains elasticity parameters that can be used to estimate the effects of employment, output, and domestic prices of such policy changes as a reduction in the level of duties on steel imports. For certain key sectors that are highly protected or subsidized and for which the accuracy of existing elasticity values is doubtful, sector-specific studies are highly desirable. The results from such studies are, however, very sensitive to the way in which the investigator formulates the model.

General Equilibrium Approaches

Multigood, multicountry trade models. As Deardorff and Stern (1985) note, one general approach to measuring the quantitative effects of nontariff trade barriers is to develop a multigood, multicountry regression model to explain actual trading patterns on the basis of factor endowments and various trade-resistance factors such as distance. The general relationships obtained are then used to estimate a particular country's trade with other countries from its unique set of factor endowments and resistance factors. The deviations between the country's actual and estimated trade patterns are taken to measure quantitatively the extent to which its trade policies are more or less restrictive than those of the collection of countries used to obtain the general relationships.

Notable applications of this technique by Saxonhouse (1983, 1988), Balassa (1986), and Lawrence (1987) have attempted to ascertain whether Japan's trade structure is consistent with its resource endowment. The results are inconclusive. Leamer (1988) uses this approach in trying to determine whether trade in individual products is distorted by unusually restrictive or export-promoting government policies. He concludes that the technique is too imperfect in explaining actual trading patterns on the basis of real variables such as factor endowments to isolate the effects of various trade measures.

Applied general equilibrium models. When major changes in protection and subsidy levels occur across industries and countries, the impact-effect measures obtained from sector-specific or other partial equilibrium approaches may be misleading. An applied general equilibrium model is needed to take full account of all the feedback effects from such changes. Among the models that have been specifically developed to examine trade policy issues are those constructed by Deardorff and Stern (1986), Dixon et al. (1982), Harris and Cox (1983), Whalley (1985), and de Melo and Tarr (forthcoming). In the more elaborate models, the effects of changes in nontariff policies across industries and countries on such variables as imports, exports, domestic production, employment, relative prices, and value added can be determined under a wide variety of assumptions about exchange rates, the flexibility of wages, and the mobility of labor and capital.

The use of applied general equilibrium models for policy analyses seems highly promising as they become more disaggregated, are extended to more countries, and are based on more reliable parameter estimates of key relationships. But until there is greater agreement among the builders of these systems on the appropriate way to model the key price- and quantity-determining relationships and greater comparability in industry detail, they are likely to serve more as useful checks on measurements of the effects of nontariff trade barriers obtained by the other methods than as the basic measurement approach.

Welfare Measures

In measuring the impact of tariff or nontariff policies, economists naturally think in terms of the comparative welfare effects of such policies. An economywide viewpoint is usually adopted, but the effects on world welfare can also be estimated. The methodologies previously described that use various direct and cross-price elasticities to arrive at price or quantity measures of nontariff policies already provide all the information needed for calculating consumer and producer surplus measures of economic welfare. In the recent EC study (Commission of the

European Communities 1988) of the effects of removing the remaining nontariff barriers among member states, price and quantity measures of these barriers were obtained for calculating the welfare gains from completing the Common Market. Other studies of the welfare effects of nontariff trade policies using a partial equilibrium approach are those by Tarr and Morkre (1984), Hickok (1985), and Hufbauer, Berliner, and Elliot (1986). With applied general equilibrium models, welfare changes are usually measured using the Hicksian concept of equivalent variation, that is, the income that would have been needed by members of the economy before the policy change to make them as well-off as they are after the policy change.

Conclusion

There are a number of techniques for measuring the effects of nontariff trade policies, none of which, unfortunately, is as simple to implement as those for measuring the effects of tariffs. As numerous studies indicate, however, taken together these techniques provide a practical and feasible means of obtaining measures of nontariff trade barriers that can be used for assessing relative sectoral protection across countries and for monitoring changes in protection and subsidization levels over time.

Tariff and subsidy equivalents of nontariff barriers are the measures with which public and private officials concerned with trade issues are most familiar and, therefore, should be the main forms of measurement used. Comparing foreign and domestic prices is the most direct means of obtaining tariff equivalents, but estimates based on known quantity changes (coupled with relevant price elasticity estimates) and on sector-specific studies should also be made as a check on the results from comparative price analyses. When good estimates of tariff and subsidy equivalents are available, they should also be used to calculate the effective rate of assistance, since this measure indicates the impact of trade distortions on the returns to domestic capital and labor more sharply than tariffs and subsidy equivalents alone.

Estimates of the quantitative effects of nontariff policies are a valuable supplemental measure and should be made where possible. In some instances, the technique used to estimate tariff and subsidy equivalents involves obtaining prior estimates of quantity changes, so this information is readily available. Such is the case when demand and supply elasticities for traded and domestic goods are used along with the data on quantitative changes to infer tariff equivalents, as well as when sector-specific and applied general equilibrium models are used. These latter models provide useful checks on other nontariff measures and will become even more useful as greater uniformity in modeling specifications and broader country and more detailed industry coverage are achieved.

Lists of nontariff trade measures and of the magnitude of their effect on trade have proved helpful in alerting government officials and others to the pervasiveness of nontariff trade-distorting policies. Frequency-type measures by themselves, however, are only a very crude measure for comparing the extent of protection or assistance across industries and countries.

Welfare measures, although regarded by economists as the best summary measure of policies that reduce economic efficiency, are unlikely to serve as a generally accepted basis for ascertaining whether a balance of concessions has been achieved in a negotiation. The wide divergence in views among negotiators about the proper welfare weights to be assigned to different groups within a country and to different countries makes it difficult to use welfare estimates for this purpose. But they can be very useful to individual countries in assessing alternative liberalization proposals, especially if the gains and losses to different consumer and producer groups across industries are separately identified so that public officials can combine these welfare changes according to their own sets of welfare weights.

In addition to determining the form in which to measure trade-distorting non-tariff barriers, investigators must decide on the types of trade barriers they wish to measure and the industry and country detail to include. Given the financial constraints on empirical research in this area, the appropriate approach initially would seem to be to focus on a limited number of sectors and countries and on nontariff measures whose price and quantity effects are significant. Concentrating on a small number of industries, such as textiles and apparel, steel, electronics, automobiles, and shipbuilding, and on major consuming and producing markets not only makes the measurement task feasible but also covers many of the nontariff trade policies of most concern to governments. Also, in order to prevent the measurement exercise from getting bogged down in disputes over what is or is not a trade-distorting policy, initial efforts to measure nontariff barriers across countries should concentrate on policies that quantitatively limit imports and exports, enforce particular prices, or clearly represent trade-distorting government subsidization.

Notes

1. Average tariffs in the industrial countries have been reduced from about 40 percent in the mid-1930s to a current level of about 5 percent.
2. The focus of the paper is on goods and services that are traded across national borders. Goods and services supplied by foreign firms within a country are also subject to trade-distorting and discriminatory government measures, but these are not considered here.
3. The European Community argued, however, that to achieve reciprocity there should be greater cuts in high-duty items than in low-duty ones. The tariff-cutting formula adopted in the Tokyo Round, by which high-duty rates were cut by a greater percentage than low rates, reflected this viewpoint.
4. The successive cross-price effects between imports and the domestically produced substitute will settle at levels at which the price and output level of the domestic variety are greater than initially and the price of imports is higher but the quantity lower than initially.
5. This threefold classification is used in the excellent survey of measurement methods by Deardorff and Stern (1986).

6. Under such arrangements as voluntary export restraints (VERs), whereby export licenses are usually allocated directly to foreign producers, p_1 is the price these producers would receive if export licenses were auctioned off by the foreign government. If the producers export to markets that are not subject to VERs, this is also the price that importers in these markets pay the producers.

7. This is part of a joint Eurostat-Organization for Economic Cooperation and Development (OECD) exercise in calculating purchasing power parities in which Eurostat collects data for EC members and OECD obtains data from non-EC members of OECD.

8. Unit values estimated from customs data are usually poor indicators of these prices.

9. In the case of VERs, for example, the export price in the tariff equivalent formula can be estimated from the price in markets supplied by foreign producers where VERs do not apply (see Hamilton 1988). However, the VERs are likely to affect the price in countries where the VERs do not apply as supplies are diverted to these countries.

10. As the OECD (1987) study of U.S. agricultural policies and their subsidy-equivalent effects documents, even finding identical agricultural products is not an easy task.

11. Levinsohn (1988) finds, for example, that to reduce total U.S. automobile imports by the same quantity as would a 1-percent rise in the price of Japanese automobiles alone requires only a 0.6-percent rise in automobile imports from all sources.

12. For a discussion of changes in the rate of protection or assistance and changes in exchange rates, see Industries Assistance Commission (1981).

References

Aw, B., and M. Roberts. 1986. "Estimating Quality Change in Quota-Constrained Markets: The Case of U.S. Footwear." *Journal of International Economics* 21: 45-60.

Balassa, B. 1965. "Tariff Protection in Industrial Countries: An Evaluation." *Journal of Political Economy* 73: 573-94.

Balassa, B. 1971. *The Structure of Protection in Developing Countries*. Baltimore, Md.: Johns Hopkins University Press.

Balassa, B. 1986. "Japan's Trade Policies." *Weltwirtschaftliches Archiv* 122 (Heft 4): 745-90.

Baldwin, R.E. 1970. *Non-Tariff Distortions of International Trade*. Washington, D.C.: Brookings Institution.

Baldwin, R.E. 1975. *Foreign Trade Regimes and Economic Development: The Philippines*. New York: National Bureau of Economic Research.

Bergsten, C.F., K. Elliot, J. Schott, and W. Takacs. 1987. "Auction Quotas and United States Policies." *Weltwirtschaftliches Archiv* 122 (Heft 4): 745-90.

Bhagwati, J., and T.N. Srinivasan. 1975. *Foreign Trade Regimes and Economic Development: India*. New York: National Bureau of Economic Research.

Commission of the European Communities. 1988. *European Economy: The Economics of 1992*. Luxembourg: Office for the Official Publications of the European Communities.

Corden, W.M. 1966. "The Structure of a Tariff System and the Effective Tariff Rate." *Journal of Political Economy* 74: 221-37.

Dardis, R. 1967. "Intermediate Goods and the Gains from Trade." *Review of Economics and Statistics* 49: 502-09.

Deardorff, A.V., and R.M. Stern. 1985. *Methods of Measurement of Nontariff Barriers*. Geneva: United Nations Conference on Trade and Development (UNCTAD / ST / MD/28).

Deardorff, A.V., and R.M. Stern. 1986. *The Michigan Model of World Production and Trade.* Cambridge, Mass.: MIT Press.

de Melo, J., and D. Tarr. Forthcoming. *A General Equilibrium Analysis of U.S. Trade Policy.* Cambridge, Mass.: MIT Press.

Dixon, P., B. Parmenter, J. Sutton, and D. Vincent. 1982. *ORANI: A Multisectoral Model of the Australian Economy.* Amsterdam: North- Holland.

Eurostat. 1988. *Purchasing Power Parities and Gross Domestic Product in Real Terms: Results 1985.* Luxembourg: Office of Official Publications of the European Communities.

Feenstra, R. 1984. "Voluntary Export Restraint in U.S. Autos, 1980-81: Quality, Employment, and Welfare Effects." In R. Baldwin and A. Krueger, eds, *The Structure and Evolution of Recent U.S. Trade Policy.* Chicago: University of Chicago Press and National Bureau of Economic Research.

Grossman, G. 1986. "Imports as a Cause of Injury: The Case of the U.S. Steel Industry." *Journal of International Economics* 20: 201-23.

Hamilton, C.B. 1986. "An Assessment of Voluntary Restraints on Hong Kong Exports to Europe and the U.S.A." *Economica* 53: 339-50.

Hamilton, C.B. 1988. "Restrictiveness and the International Transmission of the 'New' Protectionism." In R.E. Baldwin, ed., *Issues in U.S.-EC Trade Relations.* Chicago: University of Chicago Press and National Bureau of Economic Research.

Harris, R.G., with D. Cox. 1983. *Trade, Industrial Policy, and Canadian Manufacturing.* Toronto: Ontario Research Council.

Hickok, S. 1985. "The Consumer Cost of U.S. Trade Restraints." *Federal Reserve Bank of New York Quarterly Review* 10 (summer): 1-12.

Hufbauer, G.C., D.T. Berliner, and K. Elliot. 1986. *Trade Protection in the United States: 31 Case Studies.* Washington, D.C.: Institute for International Economics.

Industries Assistance Commission. 1981. *Annual Report*, 1980-81. Canberra: Australian Government Publishing Service.

Jager, M., and G.J. Lanjouw. 1977. "An Alternative Method for Quantifying International Trade Barriers." *Weltwirtschaftliches Archiv* 113 (Heft 4): 719-40.

Josling, T., and S. Tangermann. 1987. "Quantitative Measures for Negotiating and Monitoring Trade Liberalization in Agriculture." Paper presented at the International Agricultural Trade Research Consortium Meeting, Airlie House, Airlie, Virginia.

Lawrence, R.Z. 1987. "Does Japan Import Too Little: Closed Markets or Minds?" Paper presented at Brookings Panel on Economic Activity, Brookings Institute, Washington, D.C., September 10.

Leamer, E. 1988. "Measures of Openness." In R.E. Baldwin, ed., *Trade Policy Issues and Empirical Analysis.* Chicago: University of Chicago Press and National Bureau of Economic Research.

Levinsohn, J. 1988. "Empirics of Taxes on Differentiated Products: The Case of Tariffs in the U.S. Automobile Industry." In R. E. Baldwin, ed., *Trade Policy Issues and Empirical Analysis.* Chicago: University of Chicago Press and National Bureau of Economic Research.

Morici, P., and L. Megna. 1983. *U.S. Economic Policies Affecting Industrial Trade: A Quantitative Assessment.* Washington, D.C.: National Planning Association.

Moroz, A.R. 1985. *Approaches and Methodologies for Estimating Non-Tariff Barriers.* Discussion Paper No. 8508. Ottawa: Institute for Research on Public Policy.

Moroz, A.R., and G.E. Salembier. 1985. *Quantitative Assessment of the Costs and Benefits of the Footwear Import Quota.* Discussion Paper No. 8506. Ottawa: Institute for Research on Public Policy.

Nogues, J.J., A. Olechowski, and L.A. Winters. 1986. "The Extent of Nontariff Barriers to Industrial Countries' Imports." *World Bank Economic Review* 1: 181-99.

Olechowski, A. 1987. "Nontariff Barriers to Trade." In J.M. Finger and A. Olechowski, eds, *The Uruguay Round: A Handbook in Multilateral Trade Negotiations*. Washington, D.C.: The World Bank.

Organization for Economic Cooperation and Development (OECD). 1987. *National Policies and Agricultural Trade: Country Study, United States*. Paris: OECD.

Pelzman, J. 1986. "The Tariff Equivalents of the Existing Quotas Under the Multifiber Arrangement." Paper presented at Southern Economic Association Meetings, New Orleans, Louisiana, November 23-25.

Pitt, M.M. 1981. "Alternative Trade Strategies and Employment in Indonesia." In A. Krueger, H. Lary, T. Monson, and N. Akrasanee, eds, *Trade and Employment in Developing Countries I: Individual Studies*. Chicago: University of Chicago Press.

Roningen, V.D., and A. Yeats. 1976. "Nontariff Distortions of International Trade: Some Preliminary Empirical Evidence." *Weltwirtschaftliches Archiv* 112 (Heft 4): 613-25.

Saxonhouse, G.R. 1983. "The Micro- and Macroeconomics of Foreign Sales to Japan." In W.R. Cline, ed., *Trade Policy in the 1980s*. Cambridge, Mass.: MIT Press.

Saxonhouse, G.R. 1988. "Differentiated Products, Economies of Scale, and Access to the Japanese Market." Paper presented to Tenth Annual Middlebury Conference on Economic Issues, Middlebury College, Middlebury, Vermont.

Tarr, D.G., and M.E. Morkre. 1984. *Aggregate Costs to the United States of Tariffs and Quotas on Imports: General Tariff Cuts and Removal of Quotas on Automobiles, Steel, Sugar, and Textiles*. Washington, D.C.: Federal Trade Commission.

Whalley, J. 1985. *Trade Liberalization Among Major World Trading Areas*. Cambridge, Mass.: MIT Press.

Whalley, J., and R.M. Wigle. 1988. *Endogenous Participation in Agricultural Support Programs and Ad Valorem Equivalent Modeling*. London, Canada: Center for Study of International Economic Relations.

Wilkinson, B.W., and K. Norrie. 1975. *Effective Protection and the Return to Capital*. Ottawa: Economic Council of Canada.

3

Import-Increasing Quantitative Trade Restrictions

Wendy E. Takacs

This paper is an outgrowth of my doctoral thesis, which was supervised by Béla Balassa. After some years of exploring other issues, recent work has brought me back to the topic of quantitative trade restrictions. I am indebted to him for suggesting, back in early 1973, that I investigate the implications of quantitative restrictions under imperfect competition. That suggestion revealed his keen perception of areas worthy of exploration and, indeed, the future direction of the field of international trade theory. I am pleased to have the opportunity to present him with this extension of my earlier work.

Quantitative Restrictions

Quantitative trade restrictions directly limit the quantity or value of a product that is allowed to enter or leave a country. They appear in a number of forms. On the import side, a quota generally imposes a specific, preannounced upper limit on the value or volume of a specified product that can enter a country during a given period. Import quotas are administered by the importing country, usually either on a first-come, first-served basis, which entails closing the border to further imports once the quota ceiling has been reached, or through import licenses or permits issued to selected individuals or firms.

Quantitative restrictions can be applied to exports as well as imports. An increasingly popular method of protecting declining domestic industries in industrial countries has been to negotiate "voluntary" export quotas with supplying countries, particularly newly emerging suppliers whose exports are growing rapidly. These negotiated quotas are variously referred to as "voluntary export restraints," "voluntary restraint arrangements," or "orderly marketing arrangements."

Despite the general prohibition on the use of quantitative restrictions in the General Agreement on Tariffs and Trade (GATT), they remain a prevalent feature of international trading relations. Many developing countries rely heavily on licensing arrangements to restrict trade. Recent World Bank calculations using United Nations Conference on Trade and Development (UNCTAD) data reveal that a significant and growing proportion of the major industrialized countries' trade also is subject to some type of quantitative restriction. Between 1981 and 1988, the percentage of nonfuel imports subject to quantitative restrictions increased from approximately 14 percent to 16 percent in the United States and from 11 to 12 percent in the European Community. In Japan, the proportion of nonfuel imports subject to quantitative restrictions fell slightly during the same period, but remained high at over 20 percent.

These figures, which are based on the value of trade in product categories subject to particular types of nontariff trade barriers, are imperfect measures of the severity of the restrictions and should not be compared across countries. For example, very restrictive quotas allow little trade, so the proportion of trade covered would be very small. In the extreme case of embargoes, products would show up with zero weight, because no trade would occur. Despite the difficulties of interpretation, these figures do indicate that quantitative restrictions are wide-spread and that they remain an important, and probably growing, phenomenon.

One reason for the popularity of quotas among industries seeking protection is that their protective effect seems more certain than that of tariffs or tariff-like policy instruments such as countervailing and antidumping duties. A tariff or a countervailing or antidumping duty only increases the price of the imported product. The exact impact on the quantity imported is uncertain and depends on the reactions of domestic suppliers and consumers to higher prices and on the behavior of the world market price of the imported product itself. In the face of falling world prices or an appreciating home currency, a given tariff increase cannot be relied on to increase the domestic price of the imported good and, therefore, to decrease imports.

The common perception among the general public appears to be that quantitative trade restrictions will restrict import quantities with greater certainty and more effectively than price measures such as increased tariffs, countervailing duties, or antidumping duties. By directly constraining import quantities, quotas are perceived to better maintain production levels in the domestic industry, save jobs, and improve trade deficits.

Baldwin (1982) catalogs a number of reasons why trade barriers, particularly discriminatory quantitative restrictions, will fail to protect domestic industries effectively. Restrictions can be circumvented by altering the product itself or changing the degree of processing to either higher or lower stages to avoid restricted product categories. Discriminatory trade restrictions can be circumvented by transshipping goods through, or shifting production facilities to, unrestrained countries.

Moreover, if the protected industries are imperfectly competitive, the expected domestic production and employment benefits from quotas may prove chimerical. If the domestic industry consists of just one or just a few firms, quotas will not necessarily lead to higher production levels. Heuser (1939), Bhagwati (1965), and Finger (1971) have shown that in the presence of monopoly in the domestic product market, quotas can reduce, rather than increase, domestic output. This result occurs because the quota eliminates potential foreign competition and allows a single domestic producer to exploit its monopoly power. Once the quota is in place, a profit-maximizing monopolist has an incentive to reduce output to drive up the price of its product and increase profits. Similarly, quotas are likely to reduce domestic industry output when the market structure is oligopolistic, as the work of Krishna (1983) and Harris (1985) implies. In both these cases of imperfect competition, quotas would fail to maintain production levels in the industry. Lower domestic output would presumably also lower the demand for labor, so quotas would also fail to protect jobs.

Quantitative restrictions can also have a perverse effect on the balance of trade. If the restrictions take the form of negotiated quotas with exporting countries (voluntary export restraints) or if import quotas are administered by issuing licenses to exporting countries (as with the U.S. sugar quotas), then the prices paid by importers for the restrained goods are highly likely to increase because of the supply restraints. As Corden (1971, 212) notes, the quantity of imports may fall, but if import demand is inelastic, the value of imports will increase.

The purpose of this essay is to point out another potential shortcoming of quantitative restrictions that has received less attention in the literature: the imposition of quotas may actually *increase*, rather than decrease, the *quantity* of imports. I will show, in a partial equilibrium, comparative static framework, two instances in which, given market power on the part of a single domestic producer, the imposition of quotas increases the quantity of imports.

Import-Increasing Import Quotas

The first case involves the imposition of a quota above the current import level when the import-competing good is produced by only one firm in the importing country. If a quota ceiling is imposed above the current level of imports, the imposition of the quota alone can cause imports to jump to fill the quota. This result is implicit in the work of Heuser (1939) and Bhagwati (1965) and is specifically addressed by Snape (1986).

To illustrate this possibility, suppose that a single firm in the importing country produces a product that is a perfect substitute for an imported good. In figure 3.1, the demand for the product on the part of domestic consumers is shown by demand curve D. Suppose that the world market for the product can be considered competitive and that the importing country is large enough to face an upward sloping supply curve of the imported good. Given the supply of imports, the domestic firm faces a residual demand curve, D_R, obtained by subtracting the quantity of imports supplied at each price from the total quantity demanded at that price. The import supply curve is not shown explicitly in figure 3.1; the quantity supplied by foreign producers is equal to the horizontal distance between D and D_R. In the absence of trade restrictions, the domestic producer would maximize profits by producing at Q_F, where marginal revenue associated with the residual demand curve (MR_F) equals marginal cost (MC). The resulting equilibrium price would be P_F, the quantity consumed Q_F, and the quantity imported $C_F - Q_F$.

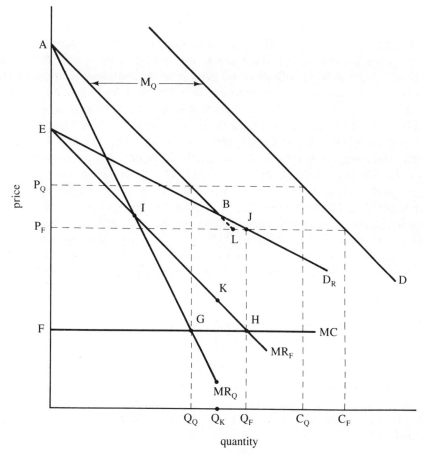

Figure 3.1 Import-Increasing Import Quota

Suppose now that the government of this importing country decides to prevent increases in imports or to protect the domestic industry by imposing an import quota, with a quota ceiling (M_Q) above the level of imports in the free-trade equilibrium. Once the quota is in place, the quantity of imports cannot increase above the quota ceiling regardless of the price charged by the domestic producer. This implies that the quota would change the residual demand curve facing the domestic producer to a line parallel to the domestic demand curve D once the quota ceiling was reached. In figure 3.1, the residual demand curve with a quota of M_Q would become the kinked line ABD_R. Given the kink in the demand curve, the marginal revenue curve would become discontinuous at the output level where the kink occurs, Q_K. For output levels up to Q_K, the relevant segment of the marginal revenue curve would be that corresponding to the segment of the quota-distorted demand curve AB, which is shown by AMR_Q. For output levels beyond Q_K, the marginal revenue curve would be the line segment KMR_F.

Given the discontinuous marginal revenue curve, there are two output levels at which marginal revenue equals marginal cost, Q_Q and Q_F. The producer would have to compare the size of profits at these two output levels to determine which one maximizes profits. Given fixed costs, this will be the output level that corresponds to the greatest difference between revenue and variable costs, or the greatest area between the relevant marginal revenue curve and the marginal cost curve. In terms of figure 3.1, this analysis would involve comparing area AGF to area EHF. Area $EIGF$ is common to both, so this is equivalent to comparing the area of triangle AIE to that of triangle IHG.

If area AIE is less than area IHG, then Q_F would remain the profit-maximizing output level. The imposition of the quota would not prompt the domestic producer to revise production or pricing decisions and the quota would be nonbinding. If AIE is larger than IHG, however, (as is the case in figure 3.1) then the profit-maximizing domestic producer would reduce output to Q_Q and raise price to P_Q. At this higher price, consumption would fall to C_Q. Given that the quantity of imports supplied at this price exceeds the quota ceiling, imports would increase to fill the quota. Extending the line segment AB downward to cross the P_F price line reveals an increase in imports of LJ, the horizontal distance between this extension and D_R at P_F. Thus, contrary to the popular perception that imposing quotas limits imports and promotes domestic production, this quota reduces domestic output and *increases* the quantity of imports.

Notice that for a quota to increase imports, the quota ceiling must be above, but relatively close to, the free-trade level of imports. As the quota ceiling increases, the AB segment of the residual demand curve and its associated marginal revenue curve AMR_Q both shift to the left. The leftward shift shrinks area AIE and increases area IHG, reducing the probability that profits would be higher at Q_Q than at Q_F.

Import-Increasing Voluntary Export Restraints

If domestic production of an import substitute is monopolized, quantitative restrictions in the form of discriminatory quotas that restrict only some suppliers also can increase the quantity of imports. A voluntary export restraint imposed by one country (or a subset of countries) at a level below its previous export level will tend to encourage increases in shipments from other nonrestraining exporters. Increases in imports from nonrestraining countries often prompt importing countries to request voluntary export restraints of those suppliers as well.

The prime example of this phenomenon is the Multifiber Arrangement, which can be traced back to Japan's agreement to limit exports of certain cotton textiles to the United States. Prompted by diversion of trade to other markets, increases in exports from other countries, and substitution of products made from other fibers, the net of bilaterally negotiated export restrictions spread to encompass trade in cotton, wool, ramie, silk, and synthetic textile and apparel products among twenty importing and thirty-four exporting countries. Similarly, the present set of arrangements that restricts the shipment of steel products to the United States began with an accord between the United States and the European Community in 1982. By the end of 1984, these arrangements had spread to include Japan, Mexico, Brazil, and South Africa. By the end of 1987, the coverage had increased to nineteen exporting countries.

Many observers have noted that increased exports from nonrestraining sources can dilute the effectiveness of export restraints as import-reducing measures. This diversion of trade is one reason that Baldwin (1982) considers voluntary export restraints ineffective, and Bhagwati (1988) refers to them as a form of "porous protection." What has not been recognized, however, is that a discriminatory quota can increase total imports of the restrained good if imposing the quota encourages increases in imports from nonrestrained sources that more than compensate for the reductions on the part of the restraining suppliers.

Figure 3.2 illustrates that the imposition of an export quota that reduces exports from one supplier can, in a comparative static sense, increase exports from non-restraining suppliers by a greater amount. Assume that a single producer of a product within an importing country faces competition from two groups of foreign suppliers, each of which constitutes a competitive industry within its own country. The good exported by each country and the domestic good are perfect substitutes. The export supply conditions of the two exporting countries are shown in the left panel of figure 3.2. The total export supply curve of both countries taken together is S, which represents the supply of imports to the importing country in the absence of trade restrictions. Country 1's export supply curve is S_1. To keep the diagram as simple as possible, country 2's export supply curve is not shown explicitly, but appears in the diagram as the distance between S_1 and S.

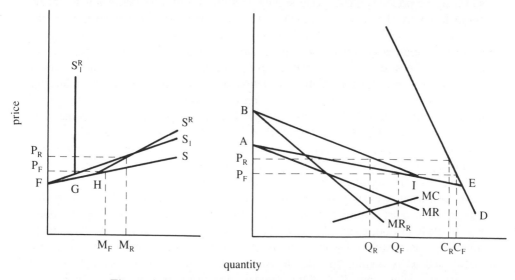

Figure 3.2 Import-Increasing Voluntary Export Restraint

The demand curve of domestic consumers or users of the product is represented by curve D in the right-hand panel of figure 3.2. In the absence of trade restrictions, the import-competing producer faces an effective demand curve for its output of AED, derived by subtracting horizontally the quantity supplied by exporters in countries 1 and 2 from total domestic demand at each price. This curve shows the residual quantity that can be sold by the import-competing producer at any given price once the quantity supplied by the competitive industries abroad has been absorbed by the domestic market. The marginal revenue curve associated with this demand curve is AMR. Profits would be maximized by producing the quantity Q_F, where marginal cost MC equals marginal revenue MR. The equilibrium price would be P_F. At that price, consumption would be C_F and imports would be M_F (equal to $C_F - Q_F$).

To illustrate how an export restraint can increase the total quantity of imports, suppose that country 1 agrees to "voluntarily" restrict its exports below the free-trade level. Country 1's export supply curve would become vertical at the export quota ceiling, as shown by the line FGS_1^R in the left panel. Assume that country 2 does not restrict its exports. This is a realistic assumption because voluntary export restraint arrangements frequently leave some important suppliers out of the agreements if they refuse to cooperate, if the political cost of including them is too great, or if joint membership in a free-trade area or common market makes it impossible to impose an export restraint. The total supply curve facing the importing country would correspondingly shift to FHS^R.

With foreign supply restricted by the export restraint, the domestic producer faces less import competition (in the sense that the increase in imports from any given price increase will be smaller) and so has an incentive to cut back output and increase price. The change in supply conditions will alter the residual demand curve faced by the domestic producer to $BIED$ and the relevant section of the marginal revenue curve to BMR_R. The profit-maximizing domestic producer would decrease output to Q_R, where the quota-distorted marginal revenue curve crosses the marginal cost curve, increase price to P_R, and decrease consumption as a result to C_R. In the case illustrated, the imposition of the export restraint by country 1 would decrease production in the importing country by more than it would decrease consumption. The result is a higher quantity of imports at the new equilibrium. This paradoxical result is more likely the less elastic is domestic demand for the restrained good, the more elastic is supply from the countries not restraining their exports, and the less marginal cost increases with output.

Tentative evidence suggests that this paradoxical result may have occurred after Japan restricted television set exports to the United States in 1977 and after the Japanese voluntary export restraint on automobile exports to France became binding in 1984. In both cases, the domestic market structure was imperfectly competitive: two dominant firms and a number of smaller firms. In the United States, Zenith and RCA dominated the television industry in 1976, although there were ten other smaller firms (U.S. International Trade Commission 1977). In France, there were two relatively large automobile firms (Peugeot-Citroën and Renault) and a few much smaller firms (Adams 1981). Although these are not cases of monopolistic market structure, collusion to exploit market power is far from implausible in an industry dominated by two large firms.

In the case of the Japanese voluntary export restraint on shipments of television to the United States, the issue is clouded by a lack of data on U.S. imports of incomplete sets before mid-1977. But data reported by Morkre and Tarr (1980) indicate that after Japan cut back exports of complete sets by about one million units and froze exports of incomplete sets in mid-1977, total U.S. imports of complete and incomplete sets increased. Between 1977 and 1978, Korean exports of complete sets to the United States more than quadrupled, while Taiwanese exports more than doubled. U.S. imports of incomplete sets from Taiwan more than doubled and imports from Mexico increased by 60 percent between the second half of 1977 and the second half of 1978.

The Japanese voluntary export restraint on automobile exports to France also may be an example of an import-increasing quota. Results reported in de Melo and Messerlin (1988) indicate that the restraint became binding in 1984 but that total French imports of automobiles increased significantly between 1984 and 1985, despite static demand, due to increased imports from other European suppliers.

Given the small number of firms in the U.S. automobile industry, one might wonder whether the Japanese voluntary export restraint increased total U.S. automobile imports by increasing imports from Europe. The evidence suggests that this was not the case. Dinopoulos and Kreinin (1988) show that the prices of European automobiles shipped to the United States increased significantly but that quantities shipped did not. This result may be due to a combination of relatively inelastic supply due to capacity constraints and the relatively competitive behavior of firms in the U.S. industry, as found by Dixit (1988) and Krishna, Hogan, and Swagel (1989).

Conclusion

The belief that quotas reduce imports and trade deficits, protect domestic industries, and save jobs is persistent and pervasive. This is the likely outcome if domestic industries are perfectly competitive, but if the protected industry is imperfectly competitive quotas may not achieve these objectives.

Imposing an import quota to protect a single domestic producer may increase the total quantity of imports if the quota ceiling is above the free-trade import level. By increasing the market power of the domestic producer, the quota may reduce the producer's profit-maximizing output level, increase the price it charges, and cause imports to jump to fill the quota.

Quantitative trade restrictions in the form of voluntary export restraints also can increase the quantity of imports. If only some suppliers adopt restraints, total imports will rise if exports from nonrestraining countries increase by more than the cutback in shipments from the restraining countries. Again, this result can occur if the voluntary export restraint increases the market power of a single domestic producer enough to cause a sufficiently large decrease in output and increase in price.

In both these cases, imposing the quota reduces domestic output (and therefore presumably employment) and increases the quantity and value of imports. While these effects certainly do not contribute to the objectives of reducing trade deficits or saving jobs, the domestic producer will enjoy higher profits.

Tentative evidence suggests two possible cases of import-increasing quotas: the 1977 Japan-United States voluntary export restraint on television sets and the Japan-France voluntary export restraint on automobiles after it became binding in 1984.

References

Adams, W.J. 1981. "The Automobile Industry." In H. W. de Jong, ed., *The Structure of European Industry*. The Hague: Martinus Nijhoff.

Baldwin, R.E. 1982. *The Inefficacy of Trade Policy*. Essays in International Finance No. 150. Princeton, N.J.: Princeton University.

Bhagwati, J. 1965. "On the Equivalence of Tariffs and Quotas." In R.E. Baldwin et al., eds, *Trade, Growth, and the Balance of Payments*. Chicago: University of Chicago Press.

Bhagwati, J. 1988. *Protectionism*. Cambridge, Mass.: MIT Press.

Corden, W.M. 1971. *The Theory of Protection*. Oxford: Clarendon Press.

de Melo, J., and P. Messerlin. 1988. *Effects of European VERs on Japanese Autos*. PPR Working Paper No. 21. Washington, D.C.: World Bank.

Dinopoulos, E., and M.E. Kreinin. 1988. "Effects of the U.S.-Japan Auto VER on European Prices and on U.S. Welfare." *Review of Economics and Statistics* 70: 484-91.

Dixit, A. 1988. "Optimal Trade and Industrial Policies for the U.S. Automobile Industry." In R.C. Feenstra, ed., *Empirical Methods for International Trade*. Cambridge, Mass.: MIT Press.

Finger, J. M. 1971. "Protection and Domestic Output." *Journal of International Economics* 1: 345-51.

Harris, R. 1985. "Why Voluntary Export Restraints are 'Voluntary.'" *Canadian Journal of Economics* 18: 799-809.

Heuser, H. 1939. *Control of International Trade*. London: George Routledge and Sons.

Krishna, K. 1983. *Trade Restrictions as Facilitating Practices*. Discussion Papers in Economics No. 55. Princeton, N.J.: Woodrow Wilson School of Public and International Affairs, Princeton University.

Krishna, K., K. Hogan, and P. Swagel. 1989. "The Nonoptimality of Optimal Trade Policies: The U.S. Automobile Industry Revisited, 1979-1985." Paper presented at the National Bureau of Economic Research and Center for Economic Policy Research Conference on Empirical Studies of Strategic Trade Policy, Cambridge, Mass., October 13.

Morkre, M., and D.G. Tarr. 1980. *The Effects of Restrictions on United States Imports: Five Case Studies and Theory*. Washington, D.C.: Federal Trade Commission.

Snape, R.H. 1986. "The Impact on Exporters of Import Restrictions." In K. Tucker and C. Baden Fuller, eds, *Firms and Markets*. London: Croom Helm.

United States International Trade Commission. 1977. *Television Receivers, Color and Monochrome, Assembled or Not Assembled, Finished or Not Finished and Subassemblies Thereof*. USITC Publication 808. Washington, D.C.: International Trade Commission.

4

Project Evaluation and Compensation Tests

Tatsuo Hatta

Béla Balassa (1974a, b) is among the pioneers in the development of the concept of the shadow price of a project in nontradable goods. The topic attracted the attention of a large number of economists and grew into a flourishing field of study. The present paper attempts to examine the relationship among project evaluation criteria, compensation tests, and the maximization of social welfare in the long run.

For project evaluation in a multihousehold economy with tariff protection, three different concepts of efficiency improvements have been used: (1) compensation tests, (2) the sum of compensating variations, and (3) shadow prices in project evaluation.

The Samuelson (1950) compensation test is the definitive measure of efficiency improvement. But it appeared so stringent that few have claimed that a given project actually passes this test. A less stringent test is the Kaldor (1939) compensation test. A project passes this test if those who gain from the project can potentially compensate those who lose. The Kaldor test may be regarded as the minimum criterion of efficiency improvement from the general equilibrium point of view.

It used to be claimed that if the sum of compensating variations of a project is positive, the project passes the Kaldor test. But Boadway (1974), Bruce and Harris (1982), and Boadway and Bruce (1984) have conclusively shown that this is not the case when the project influences the domestic price vector.[1] Chipman and Moore (1980) also discredited the compensating variation as an indicator of welfare level, but for an entirely different reason. They showed that even in a single-consumer economy, a project that gives a higher compensating variation than another may improve the utility level less than the other.

The contemporary literature on project evaluation in the presence of tariff protection began with Little and Mirrlees (1969). Early theoretical contributions to this topic include Balassa (1974a, b), Joshi (1972), Dasgupta and Stiglitz (1974), and Boadway (1974). The shadow prices of factors, and so of nontradables, were studied in the standard trade theoretic models by Findlay and Wellisz (1976) and Srinivasan and Bhagwati (1978). Diewert (1983) examined this topic in a general framework and synthesized the literature.[2]

The inner product of the project vector and the shadow price vector represents the compensated increase in the trade surplus caused by the project, that is, the increase in the amount of foreign aid the country can afford as a result of the project while maintaining the preproject utility level for everyone in the country. In this paper, that increase is called the *surplus variation* of the project.[3]

The first aim of this paper is to examine the conditions under which a positive surplus variation of a project implies that the project passes some compensation tests. In particular, we show that if the surplus variation of a project is locally positive, the project passes the Kaldor test in an economy where the utility frontier reflects a trade-off. We also establish that a project with a locally positive surplus variation passes the Samuelson test in an economy where the utility frontier reflects a trade-off and the shadow price concept of Findlay and Wellisz (1976) and Bhagwati and Srinivasan (1982) is meaningful.

Recently, the social welfare criterion rather than the efficiency improvement criterion has been increasingly used for project evaluations, as the survey by Dreze and Stern (1987) shows. There seem to be two underlying reasons for this. First, the Samuelson compensation test has been considered too stringent, so the social welfare criterion is regarded as more practical in application. Second, Chipman and Moore (1971, 1978), as well as the literature on optimal taxation, have argued that the social welfare criterion rather than the efficiency improvement criterion should be employed since a project passing the Samuelson test may reduce social welfare.

The second aim of this paper is to argue that the choice of efficiency criterion or social welfare criterion should not be absolute and that different economic situations require different criteria. We too accept social welfare maximization as the long-run target of a series of economic policies. We argue, however, that the concept of "efficiency improvement" is a useful policy criterion for the purpose of improving the long-run social welfare in an economy where numerous efficiency-seeking reforms regularly take place.

The paper first reviews the relevant literature and then presents the surplus model. After a discussion of the relationship between the surplus variation of a project and welfare improvement in a single-household economy, the paper discusses the relationship between surplus variation and compensation tests. The relationship between the Findlay-Wellisz-Srinivasan-Bhagwati shadow price and compensation tests is also discussed. Finally, the efficiency criterion and the social welfare function criterion are compared.

The Issues in the Literature

This section briefly reviews the theoretical issues in the literature that can be graphically analyzed.

The Boadway Paradox

We will call the phenomenon whereby a project with a positive sum of compensating variations fails the Kaldor test the Boadway paradox. This occurs only if the project influences domestic prices. Boadway (1974) established this paradox through the following stark example. Consider an exchange economy with two consumers, A and B, and two goods, X_1 and X_2 (figure 4.1). The initial equilibrium is I on the efficiency locus. Suppose that a project transfers income from B to A without changing the product bundle, shifting the equilibrium to point II on the same efficiency locus. This project does not enable A, the gainer, to compensate B, the loser, since the prereform equilibrium is Pareto optimal. Yet the sum of the compensating variations resulting from this project is ab, and hence positive.[4] So although this project has a positive sum of compensating variations, it fails to pass the Kaldor test.

Note that this is not a pathological example. It can readily be shown that the sum of compensating variations caused by an income transfer among consumers is always positive in an exchange economy if the initial equilibrium is Pareto optimal and if the transfer affects the price vector. Since the gainers from a transfer of income at a Pareto optimal point can never compensate the losers, Boadway's example can readily be extended to the multiconsumer and multi-commodity case.

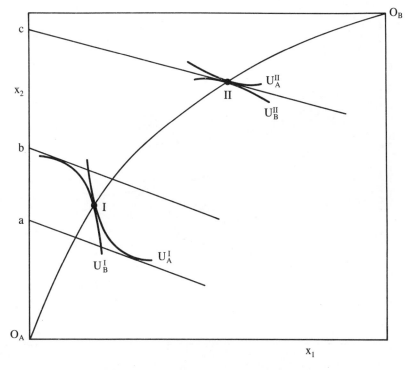

Figure 4.1 The Boadway Paradox

Ruiz-Castillo (1987) showed that if the utility functions of all consumers are identical and homothetic, the Boadway paradox does not occur. Indeed, when his conditions are satisfied, the efficiency locus of figure 4.1 is the diagonal line, and the transfer does not change the price vector. His result shows the pathological state of the economy needed for the sum of the compensating variations to serve as a meaningful efficiency improvement criterion.[5]

The Chipman-Moore Paradox

Figure 4.2 illustrates Chipman and Moore's (1980) finding that in a single-consumer economy a project that gives a higher compensating variation than another project can result in a lower utility level than the other. Project 1 brings the economy from 0 to *I*, while Project 2 brings the economy to *II*. Figure 4.2

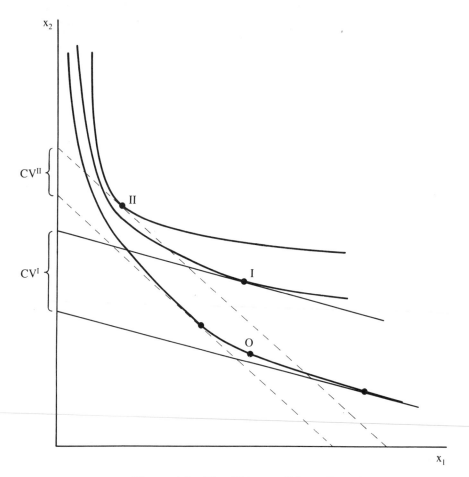

Figure 4.2   The Chipman-Moore Paradox

depicts the situation in which project 1 yields a lower welfare increase but a higher compensating variation. Notice that the Chipman-Moore paradox disappears if equivalent variation rather than compensating variation is used. This is in contrast to the Boadway paradox, which occurs whether compensating or equivalent variation is used.

Shadow Price Vector

When the public project concerns only tradables, it is easy to see why a project has to be evaluated using the world price vector rather than the domestic price vector. Figure 4.3 depicts a small open economy that has a single consumer and produces only two tradables with a fixed output bundle, Q. The consumption possibility curve is QA^0, and the consumption bundle is A^0. The slope of the consumption possibility curve represents the world price vector, while that of the dashed lines represents the domestic price vector. Suppose that the project shifts the output bundle from Q to B, pushing up the consumption possibility curve. This expansion in the consumption possibility set brings the new consumption point to A^1, improving the utility level. The value of the project bundle QB as evaluated by

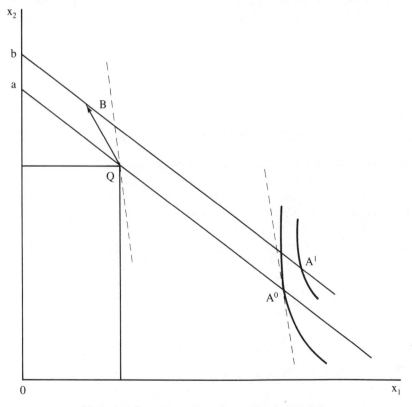

Figure 4.3   International vs. Domestic Prices

the world price is positive since the arrow *QB* lies above the initial consumption possibility curve. But its value evaluated using the domestic price vector is negative since the arrow *QB* lies below the dashed line passing *Q*. Thus the outward shift of the consumption possibility line to *BA*¹ is correctly reflected by the world price vector but not by the domestic price vector. This explains why Little and Mirrlees (1969) adopt the world price vector of tradables as their shadow price vector.

When a project is in nontradables, the shift in the consumption possibility surface it causes is no longer readily seen in a diagrammatic analysis. Also, such a project will typically change the price vector of nontradables, and the concept of the shift in consumption possibility surface itself needs refinement. In the following discussion, therefore, we have to formally extend the analysis.

The Surplus Model

Consider an economy that produces many tradable and nontradable goods. In this section and the next, we assume that a representative consumer in the economy maximizes his utility u, taking as given the nontradable and tradable price vectors denoted p^N and p^T, respectively. The compensated demand functions for tradables and nontradables, respectively, may be written as

$$(1) \qquad x^T = x^T(u, p^T, p^N)$$

and

$$(2) \qquad x^N = x^N(u, p^T, p^N),$$

Let y^T and y^N be the net production vectors of the tradable and nontradable goods, respectively. Some of the nontradables are factor inputs (e.g., labor or land), and therefore the corresponding elements of y^N will be negative. For given p^T and y^N, we define the vector $y^T(p^T, y^N)$ as the one that attains the maximum domestic market value of the tradable goods (i.e., $p^{T\prime}y^T$), subject to the given technology. We also define $p^N(p^T, y^N)$ as the vector such that for the given y^N, profit-maximizing producers produce y^T when they face the price vectors p^T for tradables and $p^N(p^T, y^N)$ for nontradables.[6]

We assume that perfectly competitive producers maximize their profits under constant-scale technology. Then we have

$$(3) \qquad y^T = y^T(p^T, y^N)$$

$$(4) \qquad p^N = p^N(p^T, y^N).$$

Net government production vectors of tradables and nontradables are given by $g^T(\alpha)$ and $g^N(\alpha)$, where α is the parameter denoting the stage of production and positive elements of $g(\alpha)$ correspond to outputs and negative elements to inputs.

The market equilibrium condition for nontradables may be written as

$$(5) \qquad\qquad x^N(u, p^T, p^N) - y^N - g^N(\alpha) = 0.$$

When u, p^T, and α are given, the system of equations 4 and 5 determines p^N and y^N. The system contains $2N$ equations and the same number of variables, where N is the number of nontradables and is unrelated to the superscript symbol N. The solution for p^N and y^N represents the price and the output vectors of nontradables that would prevail if the government kept the level of u fixed by adjusting the level of lump-sum transfers to the consumer and set the stage of the project at α in an economy that faces the international price vector of tradables p^T. The corresponding output vector of the tradables is readily found from equation 3.

We assume that tariffs τ are imposed on tradables, whose world price is p^T_*. Then we have

$$(6) \qquad\qquad p^T = p^T_* + \tau.$$

If we let s represent the trade surplus, we have

$$(7) \qquad\qquad s = - p^{T\prime}_*[x^T(u, p^T, p^N) - y^T(p^T, y^N) - g^T(\alpha)].$$

By substituting equation 5 for y^N in equation 7, we have

$$(8) \qquad\qquad s = - p^{T\prime}_* z^T(u, p^T, p^N, \alpha),$$

where

$$(9) \quad z^T(u, p^T, p^N, \alpha) \equiv x^T(u, p^T, p^N) - y^T[p^T, x^N(u, p^T, p^N) - g^N(\alpha)] - g^T(\alpha).$$

The function z^T expresses the net import demand for tradables in terms of u, α, and the price vectors of tradables and nontradables. We will call this function the *compensated import demand function* for tradables.

We consider a model consisting of equations 4, 5, and 8, which has $2N + 1$ equations and the same number of variables: p^N, y^N, and s. Parameters in this model are u, p^T, α, p^T_*, and τ. We will call this the *surplus model for the single-household economy*. A set of budget equations of each agent consistent with the surplus model exists and is discussed in the appendix, which shows that the trade surplus s is equal to the government surplus since Walras' Law and the budget equations of producers and consumers are satisfied.

The solutions to the surplus model may be written as follows:

(10) $$p^N = \boldsymbol{p}^N(u, \ \alpha; \ p^T)$$

(11) $$y^N = \boldsymbol{y}^N(u, \ \alpha; \ p^T)$$

and

(12) $$s = \boldsymbol{s}(u, \ \alpha; \ p^T, \ p^T_*).$$

We assume that a unique solution exists for p^N, y^N, and s for the initial values of $(u, \ \alpha; \ p^T, \ p^T_*)$ and that the functions $\boldsymbol{p}^N$, $\boldsymbol{y}^N$, and $\boldsymbol{s}$ are continuously differentiable in the neighborhood of these initial values. (Note that $\boldsymbol{p}^N$, $\boldsymbol{y}^N$, and $\boldsymbol{s}$ are not vector symbols but are substitutes for script symbols.) We will call this the *causality assumption* of the solution functions of the surplus model.

We will call the function $\boldsymbol{s}(u, \ \alpha; \ p^T, \ p^T_*)$ in equation 12 the *surplus function*. It represents the amount of foreign aid this country can afford to give while maintaining utility at the specified level. Thus, $\partial s / \partial \alpha$ represents the dollar amount by which this country can afford to increase foreign aid as a result of the project while maintaining its own utility level intact. We will call this efficiency improvement measure the *surplus variation* of the project. The term $-\partial \boldsymbol{s} / \partial u$ measures how much reduction in foreign aid is required to increase the utility level without changing p^T, p^T_*, and α. Since this term converts a change in the trade surplus expressed in dollar terms into the corresponding change in the utility level, we will call it the *converter term*.

In the simple case depicted in figure 4.3, the project QB increases the international market value of the output bundle of this country by ab. If the country provides foreign aid in this amount, then the consumption bundle will return from A^1 to A^0. This implies that the project enables the country to give this amount of foreign aid without changing the original utility level of the consumer. Thus in this case the surplus variation of the project is ab.

Welfare Effects: Single-Household Economy

So far we have considered the situation in which the utility level was kept constant while the trade surplus was adjusted. Let us now consider the situation in which the trade surplus is maintained at zero and the utility level is endogenously determined. We thus add the equation

(13) $$s = 0$$

to the surplus model, while treating u as a variable rather than as a fixed parameter. We will call this the *welfare evaluation model* for the single-household economy. In the welfare evaluation model, the efficiency gains, if any, are used to improve domestic welfare through a transfer from the government to the consumer, but they are not used for foreign aid.

The welfare evaluation model is specific to a given combination of p and p_*. The surplus model for the same combination of p and p_* will be called the *associated surplus model* of the given welfare evaluation model. By the "surplus function," the "surplus variation," and the "converter term" of the welfare evaluation model we will imply the respective concepts of their associated surplus model.

We assume that the solution functions of the welfare evaluation model satisfy the causality assumption. Let us write the solution function of u in this model as

(14) $$u = \boldsymbol{u}(\alpha;\ p^T,\ p_*^T).$$

Then we have

(15) $$\boldsymbol{s}[\boldsymbol{u}(\alpha;\ p^T,\ p_*^T),\ \alpha;\ p^T,\ p_*^T] \equiv 0.$$

From this we get

(16) $$\frac{\partial \boldsymbol{u}}{\partial \alpha} = \frac{\partial \boldsymbol{s}}{\partial \alpha} \bigg/ \left(-\frac{\partial \boldsymbol{s}}{\partial u}\right).$$

The welfare effect of a project in the welfare evaluation model is given by the left side of this equation. The surplus variation on the right side gives an efficiency improvement measure in dollar terms, and the converter term in the denominator translates it into utility terms.[7] Equation 16 implies that the sign of the surplus variation of a project alone cannot tell us whether the project improves the welfare level. We have the following theorem:

> **Theorem 1.** Suppose that the converter term, $-\partial \boldsymbol{s}/\partial u$, is positive at a given equilibrium of the welfare evaluation model for the single-household economy. Then a project improves welfare if and only if the surplus variation, $\partial \boldsymbol{s}/\partial \alpha$, is positive at the equilibrium.

This theorem implies that traditional project evaluation theories implicitly assume a positive converter term when they examine sufficient conditions under a positive surplus variation. In general, however, there is no guarantee that the converter term is positive. If the converter term is negative, the economy will increase its utility level by throwing away resources or by giving economic aid to other countries. This is depicted in figure 4.4, where project QB moves the consumption point from A to A', thereby reducing the utility level. In this case, when the utility level is increased by moving from A' to A, the corresponding level of resources, as measured by the international market price vector, falls. The diagram shows that this perverse outcome occurs because of the inferiority of the second good. Tariff distortions play a critical role in creating this perverse outcome.

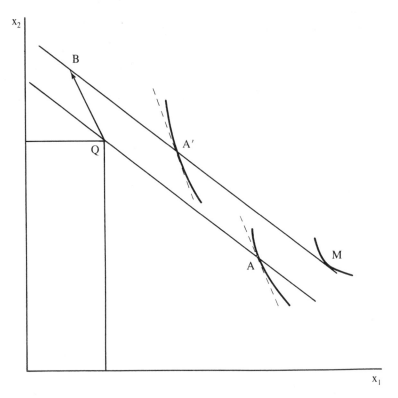

Figure 4.4 Project Under a Negative Converter Term

This phenomenon is essentially the same as the perversities in Vanek (1965), Kemp (1968), Bhagwati (1968), Foster and Sonnenschein (1970), Hatta (1973, chapter 3; 1977a), Dixit (1975), and Lloyd (1975). These studies assume that all goods are tradables. Our converter term, however, takes into account changes in the prices of nontradables. For an understanding of the nature of our converter term, the following relationship is useful:

$$(17) \qquad \mathbf{s}(u, \alpha; p^T, p_*^T) \equiv - p_*^{T\prime} z^T[u, p^T, \mathbf{p}^N(u, \alpha; p^T), \alpha],$$

which is obtained by substituting equations 10 and 12 for p^N and s in equation 8. From this we can express the converter term as

$$(18) \qquad - \frac{\partial \mathbf{s}}{\partial u} = p_*^{T\prime} \left(\frac{\partial z^T}{\partial u} + \frac{\partial z^T}{\partial p^N} \frac{\partial \mathbf{p}^N}{\partial u} \right).$$

The right side of the equation denotes the aggregate effect of an increase in the utility level on the value of net import demand evaluated by international prices. This expression decomposes the effects into two components. The first is the pure income effect under an assumed constancy of prices for both traded and nontraded goods, and the second is the indirect effect, through a change in the prices of the nontradables caused by the increased utility level.

The converter term in this form has appeared in Hatta (1973, 1977b) and Fukushima (1979, 1981) in the context of tariff reform. Hatta shows that the converter term given in equation 18 is positive if all goods are normal and if all nontradables are substitutes for all other goods. Fukushima (1981) shows in the same setting that this term is positive if a stability condition is satisfied. This term has also appeared in Woodland (1982, 222) in the context of nontraded goods theory, in Turunen-Red and Woodland (1988, equation 4.3), in the context of international transfers, and in Falvey (1988, the term m in equation 4), and Anderson and Neary (1989) in the context of quota reform.

In the following analysis, we consider mainly the situation in which the converter term is positive. In actual policy applications, however, it is important to realize that a one-dollar increase in the compensated balance of trade can imply very different levels of welfare improvement depending upon the magnitude of the converter term.

Finally, equation 17 makes it clear that the surplus variation of a project is nothing but the negative of the excess burden (or the deadweight loss) of the project, since

$$(19) \qquad \frac{\partial s}{\partial \alpha} = - p_*^{T\prime} \frac{dz^T}{d\alpha} .$$

Welfare Effects: Multihousehold Economy

The Surplus Model for the Multihousehold Economy

We now consider an economy with H households. Denote the compensated demand functions of the hth household by $x_h^T(u_h, p^T, p^N)$ and $x_h^N(u_h, p^T, p^N)$ for $h = 1, \ldots , H$; and redefine u as the vector $u \equiv (u_1, \ldots, u_H)$. Then the aggregate compensated demand functions x^T and x^N may be redefined as

$$(20) \qquad x^T(u, p^T, p^N) \equiv \Sigma_h x_h^T(u_h, p^T, p^N)$$
$$x^N(u, p^T, p^N) \equiv \Sigma_h x_h^N(u_h^h, p^T, p^N).$$

By restating the surplus model in terms of these redefined functions, we define the *surplus model for the multihousehold economy*. This model has the same variables and the same number of equations as the surplus model for the single-household economy, but the parameter u is now a vector rather than a scalar. Thus the solution functions, p^N, y^T, s can be defined as before. We again assume that the solution functions satisfy causality on the surplus model.

The Kaldor Test

There are several ways to generalize the welfare evaluation model to a multi-household economy. Letting $s = 0$ in the surplus model for the multihousehold economy and treating u as a vector variable will create more variables than equations. We will call this the *welfare evaluation model* for the multihousehold economy.

The *utility frontier* for a $(\alpha; p^T, p_*^T)$ is defined as the set of all the $(u_1, \ldots, u_H)$ satisfying

$$(21) \qquad \boldsymbol{s}(u_1, \ldots, u_H, \alpha; p^T, p_*^T) = 0.$$

We say that *the system of utility frontiers reflects a trade-off* if the following conditions are satisfied:

1. There is at least one household, say the first, for which an increase in its utility level, keeping all other arguments in equation 21 unchanged, shifts s. In other words, $\partial \boldsymbol{s} / \partial u_1 \neq 0$ for all $(u_2, \ldots, u_H, p^T, \alpha; p^T, p_*^T)$.
2. For any $(\alpha; p^T, p_*^T)$, the utility frontier is negatively sloped for each pair of households (i, j).
3. It is impossible to improve everybody's utility level by increasing foreign aid or by keeping it constant. In other words, the vector inequality $u^1 > u^0$ implies $\boldsymbol{s}(u^1, \alpha; p^T, p_*^T) \leq \boldsymbol{s}(u^0, \alpha; p^T, p_*^T)$.

When the first condition holds, the solutions for u_1 in equation 21 are differentiable functions of $u_2, \ldots, u_H, p^T$, and α and can be written as $u_1 = \boldsymbol{u}_1(u_2, \ldots, u_H, \alpha; p^T, p_*^T)$. This function represents the utility frontier of the welfare evaluation model for the multihousehold economy. By substituting this for u_1 in equation 21, we have

$$(22) \qquad \boldsymbol{s}[\boldsymbol{u}_1(u_2, \ldots, u_H, \alpha; p^T, p_*^T), u_2, \ldots, u_H, \alpha; p^T, p_*^T] \equiv 0.$$

We therefore obtain the following.

> **Lemma 1.** If the system of the utility frontiers of the welfare evaluation model for the multihousehold economy reflects a trade-off, then $- \partial \boldsymbol{s} / \partial u_i > 0$ holds for $i = 1, \ldots, n$.
>
> **Proof.** By differentiating equation 22, we can express the slope of a utility frontier as $\partial \boldsymbol{u}_1 / \partial u_i = - (\partial \boldsymbol{s} / \partial u_i) / (\partial \boldsymbol{s} / \partial u_1)$. Thus, the negative slope of the utility frontier with respect to any given commodity pair of $(1, i)$ and the continuity of the partials of $\boldsymbol{s}$ imply that all the converter terms must have the same sign at any point on the frontier for all i. If they were all negative, every household's utility would be improved by giving foreign aid or destroying goods, and hence the assumption of the theorem would be contradicted. Q.E.D.

The following definitions are concerned with shifts of utility frontiers. Suppose that the system of utility frontiers reflects a trade-off. Then we say that *a small* *project passes the Kaldor compensation test* if $\partial u_1 / \partial \alpha > 0$ at the initial equilibrium and that *a large project passes the Kaldor compensation test* if u_1 is increased when α is increased discretely, keeping $(u_2, ..., u_H; p^T, p_*^T)$ fixed.

This sets the stage for the next theorem.

Theorem 2. Suppose that the system of utility frontiers reflects a tradeoff for the given (p^T, p_*^T, α) in the welfare evaluation model for the multihousehold economy. Then

1. a small project passes the Kaldor compensation test if and only if the surplus variation, $\partial s / \partial \alpha$, is positive at the initial equilibrium, and

2. a large project passes (fails) the Kaldor compensation test if the surplus variation, $\partial s [u_1(u_2, ..., u_H, \alpha; p^T, p_*^T), u_2, ..., u_H, \alpha; p^T, p_*^T] / \partial \alpha$, is positive (negative) at every point as α is increased, keeping $(u_2, ..., u_H; p^T, p_*^T)$ constant.

Proof. By differentiating equation 22, we can express the impact of the project on the utility level of the first household as

(23)
$$\frac{\partial u_1}{\partial \alpha} = \frac{\partial s}{\partial \alpha} \bigg/ \left(-\frac{\partial s}{\partial u_1}\right).$$

The assumption of the theorem implies that the denominator on the right side of the equation is positive. From this, the first condition of the theorem follows immediately. In view of equation 22, the terms $\partial s / \partial \alpha$ and $-\partial s / \partial u_1$ in equation 23 are functions of $(u_2, ..., u_H, \alpha; p^T, p_*^T)$. From equation 23, therefore, condition 1 of theorem 2 is readily extended to condition 2. Q.E.D.

This theorem implies that if the system of utility frontiers reflects a trade-off, a positive (negative) surplus variation is sufficient for the project to pass (fail) the Kaldor compensation test. At a first glance, this finding may appear to conflict with that of Boadway (1974) that a positive sum of compensating variations is *not* sufficient for a project to pass the Kaldor compensation test. But the two findings are consistent, as was explained in endnote 3. In fact, a project can have a positive sum of compensating variations and a negative surplus variation simultaneously. For example, suppose that an income transfer causes a shift of the equilibrium from one point to another on a utility frontier, changing the prices of nontradables. Then, as we saw earlier, the sum of compensating variations associated with this transfer is positive. But the surplus variation is zero, since s is fixed on a given utility frontier. The surplus variation of the project, therefore, correctly indicates that compensation of the loser is impossible.

This example can be readily modified so that a project in nontradables results in a minor shift in the production bundle, yielding both a negative surplus variation and a positive sum of compensating variations. In that case, the negativity of the surplus variation of a project, even if it has a positive sum of equivalent variations, correctly indicates that the project fails the Kaldor test.

Evaluations of compensating variations and the surplus variation use different prices. Compensating variations are evaluated by the initial domestic market prices, while surplus variationes are evaluated by their shadow prices, representing the cost on the compensated trade surplus measured at international prices. In other words, compensating variation measures the impact of the project on expenditure, while the surplus variation measures the impact on the resource cost.

The Samuelson Test

A project that passes the Kaldor compensation test may not pass the Samuelson compensation test. To show that utility frontiers of an economy satisfying the conditions of theorem 2 can intersect with one other, let the solid curve in figure 4.5 represent the preproject utility frontier of a two-household welfare evaluation model. By tracing out u_1 for various levels of u^2, we obtain this frontier. The government moves the economy along the frontier by changing the lump-sum transfers to the two households. Theorem 2 indicates that the project can move the economy from A to the right, say to point A' under the conditions of the theorem. But this does not preclude the possibility that the surplus variation may be negative when evaluated at a different point on curve *ii*, say point B. Then the project would move the economy to the left, say, to point B', and the pre- and postproject utility frontiers will intersect as depicted in figure 4.5. The conditions of theorem 2, therefore, are not sufficient to guarantee that a project will pass the Samuelson compensation test.

In view of the celebrated Scitovsky paradox, a succession of projects each passing the Kaldor test but not the Samuelson test can eventually bring the economy to a Pareto inferior position compared to the initial situation.[8]

Let us define the Samuelson compensation test criterion in our notation for an economy in which the system of utility frontiers reflects a trade-off. We say that *a small project passes the Samuelson compensation test* if $\partial u_1 / \partial \alpha$ at every point on the initial utility frontier and that *a large project passes the Samuelson compensation test* if, starting at any point on the initial utility possibility curve, a discrete increase in α raises u_1, while keeping $(u_2, ..., u_n; p^T, p_*^T)$ fixed.

The following theorem gives a set of sufficient conditions for a project to pass the Samuelson compensation test.[9]

> **Theorem 3.** Suppose that the system of utility frontiers of a welfare evaluation model for the multihousehold economy reflects a trade-off. Then
> 1. a small project passes the Samuelson compensation test if and only if the surplus variation is positive, that is, $\partial s / \partial \alpha > 0$ at every point on the utility frontier for the given $(\alpha; p^T, p_*^T)$, and
> 2. a large project passes the Samuelson compensation test if the surplus variation, $\partial s / \partial \alpha$, is positive at every point of the utility frontier before, during, and after the project.
>
> **Proof.** Both conditions immediately follow from equation 23.

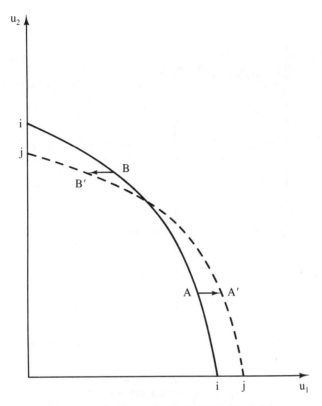

Figure 4.5 Intersecting Utility Frontiers

Thus the key condition for the project to uniformly shift out the utility frontier is that the surplus variation $\partial s / \partial \alpha$ be positive regardless of income distribution.

The literature on compensation tests was concerned principally with the welfare implications of index numbers of national income, where it happens to be the case that the surplus variation is likely to change its sign as income is transferred along a given utility frontier. This literature typically compared utility frontiers such as those corresponding to product bundles I and J in figure 4.6, where x_1 and x_2 measure the output levels of the first and the second commodities in a two-commodity economy. If the first consumer strongly prefers commodity 1 to commodity 2, he will reach a higher maximum utility level from bundle J than from bundle I. If the second consumer has the opposite taste, the reverse will be the case. Hence the utility frontiers corresponding to J and I will be similar to jj and ii in figure 4.5, intersecting in the middle. The literature concluded that the utility frontier jj intersects ii, except in the trivial case where bundle J dominates I or bundle I dominates J in both commodities.

Thus Samuelson's (1950) pessimism was appropriate in the context of national income comparison. After all, the comparison had nothing to do with efficiency

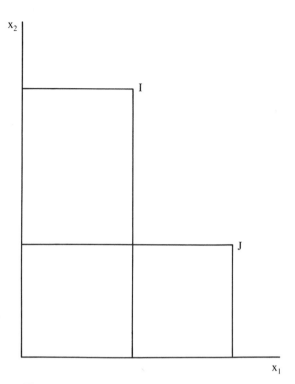

**Figure 4.6 National Income Comparison
in a Closed Economy**

improvement. In the case of distortion-removing reforms, however, the likelihood of the surplus variation changing signs is lower. For example, an efficiency improvement in production as a result of the removal of factor market distortions can give a positive surplus variation regardless of income distribution. Another example can be found in Hatta and Haltiwanger (1986), who have shown that a squeezing of the tax rates on two strong substitutes yields a positive surplus variation. An income redistribution is not likely to change the fact that pork and chicken, say, are strong substitutes.

Also, in the context of project evaluation in an open economy, we are not comparing the utility frontiers of bundles such as I and J in figure 4.6. Rather, what we are comparing is more like the utility frontiers of two consumption feasibility sets of a small open economy with different product bundles. If a shift in the output bundle from I to J in figure 4.7 shifts the consumption frontier from ii to jj, this will certainly shift out the utility frontier uniformly. In the next section, we show that this is indeed the case in the situation for which the most commonly used shadow price concept is meaningful.

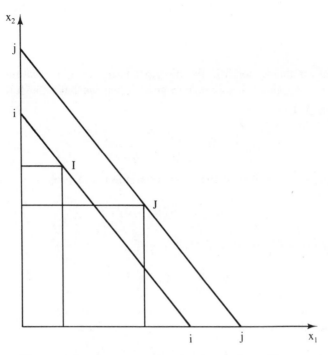

Figure 4.7 Project Evaluation in an Open Economy

Shadow Prices

We now introduce the concept of shadow prices, which applies to the surplus models of both single- and multihousehold economies.

Shadow Price and Surplus Variation

By differentiating equation 17 or by rewriting equation 19, we obtain the following:

> **Lemma 2**. The surplus variation of a project is decomposed into two terms:

$$(24) \qquad \frac{\partial \mathbf{s}}{\partial \alpha} = -p_*^{T\prime} \frac{\partial z^T}{\partial \alpha} - p_*^{T\prime} \left(\frac{\partial z^T}{\partial p^N} \right)^{\prime} \frac{\partial \mathbf{p}^N}{\partial \alpha}.$$

The first term on the right side of the equation represents the increase in the value of the output level of tradables directly caused by the project, keeping all price levels constant. This term represents the improvement in production efficiency of the new output vector. The second term represents the value of the change in the net supply of tradables induced by the price change in nontradables. The first and the second terms may be called the *output* and *price effects*, respectively. The output effect can be expressed in terms of the change in public output.

We define the *marginal tariff revenue vector of nontradables* by

$$\delta \equiv \tau' \, (\partial y^T / \partial y^N).$$

Each element of the vector δ is the marginal tariff revenue resulting from a unit increase in the output of a nontradable good. Then we have the following:

Lemma 3. Let

$$p \equiv \left[\begin{array}{c} p^T \\ p^N \end{array} \right], \quad g(\alpha) \equiv \left[\begin{array}{c} g(\alpha)^T \\ g(\alpha)^N \end{array} \right], \quad \text{and} \quad \theta \equiv \left[\begin{array}{c} -\tau \\ \delta \end{array} \right].$$

Then the output effect of the surplus variation of a project is expressed as

(25)
$$-p_*^{T'} \frac{\partial z^T}{\partial \alpha} = (p^N + \theta)' \frac{dg}{d\alpha}.$$

If $\partial g^T / \partial \alpha = 0$, this specializes to

(26)
$$-p_*^{T'} \frac{\partial z^T}{\partial \alpha} = (p^N + \delta)' \frac{dg^N}{d\alpha}.$$

Proof. Since the profit-maximizing producers produce y^N and y^T when they face the price vectors p^T and $p^N(p^T, y^N)$, we have[10]

$$p^{N'} + p^{T'}(\partial y^T / \partial y^N) = 0.$$

This, the definition of δ, and equation 6 yield

(27)
$$-p_*^T \frac{\partial y^T}{\partial y^N} = (p^N + \delta)'.$$

On the other hand, from equations 6 and 9 we have

$$-p_*^T \frac{\partial z^T}{\partial \alpha} = -(p^T - \tau) \frac{dg^T}{d\alpha} + p_*^T \frac{\partial y^T}{\partial y^N} \frac{dg^N}{d\alpha}.$$

This and equation 27 yield the lemma. Q.E.D.

Equation 26 makes it clear that the international market value of the output variation in the tradables induced by a unit increase in the output levels of nontradables is equal to $p^N + \delta$. This price differs from the producer price, p^N, by the amount of the marginal tariff revenue, δ.

In some situations, the price effect in equation 24 may disappear. Thus we obtain the following

Theorem 4 (Findlay-Wellisz-Srinivasan-Bhagwati). Suppose that the underlying production structure of the surplus model is a Heckscher-Ohlin model with an equal number of tradables and nontradables and that all tradables are domestically produced. Then the surplus variation of a project reduces to

(28)
$$\frac{\partial \boldsymbol{s}}{\partial \alpha} = (p + \theta)' \frac{dg}{d\alpha}.$$

If $dg^T / d\alpha = 0$, this specializes to

(29)
$$\frac{\partial \boldsymbol{s}}{\partial \alpha} = (p^N + \delta)' \frac{dg^N}{d\alpha}.$$

Proof. Under the provisos of the theorem, $\partial p^N(p^T, y^N) / \partial y^N = 0$ holds from the Factor Price Equalization Theorem.[11] This and $\boldsymbol{p}^N(u, \alpha; p^T, p_*^T)$ $= p^N[p^T, \boldsymbol{y}^N(u, p^T, \alpha)]$ imply that $\partial \boldsymbol{p}^N / \partial \alpha = 0$. Hence equation 24 yields $\partial \boldsymbol{s} / \partial \alpha = -p_*^{T'}(\partial z^T / \partial \alpha)$. This and equations 25 and 26 yield the theorem. Q.E.D.

Equation 29 shows that the surplus variation of a project in nontradables is equal to the domestic market value of the project vector *plus* the increase in the tariff revenue caused by the change in imports of tradables. Equation 28, therefore, shows that the surplus variation of a project is the domestic market value of the project vector plus the tariff revenue that the project yields either directly or indirectly. The shadow price vector $p + \theta$, therefore, is the price of the project vector in terms of its international resource costs.

Findlay and Wellisz (1976) and Srinivasan and Bhagwati (1978) obtained theorem 4 for the two-by-two case. Bhagwati and Wan (1979), Bertrand (1979), Bhagwati and Srinivasan (1982), Srinivasan (1982), Diewert (1983, theorem 8), and Smith (1987) generalized it to the *N*-by-*N* case. The vector $p^N + \delta$ in equation 29 will be called the Findlay-Wellisz-Srinivasan-Bhagwati (FWSB) shadow price vector of a public project.

The condition that the numbers of tradables and nontradables are equal is strong if taken literally. The implication of the Factor Price Equalization Theorem is that even when the numbers are not equal, trade mitigates the impact on the prices of nontradables caused by a project in nontradables.[12] Hence, the price effects tend to be small.

Shadow Price and the Samuelson Test

As we move along a utility frontier, the magnitude of $(p+\theta)'(dg / d\alpha)$ can potentially change only if the level of θ changes. Since τ is fixed, this implies that $\delta = \tau'(\partial y^T / \partial y^N)$ changes. If the conditions of theorem 4 are satisfied and if all the tradables are produced at every point on the utility frontier, the Rybczynski matrix $(\partial y^T / \partial y^N)(p^T, y^N)$ is independent of the vector y^N, and hence of the vector x^N in view of equation 5. Under this condition, therefore, δ remains constant even if income redistribution changes x^N, and as we move along the utility frontier, the magnitude of the surplus variation remains constant.

Theorem 5. Suppose the following conditions hold in a welfare evaluation model for the multihousehold economy:
1. The utility frontier of an economy reflects a trade-off for the given (p^T, p_*^T, α).

2. The underlying production structure is a Heckscher-Ohlin model with an equal number of tradables and nontradables.

3. All tradables are domestically produced at any point on the utility frontier before, during, and after the project.

Then a large project passes the Samuelson compensation test if and only if the initial equilibrium satisfies

$$(p + \theta)' \, dg \, / \, d\alpha > 0 \, ,$$

while the last condition degenerates into

(30) $$(p^N + \delta)' \, dg^N \, / \, d\alpha > 0,$$

if $\partial g^T / \, d\alpha = 0$.

It should be emphasized that the theorem requires us to verify that the surplus variation is positive only at the initial distribution of income. Also, the model is a standard model of international trade, which includes the well known two-by-two Heckscher-Ohlin-Samuelson model as a special case.

Bhagwati and Wan (1979) examined the conditions under which the FWBS shadow prices are stationary for a large project. Under the same conditions, an income transfer among consumers does not change the shadow prices. This is so because, in view of the definition of δ and equation 5, δ is independent of the size of the project if and only if δ is independent of x^N. The second condition of theorem 5 can be relaxed using their results.

Equity Considerations

A project passing the Samuelson criterion will not typically make every household better off; some will be made worse off. But in the real economy, losers are not likely to be compensated by a lump-sum subsidy after each project since income transfers can be distortionary, as the literature on optimum taxation emphasizes. (Transfer-induced distortions are particularly large if compensations are always made and are expected.) If compensations are not made, however, a project satisfying the Samuelson criterion may reduce the value of a reasonably defined social welfare function, as illustrated by the move from A to B in figure 4.8.

This would be a serious problem, for example, in the following situation. The World Bank is evaluating whether to finance a dam in a region of a developing country in which efficiency-seeking reforms are seldom carried out. This project passes the Samuelson compensation test, but it reduces the value of the social welfare function because it causes a major income redistribution, as in the case of the move from A to B in figure 4.8. In this instance, the project should be rejected because the acceptance criterion for this project should be based directly on social welfare, and the efficiency criteria discussed in this paper are irrelevant.

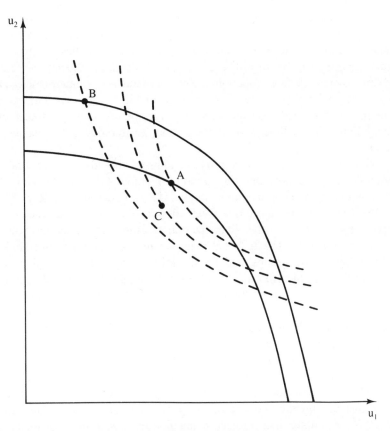

Figure 4.8   Efficiency vs. Social Welfare

The story is different if the project is being evaluated for an industrialized country in which the project is but one of many microeconomic policies aimed at improving efficiency, such as antitrust policy, tax reform, trade liberalization, financial market liberalization, or marginal cost pricing. Each of these policies will create income redistribution, and compensating the losers at each instance would be impractical. But a series of such reforms will have offsetting income distribution effects and is likely to bring about an improvement in long-run social welfare.

Hicks (1941) maintained that such offsetting income distribution effects would bring about a Pareto improvement in the long run. Hicks called this view the "creed of classical economics"; Corden (1984) called it "Hicksian optimism." Our claim here is more modest. We do not necessarily expect that the offsetting income distribution effects will lead automatically to a Pareto improvement; some people may be made worse off permanently. We only expect that partial offsetting is likely to bring about an improvement in social welfare. For example, imagine an economy consisting of consumer A, who earns $1 million a year, and consumer B, who earns $10,000 a year in the initial equilibrium. Suppose that as a result of a series of economic reforms, consumer A now earns $100,000, while consumer B earns $2 million. Consumer A's real income has dropped sharply. But this change will be regarded as an improvement in social welfare if the underlying social welfare function treats individuals symmetrically. Had the concept of a social welfare function been available to the classical economists, they might have argued that the offsetting income-distribution effects of many efficiency-improving policies would bring about an improvement in social welfare in the long run.

This view must be implicitly held by economists who advocate free trade. Thus, for example, they support the free import of automobiles to the United States despite the unemployment it causes in the U.S. automobile industry. They also advise the Japanese to import rice freely despite the damage it causes Japanese farmers. In the short run, either liberalization measure can reduce the value of the social welfare function. The fact that many economists advocate free trade, being fully aware that some groups will be severely damaged by it, implies that they believe that the loss incurred as a result of a particular trade liberalization will be outweighed in the long run by the benefits brought about by many other liberalizations. The case is even stronger if the economy has a formal system for distributing income and wealth automatically through the social insurance system, progressive income taxation, and the inheritance tax system, regardless of the cause of the plight of the transfer recipient.

In many countries, the social welfare criterion is adopted to evaluate some policies while the efficiency criterion is employed to evaluate others. It turns out, however, that mixing the two criteria is worse than consistently using either one. Suppose, for example, that project evaluation is based on the social welfare function criterion, while trade policy is based on the efficiency criterion. Figure 4.8 illustrates how sequential application of such double criteria could lead the economy to a Pareto inferior position. Assume that an efficiency-enhancing tariff reduction is carried out at the initial equilibrium at point A, moving the economy to point B. A public project that increases social welfare is then chosen, moving the economy from point B to point C, which is Pareto inferior to point A. If only one of the criteria were consistently employed, it would never lead to a Pareto inferior position. The fatal outcome of mixing the two criteria is that the transitivity of policy choice is lost.

In a modern industrial economy, a government that applies the social welfare criterion to every project is likely to attain a lower long-run social welfare level than a government that applies the efficiency criterion alone while ignoring short-run distributional effects.[13] To see this, take the case illustrated in figure 4.9. This economy is initially at point A. Two projects are being evaluated by different branches of the government: a Department of Transportation project, which would bring the economy to point B, and a Department of Housing and Urban Development project, which would bring the economy to point D. If the efficiency criterion is used to evaluate both projects, they will both be carried out, since

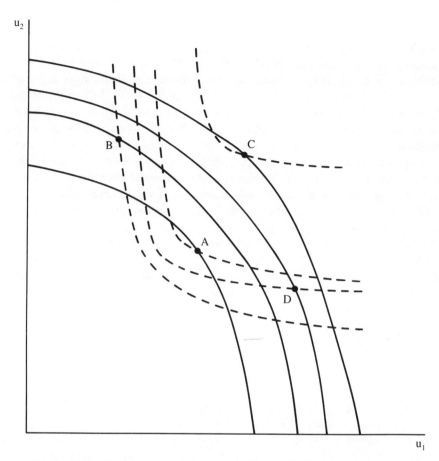

Figure 4.9   Short-run and Long-run Social Welfare Improvements

both pass the Samuelson compensation test. As a result, the economy will reach point *C*, attaining higher social welfare. If the social welfare criterion is used instead, both projects will be rejected. As a result, the economy will be stuck at point *A*, failing to attain the long-run higher welfare level of point *C*. Requiring each microeconomic policy, such as tariff reductions and public projects, to improve social welfare monotonically would severely limit policy options and would most likely prevent maximization of long-run social welfare.

The discussion in this section points to the desirability of adopting the efficiency criterion alone as the project evaluation criterion, at least in modern industrial nations.[14]

Conclusion

The debate on compensation tests during the 1930s to the 1950s led to a pessimistic view of the usefulness of efficiency criteria. This seems to have been the result largely of an unfortunate historical accident: the debate focused on the welfare valuation of national income in a closed economy, where differences in tastes among households cause intrinsic difficulties with compensation tests. Economic reforms that reduce distortions do not have such intrinsic difficulties in satisfying the Samuelson compensation test. As we have seen in this paper, public projects in an open economy can pass compensation tests under mild conditions. This is similar to the situation in which sales tax reform reduces distortions.[15] In particular, it was shown that a project with a positive surplus variation at the initial equilibrium passes the Samuelson compensation test in the situation where the FWBS shadow price is meaningful.

Another reason for the traditional pessimism regarding the usefulness of efficiency criteria is that the sum of compensating variations, which was often adopted as an efficiency criterion, is now known to be useless as a project evaluation criterion in a tariff-distorted economy. This paper has shown that the correct efficiency criterion for compensation tests is the *surplus variation*, which measures the value of the project in terms of the resource cost evaluated at international prices rather than expenditures evaluated at domestic prices. It was also shown that the concept of the shadow price of a good used in the project evaluation literature represents the increase in the surplus variation caused by a unit increase in the output of the good.

Finally, the paper examined the issue of whether to use a social welfare function or the efficiency criterion for determining whether to accept a project. There is no question that the long-run target of economic policies should be the maximization of social welfare. Also, in developing countries where efficiency-seeking policies are seldom carried out, only the social welfare function can serve as a meaningful project-acceptance criterion. In countries that carry out many efficiency-seeking policies, however, accepting only projects that increase the value of the social welfare function will unnecessarily restrict policy options. In such economies, relying solely on efficiency criteria is not only practical but is also the only way to attain a higher level of social welfare in the long run.

Appendix: Budget Equations

Since the surplus model was formulated in dual form, we did not have to make explicit the budget equations and transfers taking place between sectors. Here we make them explicit. The surplus model has four sectors: producers, consumers, the government, and the (passive) foreign sector.

Producers. Since the GNP function (defined in note 6) satisfies $e(p^T, y^N) = p^{N\prime}(p^T, y^N)y^N = -p^{T\prime}y^T(p^T, y^N)$ for all (p^T, y^N), we have

(A1) $$p^{T\prime}y^{T}(p^{T}, y^{N}) + p^{N\prime}(p^{T}, y^{N})y^{N} \equiv 0.$$

Thus profit is zero and the production sector budget is always balanced.

Consumers. Let T be the transfer the consumer receives from the government. Then the consumer's budget equation is

(A2) $$p^{T\prime}x^{T}(u, p^{T}, p^{N}) + p^{N\prime}x^{N}(u, p^{T}, p^{N}) = T.$$

If we add this equation to the surplus model, a new variable T is also added.

Government. Let S denote the government surplus. Then in view of equation 5, the government budget constraint may be written as

(A3) $$S + T = p^{\prime}(p^{T}, y^{N}) \, g(\alpha) + (p^{T} - p^{T}_{*})^{\prime}[x^{T}(u, p^{T}, p^{N}) - y^{T}(p^{T}, y^{N}) - g^{N}].$$

If we add this equation to the surplus model, the model will contain the additional variable S.

These three budget equations, definitional equation 6, and the equilibrium condition in equation 7 together imply that

(A4) $$S = s.$$

Thus the government surplus is always equal to the balance of payments surplus.

In evaluating a public project, we need not explicitly add equations A2 and A3 to the surplus model. But from these equations we can find the levels of S and T corresponding to the solutions of the surplus model.

Notes

Thanks are due to Dan Slesnick, T.N. Srinivasan, Jay Wilson, and participants of the seminars at Georgetown, Harvard, Yale, and Ohio State Universities and the State University of New York at Albany for useful comments on earlier drafts. Conversations with Kenzo Abe, Allan Feldman, Dale Jorgenson, and Makoto Okamura were also helpful.

1. Related literature includes Smith and Stephen (1975), Foster (1976), Blackorby and Donaldson (1985), and Ruiz-Castillo (1987).
2. For surveys of this literature, see Corden (1984, section 9) and Dreze and Stern (1987).
3. When the project does not affect domestic prices, the surplus variation of a project is simply the increase in the international value of the tradable goods caused by the project. It then has a monotonic relationship with the sum of the compensating variations of the project. In the case where the project affects domestic prices, however, this relationship no longer holds. This fact is consistent with our finding that the surplus variation has a close relationship with compensation tests.
4. By definition, the compensating variation of a consumer is the increase in the minimum expenditure associated with the change in utility measured by the post-reform price vector. So A's compensating variation is ac, while B's is -1 times bc.

5. He also showed that under the same assumptions, a project with a positive compensating variation passes the Samuelson compensation test.

6. Let $e(p^T, y^N)$ be the GNP function, and assume that every element of $y^T(p^T, y^N)$ is positive. Then we have the following relationships:
$$y^T(p^T, y^N) = \partial e(p^T, y^N) / \partial p^T \text{ and } p^N(p^T, y^N) = \partial e(p^T, y^N) / \partial y^N.$$
For properties of the GNP function, see Dixit and Norman (1980) and Woodland (1982, chapter 3).

7. Equation 16 is similar to equation 10′ of Hatta (1977a), in which the numerator and the denominator are called ASM (Aggregate of Substitution terms weighted by Marginal costs) and AIM (Aggregate of Income terms weighted by Marginal costs), respectively. Clearly, the compensated change in the balance of payments is a concept akin to the ASM, and the converter term to the AIM. The sign of the (closed economy) AIM is discussed in Dixit (1975) and Hatta (1973, 1977a), for example.

8. The compensation test controversy is surveyed by Samuelson (1950), Mishan (1969), and Takayama (1972). For a rigorous formulation of the issues of the New Welfare Economics, see Chipman and Moore (1971, 1978), and the literature surveyed there.

9. When $\partial s / \partial \alpha \neq 0$, the implicit function theorem implies that equation 21 defines the differentiable function: $\alpha = \alpha(u_1, \ldots, u_H; p^T, p_*^T)$. Therefore, a unique value of α corresponds to a given value of $(u_1, \ldots, u_H; p^T, p_*^T)$. This suggests that the utility frontier for the given $(\alpha; p^T, p_*^T)$ never intersects another utility frontier with a slightly higher value of α and the same value of p^T and p_*^T if $\partial s / \partial \alpha \neq 0$ holds at every point on the first utility frontier. This shows that the trade-off condition or the positivity of surplus variation is irrelevant to the nonintersection of the utility frontiers; they determine the direction of the shift of the nonintersecting utility frontiers.

10. This can be alternatively obtained as follows: differentiating equation A1 from the appendix, we have $p^{N\prime} + (\partial p^N / \partial y^N) y^N + p^{T\prime}(\partial y^T / \partial y^N) = 0$. Since $p^N(p^T, y^N)$ is homogeneous of degree zero with respect to y^N, we have $(\partial p^N / \partial y^N)y^N = 0$.

11. See Woodland (1982, 72). See also Chang (1979, theorem 5) and Kuga (1972, theorem 4). Here, the output vector of nontradables is guaranteed to remain in the interior of the cone of diversification by our condition that all tradables are domestically produced before, during, and after the project. An excellent survey of studies on the factor price equalization theorem in higher dimensions is found in Ethier (1984).

12. The reason that trade mitigates the change in the prices of nontradables is straightforward. For example, suppose the project employs labor, a nontradable. The resulting wage increase is mitigated by the reduced production of tradable goods that use labor intensively.

13. If the total distributional effects of all these microeconomic reforms in, say, a decade turns out to be so apparently skewed, compensation of net losers may be necessary to improve social welfare. But distortions associated with such a transfer will be much smaller than in the case when losers are compensated at the end of each efficiency-seeking reform, partly because the required amount of transfers is smaller as a result of offsetting effects and partly because occasional and unexpected transfers create fewer distortionary incentives than frequent, expected ones. In economies where a progressive income tax system and a social insurance system provide help to the unfortunate regardless of the cause of their plight, the need for such occasional compensations will be greatly reduced.

14. Another problem with the social welfare function criterion is that the evaluation may be sensitive to the specification of the functional forms of the utility function. At least that is the case with the estimation of the optimum taxation that takes account of distributional considerations. See Ray (1986) on this. Adopting the social welfare

criterion might imply that the economy has to rely upon the priesthood of economists, whose diagnoses differ.

15. See Hatta (1986) and Fukushima and Hatta (1989).

References

Anderson, J.E., and J.P. Neary. 1989. "A New Approach to Evaluating Trade Reform." Boston College.

Balassa, B. 1974a. "Estimating the Shadow Price of Foreign Exchange in Project Appraisal." *Oxford Economic Papers* 26: 147-68.

Balassa, B. 1974b. "New Approaches to the Estimation of the Shadow Exchange Rate: A Comment." *Oxford Economic Papers* 26: 208-11.

Bertrand, T.M. 1979. "Shadow Pricing in Distorted Economies." *American Economic Review* 69: 902-14.

Bhagwati, J.N. 1968. "The Gains from Trade Once Again." *Oxford Economic Papers* 20: 137-48.

Bhagwati, J.N., and T.N. Srinivasan. 1982. "The Evaluation of Projects at World Prices under Trade Distortions: Quantitative Restrictions, Monopoly Power in Trade and Nontraded Goods." *International Economic Review* 22: 385-99.

Bhagwati, J.N., and H. Wan, Jr. 1979. "The 'Stationarity' of Shadow Prices of Factors in Project Evaluation, with or without Distortions." *American Economic Review* 69: 261-73.

Bhagwati, J.N., R.A. Brecher, and T. Hatta. 1983. "The Generalized Theory of Transfers and Welfare: Bilateral Transfers in a Multilateral World." *American Economic Review* 73: 606-18.

Blackorby, C., and D. Donaldson. 1985. "Consumers' Surpluses and Consistent Cost-Benefit Tests." *Social Choice and Welfare* 1: 251-62.

Boadway, R.W. 1974. "The Welfare Foundations of Cost-Benefit Analysis." *Economic Journal* 84: 926-39.

Boadway, R.W., and N. Bruce. 1984. *Welfare Economics*. Oxford: Basil Blackwell.

Bruce, N., and R. Harris. 1982. "Cost-Benefit Criteria and the Compensation Principle in Evaluating Small Projects." *Journal of Political Economy* 90: 755-76.

Chang, W.W. 1979. "Some Theorems of Trade and General Equilibrium with Many Goods and Factors." *Econometrica* 32: 709-26.

Chipman, J.S., and J.C. Moore. 1971. "The Compensation Principle in Welfare Economics." *Papers in Quantitative Economics* Vol. 2. Lawrence, Kansas: University of Kansas Press.

Chipman, J.S., and J.C. Moore. 1978. "The New Welfare Economics 1939-1974." *International Economic Review* 19: 547-84.

Chipman, J.S., and J.C. Moore. 1980. "Compensating Variation, Consumer's Surplus, and Welfare." *American Economic Review* 70:933-49.

Corden, W.M. 1984. "The Normative Theory of International Trade." In R.W. Jones and P.B. Kennen, eds, *Handbook of International Economics* 1. Amsterdam: North-Holland.

Dasgupta, P.S., and J.E. Stiglitz. 1974. "Benefit-Cost Analysis and Trade Policies." *Journal of Political Economy* 82: 1-33.

Diewert, W.E. 1983. "Cost-Benefit Analysis and Project Evaluation — A Comparison of Alternative Approaches." *Journal of Public Economics* 22: 265-302.

Dixit, A.K. 1975. "Welfare Effects of Tax and Price Changes." *Journal of Public Economics* 4: 103-23.

Dixit, A.K., and V.D. Norman. 1980. *Theory of International Trade*. Cambridge: Cambridge University Press.

Dreze, J., and N. Stern. 1987. "The Theory of Cost-Benefit Analysis." In A.J. Auerbach and M. Feldstein, eds, *Handbook of Public Economics 2*. Amsterdam: North-Holland.

Ethier, W.J. 1984. "Higher Dimensional Issues in Trade Theory." In R.W. Jones and P.B. Kennen, eds, *Handbook of International Economics, 1*. Amsterdam: North-Holland.

Falvey, R.E. 1988. "Tariffs, Quotas, and Piecemeal Policy Reforms." *Journal of International Economics* 25: 175-83.

Findlay, R., and S. Wellisz. 1976. "Project Evaluation, Shadow Prices, and Trade Policy." *Journal of Political Economy* 84: 543-52.

Foster, E. 1976. "The Welfare Foundations of Cost-Benefit Analysis — A Comment." *Economic Journal* 86: 353-58.

Foster, E., and H. Sonnenschein. 1970. "Price Distortion and Economic Welfare." *Econometrica* 30: 281-97.

Fukushima, T. 1979. "Tariff Structure, Nontraded Goods and Theory of Piecemeal Policy Recommendations." *International Economic Review* 20: 427-35.

Fukushima, T. 1981. "A Dynamic Quantity Adjustment Process in a Small Open Economy, and Welfare Effects of Tariff Changes." *Journal of International Economics* 11: 513-29.

Fukushima, T., and T. Hatta. 1989. "Why Not Tax Uniformly Rather Than Optimally?" *The Economic Studies Quarterly* 40: 220-38.

Hatta, T. 1973. "A Theory of Piecemeal Policy Recommendations." Ph.D. thesis. The Johns Hopkins University, Baltimore, Md.

Hatta, T. 1977a. "A Theory of Piecemeal Policy Recommendations." *Review of Economic Studies* 44: 1-21.

Hatta, T. 1977b. "A Recommendation for a Better Tariff Structure." *Econometrica* 45: 1859-70.

Hatta, T. 1986. "Welfare Effect of Changing Commodity Tax Rates Toward Uniformity." *Journal of Public Economics* 29: 99-112.

Hatta, T., and J. Haltiwanger. 1986. "Tax Reform and Strong Substitutes." *International Economic Review* 27: 303-15.

Hicks, J. 1941. "The Rehabilitation of Consumers' Surplus." *Review of Economic Studies* 9: 108-16 (Reprinted in K.J. Arrow and T. Scitovsky, eds, 1969, *Readings in Welfare Economics*, Homewood, Ill.: Irwin.)

Johnson, H.G. 1965. "Optimal Trade Intervention in the Presence of Domestic Distortions." In R. Caves, H.G. Johnson, P.B. Kenen, eds, *Trade, Growth and the Balance of Payment*. New York: Rand McNally.

Joshi, V. 1972. "The Rationale and Relevance of the Little-Mirrlees Criterion." Oxford University Institute of Economics and Statistics *Bulletin* 34: 3-32.

Kaldor, N. 1939. "Welfare Propositions and Interpersonal Comparisons of Utility." *Economic Journal* 49: 549-52.

Kemp, M. 1968. "Some Issues in the Analysis of Trade Gains." *Oxford Economic Papers* 20: 149-61.

Kuga, K. 1972. "The Factor-Price Equalization Theorem." *Econometrica* 40: 723-36.

Little, I.M.D., and J.A. Mirrlees. 1969. *Manual of Industrial Project Analysis for Developing Countries*, Vol. 2, *Social Cost-Benefit Analysis*. Paris: OECD Development Center.

Lloyd, P.J. 1974. "A More General Theory of Price Distortions in Open Economies." *Journal of International Economics* 4: 365-86.

Mishan, E.J. 1969. *Welfare Economics: an Assessment*. Amsterdam: North-Holland.

Ng, Yew Kwang. 1979. *Welfare Economics*. London: Macmillan.

Ray, R. 1986. "Sensitivity of 'Optimal' Commodity Tax Rates to Alternative Demand Functional Forms: An Econometric Case Study of India." *Journal of Public Economics* 31: 253-68.

Ruiz-Castillo, J. 1987. "Potential Welfare and the Sum of Individual Compensating or Equivalent Variations." *Journal of Economic Theory* 41: 34-5.

Samuelson, P. 1950. "Evaluation of National Income." *Oxford Economic Papers* 2: 1-23.

Scitovsky, T. 1941. "A Note on Welfare Propositions in Economics." *Review of Economic Studies* 9: 77-88.

Smith, A. 1987. "Factor Shadow Prices in Distorted Open Economies." In H. Kierzkowski, ed., *Protection and Competition in International Trade: Essays in Honor of W.M. Corden*. Oxford: Basil Blackwell.

Smith, B., and F. Stephen. 1975. "The Welfare Foundations of Cost-Benefit Analysis." *Economic Journal* 85: 902-05.

Srinivasan, T.N. 1982. "General Equilibrium Theory, Project Evaluation and Economic Development." In M. Gersovitz, C.F. Diaz-Alejandro, G. Ranis, and M.R. Rosenzweig, eds, *The Theory and Experience of Economic Development — Essays in Honor of Sir W. Arthur Lewis*. London: Allen & Unwin.

Srinivasan, T.N., and J.N. Bhagwati. 1978. "Shadow Prices for Project Selection in the Presence of Distortions: Effective Rates of Protection and Domestic Resource Costs." *Journal of Political Economy* 86: 97-116.

Takayama, A. 1972. *International Trade*. New York: Holt-Reinhart.

Turunen-Red, A., and A.D. Woodland. 1988. "On the Multilateral Transfer Problem: Existence of Pareto Improving International Transfers." *Journal of International Economics* 25: 249-69.

Vanek, J. 1965. *General Equilibrium of International Discrimination: The Case of Customs Unions*. Cambridge, Mass.: Harvard University Press.

Woodland, A.S. 1982. *International Trade and Resource Allocation*. Amsterdam: North-Holland.

5

An Evaluation of Neutral Trade Policy Incentives Under Increasing Returns to Scale

Jaime de Melo and David Roland-Holst

> *...in developing countries where protective barriers are high and there is bias against the exports of manufactured goods, the limitations of domestic markets generally permit only the construction of plants that are below optimum size. By contrast, the disadvantages of small national markets are surmounted in countries where low protective barriers and the lack of bias against exports permit efficient-scale operations through specialization according to comparative advantage....*
>
> *Balassa (1971, 78-79)*

New developments in the theory of international trade often suggest, implicitly or explicitly, that in an imperfectly competitive environment, government intervention may be needed to achieve optimality. The most celebrated example in this new literature is the profit-shifting argument of Brander and Spencer (1984). Another example, perhaps more widely applicable, is the argument developed by Krugman (1985) showing that protection can serve as an export promotion policy under certain circumstances. These arguments have fostered a literature on strategic trade theory, which deals with conditions of imperfect competition between international trading partners.[1] The trade and development literature, on the other hand, concentrates on the implications of imperfectly competitive domestic markets.

In the first of Balassa's (1971) comparative studies on trade policies in developing countries, he argued (in the passage quoted above) that the small size of domestic markets in developing countries was a hindrance to the exploitation of scale economies. He recommended policies to promote exports as a way to break this bottleneck. In his second comparative study of trade policies in semi-industrial countries (Balassa 1982), he ascribed the superior performance of the outward-oriented development strategies in East Asia to the provision of equal incentives to sales on the home and export markets, that is, to the avoidance of home-market bias. Further, in recognition of the learning effects and externalities that accompany the establishment of new industries, Balassa (1975) recommended temporary protection to new activities, which would be gradually scaled down to an across-the-board protection level of about 10 percent. In favoring market neutrality, Balassa is not only applying the principle of nondiscrimination, but he

is also emphasizing trade policy rules or rules of thumb that have low administrative costs and do not depend on econometric evidence for their administration.

In this paper, we explore the robustness of these strategies in a setting that is
representative of semi-industrial market structures and conduct. We recognize that
production in some industrial sectors takes place under increasing returns to scale
and that pricing in tradable sectors distinguishes between domestic and export
markets. The home country is assumed to be a price-taker in both import and
export markets. Thus terms of trade are fixed, and we rule out the possibility of
strategic trade policy to exploit monopoly power in international trade, that is, the
possibility of using trade policy to shift profits to domestic firms. (By contrast,
the strategic trade literature assumes that oligopolistic interactions occur in
international markets, so that trade policy affects the home country's terms of
trade — circumstances that are more representative of developed countries than
semi-industrial ones.) The purpose of the paper is to reexamine the merits of protection, with and without neutrality of domestic and foreign sales incentives, when
some manufacturing sectors operate under increasing returns to scale and domestic
firms behave oligopolistically.

We first derive analytically the comparative statics of tariff and subsidy policy
in the setting described above, and then we derive criteria for optimal tariff-
subsidy policies. Because of intermediate linkages, the welfare effects of trade
policy changes are not generally determinate in this multisectoral, general equilibrium setting. This provides the motivation for our simulation analysis, which is
prefaced by a summary of the model and a discussion of alternative specifications
of oligopoly behavior. Next, we explore systematically the effects of tariffs and
export subsidies on welfare with a computable general equilibrium (CGE) model
of a representative semi-industrial economy with increasing returns and oligopoly
behavior in selected manufacturing activities. Finally, we return to the issues of
neutrality and optimal protection, comparing the welfare effects of trade policies
that provide only import protection for sectors with scale economies with those of
policies that combine tariffs and export subsidies.

Welfare Determinants of Trade Policy Under Increasing Returns

This section presents basic analytical results on the welfare effects of import tariffs
and export subsidies. It extends the work of Dixit (1984) and Rodrik (1988) by
encompassing export subsidies, the selling of sectoral output on different markets
(domestic and export), and imperfect substitution between domestic and imported
goods. These features are reproduced in the model structure of the empirical
application in later sections. In this setting, we show that both import tariffs and
export subsidies contribute to distortions in domestic demand. On the supply side,
our results indicate that tariff protection alone may induce producers to divert
output from exports to the domestic market rather than expanding production and
realizing scale economies. When protection and export incentives are neutral,
however, we show that scale economies can be realized that will offset or even

outweigh the welfare costs of distortions in demand. We conclude the section with the derivation of a general expression for the optimal tariff-subsidy combination. The expression takes explicit account of the linkages and cost externalities that arise under increasing returns in a general equilibrium context. The expression also shows how optimal trade policy necessitates a mixture of domestic market protection and export incentives to balance the relative profitability of sales in the two markets.

Notational conventions follow Dixit (1984). The economy has k sectors, each consisting of n_i identical firms ($i = 1,...,k$) producing output (z_i) for domestic use (y_i) and export (x_i). As in the numerical application below, firm output and sales allocation decisions are separable. Hence the allocation decision along a continuous transformation surface, $z_i = F_i(x_i, y_i)$, depends only on relative prices in the producer's domestic and export markets for output.[2] Each identical firm has a representative cost function $c_i(x_i, y_i)$. Domestic and world prices are k-vectors p and P, respectively, as are ad valorem import tariffs t and export subsidies s. Sectoral domestic prices are an inverse function $p(q)$ of domestic demands, $q_i = M_i + n_i Y_i$, themselves an aggregate of imports and domestic output for domestic use.

To evaluate the welfare effect of import and export distortions, we consider all sectors simultaneously in a general equilibrium framework. In a situation in which the government makes only lump-sum transfers and commodity preferences are those of a single representative consumer, aggregate welfare can be decomposed into three components. The first of these is consumer surplus,

$$(1) \qquad g(q) = \int_0^q p(u)du - p(q)q,$$

or the area under sectoral demand curves, net of domestic sales revenues. The second component of domestic welfare is the sum of firm profits across sectors:

$$(2) \qquad n'\pi = n'[\hat{p}y + \hat{P}(I+\hat{s})x - c(x,y)],$$

where a caret expands the vector in question into a diagonal matrix and a prime denotes a transposition. This expression accounts for revenues from domestic and export sales (which may be subsidized) and total cost. The third component of domestic welfare is tariff revenue net of export subsidy outlays, $[t'\hat{P}M - s'\hat{P}\hat{n}x]$. It reflects the direct change in domestic income due to the imposition of trade-distorting measures when world prices are fixed.

The resulting domestic welfare function is then given by

$$(3) \qquad \begin{aligned} W &= g(q) + \hat{n}\pi + t'\hat{P}M - s'\hat{P}\hat{n}x \\ &= g(q) + \hat{n}[\hat{p}y + \hat{P}x - c(x,y)] + t'\hat{P}M. \end{aligned}$$

We are interested primarily in the welfare effects of trade policies in the form of tariffs and export subsidies. Total differentiation of expression 3 gives a decomposition of the welfare effects of trade policy changes:

$$(4) \qquad dW = t'q_p(p_t dt + p_s ds) + n'(I - c_z)\, [(y_p + x_p)p_t dt$$
$$+ (x_s + y_s)\, ds] - n'(\hat{a} - c_z)\, \hat{z}\hat{n}^{-1} dn.$$

Subscripts denote partial differentiation. So q_p is the Jacobian matrix of price derivatives for domestic demand, and y_p and x_s are matrices of direct supply responses in domestic and export markets. The Jacobian c_z is the marginal cost matrix for domestic production, including (off the diagonal) cost externalities that may be conferred by sectors with increasing returns. The vector $a = \hat{z}^{-1}c(x,y)$ contains sectoral average costs.

The first term on the right side of expression 4 measures the distortionary cost in consumption and is negative when the domestic demand curve slopes downward. We have assumed that imports and domestic goods are imperfect substitutes in use and that domestic goods are imperfect substitutes in domestic and export sales. These assumptions of product differentiation imply that domestic prices are endogenous and can be affected by either tariffs or export subsidies. So, under the assumption that the aggregate demand curve is downward sloping, the first term on the right side of expression 4 indicates welfare losses from consumption distortions due to a tariff (dt), an export subsidy (ds), or a combination of the two. This term corresponds to the standard welfare costs of protection in the case of constant returns to scale.

Scale efficiency effects, which are summarized in the second term on the right side of equation 4, are slightly more complex. Note first that, with normal demand behavior, benefits from protection can arise from expansion of total output in sectors with scale economies. Domestic supply can be expected to rise with domestic prices ($y_p > 0$) and exports with the subsidy rate ($x_s > 0$). However, the net effect of each of these direct supply responses on total sectoral output depends on the extent of intermarket diversion. Rising domestic prices may induce a diversion from exports to an increasingly lucrative domestic market ($x_p < 0$), while subsidies might induce diversion in the opposite direction ($y_s > 0$). The ultimate effect on output depends on the relative magnitudes of the supply and diversion effects ($z_p = y_p + x_p$ and $z_s = x_s + y_s$) and is ultimately an empirical question. What is clear from expression 4, however, is that tariffs and export subsidies can be beneficial if domestic firms' marginal costs are below world prices. Thus, with no firm entry or exit, tariffs and subsidies can be beneficial if the efficiency gains from scale expansion exceed the distortionary costs of protection.

The third term in expression 4 represents the effects on welfare of changes in the number of firms. The negative sign indicates that, where there are scale economies, firm entry is detrimental to welfare and that the magnitude of the welfare loss increases with the degree of unexploited scale economies.

We now pose the question: What would be an optimal choice of tariff and subsidy levels with respect to our domestic welfare function? Given the qualitative symmetry of tariff and subsidy effects, it is unlikely that any policy that implements one without the other could be optimal, but their interplay may be more subtle than simple rules of thumb such as neutrality (equal rates) would imply.

We now derive optimal tariff and subsidy rates in the context of the model already presented. To simplify discussion, we assume that there is no firm entry or exit.

To maximize domestic welfare, we form the Lagrangian expression

$$(5) \qquad L(t,s) = W(t,s) + \lambda[z - F(x,y)] ,$$

which leads to first-order conditions of the form

$$(6) \qquad W_t = t'q_p + n'(I - c_z) (y_p + x_p) = \lambda(Z_p - F_x x_p - F_y y_p)$$

and

$$(7) \qquad W_s = t'q_p p_s + n'(I - c_z) (x_s + y_s) = \lambda(Z_s - F_x x_s - F_y y_s) .$$

The last two equations can be solved for the vector of optimal tariffs:

$$(8) \qquad t = - n'(I - c_z) y_p q_p^{-1} .$$

This expression shows that the optimal tariff depends on the extent of unexploited scale economies and on the elasticities of supply and demand. Conditions for a nonzero optimal tariff are initial marginal costs below world prices or falling from that level, nonzero elasticity of domestic supply, and finite elasticity of domestic demand. Expression 8 also takes account of interactions across the economy and thus derives consistent optimal policy instruments for all sectors simultaneously.

An optimal tariff-subsidy combination will be one that equates the marginal rate of transformation (MRT) between domestic and export markets with their respective relative prices, that is, one where $MRT = F_x / F_y = p / (1+s)$ in the one-sector case. More generally, the optimal tariff-subsidy combination is given by

$$(9) \qquad (I + s')F_x = \hat{p}F_y.$$

Assuming that the Jacobians F_x and F_y are diagonal, then the optimal export subsidy would be that which exactly equalizes the value of marginal domestic product between the two markets. In the numerical exercises below, we compute the vector of optimal export subsidies for a selected vector of uniform import tariffs.

Modeling Oligopolistic Domestic Markets

Since the analytical results presented above are ambiguous with respect to the effects of trade policy on welfare, we use numerical analysis to reveal the relative importance of factors affecting overall welfare. First, we describe briefly the structure of the CGE model used for the simulation exercises in the remainder of the paper.

As was the case in the analytics of the previous section, the model specifies product differentiation between exports and domestic sales and between imports and domestically produced goods in domestic demand. Again, the country is small in international markets. A Leontief technology is specified for intermediate technology. Within sectors, however, domestic and imported inputs are imperfect substitutes. This assumption of product differentiation is also maintained for sectors with scale economies. In those sectors, goods are produced by n_i identical firms. Thus all goods produced for domestic sale in the same sector are perfect substitutes, allowing us to aggregate sectoral supply across firms. Consumption demand across sectors is described by a linear expenditure system with nonunitary income elasticities of demand. Finally, value added is produced by a constant elasticity of substitution technology for two primary factors of production, capital and labor (mobile across sectors), and there is a Leontief technology between aggregate value added and aggregate intermediates. All final demands arise from a representative consumer, who also receives net tax revenues as a lump-sum income transfer. As in Harris (1984), fixed costs include capital and labor (equal weight on each).

We contrast the case of constant returns to scale (where marginal cost pricing prevails) with two pricing hypotheses in sectors with increasing returns to scale.

In the first alternative, we specify an analogue to the case of perfect competition under constant returns to scale. We assume costless entry / exit, so that the threat of entry forces incumbent firms to price at average cost. In this contestable-market scenario (omitting sectoral subscripts),

$$(10) \qquad\qquad p_z = a,$$

for each sector with increasing returns to scale, where p_z is the unit price from the constant elasticity of transformation cost function associated with the transformation function describing sales allocation to the domestic and export markets. Here p_z is the weighted sum of unit sales prices on the domestic (p) and export ($1+s$) markets and a is average costs.

In the second alternative, we assume that each (identical) firm behaves in the domestic market as a monopolist facing a downward-sloping demand curve. In equilibrium, each firms equates marginal revenue with marginal costs (c_z), that is,

$$(11) \qquad\qquad \frac{p - c_z}{p} = \frac{\tilde{\Omega}}{n\varepsilon},$$

where ε is the endogenous elasticity of demand on domestic sales given by

$$(12) \qquad \varepsilon = \varepsilon^F S^F + \varepsilon^v S^v,$$

where $F(v)$ denotes final (intermediate) demand and ε^F and ε^v are functions of the parameters describing substitution effects in intermediate and final demand. Because equation 12 is part of the system of equations that must be satisfied in equilibrium, ε is endogenous. The variable Ω is the representative firm's conjecture about the response of competitors to its output decision with respect to firm j. That is, if z_{-j} denotes the aggregate output of the remaining firms in its sectors, then $\Omega \equiv \Delta z_{-j} / \Delta z_j$. The value of Ω is obtained as follows. By choice of units, n is set equal to unity in expression 11. Since the value of ε is determined by the parameters and quantities in the model, if one takes p and c_z as data, then the value of Ω is determined by solving equation 11. We denote by $\tilde{\Omega}$ the value of the calibrated representative firm's conjecture.

We contrast two rules for determining firm entry / exit. Define

$$(13) \qquad \pi \equiv \pi_y + \pi_x ,$$

where π is profit per unit of sales and subscripts y and x denote sales to the domestic and export markets, respectively. In the first alternative, firm entry is determined to ensure that profit per unit of total sales is zero. This assumes that export subsidies allow firms to make a profit on export sales. However, since export subsidies are often justified as a way of defraying the cost of opening new markets, it is reasonable to consider the alternative case in which subsidies to export sales do not give rise to higher than normal profits. In this second alternative, firm entry is determined to give zero profit on domestic sales.

One would expect the degree of firm collusion to vary with the number of firms. The fewer the number of firms, the more collusive is behavior likely to be. To capture this effect, we add the following equation to determine conjectures:

$$(14) \qquad \tilde{\Omega} = n^{-1} ,$$

which completes the description of the model.

A Comparison of Trade Policies Under Constant and Increasing Returns to Scale

We now turn to illustrative numerical calculations based on the model outlined above. All simulations refer to the effects of a departure from free trade in an archetypal semi-industrial economy.[3]

The structure of the economy in the hypothetical free trade solution is described in table 5.1. Of the seven sectors, one is nontradables. The data on sectoral structure indicate an open economy with high trade shares in GDP. Sectoral value

Table 5.1 Sectoral Features of the Semi-Industrial Economy

Sector	Share in gross output (%)	Exports/ output (%)	Imports/ domestic sales (%)	Elasticity of substitution in production	Export supply elasticity[a]	Import elasticity of demand[a]	Cost dis- advantage ratio[b]	Domestic price elasticity of demand
Primary	8.9	4.9	40.4	2.5	0.75	1.8	--	--
Food products	9.6	2.5	6.5	1.5	1.5	2.5	--	--
Consumer goods	14.4	32.5	14.2	1.0	1.5	2.4	0.1	1.6
Producer goods	20.1	16.6	19.2	0.9	1.5	2.2	0.1	1.3
Heavy industry	7.7	31.9	41.0	0.9	1.5	1.9	0.1	1.4
Traded services	13.2	24.4	7.5	1.5	1.5	2.0	--	--
Nontraded services	26.1	--	--	0.9	--	--	--	--

a. Expenditure-compensated price elasticities. For imports (exports), expenditures (sales) on constant elasticity of substitution (transformation) aggregate of domestic and import (export) goods held constant.

b. The cost disadvantage ratio (difference between average and marginal costs divided by average cost) is a measure of unrealized economies of scale.

added ratios are quite low, indicating the strong interindustry linkages observed in a semi-industrial economy. The three sectors with increasing returns to scale account for 42 percent of gross output, 73 percent of export sales, and 51 percent of import expenses. For the simulations in this section, we assume a low and uniform cost-disadvantage ratio of 10 percent in sectors with economies of scale.[4]

Table 5.2 gives the results of simulations comparing the effects of tariff protection and export subsidization. All simulations refer to 10-percent tariff and 10-percent export subsidy rates. We contrast four scenarios: constant returns to scale (CRTS) across all sectors, contestable-market pricing for the three sectors with increasing returns to scale, and Cournot competition with total profit or domestic profit determining firm entry. The results presented in table 5.2 are for protection or export subsidization of (1) sectors with constant returns to scale only (primary, food processing, and traded services); (2) sectors with increasing returns only (consumer goods, producer goods, and heavy industry); or (3) all traded sectors.

Two measures of the welfare effects of changes in trade policy are reported in table 5.2. The equivalent variation measure is derived from the indirect utility function associated with the Stone-Geary utility function assumed for final demand. It is an aggregate measure of efficiency gains and losses in production and of efficiency losses in consumption. Equivalent variation measures how much the representative consumer would have to be compensated at the new set of prices to be indifferent to the bundle of goods now available at the initial set of prices. The second measure is the scale efficiency gain or loss from moving along average cost curves.[5] Like equivalent variation, scale efficiency evaluates the new output level at old prices, so that the measure controls for shifts in the average cost curve induced by changes in factor and product prices.

Now let us examine the results presented in table 5.2. Consider first the results under constant returns to scale in the first three columns. In the case of tariff protection, there is a welfare loss from protection regardless of which group of sectors is protected. As expected, the welfare cost of protection increases with the number of sectors being protected. Note that the corresponding welfare loss estimates for export subsidization yield very similar orders of magnitude, with the differences depending on trade volumes and substitution elasticities.

Turn now to the case of contestable-market pricing, which assumes increasing returns to scale for the consumer goods, producer goods, and heavy industry sectors. Now protection of sectors with constant returns to scale is much more costly because of scale efficiency losses when resources are pulled out of sectors with scale economies. The loss of scale efficiency occurs because firms are forced to produce higher up on their average cost curves. By contrast, protection of sectors with increasing returns to scale is much less costly because of the scale efficiency gain. Note, however, that even though protection is provided across the board for sectors with increasing returns to scale, there is a scale efficiency loss in one sector. Finally, protecting all sectors results in a larger welfare loss than under the scenario of constant returns to scale in all sectors because of scale efficiency losses.

Table 5.2 Comparison of the Welfare Effects of Tariffs and Export Subsidies under Different Pricing Conditions

Sector	CRTS			Contestable[a]			Cournot (total profit)[b]			Cournot (domestic profit)[c]		
	CRTS	IRTS	All	CRTS	IRTS	All	CRTS	IRTS	All	CRTS	IRTS	All
Ten-percent tariff												
Equivalent variation	-7	-9	-12	-50	-2	-46	12	60	78	-33	-30	-57
Scale efficiency (total)				-42	6	-34	19	69	88	-27	-22	-47
Producer goods				-14	-8	-21	9	33	42	-7	-8	-14
Consumer goods				-24	15	-8	8	15	23	-3	-6	-8
Heavy industry				-4	-1	-5	2	21	23	-3	-6	-8
Firm entry (+) / exit (-)												
Producer goods							-5	-9	-14	-1	2	1
Consumer goods							-5	-1	-5	-1	4	4
Heavy industry							-2	-1	-12	0	4	4
Ten-percent export subsidy												
Equivalent variation	-6	-19	-13	-45	52	27	52	-168	-108	18	15	36
Scale efficiency (total)				-39	74	42	57	-155	-97	24	25	46
Producer goods				-14	38	26	23	-69	-46	8	7	14
Consumer goods				-15	22	10	21	-48	-27	12	14	24
Heavy industry				-10	14	6	13	-38	-24	4	4	8
Firm entry(+) / exit (-)												
Producer goods							-8	23	15	-4	2	-1
Consumer goods							-6	11	6	-4	0	-4
Heavy industry							-9	22	13	-5	1	-4

Note: CRTS = constant returns to scale; IRTS = increasing returns to scale. All figures are basis points. Figures for equivalent variation and scale efficiency are basis points of GDP (e.g., -168 is 1.68% of GDP); figures for entry/exit are basis points of initial number of firms.

a. Pricing according to equation 10.
b. Pricing according to equation 11, with firm entry / exit determined by total profits, so that $\pi = 0$.
c. Same as note b but with firm entry determined by profits on domestic sales, so that $\pi_y = 0$.

Now, compare these results with those for export subsidization in the bottom half of the table. The subsidization results corroborate Balassa's assertion that specialization according to comparative advantage enables the disadvantages of small national markets to be surmounted in sectors with unexploited economies of scale. As before, the benefits are greatest when trade policy is confined to sectors with increasing returns to scale. The export subsidization effects dominate the tariff protection effects because of the difficulty of substituting away from imports when incentives are provided to domestic producers, and the ease of expanding sales in international markets when market share is small.

When contestable market pricing is replaced by Cournot competition, the welfare effects of trade policy are affected by three additional adjustment mechanisms: firm entry / exit (the mechanism that achieves zero profits in long-run equilibrium), the endogeneity of firm collusion, and — generally less significant — the anticompetitive effect of protection, which lowers the elasticity of domestic demand, ε.[6]

The most important of these mechanisms influencing the welfare effects of trade policy under Cournot competition is the pattern of firm entry or exit. Take the case of tariff protection, which raises the profitability of domestic sales and lowers the profitability of export sales because of induced appreciation in the real exchange rate. If firm entry or exit depends on the joint profitability of sales in both markets, then there is firm exit because sectors with increasing returns to scale happen to have high export shares in our numerical example. Firm exit allows the remaining firms to move down their average cost curves, thereby reaping the benefits of more efficient scale. If, however, one assumes that firm entry is governed by profits from sales in the domestic market alone, then there is firm entry and protection results in a welfare loss because of the loss in scale efficiency.

By symmetry, a policy of subsidizing exports has opposite effects. Export subsidization leads to crowding-in if the decision to enter depends on total profits because export subsidies lead to large profits on export sales. For the case of export subsidization of sectors with increasing returns to scale, the welfare loss amounts to 1.7 percent of GDP. If, on the other hand, one assumes that export subsidies do not give rise to abnormal profits but rather contribute to defraying the costs (and risks) of selling in new markets, there is a small welfare gain. Interestingly, in the case of export subsidization in sectors with scale economies there is a scale efficiency gain despite some firm entry.

The results presented in table 5.2 clearly show that if Cournot competition is a reasonable representation of behavior in sectors with increasing returns to scale, firm entry and exit are crucial in determining the sign and magnitude of the effects of trade policy interventions. For the illustrative trade policy interventions reported in table 5.2, one could argue that entry behavior based on total profits is the more reasonable assumption. However, one can interpret a policy of protection more broadly as one that produces home-market bias because it usually involves quotas and nontariff barriers that create barriers to entry as competition from abroad is suppressed. Then a sheltered domestic market is likely to lead to excessive firm entry because of high profits.[7]

On the other hand, the experience of successful East Asian exporters suggests that it was the provision of export incentives that put domestic producers on an equal footing with their foreign competitors. As argued by Frischtak et al. (1989, 10-11), exporters need support to make the commitment to riskier activities that have a long lead time and sunk costs for identifying suitable markets and setting up distribution channels. Under this interpretation of the costs of establishing successful export activities, subsidies (or incentives that increase the relative profit-ability of exports) are not likely to give rise to abnormally high profits and hence to induce excessive entry.

An alternative interpretation would emphasize that the appropriate policy in a setting of increasing returns to scale is to promote competition in domestic markets. This logic recognizes that imperfect competition in domestic markets can act as an export barrier by increasing the relative profitability of domestic operations. Ideally, industrial policy would be coordinated with trade policy to encourage the exploitation of efficient scale, promoting exports while avoiding excessive entry.[8]

Evaluation of Protection in Sectors with Scale Economies

We return to the issues raised in the introduction: Are there welfare gains from protecting sectors with increasing returns to scale, and how does import protection compare with neutral incentives (for example, with tariffs and export subsidies at equal rates)? To answer these questions, we report on simulations in which we contrast across-the-board tariffs of 15 percent with across-the-board export subsidies of 15 percent, both in sectors with scale economies. Protection and export subsidies are confined to the consumer, producer, and capital goods sectors. Now we assume a cost-disadvantage ratio of 20 percent, a value more in line with the unexploited economies of scale in the manufacturing sector of a typical semi-industrial country. The results of these simulations appear in table 5.3. In the constant-returns-to-scale benchmark case, there is, as before, a welfare loss from protection alone or from export subsidization alone. Neutrality, however, is less costly because the distortion introduced by the export subsidy partly offsets the distortion introduced by the tariff.

The same pattern of welfare estimates emerges under the assumption of contestable markets. However, because we have assumed a greater degree of unexploited economies of scale, the magnitudes are larger than in table 5.2. There is a welfare gain of 2.7 percent of base year GDP to be reaped from subsidizing export sales of sectors with increasing returns to scale. Note the superiority of export subsidization over import protection, which springs from our assumption that exporters face a perfectly elastic foreign demand whereas domestically produced goods face a downward sloping domestic demand curve. Hence the incentives created by export subsidization are more direct than those created by

Table 5.3 Protection and Subsidization of Sectors with
Increasing Returns to Scale

(cost-disadvantage ratio of 20 percent)

Protection/subsidy	CRTS	Contestable [a]	Cournot (domestic profit) [b]
15-percent tariff			
Equivalent variation	-18	12	-106
Scale efficiency	0	31	-88
15-percent export subsidy			
Equivalent variation	-42	274	86
Scale efficiency	0	336	110
15-percent tariff and export subsidy			
Equivalent variation	-31	281	4
Scale efficiency	0	322	27

Note: CRTS is constant returns to scale. All figures are basis points of GDP (e.g., -106 is -1.06 percent of GDP).
a. Pricing according to equation 10.
b. Pricing according to equation 11, with firm entry and exit determined by profits on domestic sales, so that $\pi_y = 0$.

protection for domestic sales. While the export demand specification deserves further scrutiny, it appears to correspond to the experience of countries that have followed an export-led development strategy.

In the contestable-market scenario, neutrality produces the largest welfare gains from trade incentives to sectors with increasing returns to scale and sustains the recommendations of Balassa (1975, 1989). In the case of Cournot competition, under the assumptions about firm entry, subsidization of exports dominates the alternative of providing equal incentives to domestic and export sales. This occurs because we have assumed that subsidies to exports do not give rise to profits (and hence do not induce firm entry) whereas protection on the domestic market gives rise to profits and induces firm entry. As we saw above, firm entry results in scale efficiency losses, an effect that comes out clearly in the case of protection to domestic sales. In that case, tariff protection results in a welfare loss that exceeds 1 percent of GDP.

It is obvious that the results under Cournot competition are quite sensitive to the determinants of the number of firms — about which little is known. In the simulations reported here, we have attempted to portray the stylized facts suggested by the comparative studies of foreign trade regimes in developing countries. These studies reveal that countries that have followed import-substitution industrialization strategies have often tended to provide made-to-measure protection for all domestic activities. This protection has, in turn, tended to create excess profit opportunities from domestic sales. When pushed to the extreme, excessive across-the-board protection of industrial activities has been shown to result in excessive firm entry.

We conclude by comparing neutrality of incentives with optimal trade policy. The "optimal" trade policy package is obtained by maximizing the value of the utility function for the representative consumer, taking tariffs as given and export subsidies as endogenous policy instruments. To facilitate the comparison with the results in table 5.2, we fix all import tariffs at 10 percent for all sectors.

The results of the calculation of these "optimal" trade policy packages appear in table 5.4. Note first that under the assumption of constant returns to scale in all sectors, the numerical calculations confirm the well-known results predicted by Lerner (1936), namely that across-the-board tariff and export subsidies at the same rates are equivalent to free trade.[9] Note also that the equivalent variation measure achieves a maximum of zero in this case because departure from free trade cannot be beneficial under constant returns to scale.

Table 5.4 Optimal Export Subsidies for a Given Ten-Percent Import Tariff on All Tradables
(cost-disadvantage ratio of 10 percent)

	CTRS	Contestable	Cournot (domestic profit)[a]
Equivalent variation	0	66 (58)[b]	55 (-6)[b]
Scale efficiency (total)		128	102
Producer goods		54	32
Consumer goods		49	52
Heavy industry		24	18
Firm entry			
Producer goods			-4
Consumer goods			-12
Heavy industry			-11
Export subsidy			
Primary products	10	-6	62
Food processing	10	-1	36
Producer goods	10	24	33
Consumer goods	10	27	25
Heavy industry	10	25	41
Traded services	10	-1	41

Note: The subsidy is in percentage points. Other figures are in basis points.
a. Pricing according to equation 11, with firm entry determined by profits on domestic sales, so that $\pi_y = 0$.
b. Corresponding equivalent variation figure under neutrality, that is, from combining a 10-percent import tariff with a 10-percent export subsidy in sectors with increasing returns to scale.

Under increasing returns to scale, Lerner symmetry still holds: across-the-board tariffs and export subsidies at the same rate are equivalent to free trade. But, as the pattern of export subsidy figures shows, neutrality is no longer optimal. Two results stand out in the contestable-market case. First, as expected, optimality requires that greater incentives be provided to sectors with increasing returns to scale. Second, the difference in welfare benefits is small between optimal trade policy and the rules of thumb advocated by Balassa (1975, 1989) — across-the-board protection (with equal incentives to exports) for manufacturing activities. Here, optimality dominates the rule of thumb of incentive neutrality by less than 10 basis points. Given the notorious lack of the precise elasticity estimates needed to calculate optimal incentives, the illustrative calculations here do not support a departure from the rule of thumb advocated by Balassa.

In the case of Cournot competition, however, the optimal pattern of export subsidies departs further from neutrality. Under this scenario, an optimal policy would encourage firm exit to reap scale economies. As the figures in the last column of table 5.4 indicate, firm exit would be achieved by providing higher export subsidies to sectors with constant returns to scale.[10] Now departure from a simple rule of thumb yields larger welfare benefits. However, the discussion of table 5.2 suggested that the results under Cournot competition are very sensitive to the determinants of firm entry, so these results should be interpreted with care.

Conclusion

This paper set out to test the robustness of Balassa's recommendation of neutral incentives to domestic and export sales in a setting where some sectors have domestic market power. We have shown analytically that the welfare effects of trade policy are more complex than they are in a setting of across-the-board constant returns to scale. In particular, we have shown, analytically and numerically, that the standard distortionary costs of protection emphasized under conditions of constant returns to scale must be amended to accommodate, among other things, the welfare effects of changes in scale efficiency. Illustrative numerical calculations also show that the magnitude of the welfare gains or losses from trade policy intervention are sensitive to the determinants of firm entry and exit.

Calculations comparing trade policies that achieve neutrality of incentives between sales to domestic and those to foreign markets found such policies to be generally superior to policies creating non-neutral incentives. Numerical results also suggest that export promotion is likely to be more beneficial than protection for sectors with increasing returns to scale. Finally, illustrative calculations of optimal trade policy packages suggest that the benefits of departing from the principle of neutrality, or nondiscrimination between domestic and export sales, may be insufficient to justify their higher administrative costs.

Notes

The research reported here is part of the World Bank research project "Industrial Competition, Productive Efficiency and Their Relation to Trade Regimes" (RPO 674-46). The numerical work is based on a model developed in de Melo and Tarr (forthcoming). The views expressed here are those of the authors and should not be attributed to their affiliated institutions.

1. See Harris (1989) and Helpman and Krugman (1989) for surveys of this work.
2. Imperfect substitutability in the allocation of sales implies that F_{xi} / F_{yi} varies along a convex transformation frontier. Lower-case letters indicate partial derivatives.
3. The archetypal economy was obtained from the free trade solution of a seven-sector CGE model calibrated to the Korean economy for the year 1982. For a description of the data set and parameters values, see de Melo and Roland-Holst (forthcoming).
4. The cost-disadvantage ratio is the difference between average and marginal costs, divided by average costs. It is a measure of unrealized economies of scale.
5. The aggregate scale efficiency measure is calculated by using current outputs as weights. For further discussion, see de Melo and Roland-Holst (forthcoming).
6. The magnitude of this effect is small for the functional forms specified here and is not reported. For a discussion of its magnitude, see de Melo and Roland-Holst (forthcoming). Also, see Devarajan and Rodrik (1989).
7. Frischtak et al. (1989) document the pervasive barriers to competition in the manufacturing sectors of developing countries. Eastman and Stykolt (1962) is an early example of a model in which protection leads to firm entry. The typical example is the automobile industry in Latin America (see Baranson 1968).
8. In this regard, the Korean experience during the 1970s is instructive. An activist industrial policy was successful in promoting the growth of large conglomerates and reaping the benefits of scale economies. While exports benefited from this policy, oligopolistic markets developed, and a vigorous antitrust policy was established in the early 1980s to promote greater competition in domestic markets. For further discussion, see Lee, Urata, and Choi (1988) and World Bank (1987).
9. Since there is no guarantee that the optimal vector of subsidies is unique, numerical verification of Lerner symmetry is a useful computational check.
10. While the results of these optimal calculations appear reasonable, there is no guarantee that the computed optima are global optima rather than local optima. Hence these results should be viewed as suggestive and subject to further scrutiny.

References

Balassa, B. 1975. "Reforming the System of Incentives in Developing Countries." *World Development* 3 (June): 365-81.

Balassa, B. 1989. *Tariff Policy and Taxation in Developing Countries.* PPR Working Paper No. 281. Washington, D.C.: World Bank.

Balassa, B., and Associates. 1971. *The Structure of Protection in Developing Countries.* Baltimore, Md.: Johns Hopkins University Press.

Balassa, B., and Associates. 1982. *Development Strategies for Semi-Industrial Countries.* Baltimore, Md.: Johns Hopkins University Press.

Baranson, J. 1968. *The Automotive Industry in Latin America.* Praeger: New York.

Bergsman, J. 1974. "Commercial Policy, Allocative Efficiency and X-Efficiency." *Quarterly Journal of Economics* 88: 409-33.

Brander, J., and B. Spencer. 1984. "Tariff Protection and Imperfect Competition." In H. Kierzkowski, ed., *Monopolistic Competition in International Trade*. Oxford: Oxford University Press.

Chenery, H. 1975. "The Structuralist Approach to Development Policy." *American Economic Review* 65: 310-16.

Corden, M. 1967. "Monopoly, Tariffs and Subsidies." *Economica* 34: 50-8.

Devarajan, S., and D. Rodrik. 1989. "Pro-competitive Effects of Tariff Reform." Working Paper, J.F. Kennedy School of Government, Harvard University, Cambridge, Mass.

Dixit, A.K. 1984. "International Trade Policy for Oligopoly Industries." *Economic Journal* 94: 1-16.

Eastman, H., and S. Stykolt. 1962. "A Model for the Study of Protected Industries." *Economic Journal* 70: 336-47.

Frischtak, C., with B. Hadjimichael and U. Zachan. 1989. *Competition Policies for Industrializing Countries*. Policy and Research Series No. 7. Washington, D.C.: World Bank.

Harris, R.G. 1984. "Applied General Equilibrium Analyses of Small Open Economies with Scale Economies and Imperfect Competition." *American Economic Review* 74: 1016-33.

Harris, R.G. 1989. "The New Protectionism Revisited." *Canadian Journal of Economics* 24: 751-78.

Helpman, E., and P. Krugman. 1989. *Trade Policy and Market Structure*. Cambridge, Mass.: MIT Press.

Horstmann, I., and J. Markusen. 1986. "Up the Average Cost Curve: Inefficient Entry and the New Protectionism." *Journal of International Economics* 20: 225-48.

Krugman, P. 1984. "Import Protection as Export Promotion." In H. Kierzkowski, ed., *Monopolistic Competition in International Trade*. Oxford: Oxford University Press.

Lee, K., S. Urata, and I. Choi. 1988. "Recent Developments in Industrial Organization in Korea." World Bank, Washington, D.C.

Lerner, A. 1936. "The Symmetry Between Import and Export Taxes." *Economica* 3: 306-13.

Melo, J. de, and D.W. Roland-Holst. Forthcoming. "Industrial Organization and Trade Liberalization: Evidence from Korea." In R.E. Baldwin, ed., *Empirical Studies of Commercial Policy*. Chicago: University of Chicago Press.

Melo, J. de, and D. Tarr. Forthcoming. *A General Equilibrium Analysis of U.S. Foreign Trade Policy*. Cambridge, Mass.: MIT Press.

Rodrik, D. 1988. "Imperfect Competition, Scale Economies, and Trade Policy in Developing Countries." In R.E. Baldwin, ed., *Trade Policy Issues and Empirical Analysis*. Chicago: University of Chicago Press.

Venables, A. 1985. "Trade and Trade Policy with Imperfect Competition: The Case of Identical Products and Free Entry." *Journal of International Economics* 19: 1-19.

World Bank. 1987. *Korea: Managing the Industrial Transition*. Washington, D.C.

6

The Food Gap of the Developing World: What We Can Learn from a General Equilibrium Modeling Approach

J.M. Burniaux, Dominique Van der Mensbrugghe, and Jean Waelbroeck

Providing enough food for the developing world is not easy. Population growth is much swifter than in developed countries, while both growth of per capita GNP and the income elasticity of demand for food exceed those in the North. It is not surprising that the tendency for food consumption to grow faster than output has been a recurrent problem of economic development.

Many attempts have been made to dramatize the problem through projections of the "food gap" of the developing world, that is, these countries' net imports of food or grain.[1] Such studies conclude that this gap will increase substantially in coming years. The findings have been used to urge developing country governments and international aid agencies to pay greater attention to agriculture in the design of economic growth strategies.[2]

This work has used simple extrapolation techniques. These involve trend projections of agricultural output and projections of demand that combine population projections with forecasts of per capita consumption, obtained by applying income elasticities of food demand to projections of per capita income. The word "simple" is not used in a derogatory sense: simple techniques should be used wherever possible in policy research. The results obtained are in any event no more than a starting point for the projections; the authors use their considerable expertise to improve these initial guesses about the prospects of various countries and regions.

The principal limitation of this approach is that it does not take into account the impact of prices on demand, or of balance of payments difficulties on the rate of exchange and the growth of GNP. These impacts are substantial. Both supply and demand of agricultural products are quite sensitive to prices, even in countries where much of agriculture is not commercialized and the population is close to the subsistence level. In very poor countries, the substitution effect of a food price increase may be small, but the income effect is large.[3]

Throughout his career, Béla Balassa has stressed that policy problems should be investigated in terms of the whole spectrum of forces that act on economies, and that the role of the price mechanism should never be overlooked. True to this spirit, we shall use applied general equilibrium analysis to reexamine the food gap problem of the developing world.

This method makes it possible to bring prices and balance of payments developments into the analysis. Assessing their impact is of course what the general equilibrium approach is good at. The authors of standard food gap projections emphasize that theirs are catastrophe scenarios that will be realized if governments do not respond to needs. History shows that governments very often do not follow the counsel of their advisers, but that thanks to the price mechanism, market economies are able to muddle through apparently insurmountable difficulties. Prices change in the process, possibly quite sharply. Groups of individuals suffer, possibly to a shocking extent. With respect to the food problem, how dire the consequences of poor policies can be is saddeningly illustrated by the recent famines in Africa. Yet no sharp breakdown occurred, no true catastrophe, in the sense of a sudden and lasting disintegration of the economic system.

We first assess what would happen should developing country governments fail to respond to the latent crisis, thereby leaving the job of dealing with the food gap crisis to the market. This will provide an opportunity to show that the pattern of hunger depends on the rate of growth in developed countries — a point overlooked in the food gap literature. We also investigate the extent to which agricultural trade liberalization under the Uruguay Round is likely to worsen the food situation in the developing world, and the impact of liberalization of nonagricultural trade in mitigating this impact. Finally, using Adelman's concept of agricultural export-led industrialization, we examine in general equilibrium terms how a shift of investment from the urban to the rural sector would affect economic growth and hunger in the South.

The Model and What It Can Do

This section covers only the model features that are crucial for the issues discussed in this study.

The Description of Agriculture

A distinctive feature of the RUNS model is its careful specification of the agricultural sector, a design choice that reflected our perception of the fundamental role of agriculture in the development process.[4] Thus in order to better pinpoint the forces that drive the rural economy, we decided that the rural and urban economies should be modeled like distinct countries. The separation of the two sectors is not done as well as we would have liked, however. For want of data, the specification of RUNS (like that of other agricultural models) identifies the rural economy too closely with agriculture. In both developed and developing countries, farm households derive a substantial income from ancillary nonagricultural activities (for example trade, transport, and simple processing such as cotton ginning, oil seed crushing, or rice milling), which national accounts and input-output conventions force us to lump into the model's urban economy. Production of these activities rises and falls with that of agriculture.

From a general equilibrium point of view, income from these nonagricultural sources affects the budget constraint of the rural population. The share of this income in farmers' earnings probably rises or falls with the evolution of technology and the organization of markets. Transport activities, for example, are less important in subsistence economies than in more monetized economies. This share probably also depends on the economic policies whose impact the model seeks to represent. Thus price and other policies that encourage farmers to stay on the land probably induce an accumulation of excess farm labor, which will seek nonagricultural local employment and so will raise the ratio of nonfarm income to total farm household income.[5] Even geography matters. For example, a farmer in densely populated Belgium can get an outside job far more easily than one who works in sparsely populated areas of Utah or New Mexico.

Recognizing that farmers have sizable nonagricultural incomes is important because this income insulates them to some extent from changes in agricultural prices. The model thus misses an important aspect of the farm economy.[6] This creates a bias in the model results: farm incomes are less dependent on agricultural protection than the model suggests.[7]

Again for want of appropriate data, RUNS assumes that farm investment adjusts to match the total of farm saving plus an exogenous contribution of public investment to irrigation and other rural infrastructure. Net private capital flows between the two parts of the economy are not taken into account. This assumption may be roughly correct in such primitive economies as those of Sub-Saharan Africa, but it is less acceptable for, say, the upper-income economies of Latin America or for poor countries such as Pakistan, where a substantial fraction of agricultural income goes to wealthy landowners who are sophisticated enough to invest their money wherever the return is highest.

Again, this induces a bias. The flow of capital between city and country is obviously responsive to the terms of trade of agriculture. Because the model does not recognize that the movement of private capital between city and country responds to market incentives, it understates the long-run impact of price policies on farm output. Again, the size of the bias probably differs between regions: it is smaller in Africa than in Latin America, where rural sectors are highly monetized and a significant share of farm income goes to rich landowners.

On the other hand, the model does take account of important phenomena that other models miss. It provides an adequate representation of the flow of labor between the rural and urban sectors, a crucial aspect of the evolution of economies.[8] The relevant equation of the model, inspired by Harris and Todaro's (1970) seminal piece, is based on the work of Mundlak (1979).

Also important to the discussion are the assumptions about competition. Agricultural markets are highly competitive, so it is unrealistic to represent world markets for agricultural products by an Armington (1969) system. Accordingly, markets for agricultural products are described as perfectly competitive.

It is well known that if supply is perfectly elastic, the assumption of perfect competition on world markets induces unrealistic behavior, characterized by wild swings in trade patterns from year to year. The standard technique for making export supply inelastic is to use the constant elasticity of transformation (CET) production function (Powell and Gruen 1968). This is based on the assumption that the goods that industries sell on the domestic and export markets are not the same, which makes it reasonable to assume a finite elasticity of transformation between them.

This is not an appropriate assumption in agriculture. For example, while the rice that the Chinese eat and the rice that they export may not be identical (they may eat some broken rice, which could not be disposed of on world markets), any reasonable guess about the elasticity of transformation between "domestic" and "export" rice would be a very large number. It is subtle differences in climate and soil structure that make the supply of individual agricultural goods inelastic. The law of comparative advantage reigns supreme on the land. Just as great Chablis cannot be produced in Flanders or flax fiber in Burgundy, there are combinations of soil characteristics and climate that are best suited to the production of each agricultural product.

Describing in full detail why the supply of particular agricultural commodities is inelastic would not have been practical. It would have been possible to use a CET whose arguments are the various outputs of the various agricultural sectors. This would have implied equal elasticities of transformation between all these goods, however.[9] This was inappropriate, because econometric evidence suggests that the supply elasticities of agricultural goods are far from uniform. Use of the CRESH function (Hanoch 1971), a well known generalization of the CET, would avoid this problem, but it is quite hard to manipulate. We have used instead a specification devised by Burniaux that is simple in design and easy to calibrate to the abundant empirical data on the supply elasticity of various agricultural products.[10]

In this specification, two conventional variables are defined, representing resources used in animal husbandry and in crop growing. Each is expressed as an input function, whose arguments are physical agricultural inputs such as land, labor, irrigation, and so on, and an output function, whose arguments are the various goods. Both functions are separable. Setting them equal generates two multi-input multi-output production functions for agriculture's cropping and animal husbandry subsectors.[11] On the input side, the RUNS specification, because it involves physical inputs as arguments of the production function, is closer to technology than production functions of the usual type. On the output side, the search for "technological authenticity" motivated a clear separation of animal and vegetal products.[12]

The "Get Your Prices Right" (GYPR) Mechanism

A crucial feature of the model is the representation of the running sociopolitical struggle between city and countryside and its economic implications for developing country economies. This struggle manifests itself in the downward rigidity of real wages and government efforts to keep food prices in line with other prices.

The representation of these forces conditions the model's response to economic shocks and is worth discussing in some detail.[13]

Modern macroeconomics emphasizes the importance of the rigidity of labor incomes. This is a fundamental element of Keynes' thinking and remains a key feature of recent work on macroeconomics. Malinvaud (1977)[14] and others have worked this idea into a general-equilibrium-with-rationing approach. Other economists have taken other approaches, including efforts to work out rigorous "microeconomic foundations" of wage rigidity. Whatever their disagreements about nuances, however, economists are agreed that wages are rigid.

It is important to note that this rigidity is not simply the result of the stubbornness of trade unions, which are often very weak in developing countries. And it is not merely wages but all urban labor incomes that are rigid. A variety of sociopolitical mechanisms impart this rigidity — from the threat of riots in Caracas to the enshrining of the privileges of particular interest groups in Brazil's new constitution. Even in India, with its high urban unemployment, trade unions are quite influential because of their ability to muster up the vote and provide the indispensable foot soldiers of electoral campaigns. The most powerful mechanism, however, is the threat of riots, which are feared by politicians throughout the developing world. Self-employed shoeshine boys in the informal sector can provoke mayhem as destructively as paid-up trade union members.[15] Paldam (1983) has shown that in Latin America, sudden falls in real wages have toppled indiscriminately democratic governments and military regimes: whichever government is in place is in danger.

For these and other reasons, governments everywhere have sought to contain increases in the cost of living, in particular in the prices of basic food products.[16] There are good arguments in favor of such policies, which can serve as short-run devices that may make it easier for the economy to adjust to unexpected events, such as sharp rises in world food prices. Increases in agricultural prices are supply shocks that raise consumer prices or production costs, reducing the real consumer wage or raising the real product wage.[17] This triggers a struggle between urban workers and producers, in which the first seek to safeguard their living standards and the second to prevent wage increases from squeezing profit margins. Even partial success by the workers (reflected in the model by wage rigidity) squeezes profit margins and lowers both output and investment. Thus the political power of the urban masses has made agricultural prices sticky. And so, at times of low world prices, has the pressure of farmers.

Such policies have significant costs. Food aid may help governments to subsidize urban consumption, but securing it may be difficult and may entail politically unattractive concessions. Keeping agricultural prices low may be achieved via subsidies, which entail large budget costs. Shifting these costs to farmers in the form of low farmgate prices discourages agricultural production and burdens the balance of payments with imports.

Downward rigidity of real wages and efforts of governments to keep food prices in line with other prices combine to generate a fundamental mechanism of RUNS which may be christened the "get your prices right" (GYPR) effect. In a barter general equilibrium model, Keynesian unemployment resulting from inadequate demand cannot exist; unemployment can occur only because the product wage (the ratio of the wage paid to workers to the prices of products sold by their employers) exceeds the market clearing result. Any event that reduces that gap — that contributes to "getting prices right" — must raise employment and GNP.

In RUNS, therefore, an increase in demand for manufactures does not increase output in direct response to aggregate demand, as envisaged by the standard Keynesian theory. Production does adapt to demand, but the response is mediated by changes in profitability that induce producers to change the amounts they produce.[18] Likewise, supply shocks that raise the product wage will make production less profitable, causing output and employment to fall. If the consumption wage is rigid (if wages are indexed even partially to the cost of living), an increase in any price but that of domestically produced urban goods tends to raise the cost of living index in relation to producer prices and hence raises the product wage in such a way that employment and output are reduced.

The mechanism does not operate in the same way everywhere. The discussion here stresses the policy trade-off between the benefits and costs of insulating domestic agricultural prices from world market prices. Countries have reacted in very different ways to this trade-off. Some countries have adopted adjusting policies, allowing domestic prices to move in parallel with world prices, while others have resolutely pursued nonadjusting policies — although not all goods are treated in the same way in a particular country (the pricing of tea in India, for example, is more "adjusting" than that of wheat).[19]

This somewhat lengthy discussion is warranted by the fact that the GYPR mechanism is a key property of RUNS, accounting for differences between its properties and those of other world agricultural models.[20] It also has a significant impact on the results obtained for individual regions, as adjusting and nonadjusting regions respond quite differently to changes in world agricultural prices.

It is worthwhile to sketch briefly the mechanisms involved. When world agricultural prices rise (for example, because of reduced agricultural protection in developed countries), domestic food prices rise by amounts that depend on whether and to what degree regions are adjusting or nonadjusting. These price increases squeeze urban output because workers, in their attempt to maintain their consumption wage, pressure their employers to raise the wage rate above the marginal product of labor (or induce the government to use a variety of devices to achieve this result). This makes production less profitable and induces producers to shed labor by closing down marginal production facilities. Agricultural output, however, increases to a degree that also depends on the degree to which regions pursue adjusting policies. This strengthens the balance of payments[21] and offsets the loss in GNP that results from the drop in urban production. The share of agriculture in total output matters: the importance of the offsetting increase in agricultural output is less in semi-industrialized countries than in less developed ones, in which agriculture is a larger share of total output.

This distinction also affects long-run economic growth: the "problem of the scissors" stressed by Preobrazhenski (1956) continues to haunt developing country governments.[22] An acceleration of urban growth increases food demand and reduces supply by drawing rural workers to city jobs. Either agricultural prices must be allowed to rise, which may cause urban unrest, or food imports must rise, which may cause widespread unrest and jeopardize growth.

These policy patterns also have a crucial impact on world markets for agricultural products. World demand for agricultural products would be virtually inelastic if all countries pursued fully nonadjusting policies.[23] Attempts by countries to insulate themselves from world market fluctuations induce a vicious circle by reducing the price elasticity of demand on world markets and making these prices even more unstable.

Given the central importance of the GYPR mechanism in RUNS, we carried out an extensive investigation of the degree to which governments have allowed fluctuations in world food prices to be passed through to domestic prices.[24] We undertook econometric studies to assess to what extent regions pursue agricultural price policies that are adjusting or nonadjusting. No attempt was made to compare degrees of real wage rigidity between countries. Wage data is quite poor in the third world, usually covering only labor incomes in the formal sector. Furthermore, casual observation suggests that wage rigidity is not stable enough to be characterized by structural relations that can be estimated econometrically. The rigidity of real labor incomes depends on the general political context. For example, the Mexican government, with a broad and stable political basis and a strong grip over its unions, can make wages adjust more easily than can a fragile democracy like Brazil's, a situation that could change completely if there were a weakening of the ruling party in Mexico. In Argentina, Peron brought unions under his control, but during other periods, they have more often than not opposed the government. In Italy, a referendum changed the system of wage indexation; of what use would econometrics be?

Subject to these doubts, the matter was resolved by a bold guess. The RUNS model covers a period that is long enough to bring about a substantial adjustment of real wages toward the wage rate that is compatible with labor market equilibrium. In the absence of solid econometric information, it was assumed that the wage rate adjusts by 0.75 percent to a 1 percent change in the equilibrium rate when the actual wage exceeds the equilibrium level. It adjusts fully to increases in that rate when the economy is at full employment.

Simulation Results

As stated above, we believe that it is legitimate to compare the model results with the food gap projections. RUNS was calibrated to judgment forecasts of agricultural production by World Bank staff. Its GNP, income elasticities of demand, and agricultural output growth rates therefore match the judgments of practical individuals whose detailed knowledge of the developing world is on the whole similar to that of the food gap projecters.[25]

The model adds three elements to their analysis:

- It completes the description of the developing economies by providing sub-models of their urban sectors.
- It closes the description of the world economy by providing forecasts of growth of developed countries.[26]
- Finally, it specifies a price system that is able to match supply and demand for all commodities and to bring foreign payments into balance.

In the food gap projections, what happens to the balance of payments is left to the imagination of the reader, who cannot avoid — and indeed is encouraged to entertain — an uneasy feeling that the projected gap is so large that balance of payments equilibrium is likely to be unattainable. In the RUNS simulations, this equilibrium is achieved willy-nilly through the impersonal and possibly cruel power of the market. All variables change to achieve this equilibrium: prices and real incomes, exports and imports of nonagricultural and agricultural goods. The food gap is not an exogenous piece of data but an endogenous variable that adjusts like all the others to bring about general equilibrium.

The RUNS Food Gap Projection in the Base Case

The base case assumptions imply that balance of payments equilibrium is not easy to achieve. The calibration describes a world of slow GNP growth in developed countries, so that they do not offer easy markets to their partners from the South.

Table 6.1 compares our food gap projections with those of other major fore-casts. The difference in results is striking. In the RUNS base case, production in developing countries increases more rapidly than consumption, a result that is in sharp contrast with the picture provided by the usual food gap projections. As the table shows, it is the demand projection that accounts for most of the difference: the projection of supply is in line with that of other forecasts.[27]

Table 6.2 sheds further light on food prospects. Per capita food consumption in developing countries grows by 0.77 percent a year, a good deal more slowly than is assumed in other projections. It is the urban population that is squeezed: its per capita consumption actually drops. How does this come about?

The food gap is too large to be financed by the foreign exchange receipts that developing countries are likely to be able to earn. Those receipts will be reduced by low growth in the developed world, which will affect the prices and volumes of developing country exports. In addition, capital flows to developing countries are expected to decline as a result of the debt crisis. The import needs of developing countries for nonagricultural products will continue to be large, however, as their underlying rate of growth remains high. Finally, as pointed out by the food gap studies, agricultural imports will tend to be buoyant.

Something has to give. What happens is that the relative price of food rises in developing countries. The real rate of exchange falls, stimulating exports and

Table 6.1 A Comparison of RUNS and Other Food Gap Projections
(growth rates)

Category	FAO 1976	UN 1976	USDA GOL 1978	FAO 1980	MOIRA 1979	RUNS (base case) 1978-86	RUNS (base case) 1987-95
Developing countries							
Population	2.7	2.7	2.7	2.3	2.2	2.3	2.3
Agricultural production	3.3	2.6	3.0	2.7	3.4	3.2	3.6
Food gap	-0.3	-1.0	-0.2	-1.0	-0.2	-0.1	0.8
Developed countries[a]							
Population			0.8		0.7	0.5	0.6
Agricultural production			2.2		2.5	1.9	2.0
Agricultural demand			1.8		1.9	1.3	1.4

a. In GOL and MOIRA projections, this category includes socialist countries.
Source: FAO 1976 (Nagle 1976); UN food conference (Nagle 1976); USDA GOL model (Rojko et al. 1978); FAO 1980 (FAO 1980); MOIRA (Linneman et al. 1979).

Table 6.2 The Food Situation in the RUNS Base Case: Per Capita Consumption
(average annual growth rates)

Category	Rural Past	Rural Proj.	Urban Past	Urban Proj.	Total Past	Total Proj.	Average annual growth rate
Developing countries							
Poor	0.34	0.48	0.79	0.63	0.48	0.53	0.6
Middle-income nonoil	0.81	1.47	1.35	1.20	1.12	1.32	1.0
Middle-income oil	0.47	0.63	1.08	1.18	0.77	0.90	1.0
All developing countries	0.44	0.67	1.05	0.94	0.69	0.79	0.8
Developed countries	1.93	3.86	1.95	2.21	1.95	2.29	0.9

Note: Past is for the period 1978-86; projected covers the period 1987-95.

discouraging imports.[28] Because of the assumed wage rigidity, urban unemployment rises, which helps the balance of payments by reducing import demand. Food consumption falls in the cities, as a result of both the fall in employment and the increase in food prices. This fall is only partly offset by increased food consumption in the countryside, where farmers consume more food because the shift in relative prices improves their income.

The scenario, therefore, is one of urban misery caused by the slow income growth in the developed world. The history of recent years, with the numerous urban food riots that have accompanied efforts of developing countries to adjust to balance of payments difficulties, shows that this is no figment of a computer's imagination.

Agricultural Trade Liberalization with Slow Growth in Developed Countries

What would be the impact on the food situation in developing countries of widespread liberalization of agricultural trade in developed countries, a principal topic of discussion under the Uruguay Round of multinational trade negotiations? The point is often made that agricultural protection among Organization for Economic Cooperation and Development (OECD) countries, by reducing world agricultural prices, alleviates hunger and poverty in developing countries. Is this argument valid in a general equilibrium context?

Liberalization of agricultural imports in the OECD area would lead to an increase in world food prices. Proponents of protection have argued that world agricultural prices are so distorted that it is meaningless to measure protection by comparing the world prices of agricultural products with their domestic prices in individual countries, as is done for example in the producer subsidy equivalent calculations in the OECD. This point is valid. We shall investigate how important it is by using RUNS to assess the rise in world prices that would occur if agricultural protection were removed in OECD countries.

The domestic price of food would rise in developing countries. The impact would be larger in adjusting than in nonadjusting countries, but there would be an increase everywhere. To the extent that food is a basic need or that, as argued by Mellor (1976), workers are more productive when they are adequately fed, this price increase would appear to be an undesirable consequence of trade liberalization. Here again, however, other less obvious mechanisms should be taken into account.

One is the terms of trade. Many developing regions are net exporters of agricultural products. An increase in agricultural prices therefore improves their terms of trade. This is a positive income effect that may offset completely or in part the negative effect just described.

A second mechanism relates to changes in rural demand. Higher food prices, by increasing the incomes of farmers, stimulate their demand for manufactures in a way that is favorable to accelerated industrialization and development (see, for example, Adelman 1984 and Adelman, Burniaux, and Waelbroeck 1989).

A third mechanism is the complex linkage between agriculture and the rest of the economy that was described above in the discussion of the GYPR mechanism. Higher food prices inflict a negative supply shock on the cities which, other things being equal, tends to reduce employment and output.

So any assessment of the impact of agricultural trade liberalization on the developing world must be based on more than the simplistic argument that, since world prices will rise, the poor will suffer. The mechanisms involved are complex: a model is needed.

The simulation assumptions are that protection is fully removed in OECD countries, that is, that domestic agricultural prices in these countries are allowed to fall to the world market level. In the United States, the PIK scheme is abolished, bringing back into production 20 percent of the land (McCalla and Josling 1985, 169). It is further assumed that developing countries do not participate in this liberalizing process.[29]

How much would world food prices rise in response to such a change? Table 6.3 shows that the results of several models are in broad agreement, although Anderson-Tyers 1 contradicts the other results.

Table 6.3 Impact of OECD Agricultural Trade Liberalization on World Prices of Agricultural Products: Comparison of RUNS and Other Models
(percentage change)

Product	RUNS	IIASA	Anderson-Tyers 1	Anderson-Tyers 2
Wheat	15.3	18.0	2.0	20.0
Rice	13.2	21.0	5.0	16.0
Coarse grain	8.5	11.0	1.0	14.0
Sugar	57.0	na	5.0	na
Meats	17.9	17.0	16.2	24.0
Edible oils	6.1	na	na	na

Source: Anderson-Tyers 1 (World Bank 1986); Anderson-Tyers 2 (Parikh et al. 1988).

Table 6.4 describes the effect of agricultural price liberalization on the chief macroeconomic variables in various regions. The key mechanisms involve the terms of trade and the powerful GYPR multiplier. The terms of trade effect works in favor of developing countries. Europe, which is by a good margin the world's chief importer of agricultural products, suffers a significant terms of trade loss. The GYPR mechanism brings about a strong expansion in the OECD area, especially in Europe, where GNP increases by 2.9 percent.

What occurs in developing countries is more complex. It is interesting that urban value added rises in "adjusting" Latin America, where there is a strong pass-through of world to domestic prices. An increase in urban unemployment would be expected. However, the region is a large net exporter of agricultural products, so the resulting terms of trade gain causes a favorable income effect, which offsets the negative GYPR impact. In addition, Latin America has significant exports of mining products and manufactures, whose world demand benefits from the increase in GNP in the OECD area.

The rural-urban price parity shifts in favor of agriculture, and urban misery worsens. This will exacerbate the conflict between farm and city that plays such

Table 6.4 Full Impact on Selected Variables of Liberalization of Agricultural Protection in OECD Countries

(percentage change relative to base case)

Region	Real income [a]	Rural val added	Urban val added	Terms of trade	Rural/urban income parity	Rural/urban price parity [b]	Food product	Food demand [c]	Food per capita rural	Food per capita urban	Food prices [d]
Low-income countries	-0.2	na	na	1.8	na	na	0.1	-0.5	na	na	1.7
Asia (excl. China)	-0.1	0.1	-0.8	3.8	5.0	1.2	0.3	-0.8	1.9	-2.7	2.4
Africa	-0.6	0.1	-1.4	1.0	6.0	4.5	0.2	-0.7	1.8	-2.9	2.5
Middle/upper-income countries	0.7	0.3	0.1	1.1	2.8	3.6	0.7	-0.3	1.2	-1.2	3.2
Latin America	1.4	0.9	0.1	7.1	6.8	6.1	1.7	-0.1	2.4	-2.3	6.6
Southeast Asia	0.9	0.2	-0.1	0.8	6.3	6.3	0.5	-1.2	2.4	-2.2	4.2
Oil producers	0.4	0.1	0.2	0	0.5	0.5	-0.1	0.0	0.3	-0.1	0.4
All developing countries	0.5	na	na	0.2	na	na	0.4	-0.4	na	na	2.3
Developed countries	1.6	na	na	-0.8	na	na	-2.4	5.2	na	na	-13.7
Europe	2.9	-3.3	2.8	-2.8	-34.0	-26.5	-5.1	8.6	2.2	12.5	-20.3
North America, Oceania	1.1	1.2	0.5	3.0	9.7	10.1	2.3	-0.5	3.6	-1.5	4.1

a. Real income is nominal value added at market prices, deflated by the consumer price index.
b. The rural–urban price parity is the ratio of rural and urban value added at factor prices.
c. Total food demand includes feed uses.
d. The food price is the ratio of an average of food prices to the consumer price index.

a key role in the politics of developing countries. A broader perspective shows, however, that nine-tenths of the absolute poor identified by the World Bank live in the countryside, and it is to rural areas that higher agricultural prices transfer the purchasing power whose loss causes this urban misery.[30]

Trade Liberalization for Nonagricultural Goods

Agricultural trade liberalization is only one aspect of the Uruguay Round negotiations. Lowered protection for nonagricultural goods is also being discussed. While reduced agricultural protection would lead to worsened terms of trade for cities and so would increase urban misery, reduced protection of nonagricultural goods would have an opposite effect. By expanding the export markets for industrial goods of the developing world, it will improve urban terms of trade, making food cheaper in relation to urban goods and improving the real incomes of urban populations.

How strong is this effect? Model estimates confirm that trade liberalization for nonagricultural goods will operate in the way described (see table 6.5), but suggest that it will only partially offset the impact of agricultural liberalization. This is not surprising, since the tariff equivalent (or the producer subsidy equivalent) of agricultural protection far exceeds the protection rate for nonagricultural products.

Table 6.5 The Impact on Key Variables of Nonagricultural Trade Liberalization in OECD Countries
(percentage change relative to base case)

Category	Real income	Total val added	Terms of trade	Food product	Food demand	Rural/urban income parity
Low-income countries	0.1	0.0	0.9	0.0	0.0	na
Asia (excl. China)	0.2	0.1	0.5	-0.1	1.0	-0.2
Africa	0.2	0.1	0.3	0.0	0.0	0.2
Middle/upper-income countries	0.3	0.1	0.6	-0.1	0.2	-0.2
Latin America	0.1	0.0	0.7	-0.2	0.1	-0.4
Southeast Asia	0.9	0.5	0.8	0.0	0.5	-0.6
Oil producers	0.3	0.1	0.5	0.0	0.1	0.0
All developing countries	0.2	0.1	0.7	0.0	0.0	na
Developed countries	0.9	0.3	-0.5	0.4	-0.6	na
Europe	1.7	0.6	-1.4	0.4	-1.1	0.3
North America, Oceania	0.5	0.2	-0.2	0.5	-0.3	0.6

Trade liberalization has the strong impact on welfare in the liberalizing regions that characterizes models with real wage rigidities. European countries gain more than the traditional developed country agricultural exporters, because their initial level of protection is higher. This enhances the boost that free trade gives to demand for the goods produced in the developing world's cities. The regions that gain are, reasonably enough, the middle-income countries, with their well-developed industries. Real income in Southeast Asia, in particular, grows by almost 1 percent. The shift in the rural-urban income parity ratio is influenced by the agricultural policies of the various regions: the change in the rural-urban income parity in nonadjusting Europe is half that in the adjusting United States.

One example illustrates the complexity of this type of model. As table 6.5 shows, nonagricultural trade liberalization in OECD countries improves the terms of trade of Africa's rural areas, but worsens it for the rural sectors of other developing countries. We interpret this difference to two factors. First, the urban sectors of Africa export very little, so they derive negligible benefits from nonagricultural trade liberalization and accelerated growth in the OECD countries. Second, Africa's agriculture, as a large exporter, benefits from the upswing in world demand that results from trade liberalization.

Increased Investment in Agriculture: A Solution?

The food gap studies use very simple analytic devices to dramatize the need to increase agricultural output. The more elaborate RUNS model confirms that developing countries will suffer from persistent food shortfalls, which will take the form of high prices rather than of large imports. How much relief, according to that model, could result from a shift in investment from the urban to the rural sector?

In the real world, the shift would to some extent take place spontaneously. The roughly 15-percent increase in world prices that would result from trade liberalization would attract private capital to agriculture.[31] There would also be an endogenous response of increased lending by the international aid agencies. (The World Bank, for example, has a 15-percent cutoff rate of return for the projects that it finances; quite a few agricultural projects would meet this condition if world prices rose by 15 percent.)

In addition to this spontaneous response, however, an additional, exogenous shift would be needed in the allocation of public funds. Successful liberalization of agricultural trade should be accompanied by a deliberate effort to increase investment in agriculture, whether in production facilities, in research, or in such activities as rural education, crop research, and extension services. In fact, RUNS finds that shifting investment from industry to agriculture has a favorable general equilibrium impact on industrial as well as on agricultural growth (see Adelman, Burniaux, and Waelbroeck 1989).

Table 6.6 shows the impact of such a shift. The impact of the assumed shift in investment is strong and goes a long way in helping to solve the problem of food shortfalls. But how realistic is this conclusion?

The model implicitly assumes that public investment in agriculture is as productive as private investment. In the past, much public investment in agriculture has been wasted, but much has been learned since then about the low returns from investment in large irrigation infrastructure projects and the difficulty of bringing to fruition integrated schemes of rural development. It is assumed that such mistakes will not be repeated.

Table 6.6 Impact on Key Variables of an Urban to Rural Shift in Investment in Developing Regions

(percentage change relative to base case)

Category	Real income	GNP			International terms of trade
		Rural	Urban	Total	
Low-income countries	0.2	2.5	-2.4	-1.0	5.3
Asia	1.2	2.4	-1.5	-0.5	8.2
Africa	-2.0	2.7	-4.6	-2.3	1.1
Middle-income countries					
Nonoil	1.4	7.4	0.4	1.1	1.5
Latin America	2.4	8.8	1.3	2.2	1.6
Southeast Asia	1.2	3.6	0.2	0.5	1.1
Mediterranean	0.5	7.2	-0.4	0.3	2.1
Oil	0.0	3.2	-0.2	0.1	0.2
All developing countries	0.8	4.8	-0.1	0.5	1.3
Developed countries	1.8	-1.0	0.7	0.6	0.2
Europe	1.3	0.1	1.0	0.9	0.6
North America, Oceania	0.5	-1.9	0.5	0.4	-0.6

Note: The shift is assumed to be a 40-percent increase in agricultural investment in the middle-income regions and a 30-percent increase in the low-income regions.

The results presented in table 6.6 illustrate the effectiveness of what Adelman (1984) has christened the "agricultural demand-led industrialization" (ADLI) strategy. The effect is positive for both developing country GNP and real income (nominal GDP deflated by the consumer price index). Not all regions gain in the same proportions, however. Reasonably enough, an improved supply of "wage goods" is more beneficial to semi-industrialized regions, with their large urban labor force, than to the less-industrialized countries in low-income Asia and, especially, in Africa.

In both of the lower-income regions, the increase in agricultural investment appears to choke off the supply of capital to industry to an extent that may be excessive, leading to a sharp rise in the price of urban goods. This reflects the large weight of agriculture in these economies. Additional aid might be necessary to alleviate such difficulties.

Conclusion

This study has used applied general equilibrium analysis to examine the food gap of the developing world. Several conclusions are of particular interest. First, the general equilibrium approach finds much lower net food imports than the food gap projections of the past two decades. The reason is simple. Developing countries will not be able to pay for these large food imports. As a result, the relative price of food will rise.[32] This finding does not mean that the food shortage highlighted by the food gap studies is a myth, but rather that the shortage is resolved by the price mechanism, at a high social cost. The price increase that occurs causes widespread misery, in particular in the cities.

The general equilibrium approach has also brought to light aspects of the problem that could not be revealed by the earlier food gap studies. One is that the food situation in developing countries is influenced by the rate of growth in OECD countries. Faster growth in those countries would boost developing country exports and improve the availability of foreign exchange. With the relaxation of the foreign exchange constraint, more food would be imported. Continuation of the recent acceleration of economic growth in developed countries would not only be cause for rejoicing among commercial banks, by easing the debt crisis, but would also help to improve the nutrition of the poor.

Another issue that has gained in precision from this analysis is the idea that agricultural trade liberalization in the developed world would worsen the food situation in developing countries. Our results confirm the conclusion of other studies that agricultural trade liberalization would raise world prices of food by about one-seventh. The clear separation of urban and rural sectors in the RUNS model makes possible the further distinction that it is the urban population whose food standards would deteriorate.[33] While nonagricultural and agricultural import liberalizations in the OECD area influence the food situation in opposite ways (although both raise the growth rate of GNP), the two effects do not offset each other because protection of the nonagricultural sector is much lower than for the rural economy.

Finally, RUNS confirms that a shift in investment from industry to agriculture would ease the food situation, assuming, of course, that the money is invested appropriately. That is hardly surprising. What is more interesting is that it also reveals that such a shift would raise industrial as well as agricultural output as a result of a positive general equilibrium feedback of agricultural on industrial growth. The operative mechanism is the GYPR multiplier, which characterizes models that involve real wage rigidities.[34]

Notes

A first version of this paper was presented in October 1989 to a World Bank / Organization for Economic Cooperation and Development conference on Implications of Agricultural Trade Liberalization on Developing Countries, and is forthcoming in the proceedings volume of this conference.

1. A recent study of this type is the International Food Policy Research Institute (IFPRI) research report by Paulino (1986).
2. The Paulino (1986) study, for example, has served as background for a number of IFPRI policy papers, dealing with such topics as food policies in the Middle East and North Africa and the role of food aid in closing the cereals gap.
3. By Engle's Law, food accounts for a large fraction of the expenditures of the poor. An increase in its price thus has a significant impact on the real value of their earnings.

4. The idea that agriculture plays a key role in the development process is of course not new: it can be traced as far back as the work of the Soviet economist Preobrazhenski (1956) in the early 1920s, which influenced our thinking.

5. This has rather clearly taken place in Germany, for example, and it is one factor that explains why outside activities account for an overwhelming fraction of the income of a large proportion of Japanese farmers.

6. Improving it in this respect is a high-priority (but costly) item in our research agenda. Census data would have to be used for this purpose.

7. The model is not alone in failing to take account of this aspect of rural life. Government policies also neglect it. Everywhere, farm parity policies focus on the ratio of agricultural to nonagricultural prices, neglecting to allow for the substantial nonagricultural incomes of farmers.

8. Indeed, the ratio of the agricultural labor force to the total population is often used as a rough indicator of the level of development. And the very term "industrializing countries" implies that the driving force in development is a shift of production factors to the industrial sector.

9. Using a multilevel CET would have made the specification more complicated without improving matters very much.

10. Important sources for data are Adams and Behrman (1976, 1984), and Rojko et al. (1978), as well as the continuing work of the Commodities Division of the World Bank. For a fuller list, see Burniaux (1987).

11. Tree crops are modeled differently. They use the same resources as other crops, but have multiyear inputs.

12. Here, the work resembles the very creative MOIRA (Model of International Relations in Agriculture) project (Linneman et al. 1979), possibly because the author of RUNS is an agricultural economist as are half of the authors of MOIRA. Coefficients for the input component of these functions are not readily available in the literature. We used the results of work undertaken for the project by Mundlak and Hellinghausen (1982).

13. In particular, this feature accounts for key differences between the simulation results of RUNS and those of other world agricultural models.

14. Malinvaud was only one of a group of people who developed this approach to macroeconomic theory and modeling. His name is cited here because of the brevity and admirable clarity of his presentation of those ideas.

15. Preserving these incomes has been a major political constraint ever since the days when citizen uprisings forced the Roman Senate to grant to the poorest citizens a free supply of bread, a privilege that their (often wealthy) descendants preserved for half a millennium. The Parisians who brought the King back from Versailles during the French revolution were shouting even more loudly for bread than for freedom. (The judgment of historians is that Marie Antoinette's "let them eat cake" was not an adequate policy response to these demands.) The triumph of Solidarnosc in Poland and the overthrow of Ceaucescu owe much to the price and scarcity of meat.

16. Mellor (for example, 1976) identified another reason to control food prices in his concept of the food wage. As we understand him, this mainly reflects the impact of nutrition on the productivity of the labor force.

17. The ratio of the wage to the cost of living and to the price of value added, respectively.

18. Which differs from the mechanism that Keynes described. In the *General Theory*, Keynes provides a very careful discussion of the way in which profits and real wages adapt to a change in demand.

19. For another view of the contrast between adjusting and nonadjusting countries, see the interesting paper by Krueger, Schiff, and Valdes (1988).

20. The mechanism is easily turned off: the program is built so that it can be switched off by changing one flag.
21. That is, in a model where the current balance of payments is exogenous, the real exchange rate is strengthened.
22. The "scissors," much discussed by Soviet economists at the time, are the gap between urban and agricultural prices, which widens as industrialization reduces rural output and increases urban food demand. Stalin solved it by collectivization, a nonmarket approach that involved setting very low farmgate prices, imposing delivery quotas, and killing farmers that disagreed — as many as 20 million peasants may have died. Today's developing country governments use gentler methods, but the problem has not gone away.
23. The price elasticity of demand would not be zero because of income effects. It would be easy to construct examples where it is perverse, that is, positive rather than negative.
24. A similar effort was a feature of MOIRA. In that model, however, full employment reigns, and there is no GYPR mechanism.
25. Indeed, World Bank economists have produced internal papers that provide their own projections of the food gap.
26. Some of the food gap projections — the FAO's, for example — also cover developed countries.
27. Not too much should be read into this, however, since the model is calibrated to reproduce the agricultural production forecasts of the World Bank's economists.
28. There is no "rate of exchange" in a barter general equilibrium model, in the usual sense of defining the ratio at which the monies of two countries are exchanged. There is no single way either of defining a "real rate of exchange"; a good choice is to use the ratio of the price of urban resources in pairs of countries (the prices of capital and labor, weighted by the shares of capital and labor in the production function).
29. There would be no pressure on them to do so, as their protection is mostly negative. Why would agricultural exporters press them to abolish import subsidies which induce them to import more? Also, as the discussion of the base case has suggested, the politically powerful urban masses will suffer from increases in the domestic relative price of food and will pressure governments to reverse them. Why, in this context, should these governments abolish the negative protection that keeps food cheap?
30. The mechanism may be even more complex in regions such as South Asia, that have a large landless agricultural labor force. It is possible then that, although the overall purchasing power of farmers increases, rural wages fail to rise, so that landless workers become poorer.
31. As mentioned previously, the RUNS model does not take adequately into account the mobility of capital between agriculture and the rest of the economy. The lack of adequate data has compelled us to make the doubtful assumption that agricultural investment equals the sum of rural savings plus exogenous government investment. Implicitly, then, the flow of private capital between the two parts of the economy does not respond to changes in incentives. This is not realistic.
32. As a result of the balance of payments pressures so strikingly revealed by the debt crisis, the prices of manufactures in developing countries would drop in relation to both domestic food prices and the prices of manufactures in the developed world.
33. As remarked earlier, this result is biased because the model fails to recognize that farmers derive part of their income from nonagricultural activities. Correcting this deficiency, which is not possible with existing data, would attenuate but not reverse this result.

34. The same mechanism also accounts for the rather large impacts of trade liberalization on GNP. Here, the RUNS simulations imply multipliers that are a good deal stronger than those that are predicted by general equilibrium models with fully flexible wages and prices (in RUNS, real wages adjust three-quarters of the way to the labor market-clearing level).

References

Adams, G.F., and J. Behrman. 1976. *Econometric Models of World Agricultural Commodity Markets*. Cambridge, Mass.: Ballinger.

Adams, G.F., and J.R. Behrman. 1984. *Commodity Exports and Economic Development*. Lexington, Mass.: Lexington Books.

Adelman, I. 1984. "Beyond Export-Led Growth." *World Development* 12: 937-49.

Adelman, I., J.M. Burniaux, and J. Waelbroeck. 1989. "Agricultural Development-Led Industrialization in a Global Perspective." In J.C. Williamson and V.R. Panchamuki, eds, *The Balance between Industry and Agriculture in Economic Development*, Vol. 2, *Sector Proportions*. IEA Conference Volumes. London: Macmillan.

Armington, P. 1969. "A Theory of Demand for Products Distinguished by Place of Production." *IMF Staff Papers* 16: 159-78.

Burniaux, J.M. 1983. "La configuration Nord-Sud du commerce des produits alimentaires: un essai projectif et une expérience d'histoire économétrique." *Recherches Economiques de Louvain* 49 (September): 3.

Burniaux, J.M. 1984. "Shifting Investment to Agriculture and the Food Dilemma: A General Equilibrium Approach." Paper presented to the IIASA Conference on General Equilibrium Modeling, Sopron, Hungary, June 18-20.

Burniaux, J.M. 1985. "Chômage, sous-nutrition, croissance: un essai d'interprétation de quelques paradoxes de l'économie mondiale à l'aide d'un modèle d'équilibre général." PhD thesis, Université Libre de Bruxelles.

Burniaux, J.M. 1987. *Le Radeau de la Méduse: Essai d'Analyse des Dilemmes Alimentaires*. Paris: Economica.

Carrin, G., J.W. Gunning, and J. Waelbroeck. 1983. "A General Equilibrium Model for the World Economy: Some Preliminary Results." In B. Hickman, ed., *Global International Economic Models*. Amsterdam: North-Holland.

Cheetham, R., S. Gupta, and A. Schwartz. 1979. *The Global Framework*. World Bank Staff Working Paper No 355. Washington, D.C.

Food and Agriculture Organization (FAO). 1980. *Agriculture Toward 2000- Twentieth Session*. Rome: FAO.

Gordon, R.J. 1987. "Productivity, Wages, and Prices Inside and Outside of Manufacturing in the US, Japan, and Europe." *European Economic Review* 31: 685-732.

Goreux, L.M., and A.S. Manne. 1973. *Multi-Level Planning: Case Studies in Mexico*. Amsterdam: North-Holland.

Gunning, J.W., G. Carrin, J. Waelbroeck, J.M. Burniaux, and J. Mercenier. 1982. *Growth and Trade of Developing Countries: A General Equilibrium Analysis*. CEME Discussion Paper 8210. Brussels: Université Libre de Bruxelles.

Hanoch, G. 1971. "CRESH Production Functions." *Econometrica* 39: 695-712.

Harris, J.R., and M.P. Todaro. 1970. "Migration, Unemployment, and Development: A Two-Sector Analysis." *American Economic Review* 60: 138-48.

Krueger, A.O., M. Schiff, and A. Valdes. 1988. "Agricultural Incentives in Developing Countries: Measuring the Effects of Sectoral and Economywide Policies." *World Bank Economic Review* 2: 255-71.

Linneman H., J. De Hoogh, M.A. Keyzer, and H.D.J. Van Heemst. 1979. *MOIRA: A Model of International Relations in Agriculture*. Amsterdam: North-Holland.

Malinvaud, E. 1977. *The Theory of Unemployment Reconsidered*. Oxford: Basil Blackwell.

McCalla, A., and T. Josling. 1985. *Agricultural Policies and World Markets*. New York: Macmillan.

Mellor, J.W. 1976. *The New Economics of Growth: A Strategy for India and the Developing World*. Ithaca, N.Y.: Cornell University Press.

Mercenier, J., and J. Waelbroeck. 1984. "The Sensitivity of Developing Countries to External Shocks in an Interdependent World. *Journal of Policy Modelling* 6: 209-350. Issue in Honor of Jan Tinbergen.

Mundlak, Y. 1979. *Intersectoral Factor Mobility and Agricultural Growth*. IFPRI Research Report No. 6. Washington D.C.: International Food Policy Research Institute.

Mundlak Y., and R. Hellinghausen. 1982. "The Inter-Country Agricultural Production Function: Another View." *American Journal of Agricultural Economics* 64 (November): 664-71.

Nagle, J.C. 1976. *Agricultural Trade Policies*. Boston: Lexington Books.

Paldam, M. 1983. "Industrial Conflicts and Economic Conditions." *European Economic Review* 20: 231-56.

Parikh, K.S., G. Frohberg, and O. Gulbrandsen. 1988. *Towards Free Trade in Agriculture*. Dordrecht: Martinus Nijhoff.

Paulino, L.A. 1986. *Food in the Third World: Past Trends and Projections to 2000*. IFPRI Research Report No. 52. Washington D.C.: International Food Policy Research Institute.

Powell, A., and F. Gruen. 1968. "The Constant Elasticity of Transformation Production Frontier and Linear Supply System." *International Economic Review* 9: 315-28.

Preobrazhenski, E. 1956. *The New Economy*. Oxford: Clarendon Press.

Rojko, A., H. Fuchs, P. O'Brien, and D. Regier. 1978. *Alternative Futures for World Food in 1985: World GOL Model*. USDA Foreign Economic Reports 149, 150, 151. Washington, D.C.: USDA.

Valdes, A., and J. Zietz. 1980. *Agricultural Protection in OECD Countries: Its Cost to Less Developed Countries*. IFPRI Research Report No. 21. Washington, D.C.: International Food Policy Research Institute.

World Bank. 1982. *World Development Report 1982*. New York and Oxford: Oxford University Press for the World Bank.

World Bank. 1986. *World Development Report 1986*. New York and Oxford: Oxford University Press for the World Bank.

Part II

Economic Reform

7

Conducting Scientific Assessments for Economic Reforms

Edmond Malinvaud

One of Béla Balassa's main concerns has long been the study of economic reforms, broadly understood, and of their impact on economic performance, particularly in developing countries which are facing the most acute difficulties. Writing here as a friend and as someone with much interest in Béla's work, I must also be recognized as an outsider in the fields of research that have concerned him. So in this essay I deal only with side issues, which I think are nevertheless important to the relevance and accuracy of the messages we economists send to others. In this context, I examine questions related to three somewhat disconnected aspects of Balassa's work on economic reform: policy evaluation, the search for appropriate measures and their uses in evaluation, and the use of intercountry comparisons. My examination has a strongly methodological cast.

The Challenge to Our Science

The organization of an economic system or the choice of a development strategy raises many issues for which economists have some competence but seldom complete answers. That is, their conclusions are rarely firm enough to be transmitted to policymakers or the general public as the basis for making the "proper" decision. This condition challenges the science of economics and each economist to an exploration of the ethics that should apply to such circumstances.

Examples of such issues abound. One is the choice between an outward-looking and a protectionist orientation of trade policy, a subject that Balassa examined repeatedly. The preference to be given to floating versus fixed exchange rates, within a more or less wide range of countries, is another case in point. The debate about the proper extent of regulation is yet another. The appropriate role, if any, of national planning and its interference with the price system are once again of widespread interest as a result of economic reforms in socialist countries. The structure of the tax system is the subject of an even more ample literature.

These examples have much in common. Most important, they concern problems about which the profession cannot remain silent. The problems are current and pressing and will be answered one way or another by politicians. More expertise on the consequences of such choices exists within economics than in any other discipline, so silence on the part of economists would mean that decisionmakers will be basing their choices on poorer information than could be available to them. At least some economists should be explaining what policy recommendations can be derived from the objective knowledge being accumulated in our science.

Having acknowledged this responsibility, it remains equally important to recognize that this knowledge remains incomplete with respect to the questions really at issue. Often in the past economic theory was claimed to imply the optimality of some form of economic organization or some development strategy. In all cases, rigorous study of the theory and of its appropriateness showed that the conclusion had been too hastily drawn and that the relevance of the theoretical results was narrower than originally claimed.[1]

Similarly, observation also yields ambiguous results. Certainly records of subsequent performance are worth looking at for countries that have made different policy choices on particular issues. The use of cross-section econometric fits can make such examination systematic. But economists have often disagreed on what such references to observation have implied. The difficulty has an obvious origin: historical cases are the results of many factors acting simultaneously, factors that are beyond the control and sometimes beyond even the perception of the economists considering these cases.

If theory alone or observation alone yields only ambiguous answers, a combination of the two may be more enlightening. Béla Balassa has combined the two, and this approach has become more and more common among economists. But even with such reinforcement between theory and observation, the conclusions reached are not unassailable and remain vulnerable to challenges with respect to their standards of rigor. In other words, varying degrees of persuasiveness and objectivity characterize the conclusions we are able to draw.

The requirement for objectivity adds another difficulty to the discussion. A scientific statement is one that asserts the likely impacts of a decision under debate in all its relevant dimensions. This statement ought to be positive, that is, value free. Thus, we can imagine a division of roles in which economists state the consequences of alternative policies and policymakers choose among the alternatives on the basis of their own value judgments concerning the desirability of the various consequences of their choices. This process would naturally lead policymakers to prefer one mode of economic organization or one strategy over another. Thus, assessments by scientists would affect the choices and so would affect the derived value judgments concerning the alternative policies themselves. This influence would, however, simply be a necessary consequence of the primitive value judgments, judgments the scientists would not have interfered with at all.

The trouble comes from the fact that this description of the process is too close to the ideal and so somewhat unrealistic. In the first place, decisionmakers may have no clear criterion for making their value judgments or may not be able to specify which dimensions of the consequences are really relevant to their choice. (A relevant dimension is not only one that has a weight in the preference function — and there are probably many — but also one in which the consequences are sensitive to the policy choice, and this the decisionmaker may not know.) Economists must therefore pay attention to what they believe is the value criterion of the policymaker, and this they can hardly do without reference to their own value judgments.[2]

In the second place, economists must make their assessments on simpler grounds than pure rigor would require because a guarded assessment would be too complex for policymakers to use. So economists cannot give full information on either the accuracy of their findings or the side hypotheses made in order to reach them. Even when a rigorous econometric procedure is used, the uncertainty of the assessment is not fully conveyed by an estimated standard error; the risks result-ing from the choice of the model should also be discussed. Similarly, the consequences depend not only on the contemplated decision but also on many aspects of the economic and social environment about which economists must make a number of reasonable hypotheses. Economists can do no more than point to a very few of these hypotheses and to the sensitivity of the results with respect to them, and they must do so in a way that does not appear to confuse the issue.

Confronted with the challenge of speaking on issues about which conclusions are still scientifically weak, economics as a profession must have ethical norms to govern such behavior. And such norms already exist: there is a good deal of agreement on what constitutes professional misbehavior with respect to assertions that are claimed or implied to be scientifically derived. With the trend toward more rigor in economic theory and more reference to econometric results, these norms are becoming progressively more stringent. But they generally remain implicit.

More open discussion of such ethical norms would not only be a sign of the growing maturity of economics but would also help to improve the quality of the contributions of our discipline to world development. I shall not attempt to define these norms here because ethical norms cannot be the outcome of the reflections of an isolated individual but should be the result of a broad collective examination. Also, focusing on special policy issues rather than on generalities may be a more appropriate way of finding out how our testimony ought to be presented.

In this search for the rules of correct behavior, attention should be given to the tendency of the general public, the media, and even scientists in other disciplines to underestimate the extent of agreement among economists. A common perception is of the clashing of opposing schools of thought, whose respective proponents give contradictory recommendations on the basis of incompatible ideological creeds. The proximity of economics to politics when major decisions are being made may lead to some confusion of their roles, but the behavior of economists surely contributes to this common misperception as well. When we address people outside our profession, do we not sometimes confuse the solid parts of our conclusions and the more tentative interpretations about which disagreement may exist? Do we not also sometimes unduly stress internal disputes that have much less importance for the layman than our outspokenness seems to imply?

New Quantitative Tools

The empirical analysis of the economic performance associated with various economic structures, development strategies, or economic policies relies heavily on macroeconomic statistics and indicators now regularly produced by official statisticians — whether as part of national accounts data or alongside them. This material, although subject to somewhat conventional definitions, has met so many needs so well that it is likely to undergo little conceptual revision. The main improvements are likely to come from more accurate data collection. But this information must often be supplemented by other indicators that researchers have to compute themselves from data of varying accessibility. Such needs have led to the creation of a large range of quantitative tools worked out in the research community along the fringes of the more traditional data collection activities. Much of this work is not yet recognized by those in charge of the standard production and diffusion of economic data — and in some cases is not even recognized in the teaching of economics. Since Béla Balassa contributed significantly to the development of this fringe activity, it is not out of place to consider it here.

This fringe is multifarious.[3] Some of the measures it contains have already been discussed extensively by official statisticians, who have no difficulty in principle in adopting them. One case in point concerns indicators of inequality in income, wealth, or standard of living; in some countries reference to a poverty line, and to the proportion of the population classified below it, has even been officially admitted. In contrast, I believe that official statisticians will not venture for long to compute measures of frictional unemployment, and the reason for this reluctance may be revealing of difficulties that may arise for other quantitative tools as well.

Like many other concepts I am concerned with here, the concept of frictional unemployment entails comparisons of an ideal alternative situation with the real one. In this case, the ideal situation is that of equilibrium of supply and demand in the labor market at the aggregate level. If macroeconomists want a measure of frictional unemployment and of its changes through time, it is precisely because the ideal situation of equilibrium plays an important role in any application of macroeconomic theory, that is, in any assertion about the likely consequences of policy changes. But this concept of equilibrium, which is well defined in the theoretical models, has no obvious transposability to real countries, where workers with many different qualifications live in many different places and where perceptions differ between employers and employees concerning what ought to constitute equilibrium of the market. Understandably, statisticians are reluctant to take on the role of making the transposition in such a difficult and debatable context.

Although not evaluated within the context of standard official statistics, a measure of full-employment budget surplus, which is meant to characterize a country's fiscal policy stance, has often been computed, at least in the United

States. The measure is usually computed by economists working for the administration or by others outside the administration as a tool for disputing administration policy. Since it refers to full employment, this concept relies on a measure of the rate of frictional unemployment (the rate of frictional unemployment at full employment). But this measure is not usually the object of deep scrutiny, and making a conventional hypothesis about it appears to be admissible. Such a casual approach is probably explained by the fact that, as soon as attention focuses on fiscal policy itself and not on the state of the labor market, the definition of full employment becomes a less sensitive issue. Rigor, however, requires closer scrutiny and, to begin with, a more precise definition of what the concept of full-employment budget surplus is intended to capture. In this context, full employment may turn out to be a proxy for some other notion concerning overall economic equilibrium.

Also for purposes of fiscal policy evaluation, but for many other purposes as well, it is often considered necessary to correct national account figures for the effects of inflation: capital gains or losses due to changes in the price level are then treated as positive or negative income. In cases of protracted inflation, the corrections are so significant that they ought to be made by official statisticians, notwithstanding both the conventional nature of some of their hypotheses and the difficulty in collecting some of the required data (see Hibbert 1982).[4]

Some of the recently developed quantitative tools are intended to characterize less aggregated and more structural features of the economy. For example, an extensive literature has developed on the measurement of the cost of capital, on its variation according to mode of financing, and on effective rates of taxation. Of particular interest also are measures of the extent of protection and subsidy in the goods market, a field to which Balassa made substantial methodological contributions and in which he promoted large-scale empirical work. The vast amount and quality of effort that went into this work culminated in the two books published under his leadership (Balassa and Associates 1971 and 1982). His book *Development Strategies in Semi-Industrial Economies* (1982) is now the standard methodological reference for both the definition of the concepts (nominal, effective, and net effective rates of protection or subsidy) and workable estimation procedures. The detailed study of twelve countries had to cope with numerous obstacles that made proper measurement difficult, but the result was to provide a wealth of data that shows how diverse are the protection policies and practices of semi-industrial countries. Such data permit an important aspect of development strategies to be characterized for the respective countries and contrasted among them.

The various quantitative tools mentioned above, and others as well, have in common the fact that they may be viewed as intermediate products. These tools are the result of the more or less elaborate processing of available data from standard collections of macroeconomic statistics or from microeconomic sources of information. In turn, they are intended to serve in the analysis of other questions; they are more interesting as input for this analysis than as end product. Concerning this common feature, I should like to make a few comments.

First, we ought to be aware of the large role this kind of intermediate data processing now plays in our discipline. Many of us used to think of only two industries dealing with observations in positive economics: (1) official statistical agencies collecting data and computing general-purpose aggregates and indices and (2) applied econometrics for estimating structural parameters and testing hypotheses. The important intermediate work being done between these two processes and contributing to our knowledge of the economy must now be recognized, particularly since its methodology may raise questions that do not arise in either of the two more traditional industries.

I believe that the rationale for the existence and importance of this production of intermediate indicators lies in the exploratory nature of some of our investigations, even when we want to assess the impacts of alternative policies. Indeed, in many areas of economics, research does not operate within the confines of a complete, given theoretical model. While the general concern of the research is usually clear, even the precise questions to be answered may not be formulated until after a first examination of the reality at issue. Once the questions have been formulated precisely, it may still be unsatisfactory to limit the search for an answer by making all the side hypotheses that reliance on a model would require. In such cases, measurement of precisely defined but unfamiliar concepts appears to be a necessary first step for a fruitful exploration, whereas direct estimation or resolution of a model would seem premature since it would have a good chance of missing the mark.

I will illustrate this point here with just one example. It has sometimes been suggested that the use of a general equilibrium model would permit direct evaluation of the effect of protection on resource allocation in a given economy and that computation of effective protection rates is therefore unnecessary. Such a suggestion relies on an unrealistic assumption, namely, that we agree from the start, and will still agree at the end, to consider the general equilibrium model as perfectly suitable. It seems to me that we will make greater progress in our investigations by instead assuming an agreement about the formulas to be applied for calculating indicators of protection. I feel confident that readers of the two books published under Balassa's leadership will agree on this point.

Improving the methods for producing such intermediate quantitative tools is the responsibility of those in the various fields that use these tools, and by and large, this has been the case. I would, however, like to make one general comment. I believe that the definition, calculation, and discussion of these intermediate indicators play an important role in improving the efficiency of the whole chain from observation to inference. Pausing at an intermediate stage enables us to spot more clearly than otherwise the deficiencies in accuracy or relevance of the available statistical material and so can provide useful feedback to statisticians for improving their work. By contrast, the end results of econometric studies are based on too many hypotheses and too much processing to reveal any weaknesses in the database. In addition, the conceptual work done at the intermediate level must take into account real features that theory tends to neglect. This process may stimulate reexamination of the theory and possibly a reformulation that will make it more satisfactory. In this way, the science of economics is improved for all its applications, most notably for those concerning economic systems or development strategies.

A second issue concerns whether the calculation of these new quantitative indicators, once they have proven their workability and usefulness, should become the regular responsibility of official statisticians. These statisticians have two objectives: making existing statistics more accurate and creating new statistics that provide more relevant information. They tend to give priority to the first objective, in particular because the accuracy of their data is often overestimated. Some users of statistics, however, assign greater priority to the production of new statistics. That is how national accounts data, for example, came to be regularly computed or, more recently, how statistics on the environment came to be developed. Perhaps it is time for economists once again to press for a few additions to the list of indicators regularly computed for their use.

Intercountry Comparisons

Reports on the situation in various countries of the world strongly influence the general public's judgment about the relative performances of alternative economic systems and the relative success of alternative development strategies. Often these reports rely more on colorful but partial descriptions, even on impressions, than on objective assessments. Nevertheless, they are very influential. While there is nothing intrinsically wrong with this state of affairs, the process must be sufficiently controlled that it does not lead to false conclusions on important issues. Ensuring that this does not happen is clearly the responsibility of economists, whether they like it or not.

Thus, rigorous intercountry comparisons become more than a means of econometric inference, on a par with cross-section analyses of samples of individual observations or aggregate time-series analyses. Intercountry comparisons are also required to enable economists to fulfill their necessary role of objective witness. Many of us feel uncomfortable about assuming this role because the issues are often ill-defined, the proper information is not available, or conclusions cannot be reached without a loosening of scientific standards. At least some of us, however, must leap into the fray. One of those who has done so consistently is Béla Balassa, who has repeatedly contributed to the effort made by the profession to improve the objectivity of commonly held views about economic matters. Commenting on the difficulties of this activity is a way of paying tribute to his work.

But not even economists have been immune to the potential versatility and attraction of simply accepting the dominant views about relative economic performance and the economic prospects of various countries, particularly developing countries. And yet how different is the common economic wisdom of today compared with what was said or written by economists twenty years ago, for example. Part of the explanation for this divergence stems from the enormous amount of misinformation that has been disseminated about a large part of the world — misinformation that was, moreover, favored by ideas promoted in some intellectual quarters. But it is also true that the normal process of science leads to revisions of assessments as new evidence is found, and that many of us had in good faith underestimated the difficulties of development. These explanations notwithstanding, I believe that some of us have too easily accepted and repeated what was commonly being propounded without making the investigations that as economists we should have made.

With respect to the future rather than the past, we must first note that databases now exist for enabling valid intercountry comparisons. Of course, the wealth and quality of the data vary substantially from one country to another and are still poor in many cases. This means that any research project dealing with a wide range of countries must begin with a scrutiny of the value and comparability of available statistics. But lack of data is no longer a legitimate excuse for failing to take on such analyses.

The main difficulty with respect to scientific assessments of objective inter-country comparisons concerns the interpretation of observed facts. Any two given countries or groups of countries will always have many features other than eco-nomic ones in which they differ. It would therefore be presumptuous to assume that their differences in performance derive only from differences in their eco-nomic system, development strategy, or economic policy. Even when several countries are considered simultaneously with the help of econometric regressions or otherwise, the difficulty remains: giving a causal interpretation to a correlation is always a delicate operation.

Although this point appears to be trivial or obvious as a general principle, it is often forgotten in particular applications. To make this issue clearer, let us refer here to a question that I have considered seriously during the past years, namely the influence of an increase in real wages on employment and unemployment. Intercountry regressions of the growth of employment on the growth of the real wage rate and the growth of GDP yield a significant negative coefficient for wages, a result that has been presented as proof of the detrimental influence of wage-push forces on employment. However, the regressions also happen to be quite consistent with the fact that, along an equilibrium growth path, the real wage rate grows at the same speed as labor productivity; so intercountry disparities in real wage increases may simply reflect intercountry disparities in productivity growth. This means, for example, that I cannot interpret the regressions as providing support for my belief that high real wages played some role in the deviation of European economies from their full employment growth path in the 1970s.

This does not mean that intercountry comparisons should be dismissed. On the contrary, they play and must continue to play an important role in shaping our ideas, particularly with respect to medium- or long-run phenomena for which the information provided by time-series data is relatively less rich. Nor does it mean that econometric procedures are out of place in intercountry comparisons. On the contrary, making these comparisons more systematic helps to reduce the impact of the fundamental difficulty I have been discussing. Like many other economists, I am inclined to think that simultaneously considering a large number of countries can reduce the biases deriving from the many neglected regressors, although extending the number of countries may not always be wise if it comes at the cost of too great an increase in the heterogeneity of the sample.

But I believe that the difficulty should be kept in mind when we draw conclusions from evidence found in intercountry comparisons. This evidence must always be included within a larger analytical and empirical package. Doing so will, first, provide a framework for a proper interpretation of the results and a proper identification of neglected factors and, second, contribute other evidence from aggregate time series or cross-sections of individual observations that will support, complement, or contradict the interpretation first given.

Returning here in the conclusion to my comments at the starting point of this modest tribute to Béla Balassa, I wish to stress again that scientific assessments about the outcomes of alternative systems or policies are expected from us as economists. They require that we aim at the highest feasible standard of rigor, a standard that is unfortunately much lower in practice than in pure theory. Progress can also come from a continuous effort to decompose the big issues into more precisely defined questions, to collect and process data with an enriched kit of tools, and to systematically confront all the evidence coming from the many analyses and observations at our disposal.

Notes

1. For instance, Krugman (1987) wrote that free trade "can never again be asserted as the policy that economic theory tells us is always right." Actually, the same sentence could have been written decades ago on the basis of the then available theoretical results to be found, in particular, in the readings collected by Ellis and Metzler (1949).
2. This point is forcefully argued by Blaug (1980) — even a bit too forcefully argued I would say, given my experience as a technocrat and policy adviser (see "The economist as a technocrat," pp. 149-52).
3. For the sake of brevity, I do not consider here the extended measures of national income and product that have been proposed and evaluated by a number of research workers (see, for instance, Eisner 1988).
4. I had occasion to show the importance of the correction for a proper measurement of the disequilibrium (or distortion) of the system of remuneration rates in France during the 1980s (Malinvaud 1983). I was glad to see that Béla Balassa found my results to be meaningful for his analysis of French economic evolution (Balassa 1984).

References

Balassa, B., and Associates. 1971. *The Structure of Protection in Developing Countries.* Baltimore, Md.: Johns Hopkins University Press.

Balassa, B., and Associates. 1982. *Development Strategies in Semi-Industrial Economies*. Baltimore, Md.: Johns Hopkins University Press.

Balassa, B. 1984. "French Economic Policies Under the Socialist Government: Year III." *Tocqueville Review* VI (Spring-Summer). Reprinted in B. Balassa, 1985, *Change and Challenge in the World Economy*. London: Macmillan.)

Blaug, M. 1980. *The Methodology of Economics*. Cambridge: Cambridge University Press.

Eisner, R. 1988. "Extended Accounts for National Income and Product." *Journal of Economic Literature* 26 (December): 1611-84.

Ellis, H., and L. Metzler. 1949. *Readings in the Theory of International Trade*. Philadelphia: Blakiston.

Hibbert, J. 1982. *Measuring the Effects of Inflation on Income, Saving, and Wealth*. Paris: Organization for Economic Cooperation and Development.

Krugman, P. 1987. "Is Free Trade Passé?" *Journal of Economic Perspectives* 1: 131-44.

Malinvaud, E. 1983. *Essais sur la théorie du chômage*. Paris: Calmann-Lévy.

North

8

France, the German Republics, and European Economic Integration

Charles P. Kindleberger

Béla Balassa and I go back to the summer of 1960, when we were both in Paris. I have the distinction, moreover, of having been the Balassas' first guest at dinner as his wife Carol started her second simultaneous career, after economics, as a gourmet cook. Since that time we have kept in touch, more or less, as Béla moved from Yale to Johns Hopkins and the World Bank. My balance-of-indebtedness to him on reprint account is enormous. While as economists I assume that we both dislike bilateral as opposed to multilateral exchanges, he nonetheless wrote for my festschrift on "Effective Rates of Protection in Developing Countries," which combined two of his deepest interests and fields of specialization: international trade policy and economic development. I respond now by turning to two other areas of great interest to him: French political economy and European economic integration.

Of the close to 300 items in his bibliography, 11 at a rough count relate to France, the country we all love best next to our own, and 21 to economic integration in Europe. On the topic of integration, Béla has been characterized by Fritz Machlup as "one of the most productive contributors to the literature," beginning as far back as an article and a book in 1961 (Machlup 1977, 269; Balassa 1961a,b). It is of interest that economic integration featured more importantly in his early books and papers, and France more in the later years, an externality, I suspect, of his interest in gastronomy that has led to the successive editions of the privately printed *A Primer in Culinary Economics* — to each new appearance of which his friends and colleagues look forward eagerly, and which they take to Europe and lend to friends.

Of course, a fifth interest of this Renaissance economist of wide-ranging expertise and prodigious productivity is his native Hungary. I write this paper in November 1989, caught up in the revolutionary excitement of Eastern Europe. The paper grazes the subject tangentially, as it focuses on France, the European Economic Community (EEC), and both the Federal Republic of Germany and the Democratic Republic of Germany.

My own research has gone into economic history rather than contemporary issues. I have not kept up as much as perhaps I should have, beyond ordinary newspaper reading, with the unfolding of economic policies and events in France or the EEC or with the financial manifestations of the European Monetary System and the European Currency Unit. Moreover, French policies, the Common Market, and the place of Eastern Europe in the future of Western Germany and of Western Europe as a whole are all in flux at this moment. In the absence of hard data, and in the midst of change, one can only speculate on the impact of German *ostpolitik* on the EEC, especially on how it will affect France, the other leader in the EEC beside the Federal Republic. But first a touch of political-economy history.

The Evolution of European Integration

The European Economic Community

President Charles de Gaulle was agreeable to the Rome Treaty of 1957, which sprang from the French initiative of Jean Monnet, when it appeared that France would lead the Common Market. He conceived of the Common Market not as a waystation on the road to a United States of Europe but simply as a confederation of *patries*. That is, he viewed it as an alliance, as opposed to a federation in which the constituent states give up important powers.

The British made an early mistake, cobbling together the European Free Trade Association (EFTA) among countries on the European periphery. Within Béla Balassa's broad definition of economic integration — the absence of government discrimination between domestic and foreign economic interests — economic integration was possible within EFTA (Balassa 1961b). But under a tighter definition based on the criterion of factor-price equalization, it was not. Even if governments did not discriminate, factor-price equalization was unlikely to be achieved through factor movements — except possibly for capital — and equalization through trade would fail as a result of high transport costs among widely separated economic states. But EFTA was a mistake not only because of the unlikelihood of developing dense trade among Great Britain, Norway, Denmark, Sweden, Austria, Switzerland, and Portugal — to list them clockwise — but also for political reasons.

British economic foreign policy, as revealed during the Marshall Plan, was not working. The major elements of this policy were to maintain the "special relationship" with the United States, to keep the Commonwealth and the sterling area together, and to move into Europe no further than the point of no return (Hogan 1987). The special relationship with the United States collapsed, if not during the Marshall Plan — when the United States treated Great Britain as merely one among the group, although perhaps giving it more assistance than other European countries — then at least at Suez in 1956. Also, the Commonwealth was breaking up, with India's independence, South Africa's moral isolation over apartheid, and Australia's gradual shifting of its trade first to the United States and then to Japan. In addition, the sterling area was proving to be a drain on British reserves rather than a plus. In 1962, therefore, after an intense debate in Great Britain that divided each party and the ranks of economists, the country petitioned to join the Common Market.

But in January 1963, President Charles de Gaulle said "*non.*" The smaller members of the EEC, especially the Netherlands and Belgium, strongly wanted British membership to dilute the dominance of France and the Federal Republic of Germany. Germany and Italy were also in favor of British membership, if less fervently so. France, however, said "no" because it still hoped to take the lead in the EEC and was fearful that British membership would increase the opposition to that role.

By the 1970s, it seemed clear that West Germany and not France would take the leading part in the EEC. When Great Britain reapplied, the French responded positively. There was no change in the attitude of the Low Countries or Italy. Unlike France, Bonn was not particularly interested in the politics of the EEC, believing itself strong enough to safeguard its interests. Because Germany's political ambitions had been moderated by the defeats of 1918 and 1945, it did not assert a strong leadership role as Prussia had done in the unification of the Reich in 1871 or Piedmont had done in the unification of Italy in 1860. The West German economy continued to gain in strength, however, and France continued to widen the Common Market. The six original members became seven, eight, and nine with the additions of Britain, Ireland, and Denmark, and then membership swelled to twelve as Spain, Portugal, and Greece became — rather unequal — members.

Monetary Integration
But the European idea kept growing, if not at the highest levels of government in France and West Germany, then at least among the smaller countries and among the voters who elected representatives to the European Parliament at Strasbourg. The pressure was on to move beyond the elimination of internal tariffs, which is relatively easy, to the harmonization of taxes and regulations, which is necessary before the border guards can be fully dispensed with.

Agreement was reached to do this rapidly, by 1992, despite the enormous amount of detailed, tedious, and politically difficult work entailed in equalizing value added and excise taxes and adopting common standards on pure food and drugs, antipollution measures, and ultimately perhaps, common laws on negotiable instruments, insurance liabilities, legal tender, and the like. Some naive economists regard the opening up of markets as a simple task that can be accomplished by a flick of the wrist. They would do well to review the enormous amount of work that was required to put West Germany's monetary reform in place in 1948. This reform, involving only a single country, took forty experts working for two months in Rothwesten to devise the appropriate regulations that would need to be enacted to enable the change of currency (Möller 1976). It should also be remembered that the adoption of a common tariff nomenclature, which is required for a common market although not for a free-trade area, took several years to work out.

Thus, except perhaps to unsophisticated enthusiasts, achieving the goal of 1992 looked difficult enough without the complication of the movement to a common monetary standard, the European Monetary System. An enormous amount of literature had grown up in the 1960s and 1970s on parallel currencies, monetary agreements, coordination of macroeconomic policy, and the like, and progress continued to be made, although slowly and with a number of setbacks. The Werner Plan, the All-Saints Manifesto of November 1975, and the Optica Group dominated the discussion for a time and then faded into obscurity, until finally in January 1979 the European Monetary System was established.

Slowly, devaluations of the weaker European currencies against the others grew less frequent and smaller, and rates of inflation began to converge. Progress in denominating loans and prices in the European Currency Unit rather than in dollars, deutsche marks, sterling, or another local currency moved at glacial speed. Little attention seems to have been paid to the fact that, historically, monetary unification came after rather than before political union and that it came with the adoption of an existing dominant currency rather than through the creation of an artificial one. The mark of 1872 and the Reichsbank of 1875 were basically the Prussian thaler and the Prussian National Bank, although the thaler was renamed after the Hamburg currency. Identification of money with sovereignty is evident even in the names of some coins: the sovereign, the crown, the *real* (royal), and the *louis d'or*. In more modern times, this identification is evoked by the memory that the split of East and West Germany occurred with the blockade and the airlift of June 1948, when the three western occupation authorities tried to introduce the deutsche mark, their new, reformed currency for the Trizone, into the Soviet zone of occupation.

In recent decades, France has been somewhat on the defensive vis-à-vis the Common Market. French planning, it was asserted, broke down (and was replaced by *déplanification*) because French borders were open to the rest of the Community. Planning, it was argued, had to be adopted by the entire Common Market or it could not obtain in a single part. Similarly, the Socialist president, Mitterrand, elected in May 1981, abandoned the program of nationalization that the French left had dreamed about since the failure of the Cartel des Gauches in the 1920s (Jeanneney 1977) because of the flood of imports from the Common Market that followed.

Europe 1992

Then, along came Jacques Delors, the French Commissioner at the EEC, who took up the Jean Monnet role of attempting to accelerate European integration. Disregarding the historical experience that monetary integration follows political integration, he sought to accelerate the development of a single currency and a single central bank in the Common Market. Meanwhile, the French, the West Germans, and especially Margaret Thatcher's United Kingdom were, if not opposed in all cases, at least profoundly skeptical.

The Delors report of the spring of 1989 calling for a central bank of Europe was ambiguous enough to permit different interpretations. German enthusiasm for it is moderate, but couched in terms that seem to view it as another Federal Reserve System such as that delineated in the U.S. Act of 1913: twelve regional banks, with their separate regional money and capital markets, presided over by a central federal reserve board whose role is to achieve coordination. This concept accords more with the intentions of the framers of the Federal Reserve Act than with the reality of the system as it operates in the United States.[1] The same process would be likely to occur with any European central bank that functioned as more than a club of central bankers, like the Bank for International Settlements. A European central bank that had an impact on monetary policy through instruments such as open-market policy, discount policy, and the like rather than merely through moral suasion and example would be likely, in the absence of foreign-exchange and capital controls, to put existing central banks in the smaller countries, including probably France as well as Italy, into walk-on roles.

There are, moreover, complex questions about how a European central bank would be organized. Would it be independent of the Commission, as the Bundesbank is independent of Bonn, or would it be owned by and subservient to government, at least to some extent, as are the Bank of France and the Bank of England? If France pushes ahead with European monetary integration, is it likely to find that its relationship to the Bundesbank resembles that of the Federal Reserve Bank of Kansas City to the Federal Reserve Bank of New York? This is evidently what Prime Minister Margaret Thatcher believes, as she fights for a less extreme position than that of the Delors initiative on the European currency and the European central bank. The Federal Republic of Germany is almost equally opposed in principle to giving up its sovereignty to a European central bank, but goes along passively in quiet confidence that when the final decisions are made, it will have the power to ensure that things come out its way.

The German Republics

We come now to November 1989 and the tearing down of the wall between the two Germanies. West German economic and general foreign policy, even before the events of 1989, had been somewhat schizophrenic. Thus the Federal Republic of Germany lined up solidly with the EEC, NATO, the Organization for Economic Cooperation and Development, and the West in general while pursuing its own ostpolitik. Part of this ostpolitik was the provision of credits to the Democratic Republic of Germany. Now, with the wider dissolution in Eastern Europe — in Poland, Hungary, Bulgaria, the Soviet Union, and most recently, Czechoslovakia and Romania — demands on German resources for assistance in the form of grants and loans will be high. That there will be no trade-off with assistance to Spain, Portugal, Greece, and Ireland or to the poorer regions of France and Italy is unimaginable.

Notions of a new Marshall Plan seem inapposite. The Marshall Plan provided assistance to recover the *status quo ante* and to reinvigorate an economic system that had existed twenty years earlier. In the Soviet case, at least, we need to go back almost eighty years to 1910 or so for any experience with free-market pricing and resource allocation with consumer sovereignty, and for the rest of Eastern

Europe, back at least fifty years to 1939, a year that ended a decade of only limited economic success. Furthermore, the Marshall Plan metaphor never fit Third World countries or impoverished areas of the United States such as Harlem or the Indian reservations. Thus, while it may be going too far to say that Eastern Europe has completely lost all kinesthetic memory of how market economies behave, the truth is not far from that.

One possibility, then, is that West German attention and resources will be diverted from the West to the heroic tasks that await the world in the East. Another is that the Federal Republic will be strengthened by an infusion of skilled, assimilable labor, hungry to restore its lost middle-class status through the rebuilding of assets and ready for hard work and high savings, much as were the refugees from east of the Oder-Neisse line in 1946-61, before the wall went up.[2]

However, there are minuses to such immigration as well as the big plus. I have hypothesized that the limits to growth from an unlimited supply of labor in Europe as a whole in the period up to 1973 came as a result of three forces. One was the exhaustion of skills among south Italians, Spanish, Portuguese, Yugoslavs, and Turks. A second was social and political resistance to further dilution of national cohesion; the Swiss, for example, refused to take in any more immigrants when their number reached a third of the national work force. And third was the pressure of large infusions of workers on the infrastructure, especially housing, education, and health care.

The first wave of immigration brings young, single men who need no additional schooling, can be housed in dormitories, and are by and large healthy. In the later stages, families arrive, which calls for substantial investments. The assimilation problem is not entirely eliminated by the fact that the new migrants will come from East Germany, although it is far milder than would be the case were race, language, appearance, and the like to differ markedly. The infrastructure problems may be more acute, however, because the East Germans aspire to equality with Germans in the West. Thus, to the pressure on resources for providing aid to Eastern Europe as a whole may be added demands for enlarging the super-structure within the combined Republics. Under these conditions, West German contributions to the EEC and the Third World will diminish.

The initial reactions from France are by no means its ultimate ones, but it is instructive to catalogue them. When President Mitterrand spoke to the European Parliament at the end of October, he made no mention of ostpolitik or of the possibility of German reunification. When the wall came down on November 9, President Mitterrand's formal reaction was that if the two Germanies wanted reunification, France would not oppose it: the two Germanies could do as they chose.

It is by no means clear that this is Mitterrand's real position, as opposed to the proper diplomatic and politic expression for a time of great change and emotional excitement. The more traditional French position, as wryly expressed by François Mauriac, is that the French are so fond of Germany that the more German states there are, the better they like it (*The German Tribune*, November 12, 1989). This feeling was clearly expressed in the immediate days after World War II, as the French fought hard to dismember Germany, at least to sever the Ruhr (and the Saar) from West Germany. And if France feared dominance by the German economy before reunification, the addition of the 16 million people of the People's Republic — itself the tenth largest industrial state in the world — would make the disproportion between the French and the German economies that much greater, with 80 million Germans and only 50 million French people. And indeed, a week after Mitterrand's comments, Jean François-Poncet, a former French foreign minister, expressed concern in *Le Figaro* (November 13) that a reunification of the two Germanies would create an economic and political colossus certain to tower over Europe.

A week later, however, Dominique Moisi, editor of *Politique Etrangère*, suggested that there were three alternative attitudes for France: optimism, skepticism, and pessimism. The optimists regard the collapse of totalitarian Communism in Eastern Europe as an opportunity for the rebirth of Europe. Skeptics fear the clash of ostpolitik with Western European unity. And pessimists anticipate German domination unrestrained by the Soviet Union on the one hand or American protection on the other. But Moisi's op-ed article in *The New York Times* (November 20, 1989) adduces one reason for optimism that may be unsettling to determined integrationists. France need have no inferiority complex vis-à-vis a united Germany, she states, because France and Great Britain together have the economic power to balance Germany. This echo of the balance-of-power system of international politics that broke down so decisively in 1914 and 1939 makes me, for one, uneasy.

Implicit in French fears of a large, strong, and growing German economy is the worry that the country once again, as in 1870, 1914, and 1939, would attempt to dominate Europe. My optimism about the future of Europe, despite the fears of some in France and elsewhere, rises from a belief that Germany, after defeats in two world wars, has lost all chauvinistic desire to be number one in Europe or in the world. Germany, along with Japan, has been a follower of U.S. leadership in the decades of the 1960s, 1970s, and most of the 1980s. While a faltering of U.S. leadership has made both countries more assertive, to be sure, both seem unready, as far as can be observed, to push ultranationalist goals at the expense of international goals. France itself lost much of its aggressiveness in 1815 after nearly a quarter of a century of war. Germany, as Joseph Alsop suggested to me in 1946, may well subside in the same fashion.

Ostpolitik and European Integration

In the aftermath of the Eastern European revolution of November 1989, ostpolitik affords the Federal Republic of Germany an excuse to slow down the headlong pace of European integration set by the grass-roots supporters of the European Parliament and by the political ambitions of Jacques Delors. Such a slowdown would also be satisfactory to Prime Minister Thatcher and perhaps, although he is unwilling to say so, to President Mitterrand and many others in France. The detailed work of harmonization, moreover, may require more than the three years remaining until the end of 1992. But a slowdown is not the same as a U-turn. The underlying political forces for economic integration and, ultimately, political federation on a Europe-wide basis seem to me so powerful as virtually to ensure achievement of the goals of the integrationists over time. There may be setbacks, as with the successive proposals for monetary unification, but I believe that there can be no turning back.

Timing and pacing have complex political dimensions: when to approach a goal step by step, inch by inch, and when to make a break for it — as in setting the ambitious goal of 1992 as the year of economic integration. Take two very different examples concerning wartime production in the United States. During World War II, President Roosevelt announced a goal of 50,000 airplanes a year; the number stunned the industry and the country, but galvanized it into immediate action. In another case, an astute political scientist told me after the war that the only way the United States was able to export 50 million tons of coal a year was to push here and push there, but without terrifying the industry by indicating the distant target.

The European Economic Community may not reach its 1992 targets, and this may be due in some part to West German preoccupation — and that of the rest of the world as well — with the economic and political problems of East Germany and Eastern Europe in general. The optimists in France, like Jean Monnet, Jacques Delors, and Dominique Moisi, may be outnumbered at the moment by the skeptics and pessimists. In the long run, however, they will prove right.

Notes

1. With the financial demands of World War I, New York emerged as the center of a nationwide money and capital market, with much smaller "provincial" markets in Chicago, Boston, and Philadelphia. The independence of the regional Federal Reserve banks was largely fictitious. On occasion, they would delay changes in the rediscount rate for a day or so, to make it appear that there was independent decisionmaking.
2. That period in Europe has been described as one of super growth, following the Lewis model of growth under unlimited supplies of labor. In West Germany, there was the further gloss that German immigrants from the east after World War II were superior in quality to the lumpenproletariat of the Marxian model or the ordinary labor in the Lewis model because of their greater range of skills and their education and class standing. Also important was the greater readiness of impoverished middle-class people to work hard and save to return to a lost social status than that of ordinary labor, which is for the most part reconciled to its place in the social scheme of things (Kindleberger 1967).

References

Balassa, B. 1961a. "Towards a Theory of Economic Integration." *Kyklos* 1: 1-17.

Balassa, B. 1961b. *The Theory of Economic Integration*. Homewood, Ill.: Richard D. Irwin.

Hogan, M.L. 1987. *The Marshall Plan: America, Britain, and the Reconstruction of Western Europe, 1947-1952*. Cambridge: Cambridge University Press.

Jeanneney, J. 1977. *Leçon d'histoire pour une gauche au pouvoir: La faillité du Cartel (1924-1926)*. Paris: Seuil.

Kindleberger, C. P. 1967. *Europe's Postwar Growth: The Role of the Labor Supply*. Cambridge, Mass.: Harvard University Press.

Machlup, F. 1977. *A History of Thought on Economic Integration*. London: Macmillan.

Moisi, D. 1989. "Germany's Unity, Europe's Rebirth." *The New York Times*, November 20, p. A23.

Möller, H. 1976. "Die westdeutsche Währungsreform van 1948." In Deutsche Bundesbank, ed., *Währung und Wirtschaft in Deutschland*, 1876-1975. Frankfurt am Main: Fritz Knapp GmbH.

9

The 1992 European Integration Program and Regional Development Policies

Paul De Grauwe

Progress toward a single European market has reached the point of no return. It has generated a new optimism about the economic and technological prospects of Europe that has accelerated investment activity, giving new impetus to economic growth. Not everyone shares this optimism, however, and some express concern that not all regions in Europe will share in the economic benefits of the 1992 program.

Are these fears justified? Are the rich regions going to be net gainers, and the poor regions net losers, as is sometimes claimed? Is a single European market likely to increase or reduce the disparities in income between regions? Can regional policies help lagging regions take off along a cumulative growth path? These are some of the questions analyzed in this paper. But first, let us examine some of the broad characteristics of the 1992 program.[1]

The 1992 Program for a Single European Market

Although tariff barriers have been eliminated within the European Community (EC), many nontariff barriers have sprung up in their place. Nontariff barriers have increased over the years and in many cases have offset the positive effects of tariff elimination. As a result, it is probably no exaggeration to say that the level of protection was higher before the launching of the 1992 program than at the end of the 1960s.

The nature of the nontariff barriers is well known. First, there are many national differences in technical and safety regulations. These differences tend to segment national markets and make it costly for producers to sell their products in other countries. Second, there are costs from cross-border transactions. These arise from differences in value added tax rates and from cumbersome customs regulations. These costs make it very difficult for consumers to comparison shop and order goods and services from the least-cost country. Third, public procurement policies protect local producers from foreign competitors by guaranteeing an outlet for their products. The most notorious examples of such policies are in construction, tele-communications, railway equipment, and defence sectors. Finally, despite the commitment to the free movement of labor and capital, there are still many restrictions on the movement of factors of production.

It is now generally believed that these nontariff barriers have handicapped European firms, making them less competitive than firms outside Europe, and that eliminating these barriers will lead to large gains for Europe. But what exactly are the economic gains that can be expected to result from the creation of a single European market? The analysis of the gains from economic integration has been a major part of Béla Balassa's professional work. His first major contribution to the issue, *The Theory of Economic Integration* (Balassa 1961), still serves as the basic work in this field. Much of the discussion in this paper, therefore, finds its roots in his work.

Three types of gains from a single European market have been identified: gains from a better use of comparative advantage, gains from larger markets, and gains from greater competition.

Countries and regions are differently endowed. For example, some regions have abundant sunshine and natural resources, while others may have cheap and abundant labor. Still others may have expensive but highly skilled labor. Free trade allows each of these regions to better exploit its *comparative advantages*. This will increase economic efficiency and thereby allow these regions to increase their welfare.

A second major economic gain from the 1992 program will come from the increase in the size of markets as a result of the elimination of trade barriers. Larger markets will allow firms to better exploit *economies of scale*, both static and dynamic. Firms that expand in response to the larger markets will be able to produce at a lower point on their average cost curves. This static effect of the single European market is likely to be important in industries that are now heavily protected and operate at too small a scale. Examples are telecommunications, railway equipment, and defense industries, which have been protected by public procurement policies. For example, each country in Europe has its own railway equipment industry, and there are now sixteen such manufacturers in Europe, compared with two in the United States. The result is high-cost equipment in each European country (EC Commission 1988).

There are also dynamic economies of scale to be realized as a result of larger markets. Many economic activities require considerable experience to build up expertise and knowledge. This experience is achieved by the scale of production over time. Again taking the example of the telecommunications industry, this learning by doing effect is likely to be important. National protection, however, keeps each European firm small, preventing firms from acquiring the same skills and knowledge as their non-European competitors.

A third gain from the elimination of trade barriers within Europe will come through the profound effects on the *intensity of competition*. Consumers will be able to shop around more freely than they do today. This will increase the level of competition and will affect the way many firms, which are now heavily protected, conduct their business. More particularly, increased competition will reduce price-cost margins, intensify the search for cost-cutting techniques, and stimulate technological innovation.[2]

Costs and Benefits for the Less Developed Regions

The 1992 program will produce large gains, but it will also produce losers. How evenly will the gains and losses be distributed among the many regions in Europe? Will the rich regions be net gainers and the poor regions net losers, as is sometimes argued? Is the single European market likely to increase or decrease the disparities in income between regions?

Experience from the Earlier Economic Integration
In trying to answer these questions, let us first look at the past. What happened to the income disparities between the rich and the poor regions during Europe's first move toward integration in the 1960s?

Let us compare per capita income (in EC Units of Account) in the richest and poorest EC regions (Robson 1980):

Year	Southern Italy	Hamburg	Relative difference
1960	306	2098	6.9
1970	965	5437	5.6
1974	1323	8705	6.6

What is most striking about these figures is the near lack of change in the relative positions of the richest and the poorest regions during this first phase of economic integration.[3] The integration process does not seem to have increased or reduced the disparities in income in Europe. It could be, of course, that this stable regional distribution of income was achieved through vigorous regional policies, which tended to offset the widening disparities produced by the integration process. As I argue later in this paper, however, in the discussion of the role of regional policies in a single European market, such policies have been quite ineffective in bridging the income gap between regions.

Potential Effects of the 1992 Integration Program
Now let us look to the future and ask the same question about what effect a single European market will have on the regions of Europe. To begin with, economic integration has two fundamentally different effects on regional economic development. One is positive, the other can be negative, although it is not necessarily so.

Comparative advantage effects. The first effect follows from the theory of comparative advantage, which says that with free trade, countries and regions will specialize in the activities in which they have a comparative advantage. Most poor regions have an abundance of cheap labor, so free trade and economic integration will lead them to specialize in relatively labor-intensive activities. This, in turn, will put upward pressure on wage levels in these poor regions. The opposite will occur in rich regions, which are usually endowed with a large capital stock and so will specialize in capital-intensive activities, a process that tends to depress wages. The comparative advantage effect, therefore, will lead to a narrowing of the income gap between poor and rich regions.

Similar forces will tend to equalize the return on capital in different regions. In the rich regions where capital is abundant, its return is low, while in poor regions where capital is scarce, its return is high. The process of market integration, therefore, will lead to outward investment from the rich regions to the poor regions. This will lead to a dynamics that will tend to equalize rates of return.

Economies of scale effects. This view that economic integration contains a dynamics that tends to reduce regional income inequalities has a long tradition based on the Heckscher-Ohlin trade model.[4] There are, however, other forces working in the opposite direction that may lead to greater regional inequality following a process of market integration. These phenomena have to do with economies of scale, both static and dynamic.

Let us concentrate on the *static* economies of scale first. The enlargement of markets will make it possible for firms to exploit economies of scale. Inefficient plants will be forced to close, and activities will be concentrated in fewer and larger plants. This process will lead to divergent regional effects, with the gainers being the regions in which the activities are concentrated. The phenomenon of economies of scale leads to agglomeration effects in some places. The reverse of that coin is depopulation in other places.

Dynamic economies of scale lead to similar agglomeration effects. Large-scale production leads to the accumulation of experience and technological knowhow. Over time, this allows for productivity gains, which in turn increase competitiveness and stimulate more production. Economic growth becomes a *cumulative* process in a world where dynamic economies of scale are important. This process of cumulative growth is reinforced by the external effects of technological knowhow. Producers in a region will profit from the technological and scientific performances of other producers in the region. Workers trained in one firm will bring their technical expertise with them when they move to other firms.

Thus, once a region is able to attract a significant amount of productive activities, it may find itself on a cumulative growth path. Regions that are unable to attract or to engender these activities will experience difficulties in taking off on a growth path. These phenomena of economies of scale and externalities suggest that market integration may lead to increasing divergences in regional income levels.[5]

Level of Aggregation and Measurements of Costs and Benefits of Integration
In considering what the effect of economic integration will be on regional development, therefore, we see that the comparative advantage effect leads to a convergence of regional incomes while the economies of scale effect leads to a divergence. Which of the two effects will prevail when a single European market

comes into existence is difficult to predict. This is the same conclusion Balassa reached in his *Theory of Economic Integration*. The evidence of the 1960s and the early 1970s in the EC seems to indicate that the effects of these two phenomena have tended to offset each other.

This conclusion, however, is sensitive to the level at which we aggregate regions. If we look at sufficiently large regions, such as the Iberian Peninsula versus northern Germany and the low countries, the equalizing effects of economic integration tend to dominate. This follows from the fact that these regions are large enough to attract many large-scale production processes. Comparative advantage becomes the more important of the forces accompanying integration. Thus the Iberian Peninsula and Italy have been catching up with the northern part of Europe since the early 1960s, as the following data show (EC Commission 1988, table 7):

GDP per Capita as %
of German GDP per Capita

Year	Italy	Spain
1960	66	28
1970	71	36
1987	73	39

Since the early 1960s, Italy and Spain have experienced a substantially higher real GDP growth rate than Germany, which has allowed them to narrow the income gap with Germany.[6] Viewed from this perspective, it seems likely that the single European market will allow the southern part of Europe to accelerate the process of catching up with the north.

However, if we disaggregate the regions sufficiently, the economies of scale and the cumulative growth effects seem to become more important, leading to increasing regional income gaps. This may have been the phenomenon underlying the divergence in economic growth between the north and the south of Italy in the postwar period.[7] It may also explain the fact that two small countries in Southern Europe, Portugal and Greece, have experienced increasing income gaps with the north, as the following data show (EC Commission 1988, table 7)[8]:

GDP per Capita as %
of German GDP per Capita

Year	Greece	Portugal
1960	33	23
1970	27	14
1987	24	19

To summarize, the single European market is likely to speed the process of convergence of income levels between northern and southern Europe. Its regional effect at a more disaggregated level is unclear. Two implications can be drawn from the discussion, however. First, because of the economies of scale effects of integration, some regions will gain more than others. Second, it is impossible to predict which regions are most likely to gain. Thus, for example, Sicily may profit more than Sardinia, but the reverse could as easily be the case. There is no way to predict the outcome. At this subregional level, historical accidents may help to shape the outcome. For example, the decision by multinationals to invest in one region rather than another may be based on some marginal differences between the regions. This decision, however, may have large implications for the future growth of the region that is chosen by the investors. That region may profit from the dynamic effects described earlier, which will lead to increased competitiveness and cumulative growth.

Recent growth theories (see Romer 1986) have also stressed this cumulative aspect of economic growth. In these models, in which dynamic economies of scale play an important role, small changes in initial conditions may completely change the future growth path of a country or region. A similar process occurs in models in which the expansion of one sector has spillover effects on aggregate demand, stimulating the growth of other sectors (see Murphy, Shleifer, and Vishny, 1989).

Can Regional Policies Be Useful?

Since the early days of the integration process in Europe, regional policies have been considered a necessary complement of trade liberalization. This has led to a proliferation of regional policies on the part of both the national authorities and EC institutions. It also led to the recent decision to double the budget of the EC's regional fund in anticipation of the single European market. The theory underlying these regional policies is that the processes of economic integration, if left to proceed uncontrolled, will make the rich regions richer and the poor regions poorer.

As we have seen, however, economic theory does not allow us to draw that conclusion. What it does tell us is that while some poor regions may become poorer, other poor regions will become richer as a result of the opening up of markets. In addition, the theory tells us that we will generally have great difficulty predicting which region(s) will move up into the league of high performers. We are still left, however, with the question of whether the movement toward a single European market should be accompanied by intensified regional policies aimed at helping regions that fail to capture the benefits of a single market. Can governments help regions to take off along a cumulative growth path?

The answer to this question is that it depends on what these regional policies are. Some sets of policies are certainly conducive to the economic development of a region. These include policies for the provision of public goods, such as an educational system, transportation and communication infrastructure, and a reliable legal system. The existence of these public goods makes it easier for a region to exploit its comparative advantages and increases its chances of moving along a cumulative growth path. A favorable business climate is also important to success, and this can be stimulated by government policies that minimize price and regulatory distortions.

Quite often, however, far more extensive and interventionist regional policies are proposed. Proponents of regional policies often argue for active government intervention in production and investment. In their view, government must stimulate particular industries and firms by subsidizing the industrial activities it considers important to regional development.

The economies of scale effects (both static and dynamic) of the integration process appear to strengthen the case for a regional development policy based on targeting particular industries, at least in theory. If the right industries are selected, a government subsidy can give an initial advantage to the regional firms in that industry. These firms will then be able to "slide down" their average cost and learning curves quicker than competitors in other regions. As a result, they will also obtain a competitive advantage. Such a policy, if applied in the right industries, may put the region on a cumulative growth path.[9]

Although such policies can, in principle, be used to correct what is in essence a market failure, their practical implementation requires the existence of a benevolent, well-informed, and powerful government. Unfortunately, we are unlikely to have such governments. In other words, to be convincing, these proposals for regional industrial targeting must face the issue of whether governments in Western political democracies are able to perform the tasks required for the success of these policies. This question relates to the *political economy of subsidies* and has been analyzed in great detail by the "collective choice" theorists.[10] In order to analyze this question, we need to look briefly at the demand and supply for subsidies and protection.

The Political Economy of Industry Targeting

Let us start with the demand side. As soon as a government announces a policy of industry targeting in a particular region — that is, a policy that will favor, in a discriminatory way, some firms and industries — economic agents will spend resources in an effort to profit from these favors. In a world of scarcity, economic agents will not limit their competition for scarce resources to the economic market, but will compete in the political market as well. By announcing policies that will favor certain economic activities in particular regions, the government stimulates this rent-seeking behavior by providing an incentive for economic agents to increase their efforts to obtain favors through the political market.[11]

On the supply side are the subsidy and protection favors generated by the government. In traditional welfare analysis, it is assumed that government knows and pursues a social welfare objective. That is, the government is assumed to be well-informed and benevolent. But as the public choice literature points out, this is a very arbitrary assumption that implies that there are two kinds of agents in society. One class (the consumers and the producers) pursues individual welfare objectives, while another class (politicians and civil servants) pursues a social welfare objective. It is not clear, however, where these two classes of individuals come from nor, if two types of individuals actually exist, how the altruistic types are selected into the political and bureaucratic institutions.

A more realistic and useful starting point is to assume that individuals, including politicians and civil servants, pursue objectives of individual welfare. Then one can analyze how and under what institutional conditions these individuals will perform acts that are also consistent with the general welfare (much in the same way as Adam Smith analyzed the conditions under which self-interested individuals in markets will act in ways that improve the general welfare).

Given this basic assumption, one can ask how the supply of subsidies and protection will be organized. In a system in which politicians compete with each other to obtain or preserve power, the subsidies are likely to be used to further these objectives. This does not necessarily mean that the distribution of these favors may not be in the general regional interest. If the general welfare objectives of industry targeting in a region can be clearly identified, it is in the politicians' interest to seek the political support needed to pursue these policies. If many people will benefit from these policies, the astute politician will organize the support needed to realize them, and thereby also enlarge his power base. If, however, the social welfare objectives cannot be easily identified, or if no consensus can be reached on the nature of the social welfare involved, it is more likely that special interests will dominate in the distribution of the favors in a region.

The results of this competition for scarce resources in the political market are difficult to predict, since they depend on the peculiarities of political institutions (for example, the electoral system). In some countries and regions, these institutions will favor large companies with strong labor unions. In other countries and regions, favors will be spread thinly across many firms and industries. In general, however, the subsidies will typically go to those who have exerted the greatest political pressure. Governments in political democracies have great difficulty resisting this pressure and selecting regional projects in an economically rational way.

Thus, there is no presumption that the distribution of subsidies and favors through the political market will stimulate the projects that will most benefit the development of a region. So although the existence of economies of scale and learning effects creates a scope for government intervention, its implementation requires such strong assumptions about what governments can do in a democratic society as to make them impractical. In fact, it can be argued that industry targeting at the regional level, when put into practice, is often more harmful than beneficial to the development of a region. There are two main reasons for drawing this pessimistic conclusion, and they are both related to the effects of subsidies on the workings of the market system.

First, when government stimulates a particular project in a region, scarce resources have to be attracted from elsewhere, and some of these resources will come from the region itself. If there is sufficient unemployment of the needed factors of production in the region — say labor — this can be done without affecting the regional wage rate. However, if this is not the case, regional subsidies will lead to an increase in the regional wage rate. This, in turn, will make nonsubsidized projects in the region more costly and less competitive, and they will be crowded out.

This phenomenon is not necessarily a problem if the selection process for targeting particular projects is based on criteria of economic efficiency. After all, when private investors decide to invest in a region, they will also draw resources away from the rest of the region, thereby increasing their prices. The problem arises, as was argued above, when the selection of individual projects through the political market is dominated by political rather than economic efficiency considerations.

There is some evidence that regional policies have created such problems. In the Mezzogiorno (southern Italy), for example, regional subsidies stimulated large industrial projects that did not correspond to the comparative advantage of the region. These projects have destroyed much of the surrounding economic fabric and have contributed to the creation of regional economic wastelands.

The Efficiency Costs of Regional Industry Targeting
Another way in which regional subsidy policies may be harmful to a region is through their X-efficiency effects. Subsidies, because they protect recipients from external competition, may lead protected firms to pursue cost-minimizing strategies with less vigor than firms that are less protected. The reduced competition also weakens incentives to innovate and to look for new products and production techniques. In the long run, subsidized and protected firms may be less able to withstand international competition. As a result, these firms may become permanently dependent on the subsidies.

These potentially cost-increasing effects of subsidies need to be considered alongside the potentially cost-reducing effects deriving from the existence of dynamic economies of scale. Through the learning effects resulting from economies of scale, subsidies allow firms to slide down their learning curves faster than their competitors and to reduce costs faster.[12] It is difficult to decide a priori which of the two effects will prevail. It cannot be excluded, however, that the cost-increasing effects of subsidies may be larger than the cost-reducing effects coming from the exploitation of the dynamic economies of scale.

A regional subsidy may create the condition for cost-saving by allowing firms to "learn by doing." But while doing may be necessary for learning, it is certainly not sufficient. Firms also need a competitive environment that forces them to learn quickly from their experience (see Bhagwati 1988, 97). Without such competition, firms may have only a weak incentive to translate experience into cost-saving measures. In other words, subsidies are a two-edged sword. They create the possibility for cost-saving by making the rapid accumulation of experience possible. At the same time, they reduce the level of competition and so reduce the pressure on subsidized firms to forge the link between learning and doing.

Thus government policies for regional development through selective assistance to potential "industry champions" have a low probability of success. In the light of these observations, it would clearly be a grave mistake for the representatives of the poorer regions in Europe to use the occasion of the 1992 program to try to obtain more subsidies for pursuing policies of industrial targeting at the regional level. Such regional subsidies are likely to be ineffective and may even do more harm than good with respect to the economic development of the poorer regions of Europe.

Conclusion

How will the move toward a single European market affect Europe's regions? Will it benefit the rich regions at the expense of the poorer ones, or will the gains of the single market be shared equally by all regions? In analyzing these questions, we argued that there are two forces accompanying market integration that have quite different effects on regional development. One force leads to convergence of regional income levels, as economic integration induces regions to specialize according to their comparative advantages. This process will lead poor regions to specialize in labor-intensive production. As a result, wage levels in the poor regions will tend to increase faster than in the rich regions.

A second force inherent in the integration process that may lead to divergence of regional income levels derives from the existence of economies of scale (static and dynamic) and of externalities. By enlarging the size of markets, the single European market will make it possible to exploit these economies of scale and externalities. Inevitably, this process will profit some regions more than others. Some regions may profit from cumulative growth effects, while others may fail to capture these positive effects. The possibility that some smaller regions will actually be harmed cannot be ruled out.

One of the characteristics of the economies of scale effects of economic integration is that a small initial advantage to a particular firm can lead to large gains by accelerating the learning process and allowing the firm to acquire a competitive advantage. This feature of the integration process tempts the authorities to give an extra push to local producers by subsidizing them. This has become one of the major justifications for regional policies.

This paper has argued that it would be a mistake to use the 1992 program to increase efforts to target industries at the regional level. Analysis based on the political economy of subsidies shows that, in political democracies, it is very difficult for the political authorities to hold out against the pressure of those who try to capture subsidies. As a result, the distribution of subsidies and other favors is more likely to reflect a political balance of power than the comparative advantages of a region. In the end, such regional policies may do more harm than good.

But not all government regional policies are harmful or of dubious benefit. Poor regions can be helped by improvements in the supply of public goods, in particular educational services, infrastructure, and a solid legal system. If government regional policies are geared toward these objectives, they can help the poorer regions of Europe profit from the economic gains of a single European market.

Notes

1. For a more detailed analysis, see EC Commission (1988).
2. For a discussion of these effects, see EC Commission (1988).
3. Some observers have looked at the evolution in the *absolute* rather than the relative disparities in income and have noted that the absolute difference has increased. This seems to be the wrong way to view changes in income distribution. It is equivalent to saying that if everybody's income doubles, the income inequality increases, because the absolute difference between the highest and the lowest incomes increases.
4. For a presentation, see, for example, Ethier (1988) or Caves and Jones (1986).
5. This view of the unequal regional effects of economic integration has been elaborated by Myrdal (1957) and Kaldor (1966). For a synthesis, see Balassa (1961, chapter 9). In the French economic literature, this view has found expression in François Perroux's concept of "pole de croissance." This idea has been very influential in the devising of regional policies in Southern Europe. Recently, the "new" growth theory has incorporated some of these ideas (see Romer 1986 and, more recently, Murphy, Shleifer, and Vishny 1989).
6. Note that although Spain did not become a member of the EC until 1986, it has followed export-oriented growth strategies since the early 1960s, allowing it to progressively integrate its economy into the European economy. There is evidence that its recent membership in the EC has accelerated economic growth in Spain. For more analysis on the effects of export-oriented growth strategies, see Balassa (1980 and 1982).
7. A recent paper by d'Antonio, Colairo, and Leonello (1988) provides evidence that the patterns of input-output linkages between northern Italy and Mezzogiorno favor the north.
8. There are alternative explanations, however, for conditions in these two countries. Both countries have until recently heavily protected their domestic markets. The increasing income gaps may be the result of these inward-looking strategies, which have left their domestic producers very uncompetitive. Another explanation may be the volatile macroeconomic policies of these two countries, which may have led to an environment unconducive to investment and growth.
9. The so-called "new" trade theory has stressed this point in many recent publications. See, for example, Krugman (1987).
10. See, for example, Olson (1962) and Buchanan (1980). For an application in trade theory, see Bhagwati (1982).
11. See the classic article on this type of behavior by Krueger (1973).
12. The infant industry argument is based on similar reasoning, but the argument here emphasizes the externalities created by knowledge, which are not internalized in a free market system.

References

Balassa, B. 1961. *The Theory of Economic Integration*. London: Allen & Irwin, 1961.

Balassa, B. 1980. *The Process of Industrial Development and Alternative Development Strategies*. Essays in International Finance No. 141. Princeton, N.J.: Princeton University.

Balassa, B. 1982. *Development Strategies in Semi-Industrialized Countries*. Baltimore, Md.: Johns Hopkins University Press.

Bhagwati, J. 1982. "Directly Unproductive, Profit Seeking (DUP) Activities." *Journal of Political Economy* 90: 988-1002.

Bhagwati, J. 1988. *Protectionism*. Cambridge, Mass.: MIT Press.

Buchanan, J. 1980. "Rent Seeking and Profit Seeking." In J. Buchanan, ed., *Towards a General Theory of the Rent Seeking Society*. College Station, Texas: Texas A & M Press.

Caves, R., and R. Jones. 1986. *World Trade and Payments*. Boston: Little, Brown.

d'Antonio, M., R. Colairo, and G. Leonello. 1988. "Mezzogiorno / Centre-North: A Two-Region Model for the Italian Economy." *Journal of Policy Modelling* 10: 437-51.

EC Commission. 1988. *European Economy: The Economics of 1992*. Luxembourg: Office for the Official Publications of the European Communities.

Ethier, W. 1988. *Modern International Economics*. New York: Norton.

Kaldor, N. 1966. *The Causes of the Slow Rate of Growth of the United Kingdom*. Cambridge: Cambridge University Press.

Krueger, A.O. 1973. "The Political Economy of the Rent-Seeking Society." *American Economic Review* 64 (June): 291-303.

Krugman, P.R., ed. 1987. *Strategic Trade Policy and the New International Economics*. Cambridge, Mass.: MIT Press.

Murphy, K., A. Shleifer, and R. Vishny. 1989. "Industrialization and the Big Push Stage of Industrial Development." *Journal of Political Economy* 97: 1003-26.

Myrdal, G. 1957. *Economic Theory and Underdeveloped Regions*. New York: Duckworth.

Olson, M. 1962. *The Logic of Collective Action*. Cambridge, Mass.: Harvard University Press.

Robson, P. 1980. *The Economics of International Integration*. London: Allen and Irwin.

Romer, P. 1986. "Increasing Returns and Long Run Growth." *Journal of Political Economy* 94: 1002-37.

10

The Discipline of Imports in the European Market

Alexis Jacquemin and André Sapir

Both theoretical and empirical research suggest that import competition within European markets serves as a major constraint on the price-cost margins of domestic firms. The program for the completion of the European Community's (EC) internal market by 1992 is based largely on a strengthening of European competition through the removal of the remaining barriers to intra-EC trade. According to the European Commission's assessment of the economic effects of this liberalization (Emerson et al. 1988), the overall result will be a significant gain in welfare.

Imports from the rest of the world also exercise an important trade discipline on European market performance. In fact, various arguments suggest that the disciplinary effect of these imports may be stronger than that of intra-EC imports. In that case, a further opening of the European Common Market to world imports would lead to an even more dramatic competitive impact on EC industrial price-cost margins than is expected from the 1992 program alone.[1]

In this paper, our analysis encompasses two areas to which Béla Balassa has contributed immensely over the past thirty years: economic integration and trade liberalization. Starting with his celebrated work on *The Theory of Economic Integration* (1961), Balassa has shown that regional integration can, as it has in Europe, produce important welfare gains. At the same time, he has always emphasized the virtues of trade liberalization on a more global scale.

The paper investigates empirically the discipline imposed by intra-EC and extra-EC imports on European industry performance. It first examines the theoretical arguments for the role of trade, actual and potential, as a discipline argument and the possible influence of the origin of imports, and then sets out the econometric model and its results. Sectoral aspects of trade liberalization are also discussed.

Imports as a Discipline Argument

Various oligopoly models have incorporated international factors and derived equilibrium relations that have identified the role of imports (see Caves 1980 and Jacquemin 1982). The Cournot-Nash model with homogeneous products is straightforward in establishing a negative association between the domestic price-cost margin (or, with constant variable costs, the industry rate of gross return on domestic sales) and the rate of imports. In this model, each firm calculates its optimal policy and treats the output of rivals (imports as well as domestic producers) parametrically.

By contrast, the dominant-firm model distinguishes between a fringe of small firms, which take price as given, and the members of the dominant group of firms, which take the fringe's reaction function as given. In this case too, the various equilibria show a negative link between the price-cost margin and the rate of imports. However, the interpretation of the variables depends on the identity of the members belonging to the two groups. If foreign producers are treated as the competitive fringe and the domestic industry as the cartel, trade emerges as a discipline argument immediately. But when foreign producers form the dominant group (usually multinationals) and domestic firms are the fringe, discipline is imposed not by imports but by domestic firms' output (Geroski and Jacquemin 1981). A basic implication, then, is that the nature of the link between profits and import penetration depends on the nature of imports and the origin of trade discipline.

With respect to the *nature of imports*, several characteristics can diminish the procompetitive force of imports. An important one is the existence of product differentiation at the level of firms and industries, which implies the existence of monopolistic competition and market power. Such product differentiation tends to reduce the intensity of import discipline and to favor intraindustry trade. Also important is the role of intrafirm trade in the case of domestic firms that have a multinational base that controls imports, a condition that increases the prospects of effective market cartelization. Related to the issue of the nature of imports is the role of barriers to trade, whether natural or artificial. Among the natural barriers are the existence of important scale economies and differences in preferences, habits, language, culture, and incomes, all of which can limit the entry of imports. Artificial barriers include various tariff and nontariff obstacles such as technical norms and public procurement policies. More generally, the disciplinary role of trade depends on the elasticity of foreign supply with respect to domestic price. This elasticity is only partly reflected in the current flow of imports since they can be restricted by various entry barriers.

With respect to the *origin of trade discipline*, the question to be tested is whether the import discipline imposed on European industrial profitability is stronger for imports originating outside the EC than for those of Community origin. An a priori reason for expecting this to be the case is the evidence associating European integration with a growing complementarity and division of labor and with increased intraindustry and intrafirm trade (Greenaway 1987). Thus, for example, the heavily intraindustry cast of intra-EC imports could reduce their competitive effect. Certain characteristics of market conduct within the Common Market also can reduce competition: various horizontal and vertical agreements, dominant positions permitting price leadership, and intrafirm trade and corresponding restrictive practices, including transfer pricing. These types of market behavior can be expected to be less effective for imports coming from the rest of the world.

Finally, the specific effects of imports on industrial price-cost margins must be disentangled from the role of various characteristics of industry, such as capital intensity and technology, which are also expected to be related to profitability.

Given the multiplicity of possible configurations of market conduct and structure, it is difficult to provide a single model encompassing the various alternatives. Our empirical analysis is more modest. It is intended to determine empirically the extent to which intra- and extra-EC imports exercise a different impact on profit margins, taking into account the interaction between profits and imports. The flow of imports will be endogenously determined by various structural features of industry, which themselves exert a differential impact according to the origin of the imports. Furthermore, the effects of trade on industry performance will be allowed to vary according to the source of the threat or discipline.

Methodology and Empirical Results

To test whether imports from inside and outside the EC exert a different disciplinary effect on price-cost margins, we postulate the following structure-performance equation:

$$(1) \qquad \Pi_i = \alpha_1 + \beta_1 \, m_i^i + \beta_2 \, m_i^e + \sum_{j=1}^{J} \gamma_{1j} \, X_{1j} + \varepsilon \,,$$

where i denotes the industry, Π is the price-cost margin, m^i is intra-EC import penetration, m^e is extra-EC import penetration, X is a set of variables characterizing industry performance, and ε is a zero-mean, normally distributed error term.

Ordinary least squares estimation of equation 1 is likely to lead to biased and inconsistent parameter estimates since, as noted by Pugel (1984), there is a simultaneity problem in considering price-cost margins and import penetration. Not only is import penetration expected to influence (negatively) profits, but profits are also expected to influence (positively) import penetration: the higher the level of profits in a domestic industry, the greater the attraction for foreign firms to enter that market. To solve this simultaneity problem, an instrumental variable procedure is used, wherein m^i and m^e in equation 1 are replaced by their estimated values.

The empirical analysis is conducted for the "Big Four" EC members (France, Germany, Italy, and the United Kingdom) for 1983. It relies on a recently developed database on European industry that covers over one hundred manufacturing sectors and permits analysis at a rather disaggregated level (three-digit NACE).

Profitability, or the price-cost margin, is defined as value added at factor cost minus payroll divided by total sales. It is computed as a three-year average centered on 1983. Following the conventional literature on industry performance, we associate the level of price-cost margins with a number of variables reflecting industry structure and conduct, including import competition.

In considering the effects of trade on profitability, we distinguish the effects of both actual imports and potential imports and of intra-EC imports and extra-EC imports. *Actual* import competition is measured by means of import intensity, defined as the ratio of imports to apparent consumption. The *potential* pressure of imports is measured using dummy variables for trade barriers. In the case of nontariff barriers affecting intra-EC trade, the dummy variable takes the value 1 for sectors characterized by strong and medium nontariff barriers and 0 for other sectors.[2] Barriers against extra-EC imports are reflected by the common external tariff, measured as the ratio of duties collected by Belgian customs to the value of extra-EC imports.

As already mentioned, we expect import intensity to have a negative impact on price-cost margins, with extra-EC imports exerting a stronger effect than intra-EC imports. In contrast, we expect trade barriers (both tariff and nontariff) to reinforce the market power of domestic firms, and so to be positively associated with profitability.

The remaining explanatory variables of the industry performance equation are traditional indicators of structure and behavior: the extent of industry demand, the importance of economies of scale, the intensity of research and development (R&D), and the degree of product differentiation. The rate of growth of consumption in Organization for Economic Cooperation and Development (OECD) countries is used to identify sectors of *fast-growing world demand*; this variable is expected to exert a negative influence on profits since market growth facilitates entry. To determine the importance of *economies of scale*, we used British data on the output achieved in each industry by the largest plants that account for 50 percent of total output; the existence of scale economies is likely to have a positive impact on profitability since scale economies are positively correlated with concentration and may also reflect barriers to small-scale entry.[3] The *intensity of R&D* is measured by the ratio of R&D staff to total staff. R&D activities are clearly important to maintaining profitability in an international context since worldwide competition has become increasingly technological. *Product differentiation* is captured by a dummy variable that takes a value of 1 for consumer goods and 0 otherwise. We expect product differentiation to be associated with reduced intensity of competition and increased profits.

The regression analysis covers all the available observations (265), which were obtained by pooling the observations for each of the Big Four countries.[4] The pooling was necessary because data on several explanatory variables were missing for some industries in some countries. Preliminary testing of the data indicated that *country dummies* would be needed in order to capture differences in profitability among the four large EC members in 1983 that were not accounted for by the other explanatory variables.

The results of the regression analysis of profitability appear in table 10.1. The estimates of the coefficients are generally consistent with our expectations, and the summary statistics (R^2 and F-statistics) are relatively high. Trade barriers, economies of scale, R&D, and product differentiation are all positively associated with large price-cost margins. In contrast, the intensity of imports and the growth of demand tend to impose a constraint on profitability. Our estimates also showed that industries across the board in France, Italy, and the United Kingdom had significantly higher price-cost margins than did German industries.

A major finding of the analysis is that only imports from outside the EC exert a significant disciplinary effect on price-cost margins. Imports from within the EC seem to exert no disciplinary effect at all.

Table 10.1 Regression Analysis of Determinants of EC Industrial Price-Cost Margins

Variable	Regression result
Constant	16.466
	(17.04)
Intra-EC imports	-0.008
	(-0.06)
Extra-EC imports	-0.380
	(-3.55)
Intra-EC, strong nontrade barriers	2.356
	(2.16)
Intra-EC, medium nontrade barriers	1.093
	(1.08)
Common external tariff	0.203
	(1.84)
Demand growth	-0.315
	(-1.83)
Economies of scale	20.461
	(3.24)
Research and development	0.414
	(4.44)
Product differentiation	2.211
	(1.85)
France	2.557
	(1.90)
Italy	4.894
	(5.60)
United Kingdom	3.553
	(4.74)
R^2 (adjusted)	0.316
F-statistic	11.17

Note: Figures in parentheses are t-statistics.

Another interesting finding concerns the potential effect on price-cost margins of the removal of the common external tariff and intra-EC trade barriers. The estimated coefficients show that potentially important barriers to trade within the EC do indeed protect European producers and, consequently, raise their profit margins. However, this protection is limited to the sectors that are subject to the highest nontariff barriers.[5, 6]

Sectoral Aspects of Trade Liberalization

Increasing competitive pressure will result from the elimination of nontariff barriers and the increased flow of imports from both inside and outside the EC. Whatever the efficiency gains, this situation is bound to entail adjustment costs as well. Policy measures will need to be devised in order to make this greater competition acceptable. When formulating these measures, a distinction might usefully be made between traditional and high-tech sectors. In the traditional sectors, specialization is based on comparative advantage, and production is undertaken by a large number of firms. In the high-tech sectors, there are significant economies of scale, learning, and scope, and competition takes place between a limited number of large firms. If products are differentiated, trade remains largely within the same industry and can be increased by competition. If products are homogeneous, competition results in an expansion in production in certain firms in certain countries, and in a contraction of activity, or even closure, in others.

For traditional sectors, a more efficient worldwide division of labor is desirable, although it may lead to considerable structural adjustment costs, especially in certain labor-intensive industries. For instance, empirical studies of the textile and clothing sector suggest that the removal of tariff and nontariff barriers would enhance the welfare of both developing and industrial countries but would entail significant adjustment costs for labor.

For the high-tech sectors, open policies toward the outside world are also desirable. They can lead to improved efficiency in production by lowering unit costs, lessening the threat of monopoly power in the domestic market, and extending the product range. However, such policies may also facilitate the creation of global dominance in some industries and the transfer of monopoly rents to specific oligopolists and countries. Empirical studies suggest that in certain sectors, such as aviation or electronic components, strategic commercial policies can secure net gains for those who initiate them, but often at the expense of the rest of the world. In view of the large possible gains, it is inevitable that the authorities, already under pressure from various lobbyist groups, will be increasingly tempted to apply such policies. This risk is especially great under the present climate of drift toward the formation of economic blocs and the adoption of noncooperative attitudes.

What these findings mean in practical terms is that the potential benefits of a simultaneous process of internal and external liberalization of the single European market can only materialize if the competitive process is accepted, implying a consensus on the long-term outlook and the accompanying policies to be adopted both internally and externally.

For the traditional sectors, there must be an acceptance of a gradual shift in specializations and methods of production toward a worldwide division of labor in line with the dynamics of comparative advantage. Far-reaching structural adjustment policies, designed to encourage rather than withstand change, must be implemented at the sectoral level. This would involve either pulling out of certain areas or retargeting production toward the upper end of the market. These policies are particularly urgent in southern Europe, where adjustments have been very limited despite the increasing competition in labor-intensive activities that these countries face from developing nations.

In high-tech sectors, a policy of international consultation should be implemented to ensure genuine worldwide cooperation and avoid the pitfalls of bilateralism or anticompetitive behavior. Here, too, urgent action is called for, since Europe's relative position in the growth sectors has slipped in recent years in contrast to the case of Japan and the newly industrialized countries of Southeast Asia, with their particularly effective export policies. There must be no retreat into isolation; on the contrary, an outward-looking strategy must be developed in conjunction with the liberalization of the internal market.

Conclusion

This paper developed an empirical model to examine the influence of import discipline on European industrial price-cost margins. A general finding is that both potential and actual competition induced by imports are effective in narrowing price-cost margins. Furthermore, trade discipline was found to vary not only according to certain characteristics of industry but also according to the origin of imports: only imports from outside the EC were found to exercise a significant impact.

The liberalization of the European market will indeed increase the competitive pressure on European industry and create a constraint on the exercise of market power. Today, a main competitive pressure comes from the discipline imposed by imports from outside the EC; tomorrow, it will come from the removal of the barriers to potential intra-EC competition. A recent study by Neven and Röller (1990) even suggests that the elimination of these barriers will increase extra-EC imports more than intra-EC imports, so even in the case of potential competition, the main pressure could come from the rest of the world rather than from within the Community.

In presenting a strategy for making the dual (internal and external) liberalization acceptable, a distinction was drawn between traditional and high-tech sectors. In both types of sector, it is important for the EC to supplement and balance its trade concerns with longer-term structural policies. Only such an approach will ensure that the EC's international relations are based on stable, multilateral cooperation.

Notes

The authors are grateful to Isabelle Pouplier for excellent research assistance and to Victor Ginsburgh, Herbert Glejser, Khalid Sekkat, and Alan Winters for helpful comments and suggestions on an earlier version of the paper.

1. See Sapir (1989) for a discussion of the external impact of the 1992 program.
2. These two variables were constructed on the basis of a recent study by Buigues and Ilzkovitz (1988) identifying the most fragmented EC markets. This study uses two indicators of market fragmentation. The first is a set of eight trade barriers: technical standards and regulations, public procurement, administrative barriers, frontier formalities, differences in value added taxes and excise duties, transport regulations, capital market controls, and implementation of EC law. The other indicator is a measure of price discrepancies between member states.
3. Recent studies suggest that, contrary to traditional wisdom, concentration itself is not generally correlated with price-cost margins (see Schmalensee 1989). While our own data are not extensive enough to permit us to examine concentration over a sufficiently large sample, a simple correlation analysis over a reduced set of observations shows a rather strong link between concentration and economies of scale.
4. All (processed) agricultural sectors have been omitted from the sample because profitability there was thought to be conditioned by a rather different set of factors than is the case for manufacturing industries.
5. According to Buigues and Ilzkovitz (1988), these sectors include activities in which public procurement regulations have considerable influence (such as boilermaking, railway equipment, and shipbuilding). The removal of these barriers should result in a significant lowering of price-cost margins.
6. It is common in regressions of price-cost margins to introduce a capital-intensity variable to correct for measurement problems. The use of such a variable does not affect the results.

References

Balassa, B. 1961. *The Theory of Economic Integration.* Homewood, Ill.: Richard Irwin.

Buigues, P., and F. Ilzkovitz. 1988. "Les enjeux sectoriels du marché intérieur." *Revue d'Economie Industrielle* no. 45: 1-21.

Caves, R. 1980. "Symposium on International Trade and Industrial Organization." *Journal of Industrial Economics* 29: 113-218.

Emerson, M., M. Aujean, M. Catinat, P. Goybet, and A. Jacquemin. 1988. *The Economics of 1992.* Oxford: Oxford University Press.

Geroski, P., and A. Jacquemin. 1981. "Imports as a Competitive Discipline." *Recherches Economiques de Louvain* 47: 197-208.

Greenaway, D. 1987. "Intra-Industry Trade, Intra-Firm Trade and European Integration: Evidence, Gains and Policy Aspects." *Journal of Common Market Studies* 26: 154-72.

Jacquemin, A. 1982. "Imperfect Market Structure and International Trade: Some Recent Research." *Kyklos* 35: 75-93.

Neven, D., and L.H. Röller. 1990. *European Integration and Trade Flows.* London: Center for Economic Policy Studies.

Pugel, T.A. 1980. "Foreign Trade and U.S. Market Performance." *Journal of Industrial Economics* 29: 119-30.

Sapir, A. 1989. "Does 1992 Come before or after 1990? On Regional versus Multilateral Integration." In R. Jones and A.O. Krueger, eds, *The Political Economy of International Trade*. Oxford: Basil Blackwell.

Schmalensee, R. 1989. "Inter-Industry Studies of Structure and Performance." In R. Schmalensee and R. Willig, eds, *Handbook of Industrial Organization*. Amsterdam: North-Holland.

11

Is Japan an Outlier Among Trading Countries?

T. N. Srinivasan

Among Béla Balassa's many friends, admirers, and colleagues, I am one whose association with him — in all three capacities — dates back to the early days of his life and career in the United States. I entered Yale's graduate program in economics just a few months after Béla. We may even have taken some of the same courses, including Professor Robert Triffin's stimulating course in International Economics. We have kept in close touch since those days. Our contacts have included my rewarding three-year stint at the World Bank Development Research Center, for which Béla was at the time a senior consultant — and which has since been sacrificed in one of the Bank's periodic rituals called reorganization. Although we do not always agree on policy matters, our disagreements are far fewer than our common views on many policy issues facing developing countries. It is with deep affection and admiration, not only for his professional contributions but also for his extraordinary strength of character and will that make him function so effectively in circumstances that would have defeated almost anyone, that I offer this contribution to his festschrift.

Béla has contributed to so many policy debates that one has a wide choice of topics on which to write for his festschrift. Among these issues are Japan's foreign trade policies and Japan's role in the world economy, topics on which he has written, singly and with Marcus Noland. Many of the contributors to this literature, including some distinguished economists, seem unable to avoid accusations of mercantilism and what must frankly be called jingoistic overtones. In contrast, Balassa and Noland (1988) provide a comprehensive and sober discussion of the microeconomic and macroeconomic aspects of Japan's trade and current account surpluses. One of the many empirical results reported in the study is that Japan is "an outlier as far as import shares are concerned. Japan is different from other countries in that it imports substantially less than what would be expected on the basis of international comparisons of the national attributes of industrial countries" (Balassa and Noland 1988, 253-54). I focus on this result — that Japan imports too little — which has also been reported by other studies using different methodologies.

In examining measures of import shares as a proportion of GNP, I look first at the implications of using an extension of the simplest version of the Krugman (1979) model of intraindustry trade. This allows for the use of natural resources in production, an exogenous capital outflow, and the presence of nontraded goods. I conclude that there is no theoretical presumption that, but for trade barriers, all industrial countries would have identical import ratios. After exploring the implications for import shares of assuming identical and homothetic tastes among countries and the absence of natural and policy-induced trade barriers, I critically review some of the econometric studies including Balassa (1986), Balassa and Noland (1988), Lawrence (1987), Leamer (1988), and Saxonhouse (1983, 1986a, b, 1988). Even if some of the estimation biases of these studies are ignored and their findings are accepted, it does not necessarily follow that governmentally imposed and other invisible trade barriers are the *causal* factor explaining low Japanese imports.

In the following section, I offer some remarks on macroeconomic and other considerations that may be more important in explaining Japan's trade and current account surpluses than the alleged trade barriers. I conclude with a brief discussion of the implications of the unilateral U.S. action against Japan under the U.S. Trade Act of 1988, arguing that it is a retrograde step from the perspective of maintaining a liberal multilateral trading regime, an objective close to Béla's heart.

Import Shares and Features Distinguishing Japan from Other Major Trading Countries

In examining whether Japan imports too little, one can look at various measures of import penetration, such as the share in GNP of all imports from all sources (or from particular sources), of manufactures imports (or share of manufactures imports in domestic use of manufactures), of intraindustry trade, and so on. Each of these measures is of interest, with its particular relevance depending on the policy issue being addressed. It is fair to say, however, that much of the debate has focused on the manufacturing sector. For example, on the basis of less formal evidence, Krugman (1987), in commenting on Lawrence (1987), concludes that Japan should be importing roughly twice the manufactures it is importing. It is also argued that Japan engages in too little intraindustry trade arising from the presence of increasing returns to scale in production and product differentiation. It is appropriate to use a model that incorporates these features. It is also essential that the model be capable of incorporating some of the important characteristics that distinguish Japan from other major trading nations.

One such distinguishing feature is Japan's heavy dependence on imports of natural resources, particularly crude petroleum. To look at the implications of this for the import penetration ratio in manufacturing, let us consider a simple extension of the Krugman (1979) model of intraindustry trade. We begin by postulating that a unit of output of any variety of manufactured product requires γ units of natural resources. In our two-country model, we assume that (1) the foreign country is the exclusive supplier of this resource; (2) each variety of manufactured product is produced in both countries by the same technology (i.e., the feasibility of costless product differentiation is assumed), which involves a fixed cost of α units of labor and a marginal cost of β units of labor per unit of output; (3) all consumers in both countries have the identical utility function, $\sum_i c_i^\theta$, where c_i is consumption of variety

i; (4) there are L consumers at home and L^* consumers abroad, each of whom supplies a unit of labor; (5) producer behavior is described by Chamberlinian monopolistic competition of the large group; and (6) there are no barriers to trade.

It is easy to show that as long as the endowment of natural resources abroad, R^*, is not too large relative to the aggregate labor endowment $L + L^*$, resources will be positively priced in the trading equilibrium in which wage rates are the same in both countries. This equilibrium, with labor as the numeraire, is as follows, where r is the price per unit of natural resources, p the price of each variety produced or consumed in either country, n (n^*) the number of varieties produced at home (abroad), x the output of each variety, c (c^*) the per consumer consumption of each variety at home (abroad), and S the exogenously specified trade surplus of the home economy in units of labor.

(1)
$$r = \left(\frac{\gamma\theta(L+L^*)}{R} - \beta \right) \frac{1}{(1-\theta)\gamma}$$

(2)
$$p = \frac{\beta + \gamma r}{\theta}$$

(3)
$$n = \frac{L}{\alpha} \left(\frac{(1-\theta)(\beta+\gamma r)}{\beta+(1-\theta)\gamma r} \right)$$

(4)
$$n^* = \frac{L^*}{\alpha} \left(\frac{(1-\theta)(\beta+\gamma r)}{\beta+(1-\theta)\gamma r} \right)$$

(5)
$$x = \frac{\alpha\theta}{(1-\theta)(\beta+\gamma r)}$$

(6)
$$c = \frac{L-S}{(n+n^*)pL}$$

(7)
$$c^* = \frac{L^*+S+rR}{(n+n^*)pL^*} .$$

It is clear that as long as $\frac{\gamma\theta(L+L^*)}{R} \geq \beta$, this equilibrium is well defined.

Now, the import penetration ratio of manufactures for the home (foreign) economy, denoted by m ($m*$), is the ratio of the value of home (foreign) imports, $pn*cL$ ($pnc*L*$), to home (foreign) GNP, L ($L*+rR$). The total value of imports (manufactures plus natural resources) for the home economy equals the value of its exports net of trade surplus, ($pnc*L*-S$), so that the total import penetration ratio $\tilde{m}$ is $pncL* - S / L$. Since the foreign economy imports only manufactures, its total imports equal its manufactured imports, so that $\tilde{m}* = m*$. Thus,

(8)
$$m = \frac{pn^*cL}{L} = pn^*c$$

(9)
$$\tilde{m} = \frac{pnc^*L^* - S}{L}$$

(10)
$$m^* = \frac{pnc^*L^*}{L^* + rR}$$

(11)
$$\tilde{m}^* = m^*$$

(12)
$$\frac{m}{m^*} = \left(\frac{L^* + rR}{L^* + rR + S}\right)\left(\frac{L-S}{L}\right)\left(\frac{L^*}{L}\right)$$

(13)
$$\frac{\tilde{m}}{\tilde{m}^*} = \left(\frac{pnc^*L^* - S}{pnc^*L^*}\right)\left(\frac{L^* + rR}{L}\right) = \left(1 - \frac{S}{pnc^*L^*}\right)\left(\frac{L^* + rR}{L}\right).$$

Let us use equations 12 and 13 to simulate the expected import penetration ratios in the United States and Japan by pretending that these are the only two countries in the world and that both produce and consume only differentiated manufactured products. Thus, products of all other industries, including mining, agriculture, and services, are viewed as if they are different varieties of the manufactured product. We will ignore the fact that observed data for the two countries would obviously be inconsistent with these assumptions. It should be noted that we are focusing on the *ratio* of the import penetration ratios of the two countries rather than on absolute values. The reason, or rather the hope, is that although the obvious inadequacies of the model and the stylized data used in estimation will result in imprecision in the estimates of the absolute values, the ratio will be better estimated.

In equation 12, the first term represents the ratio of foreign income to expenditure, and the second term represents the ratio of home expenditure to income. Available data (see appendix for details) suggest that in 1987 the current account deficit of the United States was 3.16 percent and the surplus of Japan about 3.64 percent of its GNP, so the product of the first two terms is 0.93. If we identify L (L^*) as Japanese (U.S.) input of labor hours (note that total employment in Japan [U.S.] in 1987 was 59 [114] million persons) and allow for the fact that the Japanese work more hours per week (43.6 hours versus 38.0 hours in the United States in industry in 1985), we get L^* / L equals 1.68. Thus, equation 12 leads one to expect that the Japanese import penetration ratio would be about 1.56 times that of the United States; however, the actual figures in 1987 were 8.9 percent for Japan and 10.7 percent for the United States.

The first term of equation 13 is one minus that share of the home country's (Japan's) current account surplus in exports, and the second term is the ratio of foreign to domestic income. Given that Japan exported 12.68 percent of its GNP and ran a current account surplus of 3.64 percent of GNP in 1987, the first term is 0.71. Using the 1987 GNP and exchange rates, the second term comes to 1.90. The product of the two terms is 1.35, suggesting that Japan's total import penetration ratio should be nearly 35 percent greater than that of the United States.

The ratios derived from this rather simple, even simplistic, model should not be taken too literally, of course. Clearly, the United States and Japan do not produce only manufactured goods nor is labor the only nonresource input into production. Both trade with other countries besides each other. A significant proportion of output is nontraded, and the share of intermediate goods in trade is also significant. All these factors imply that the actual total import penetration ratios do not quite correspond to their theoretical counterparts in equations 12 and 13. But even with all these caveats, the numbers are as suggestive as the estimates from the flawed econometric studies reviewed below. One has to look for factors assumed away by the model, such as differences in technology, preferences, or possible trade barriers to explain the difference between the actual import penetration ratios and those predicted by the model.

Another factor that has been suggested as a possible explanation for Japan's low import penetration ratios is that Japanese consumers have to spend a higher proportion of their income for nontraded goods such as services and land rental because of their high relative prices. To explore this, let us modify the Krugman model by introducing a nontraded good. Assume that it takes one unit of labor at home and δ units abroad to produce a unit of a nontraded good, where $0 < \delta < 1$, that is, it takes less labor abroad than at home to produce it. Assume that the nontraded good enters the utility function as just another variety of manufactured good. For simplicity, assume that no natural resources are needed for its production. It is easily seen that if q (q^*) is the home (foreign) price of the nontraded good in units of labor and if Q (Q^*) is its home (foreign) consumption (and production), then in equilibrium,

$$p = \frac{\beta}{\theta} \qquad (14)$$

$$x = \frac{\alpha\theta}{\beta(1-\theta)} \qquad (15)$$

$$q = 1 \qquad (16)$$

$$q^* = \delta \qquad (17)$$

$$Q = c\left(\frac{\beta}{\theta}\right)^{-1/1-\theta} \qquad (18)$$

$$Q^* = c^*\left(\frac{\beta}{\delta\theta}\right)^{-1/1-\theta} \qquad (19)$$

$$n = \frac{(1-\theta)L}{\alpha}\left\{1 - c\left(\frac{\beta}{\theta}\right)^{-1/1-\theta}\right\} \qquad (20)$$

$$n^* = \frac{(1-\theta)L^*}{\alpha}\left\{1 - c^*\left(\frac{\beta}{\theta}\right)^{-1/1-\theta}\right\} \qquad (21)$$

$$c = \frac{1-s}{(n+n^*) + \left(\frac{\beta}{\delta\theta}\right)^{-1/1-\theta}} \qquad (22)$$

$$c^* = \frac{1-s^*}{(n+n^*) + \left(\frac{\beta}{\delta\theta}\right)^{-1/1-\theta}} \qquad (23)$$

where $s = \dfrac{S}{L}$ and $s^* = \dfrac{S}{L^*}$ and $(n+n^*)$ is the solution of

$$(24) \quad (n+n^*)\frac{\alpha}{1-\theta}=(L+L^*) - \frac{(1-s)L\left(\frac{\beta}{\theta}\right)^{-1/1-\theta}}{(n+n^*)+\left(\frac{\beta}{\theta}\right)^{-1/1-\theta}} - \frac{(1+s^*)L^*\left(\frac{\beta}{\delta\theta}\right)^{-1/1-\theta}}{(n+n^*)+\left(\frac{\beta}{\delta\theta}\right)^{-1/1-\theta}}.$$

A unique positive solution exists as long as $L + L^* > \frac{\alpha}{1-\theta}$. The import penetration ratios are then

$$(25) \quad m = \frac{(pn^*c)L}{L}=pn^*c$$

$$(26) \quad m^* = \frac{(pnc^*)L^*}{L^*}=pnc^*,$$

so that

$$(27) \quad \frac{m}{m^*} = \frac{n^*}{n}\frac{c}{c^*} = \frac{L^*\left\{1-c^*\left(\frac{\beta}{\delta\theta}\right)^{-1/1-\theta}\right\}}{L\left\{1-c\left(\frac{\beta}{\delta\theta}\right)^{-1/1-\theta}\right\}}\frac{c}{c^*}.$$

If we let $\delta \rightarrow 0$, so that the nontraded good becomes free abroad while still requiring one unit of labor to produce at home, from equation 23 it can be seen that

$$c^* \rightarrow \frac{1+s^*}{n+n^*}, \quad c^*\left(\frac{\beta}{\delta\theta}\right)^{-1/1-\theta} \rightarrow 0, \quad n^*, \rightarrow \frac{(1-\theta)L^*}{\alpha},$$

and so on. It would appear that m / m^* will decrease as δ decreases, raising the presumption that it will tend to a value less than one. In any case, the first term of equation 27 is the ratio of foreign employment in traded goods production to home employment and the second term is the ratio of per worker consumption of traded goods at home relative to that abroad. Japanese and U.S. data for 1987 suggest that employment in traded-goods-producing sectors (narrowly defined as agriculture, mining, and manufacturing) was 25.15 million in the United States and 19.22 million in Japan. As noted earlier, hours of work per week in industry in 1985 were 38.0 in the United States and 43.6 in Japan. Total domestic consumption of traded goods per worker in 1986 was $11,223 in the United States and $9,683 in Japan. These figures lead to a value of 1.00 for m / m^*, suggesting that Japan's total import penetration ratio should be about the same as that of the United States instead of being lower. Once again, this calculation based on the model should not be taken too literally for the reasons already mentioned.

Econometric Tests

Instead of working with a very simple but analytically tight theoretical model of intraindustry trade with increasing returns in a world of two countries, let us see how far we can get without explicitly specifying production technology and factor endowment. Consider a multicountry world without transportation costs or trade barriers. The price of a commodity in terms of a common numeraire will be the same in all countries. Let preferences be homothetic and identical across countries. By definition, C_J, the value of Japanese consumption of manufactured products, is

$$(28) \qquad C_J = \sum_i C_{iJ} = \sum_i Q_{iJ} + \sum_i M_{iJ} - \sum_i X_{iJ} \ ,$$

where Q_{iJ}, M_{iJ}, X_{iJ} are, respectively, Japanese production, imports, and exports of the ith manufactured product. Hence the share m_J^N of *net* imports of manufactures in consumption is given by

$$(29) \qquad m_J^N = \frac{\sum\limits_i C_{iJ} + \sum\limits_i Q_{iJ}}{\sum\limits_i C_{iJ}} = 1 - \frac{\sum\limits_i Q_{iJ}}{\sum\limits_i C_{iJ}} \ .$$

Under the assumption of identical and homothetic preferences,

$$(30) \qquad C_{iJ} = \phi_i \ (p) \ E_J$$

and

$$(31) \qquad c_{iW} = \phi_i \ (p) \ E_W \ ,$$

where p is the vector of equilibrium prices of goods entering the consumption basket, E_J and E_w are, respectively, Japanese and world expenditure levels, and $C_{iw} = Q_{iw}$ is the value of consumption (equal to the value of production, assuming no inventory change) of manufactures in the world. Denoting by s_J^P and s_J^E, respectively, the Japanese share $(=\sum Q_{iJ}/Q_{iW})$ in world production of manufactures and world expenditures, and substituting in equation 29, we get

(32)
$$m_J^N = 1 - \frac{s_J^P}{s_J^E} .$$

If the manufacturing sector produces a single homogeneous product, Japan will either import or export that product, but not both. If it imports it, m_J^N will be the share of imports; if it exports the product, m_J^N will be the negative of the share of exports in domestic use. This equation is the starting point for several of the econometric studies of Japan's trading structure, particularly those of Saxonhouse.

Suppose that the manufacturing sector consists of a number of varieties of the same product denoted by i, with each country producing a different variety. Then it follows that $\Sigma Q_{iJ} = Q_{JJ} = Q_{Jw}$. In other words, Japan's total output of ΣQ_{iJ} manufacturing consists of the output Q_{JJ} of the Japanese variety J; it also equals the world output of variety J since, by assumption, no other country produces this variety. Further, it also implies that $M_{JJ} = 0$, $X_{iJ} = 0$ for $i \neq J$, that is, that Japan does not (and indeed cannot) import the Japanese variety or export any non-Japanese variety. Since Japanese exports X_{JJ} by definition equal the rest of the world's consumption of variety J, given the assumption of identical and homothetic preferences, we get $X_{JJ} = (1 - s_J^E)Q_{JJ}$. Hence m_J, Japanese imports as a share of Japanese consumption, is given by

(33)
$$m_J = \frac{\sum\limits_{i \neq J} M_{iJ}}{\sum\limits_i C_{iJ}} = \frac{\sum\limits_i C_{iJ} - Q_{JJ} + X_{JJ}}{\sum C_{iJ}} = 1 - \frac{s_J^E Q_{JJ}}{s_J^E \sum\limits_i Q_{iW}} = 1 - s_J^P .$$

Thus the share of Japanese imports of manufactures in consumption equals the rest of the world's share in production. One could rewrite equation 33 by noting that Japanese consumption of manufactures, ΣC_{iJ}, equals $(s_J^E / 1 - s_J^E)$ times the rest of the world's consumption and that Japanese consumption of variety J, $Q_{JJ} - X_{JJ}$, equals $(s_J^E / 1 - s_J^E)$ times its exports, X_{JJ}, so that

(34)
$$m_J = 1 - x_J ,$$

where x_J is the share of the Japanese variety in the rest of the world's consumption. Equations 33 and 34 form the basis for the regressions run by Lawrence (1987). It is easy to see that these two equations continue to hold if Japan produces more than one variety of the manufactured products as long as the same set of varieties is not produced elsewhere.

According to equations 32, 33, and 34, there is no presumption that Japanese import penetration ratios have to be similar to those of other industrial countries or that they have to have a similar increasing trend over time, although by the assumption of homothetic preferences the ratio of consumption of manufactures to expenditure is the same across all countries. The ratios will be similar only if s_j^P / s_j^E (or s_j^P in the case of differentiated products) is similar to that of other comparable countries. Unless it is postulated that the levels and trends in the factors (technology, factor endowments, productivity trends, and so on) that determine s_j^P / s_j^E are the same in Japan as elsewhere, such a strong conclusion cannot follow. We should hasten to add, however, that none of the econometric studies discussed below attempts to test this extreme version. Rather, they test the hypothesis that s^P / s^E (or s^P, as the case may be) is determined by the same function of the same factors in Japan as elsewhere. Hence, for these authors, the relevant question is not whether Japan's import penetration ratio is lower than that of, say, the United States or the EC but whether it is lower than can be explained by the differences in the levels of the factors that determine s^P / s^E in Japan as compared to the United States or the EC.

There are alternative econometric approaches to explaining import penetration ratios. One approach is to derive the import penetration ratio from a theoretical model. Equation 32, 33, or 34, supplemented by a theory of what determines s^P / s^E or s^P, would be such a model. From the theoretical model one proceeds to its econometric specification and estimation, as indeed Saxonhouse and Stern (1988) do. They relate net exports of individual sectors linearly to factor endowments and derive this relationship from an appeal to the Heckscher-Ohlin model. Leamer (1988) also follows the same approach. Saxonhouse and Stern also derive an estimating equation that is based on the Helpman-Krugman model of product differentiation and economies of scale and in which factor endowments are included as explanatory variables. This estimating equation is also used in the later study of Saxonhouse (1988). Another approach is an eclectic one that proceeds *directly* to an econometric specification relating import penetration ratios to some set of explanatory variables and estimates the relationship. Although the choice of the explanatory variables may be informed by theory, there is no pretense that the estimated relationship is being deduced from a tightly structured theory. The studies of Bergsten and Cline (1987), Balassa (1986), and Balassa and Noland (1988) fall into this category. The study of Lawrence (1987) shares some features of both approaches. In our view, however, its theoretical underpinning is not significant enough for it to be classified under the first approach.

For testing whether Japan is different from the rest of the world, once again there are at least two possible approaches. In the first, the model explaining import penetration is estimated without including Japanese observations, and the predictions for Japan from the estimated model are statistically compared with their actual values. This is the approach of Saxonhouse. In the second approach, a dummy variable taking the value of one for Japanese data and zero for others is included among the set of explanatory variables of the model. The model is estimated with data from all countries including Japan. This is the approach of Bergsten and Cline (1987), Balassa and Noland (1988), and Lawrence (1987).

The two approaches are not equivalent, except when the data consist of a single cross-section. In this case, the residual for Japan in the first approach is the coefficient of the dummy in the second if both approaches have the same explanatory model and only the non-Japanese observations determine the parameters (other than the dummy) in both. If we assume that the model explains the data from other countries satisfactorily, then in the first approach a *failure* of the model to predict Japanese import penetration ratios means that the estimated explanatory model is inadequate for Japan. This means that either a model with a different set of explanatory variables or the same model with a different set of coefficients than the estimated ones is appropriate for Japan. However, in the second approach, if the model satisfactorily explains all observations, Japan could be different only in the sense that the average or mean import penetration ratio for Japan at any given value of explanatory variables is different from that of other countries. In other words, the behavioral difference between Japan and other countries, if any, is assumed to take this specific form, and Japanese observations influence the estimates of all other parameters.

The first approach allows for Japan to differ from others more generally. If there is more than one cross-section one cannot, in principle, rule out the possibility that the second approach leads to the conclusion that Japan's behavior is no different from that of others (that is, the coefficient of the dummy variable for Japan is statistically insignificant) yet there may be a distinct pattern to the residuals of Japanese observations from the predictions of the model, suggesting that Japan's behavior is indeed different.

From a statistical testing point of view, the second approach is simpler in that it reduces to the question of whether the dummy variable has a coefficient significantly different from zero. In the first approach, particularly when data from a single cross-section are used, one needs to construct "tolerance intervals" (Srinivasan 1979), within which the Japanese observations can be expected to lie if the model estimated for other countries were to be applicable. These intervals are different from forecast intervals. Saxonhouse uses the somewhat inappropriate forecast interval for his test. With a single cross-section, the forecast interval test and the dummy variable test are equivalent if the same explanatory model is used.

Finally, the most important point is that either approach can answer only the question of whether Japan's behavior is different from that of others but not why it is different — if it is. Thus, there is no basis for concluding that the difference in behavior as indicated, for example, by the studies of Lawrence (1987) or Balassa and Noland (1988) is due to trade barriers. Even if additional evidence of the existence of trade barriers — that was not incorporated in the econometric model — is presented alongside the econometric test (as is done by Balassa and Noland) to reach this conclusion, such evidence has to be viewed on its own merits alone. It cannot have any rigorous statistical standing analogous to conclusions based on an econometric test.

Let us turn briefly to the individual studies. As mentioned earlier, Lawrence's regressions are derived from equations 33 and 34. However, he regresses the logarithm of the import penetration ratio against the logarithm of output (or export) share and other variables. Since the logic of the economic argument resulting in equations 33 and 34 suggests a linear relationship between the variables themselves and not their logarithms, Lawrence's regression is misspecified. Also, he includes a distance variable without any justification from theory about why its effect should be *additively* separable from that of the production or export share. If that is in fact not the case, the model is misspecified. Further, as Saxonhouse, among others, has pointed out, the regression suffers from a potential simultaneity bias since, obviously, imports, production, and exports are jointly determined. Hence production (or export) share cannot be viewed as an exogenous variable in the regression.

The problems of misspecification and endogeneity of explanatory variables are just as serious in Lawrence's import demand equations. The price elasticities from these equations are used to argue that "normal" price elasticities combined with evidence of underimporting could indicate tariffs or inadequate competition in the distribution system (Lawrence 1987, 539). After all, import demand is by definition *excess demand*. In a structural model, import demand will be the difference between domestic demand and domestic supply, each of which will be specified as a function of appropriate explanatory variables. Even if Lawrence's estimated equation is viewed as a reduced form (thus ignoring the possible endogeneity of GNP and relative import price for a large trader such as Japan), the coefficient of the relative price variable cannot be interpreted as a demand elasticity.

Finally, one could argue that what Lawrence has shown is that the "frictionless" model based on equations 33 or 34 does not fit the data. After all, the estimated values of the intercept coefficients of production or export share differ significantly from the values to be expected from a frictionless model. As such, if the *estimated model* cannot be rationalized by an appeal to theory, the finding that Japan under-imports relative to the predictions of such a model is neither here nor there. We can illustrate this by an extreme example. Suppose we have data on import penetration ratios for 1989 for 100 countries other than Japan. If we include in a linear regression some ninety-seven arbitrary explanatory variables besides a constant term and dummy for Japan, we are likely to get a very high R^2 (though not high $\bar{R}$)! Surely, even if the dummy turns out to be significantly negative, not much analytical or policy significance can be inferred from it.

Balassa and Noland (1988, appendix C), who build on the earlier work of Balassa (1986), regress the share of each of *three* categories of imports (primary, manufactured, and total) from each of *three* sources (developing countries, industrialized countries, and the world) on a set of explanatory variables including logarithm of per capita income, logarithm of population, arable land per capita, per capita value of mineral production, per capita value of oil production, a transportation cost variable, and dummy variables for Japan, the EC, and the European Free Trade Association. The equations were estimated with annual data for the period 1973-83 for eighteen industrial countries. The estimated coefficient of the dummy variable for Japan is significantly negative for manufactured and total imports from all three sources and significantly positive for primary imports from the world as a whole.

As is the case with Lawrence's import demand equation, this study should also be interpreted as a reduced form of an unspecified structural model. It is obvious how the estimated model is related to received theory. In addition, some of the explanatory variables cannot be considered exogenous. For example, while oil or mineral endowments can be reasonably viewed as exogenous, oil production and mineral production are certainly endogenous. It is also not evident why per capita (rather than per unit of total output) production of these resources is the appropriate explanatory variable. In any case, a similar specification by Bergsten and Cline (1987) with a subset of explanatory variables used by Balassa and Noland for total imports led to an insignificant coefficient for the dummy variable for Japan. Although some of the criticisms by Balassa and Noland of the Bergsten and Cline study are well taken, the fact that neither model is based on a reasonably well-specified theory makes it difficult to draw any strong policy conclusions from either the statistical significance or lack thereof of the dummy variable for Japan.

Saxonhouse has examined Japan's trade structure in great detail in several papers, but the focus here is on the most recent paper (1988). His starting point is that in a frictionless world with each country j producing its own variety of sector i output, identical and homothetic preferences across countries, and balanced trade, the imports M_{ij}^+ of sector i varieties into country j will equal $S_j(Q_i - Q_{ij})$, where S_j is country j's share of world income, Q_i is the world output of sector i varieties, and Q_{ij} is country j's output of its own sector i variety. Similarly, exports X_{ij}^+ by country j of its own variety of sector i product equal $(1 - S^j)Q^j$. Once factor price equalization and the equality of number of goods and factors are assumed, equations for Q_{ij}, Q_i, S_i can be written in terms of the factor endowments of country j and world factor endowments. With the additional twist that only the prices of efficiency units of factors are equalized across countries, Saxonhouse estimates the parameters of the model, including factor efficiency coefficients.

Although Saxonhouse's estimating equations appear to be grounded in sound theory, there may be a problem in estimating a model with sixty-one sectors and only six factors when the theory assumes an equal number of goods and factors. Also, as Balassa and Noland point out, the factor efficiency coefficients may in fact reflect trade barriers, in which case a simultaneity bias may arise if the residuals from the regression also partly reflect the effect of trade barriers. Further, there may be heteroscedasticity in residual variances since Saxonhouse estimates absolute values (rather than shares of GNP or apparent use) of imports. Finally, as already mentioned, there is a statistical problem with his use of a forecast interval or an equivalent t-test to test whether Japan's behavior is consistent with the predictions of the model estimated by excluding Japanese observations.

By far the most careful econometric specification, well grounded in theory, is that of Leamer (1988), although his study is not aimed at analyzing Japanese trade behavior. His model uses the trade-intensity ratio (exports plus imports divided by

GNP) as the dependent variable and resource endowments and distance to markets as the basic explanatory variables. As he points out, "trade barriers are *assumed* to be . . . the only important omitted variables and these are *uncorrelated* with the included variables" (emphasis added). As he readily admits, these are extremely strong assumptions. The basic theoretical model is the standard Heckscher-Ohlin-Samuelson model with identical and homothetic tastes, constant returns to scale, equal numbers of goods and factors, and factor price equalization. Thus the predicted net trade N_{ij}^* of sector j in country i is $\beta_j' V_i$, where V_i is the vector of resource endowments and β_j is a vector of parameters depending on tastes, technologies, and prices. The residual E_{ij} - N_{ij} - N_{ij}^* is, as mentioned earlier, assumed to reflect the effect of trade barriers. A measure of openness defined by Leamer is

$$\left[\sum_J \left| N_{ij}\right| - \left| N_{ij}^*\right| \right] / GNP_j .$$

Another measure is

$$\sum_J \left| N_{ij}\right| / \sum_J \left| N_{ij}^*\right| .$$

Countries are ranked by degree of openness using one of these measures. Japan turns out to be moderately open. However, Leamer admits to a "feeling of skepticism regarding the usefulness of the adjusted (for size of economies as measured by GNP) trade intensity ratios as indicators of trade barriers — what seems clear is that, in the absence of direct measures of barriers, it will be impossible to determine the degree of openness for most countries with much subjective confidence" (Leamer 1988, 198-99). This conclusion applies equally to all the econometric studies reviewed in this section.

Finally, *none* of the econometric studies reviewed is dynamic. It is hard to reconcile the static equilibrium model of the theory with its estimation from observations that most certainly do not represent equilibria but disequilibrium to various shocks.

Summary and Conclusions

The discussion of the preceding two sections leads one to conclude that there is no basis in trade theory for the hypothesis that Japan's import penetration ratios ought to be comparable to those of other high-income industrial countries. Furthermore, empirical studies purporting to show that Japan imports too little for a country at its stage of development and with its income are subject to serious biases. On the other hand, simulations from a rather tightly structured but very simple model of increasing returns to scale and intraindustry trade also suggest that Japan's import penetration ratios are low. However, the model is simplistic, and the assumptions on which the simulations are based are too gross for the results to be taken as anything more than suggestive. In any case, none of the empirical studies and simulations *directly* links the observed import penetration ratios of Japan with appropriately defined and measured indicators of the extent of barriers to trade. Yet the fact that the simulations as well as the econometric studies, in spite of the differences in their methodology, sources, and extent of bias, all point in the same direction suggests that the issue of whether there are subtle but effective barriers to imports in Japan will remain an open question pending a satisfactory empirical analysis.

What about other determinants of trade volumes and patterns? Clearly, if trade is balanced, then the value of imports equals the value of exports. As such, a low share of imports in income means a low share of exports as well. Thus, one could argue that if the barriers erected by Japan's trading partners against imports from Japan restrained Japan's exports, then those barriers, rather than impediments erected by Japan, would explain Japan's low import / GNP ratios. Indeed, barriers against Japanese exports predate the current era of "voluntary" export restrictions. It should also be noted that Japan's massive trade and current account surpluses and the increase in U.S. and other industrialized country import penetration ratios are of fairly recent origin, while Japan's import penetration ratios have been relatively constant for a much longer time.

It is well known, although sometimes forgotten, that the current account balance is primarily a macroeconomic phenomenon. Trade policy interventions, such as import protection or export subsidization, that are aimed at affecting the *patterns* of trade would not influence this balance, at least as a first approximation. Nor is there anything abnormal in terms of either economic theory or historical experience in a country's accumulating a substantial fraction of its income as current account surpluses — Great Britain in the nineteenth century and the United States in the post-World War II era (until recently) both did so.

That households in Japan save a substantially higher proportion of their income than do households in trading partner countries, that nonhousehold sectors including government have not offset this, and that aggregate savings exceed domestic investment imply, through the national income and expenditure identity, high current account surpluses. A number of factors influence Japanese savings and investment, and many of them are discussed by Balassa and Noland (1988). Several measurement problems, such as treatment of depreciation, and accounting conventions, such as the classification of purchases of consumer durables as consumption, also lead to an exaggeration of Japanese savings ratios (Hayashi 1986). Furthermore, the aging of the Japanese population suggests that the household savings rate will begin to come down as the dissavings of the elderly comes to dominate the savings of the young.

It is sometimes suggested that the Japanese tend to buy Japanese products even when cheaper imports are available. To attribute this behavior to Japanese tastes is of course no explanation. In any case, there can be a valid economic basis for such behavior where the market price of a product is only one of its many characteristics. After all, most economic transactions have changed considerably from the old pattern of transactions between anonymous agents involving homogeneous products whose characteristics are common knowledge. Today's transactions are in fact package deals, involving alternative combinations of such factors as quality (itself multidimensional), speed and certainty of delivery, and after-sales services. Agents involved in such transactions are likely to have dealt with each other over an extended period, and the transactions are often governed by implicit contracts. Reputation and trust are essential features of such contracts. Given these conditions, it is not irrational or peculiar for Japanese consumers to continue to buy Japanese products until the foreign supplier has established a good reputation. On the other hand, if indeed there are barriers to entry, foreign producers will be unable to establish their reputation.

The United States has recently named Japan, along with Brazil and India, as a target for possible action under the Super 301 section of the Omnibus Trade Act of 1988. Such a move would be a unilateral action, taken without any recourse to the appropriate forum within the General Agreement on Tariffs and Trade (GATT). Leaving aside the issue of the effectiveness of such a threat in opening Japanese markets for U.S. exports, can it be rationalized under the articles of the GATT? Jagdish Bhagwati (forthcoming) puts the issue as follows: first, if underimporting by Japan is established beyond dispute and is viewed as prima facie evidence that Japan is cheating on the obligations it accepted in successive GATT rounds of multilateral trade negotiations, then Article XXIII of the GATT may apply. Article XXIII refers to "impairment" of the benefits extended to other members, entitling them to withdraw their own concessions if the situation is not remedied. Thus, according to this argument, Japan is not being asked to liberalize unilaterally but only to observe the commitments it undertook in the GATT rounds. Second, the GATT negotiations are based on the reciprocal exchange of concessions. If other GATT members, having failed to take Japan's business practices and buyer preferences accurately into account, overestimated the impact of Japanese concessions on their exports to Japan, they are entitled to reopen the issue on the grounds that the original exchange was not really a matching or balanced one.

Neither argument is really persuasive. Strictly speaking, the agreements in various rounds of negotiations related largely to tariff cuts, and Japan has fulfilled the commitments it undertook in this regard. Whether tariff concessions have been offset by increases in nontariff barriers is another matter. (In any case, few GATT signatories, including above all the United States, are entirely innocent in their use of GATT-sanctioned or GATT-inconsistent nontariff measures.) Complex issues are involved in the question of whether GATT signatories overestimated the impact of Japanese concessions and, if so, what the appropriate remedy should be. On the one hand, one should in principle assume that negotiators are fully informed and have rational expectations when they come to an agreement. If an agreement can be reopened because a party to it claims to have been uninformed or to have had the wrong expectations, the system will have no stability. On the other hand, only in the never-never land of the Arrow-Debreu model are all future contingencies common knowledge so that agreements can be written specifying the actions required of each party in each contingency. In the real world, all contracts are necessarily incomplete.

The option of renegotiation improves the efficiency of the system, and so the reopening of past agreements prior to their expiration should not be altogether ruled out.

Nor, as a practical matter, is it necessarily the case that negotiators know the implications of their own proposals. For example, Brown and Whalley (1980) used a computable general equilibrium global trading model to compare the welfare effects of the tariff-cutting proposals of the United States, EC, Japan (two), and Canada (two) with the compromise formula, proposed by Switzerland, that was actually adopted during the Tokyo round. They found that the United States would have gained the least with its own proposal and the most under one of the Canadian proposals. Japan would have gained considerably less under either of its own proposals than under the U.S. proposal or one of the Canadian proposals. This is hardly surprising, given the immense complexity of computing the general equilibrium effects of tariff cuts. And yet the results do not necessarily contradict the presumption of rational expectations and behavior on the part of negotiators. Gains in consumer welfare may not have been their sole objective. And strategic behavior may have been involved as well. If one knows that one's proposal will be viewed with suspicion and will eventually be changed, the better strategy may not be to offer a proposal that promises the most gains but rather to obtain these gains through modifications of others' proposals.

The argument that a successful action by the United States in opening contested markets will improve the functioning of the multilateral trading system is disingenuous. If indeed the affected countries are maintaining trade barriers in violation of their commitments as signatories of the GATT, it is very likely that a successful U.S. action under Super 301 will simply induce them to open their markets to exports from the United States at the expense of exports from less powerful competitors to the United States in their markets.

Unfortunately, action under Super 301 is only the latest instance of a trend away from a rule-based multilateral liberal trading regime toward bilaterally negotiated arrangements for politically managed trade. Other examples include voluntary export restraints and voluntary import expansion involving quantitative targets. This trend characterizes not only U.S. trade policy but that of other Organization for Economic Cooperation and Development countries as well. And managed trade arrangements can also be negotiated multilaterally — the most notorious example is the Multifiber Arrangement. While it originated as a short-term arrangement in 1961 relating to trade in cotton textiles, it has been extended many times and its coverage expanded. Both developed and developing countries were willing to negotiate this arrangement despite its obvious conflict with the principles of the GATT. Now, instead of strengthening the GATT by using its procedures to settle trade disputes, the United States, with its unilateral Super 301 action, has arrogated to itself the right to be simultaneously prosecutor, jury, and judge. The risk is that such a step may end up destroying the GATT while invoking the principles that embody it.

Appendix

Gross National Product 1987

Japan (billion yen)	345,292
USA (billion dollars)	4526.7
Japan (billion dollars; 144.64 yen = 1 dollar)	2387.3
Ratio of U.S. GNP to that of Japan	1.896

Source: IMF (1989; for Japan, pp. 311, 312; for the United States, p. 548).

Exports, Imports, and Current Account Balance, 1987

	Exports	*Imports*	*Current Account*
Japan (billion yen)	43,817 (12.68)	30,748 (8.90)	87* (3.64)
USA (billion dollars)	332.0 (7.33)	484.5 (10.70)	143.09 (3.16)

*Billion dollars. Figures in parentheses are percentages of GNP.
Source: IMF (1989; for Japan, p. 312; for United States, p. 548).

Employment and Working Hours

	*Total**	*Agriculture mining, and manufacturing**	*Working hours per week*
USA	114	25.15	38.0
Japan	59	19.22	43.6

*Millions of people.
Source: Employment data for 1987 are from
OECD (1989, 25, 91, and 107); working hours are
from Foreign Press Center (1987, 56).

Consumption of Traded Goods (1986)

USA		
	Total personal consumption of durable and nondurable goods (billion dollars)	1341.8
	Labor force (million)	119.5
	Per worker consumption	$11,228.5

Source: Council of Economic Advisers (1988, 264, 284).

Japan   (a)   Total per household consumption expenditure
per month less spending on housing, medical
care, education, reading and recreation $1283

           (b)   Total population (1985; million)   121.05

                Household size (1985)   3.22

                Number of households (1985; million)   37.59

           (c)   Labor force (1985; million)   59.63

                Workers per household   59.63 / 37.59 =   1.59

           (d)   Consumption of traded goods per
worker per year = (1283 x 12) / 1.59 =   9683

Source: (a) Keizai Koho Center (1988, 86); (b) Foreign Press Center (1987, 10 and 16); (c) OECD (1989, 29).

Note

I wish to thank Koichi Hamada for permission to draw on our joint work on the Japan-U.S. trade problem. I also thank Jagdish Bhagwati, Robert Lawrence, Hugh Patrick, and Gary Saxonhouse for their valuable comments on an earlier version without implicating them in my conclusions and errors.

References

Balassa, B. 1986. "Japan's Trade Policies." *Weltwirtschaftliches Archiv* 122: 745-90.

Balassa, B., and M.H. Noland. 1988. *Japan in the World Economy*. Washington, D.C.: Institute for International Economics.

Bergsten, F., and W. Cline. 1987. *The United States-Japan Economic Problems*. Policy Analysis in International Economics No. 13. Washington, D.C.: Institute for International Economics.

Bhagwati, J.N. Forthcoming. "U.S. Trade Policy Today." *The World Economy*. Department of Economics, Columbia University.

Brown, F., and J. Whalley. 1980. "General Equilibrium Evaluations of Tariff-Cutting Proposals in the Tokyo Round and Comparisons with More Extensive Liberalization of World Trade." *Economic Journal* 90: 838-66.

Council of Economic Advisers. 1988. *Economic Report of the President*. Washington, D.C.: U.S. Government Printing Office.

Foreign Press Center. 1987. *Facts and Figures of Japan*. Tokyo: Foreign Press Center.

Hayashi, F. 1986. "Why Is Japan's Savings Apparently So High?" In *NBER Macroeconomic Annals*. Cambridge, Mass.: National Bureau of Economic Research.

International Monetary Fund. 1989. *International Financial Statistics*. Washington, D.C.

Keizai Koho Center. 1988. *Japan 1988: An International Comparison*. Tokyo: Keizai Koho Center.

Krugman, P. 1979. "Increasing Returns, Monopolistic Competition and International Trade." *Journal of International Economics* 9: 409-79.

Lawrence, R.Z. 1987. "Imports in Japan: Closed Markets or Minds?" *Brookings Papers on Economic Activity* 2: 517-48.

Leamer, E. 1988. "Measures of Openness." In R. E. Baldwin, ed., *Trade Policy Issues and Empirical Analysis*. Chicago: University of Chicago Press.

Organization for Economic Cooperation and Development. 1989. *Labor Force Statistics: 1967-1987*. Paris: OECD.

Saxonhouse, G.R. 1983. "The Micro- and Macro-Economics of Foreign Sales to Japan." In W. R. Cline, ed., *Trade Policies in the 1980s*. Cambridge, Mass.: MIT Press.

Saxonhouse, G.R. 1986a. "Japan's Intractable Trade Surpluses in a New Era." *The World Economy* 9: 239-58.

Saxonhouse, G.R. 1986b. "What's Wrong in the Japanese Trade Structure?" *Pacific Economic Papers* 137 (July): 1-36.

Saxonhouse, G.R. 1988. *Differentiated Products, Economies of Scale, and Access to the Japanese Market*. Seminar Discussion Paper No. 288. Research Seminar in International Economics, Department of Economics, University of Michigan, Ann Arbor, Michigan.

Saxonhouse, G.R., and R. Stern. 1988. *An Analytical Survey of Formal and Informal Barriers to International Trade and Investment in the United States, Canada, and Japan*. Ann Arbor, Mich.: University of Michigan.

Srinivasan, T.N. 1979. "Tolerance Intervals." Yale University, New Haven, Conn.

12

Export Targeting and Japanese Industrial Policy

Marcus Noland

Perhaps no topic in trade policy has provoked more controversy in recent memory than that of the impact of industrial policies on Japan's trade pattern. Proponents of industrial policy have long argued that the Japanese government has used a variety of policy instruments to affect resource allocation, promote industrial upgrading, and enhance welfare (see, for example, Shinohara 1982). More recently, researchers have demonstrated the theoretical possibility of welfare-enhancing industrial policies (see, for example Itoh and Kiyono 1987 and Okuno-Fujiwara 1988) and have begun to evaluate Japanese industrial policy in terms of modern strategic trade policy theory (Tyson and Zysman 1989).

But it is one thing to demonstrate the theoretical possibility of welfare-enhancing industrial policies and quite another to actually implement them. Implementation, at a minimum, would require that policymakers identify the correct sectors for targeting and design the proper instruments to execute the policy. Most mainstream economists remain skeptical that this can be done (see, for example, Trezise 1983, Schultze 1983, and Komiya 1988).

One noticeable aspect of the industrial policy literature (other than its frequently polemical tone) is the dearth of positive analysis.[1] Surprisingly, there has been very little empirical modeling of the possible impact of industrial policy measures. There has been no attempt simply to correlate measures of actual policy intervention with outcomes as a first step in determining the magnitude and direction of policy impact.

This neglect may be due in part to the inherently unquantifiable nature of some of the policy tools. Administrative guidance and the encouragement of cartels are not amenable to quantification. Nonetheless, other direct policy interventions are subject to systematic quantification and analysis, and it is these interventions that this study examines. First, the tools of Japanese industrial policy are surveyed, and multisectoral data on effective rates of protection, capital subsidies, and research and development (R&D) subsidies are presented. These data are then regressed against Japanese exports. As it turns out, the capital and R&D subsidies are shown to be correlated with both contemporaneous Japanese comparative advantage and its subsequent evolution.

Several possible explanations for these results are discussed. One possibility is that the observed policies have simply conformed to the underlying pattern of comparative advantage and have had no independent impact on the trade pattern. This possibility is investigated through cross-country regressions of factor endowments on trade. These are used to generate counterfactual data on Japanese exports to control for the influence of factor endowments on Japan's trade specialization. The deviations of observed export shares of national income from their predicted values are then regressed against the industrial policy variables. If industrial policy measures have had no impact on the trade pattern, then the estimated coefficients on these variables should be insignificant. Estimates for the subsidy measures are in fact insignificant, although protection appears to depress the export level.

Industrial Policy Tools

Saxonhouse (1983) has identified five policy instruments that the Japanese government might use to promote favored industries directly: protection from foreign competition, direct subsidies, subsidies through the tax code, preferential access to credit, and special aid through government procurement. This list, while not exhaustive, provides a convenient starting place to review Japanese industrial policy. These instruments are discussed under the broad categories of effective rates of protection, capital subsidies, and subsidies to research and development.

Effective Rates of Protection
In manufacturing, Japanese tariffs were historically higher than those maintained by the United States and the European Community (EC). Through successive rounds of reductions, Japan has lowered tariffs on manufactures so that they are generally comparable to (if not somewhat lower than) those of the United States and the EC. In the high technology area, which is of special industrial policy interest, Japan in the 1970s had special tariffs on integrated circuits and computers (and computerized numerically controlled machine tools, which were classified as computers), but these were eliminated after the signing of the Tokyo Round agreements in 1979.

Quotas are limited mainly to light industry (textiles, apparel, shoes, and leather products) and affect mostly the less developed countries. Other nontariff barriers, especially discriminatory standards, testing, and certification requirements, are more ubiquitous and may involve a significant amount of import suppression (Leamer 1989a, b). There is also extensive anecdotal evidence of "invisible barriers" — informal government and private practices that restrict imports. Their quantitative significance is difficult to evaluate, and estimates of their aggregate importance vary widely (see Balassa and Noland 1988, app. C). In the high technology sector, prominent examples of these nontraditional import barriers include the apparent closure of the Japanese semiconductor market in the early 1980s (Baldwin and Krugman 1986), exclusionary public procurement practices in supercomputers, and the prohibition of government procurement of foreign satellites (USTR 1989).

Effective rates of protection (ERPs), computed by Shouda (1982) from tariff data and the Japanese input-output table, are shown in table 12.1.[2] In 1968, ERPs were greater than 10 percent in all manufacturing sectors except publishing, where the ERP was negative. The highest ERPs — more than 40 percent — were in food processing, textile products, and transportation machinery. The estimates for food processing and textile products are probably upwardly biased indicators of the true ERPs, however, since major inputs to these products were subject to quota protection that was not included in the ERP calculation.

Table 12.1 Effective Rates of Protection for Industrial Goods in Japan, 1968, 1975, and 1987

Industry	1968	1975	1987[a]
Traded Goods	24.9	19.3	15.8
Primary	5.9	5.5	4.5
Agriculture	7.6	9.4	7.6
Forest	-1.0	-0.1	-0.1
Fishery	13.9	8.2	6.7
Mining	-0.6	-0.7	-0.5
Manufacturing	26.7	20.6	16.9
Food processing	45.4	55.6	54.1
Textile spinning	21.0	10.8	12.5
Textile weaving	33.6	92.6	94.2
Textile products	41.0	35.4	35.1
Wooden products	18.7	8.9	6.6
Pulp and paper	21.9	21.9	13.5
Publishing	-3.4	-3.3	-2.3
Leather and rubber	26.0	23.5	22.0
Chemicals	18.9	15.7	12.3
Petroleum and coal Products	10.9	6.7	7.0
Nonmetallic mineral products	17.7	8.8	6.4
Iron and steel	28.9	20.8	14.9
Nonferrous metals	31.0	32.2	20.1
Metals products	18.7	8.6	6.3
General machinery	17.9	8.2	6.2
Electrical machinery	21.0	13.4	6.5
Transport machinery	45.4	5.4	1.4
Precision machinery	27.3	8.7	7.2
Miscellaneous products	28.0	20.4	9.9

Note: Effective rates of protection are based on tariffs only.
a. Estimated.
Source: Shouda (1982).

By 1975, ERPs had fallen for most manufacturing categories. The reductions were most dramatic in the machinery sector; ERPs fell by approximately 40 percentage points for transportation and by 20 percentage points for precision machinery. Excluding the aberrant cases of food processing and textiles, estimated ERPs for 1987 (based on tariff cuts agreed to under the Tokyo Round negotiations) are under 10 percent for most manufacturing categories. Thus, rates of protection have generally fallen over a twenty-year period. Although these calculations are based on tariff protection only and the sectors are relatively aggregated, the distinct impression emerges of a gradual liberalization in most manufacturing sectors.

Capital Subsidies

A second tool for promoting industries is direct subsidies. But conventional wisdom among economists is that direct subsidies have played little role in fostering changes in Japan's trade specialization. Indeed, more than 90 percent of on-budget subsidies go to the declining sectors of agriculture, forestry, fishing, and coal mining (Ogura and Yoshino 1988, table 1). One study by the Japanese government found that only one sector, food processing, received direct subsidies exceeding 0.1 percent of GDP originating in that sector (Saxonhouse 1983).

Sometimes overlooked, however, is the role of indirect subsidies through the tax system and off-budget finance. The primary source of subsidized capital is the Fiscal Investment and Loan Program (FILP), under the control of the Ministry of Finance Trust Fund Bureau. This off-budget program is about half the size of the general accounts budget and has been a powerful policy tool. Using FILP as a second or "shadow" budget, bureaucrats were able to address priorities not met in the general accounts budget.

Funds for the FILP come mainly from the postal savings system. Private sector investments are also financed through public financial institutions such as the Japan Development Bank, the Export-Import Bank, and the Housing Loan Corporation. Although in the early postwar period much of FILP finance went into strengthening industry, the share of FILP funds going to industry has steadily fallen, while housing, regional development, and other activities have received larger shares.

The public financial institutions offer loans at rates below the prevailing market interest rate. This implicit subsidy has been calculated as the difference between interest rates charged by private and public sector financial institutions multiplied by the amount of government financial institution loans:

$$(1) \qquad\qquad LOANSUB_i = L_i^* \, (rp_i - rg_i),$$

where L is the amount of public financial institution loans, rp and rg are private and government financial institution interest rates, and the subscript i indicates industry.[3]

A second source of implicit capital subsidy is the tax system.[4] In computing corporate income, corporations are allowed to deduct the acquisition cost of machinery and equipment from their annual incomes over a number of years, depending on the stipulated asset life. This system spreads the tax reductions over a certain period of time, but it does not take into account interest costs and inflation over the relevant period. Hence the longer the stipulated asset life, the longer the period over which the tax saving arising from depreciation is spread and the lower the present value of the tax reduction. The corporate tax burden with respect to investment goods can thus be reduced by shortening stipulated asset lives, even without changing tax rates.

Special depreciation schemes have existed in Japan throughout the postwar period. The most important of these had the effect of subsidizing certain classes of investment goods.[5] In addition, an export-based special depreciation system existed from 1961 to 1972.[6] The special tax depreciation can be thought of as an interest-free loan. Thus, the subsidy value of the special depreciation provisions is the implicit interest burden reduction associated with the loan, or

$$(2) \qquad TAXSUB_i = [\sum_{l}^{l_1} (SPDEP*t)(1-rp_i)^{l_i}]*rp_i,$$

where *SPDEP* is the amount of the special depreciation, t is the corporate tax rate, l is the average lifetime of capital, and r is the effective rate of interest.[7]

An indication of the quantitative significance of the implicit capital subsidies is given in table 12.2, which reports the implicit capital subsidy to investment ratio for twelve industries in 1968, 1976, and 1984. In general, the low interest rate loans have been of greater quantitative significance than the special depreciation provisions. With the exception of mining, where investment has been weak and the involvement of public financial institutions high, the implicit capital subsidy to investment ratio has been low — generally less than 5 percent. After mining, the greatest beneficiary of the reduced interest burdens has been the transportation machinery industry, which includes shipbuilding, motor vehicles, and aircraft.[8]

Table 12.2 Capital Subsidy-Investment Ratio for Selected Industrial Goods in Japan, 1968, 1976, 1984
(percentages)

Industry	1968			1976			1984		
	Loan	Tax	Total	Loan	Tax	Total	Loan	Tax	Total
Mining	9.38	1.36	10.74	13.28	1.48	14.76	3.83	1.29	5.12
Food processing	0.65	0.49	1.14	1.24	0.81	2.05	0.51	0.46	0.97
Textiles	0.66	1.60	2.26	2.59	0.88	3.47	0.22	0.51	0.73
Pulp and paper	0.01	0.26	0.27	0.03	0.66	0.69	0.03	0.42	0.45
Chemicals	0.71	0.54	1.25	1.63	0.39	2.02	0.44	0.17	0.61
Iron and steel	0.50	0.87	1.37	1.39	0.58	1.97	1.52	0.96	2.48
Nonferrous metals	0.48	0.46	0.94	8.40	0.34	8.74	0.62	0.35	0.97
Metal products	0.85	1.16	2.01	1.52	0.75	2.27	0.57	0.63	1.20
General machinery	0.35	0.50	0.95	2.02	0.43	2.45	0.28	0.20	0.48
Electrical machinery	0.37	0.84	1.21	1.25	0.47	1.72	0.39	1.45	1.84
Transportation machinery	2.95	0.79	3.74	3.76	0.71	4.47	0.56	0.20	0.76
Precision instruments	na	na	na	0.54	0.47	1.01	0.05	na	na

Source: Ministry of Finance; Ogura and Yoshino (1985); Economic Planning Agency, *Gross Capital Stocks of Private Enterprises*.

Research and Development Subsidies

Certain tax and budget policy provisions have been used to promote high technology sectors beyond the relatively uniform low subsidy ratios reported in table 12.2. There are special depreciation provisions for the purchase of numerically controlled machine tools, computers and terminals, computer-aided design equipment, and industrial robots. Additional tax incentives exist for the use of these products by small businesses, although the amounts appear to be relatively small. Other special tax provisions exist for the software industry.[9]

The Japanese computer and robotics industries have been further assisted by the Japan Development Bank and by Small Business Finance Corporation funding, including the establishment of special leasing corporations to encourage the leasing of Japanese computers and robots, especially by small firms. Unlike the tax provisions, which are justified on the ground of promoting the diffusion of new technologies and do not discriminate between domestic and foreign products, the leasing schemes specifically apply to Japanese-made equipment. The amounts of money involved appear relatively small, however.

The government has also promoted high technology sectors through direct subsidies to R&D activity, special deductions for R&D costs, and the provision of low-interest loans by public financial institutions. Tax preferences have been provided through a variety of schemes.[10] The most important channel in quantitative terms has been the system of research contracts on large-scale industrial technology R&D established in 1966. Of particular significance were subsidies to promote the development of computers in the 1970s and research contracts on next-generation industrial technology (new materials, biotechnology, and new electronic devices) in the 1980s.

Private R&D has also been subsidized through the provision of low interest loans by public financial institutions for "financing development of new technology."[11] Private R&D activities are provided indirect support by a number of government-supported institutions. These include national and public research institutes, private nonprofit research organizations, special public corporations, and the mining and manufacturing technology research associations (such as the Very-Large Scale Integration Research Association).

In quantitative terms, the direct subsidies are the most important component of government R&D support, running about twice the size of the tax provisions in recent years. Implicit subsidies through the provision of low interest loans have been relatively unimportant. Government support for research organizations is approximately as large as direct subsidies.

Assessing the sectoral pattern of R&D support is difficult. Direct subsidies from the government, public corporations (such as Nippon Telephone and Telegraph), and special public corporations are reported at the sectoral level. Special R&D tax deductions are reported only at the aggregate level. The amount of sector-specific indirect support through the research associations is difficult to ascertain, partly because individual associations frequently encompass more than one sector and partly because the budgets of these organizations include private as well as government funding.

Data on the government subsidy share of total R&D expenditures are reported in table 12.3. Government support of R&D activities is low; total government support (allowing for nonsubsidy financing) is certainly less than 5 percent of total R&D expenditures for the economy as a whole, far less than the comparable figure for the United States. In terms of individual sectors, government R&D support as a share of total R&D has been highest in the declining mining industry. After mining, support has been highest in the energy-related sector of petroleum and coal products and, as in the case of capital subsidies, the transportation equipment industry, which includes aerospace.

Table 12.3 Government Subsidy Shares of Total Research and Development, 1968, 1976, 1984

Industry	1968	1976	1984
Mining	3.2	3.2	14.0
Food processing	0.0	0.1	0.4
Textiles	0.7	0.2	1.1
Pulp and paper	0.8	0.3	0.0
Chemicals	0.5	0.3	0.8
Petroleum and coal Products	1.0	0.3	7.2
Nonmetallic products	1.0	0.8	1.8
Iron and steel	0.2	0.6	1.7
Nonferrous metals	0.8	1.5	2.9
Metal products	0.1	0.2	0.2
General machinery	1.4	2.2	1.2
Electrical machinery	1.7	1.5	1.4
Transportation machinery	1.0	4.4	4.7
Precision instruments	1.8	0.3	0.1

Source: *Kagaku Gijutsu Kenkyu Chosa Hokoku* (Report on the Survey of Research and Development), various issues.

Perhaps of equal or greater importance than its role as a provider of R&D funds has been the government's role as "doorman...determining under what conditions capital technology and manufactured products enter and leave Japan" (Borrus, Tyson, and Zysman 1986, 98). Put another way, the Japanese government has used its various policy levers to bargain with foreigners from the standpoint of a monopsonist. Goto and Wakasugi (1988) provide the example of royalty payments on imports of an Austrian steel production technology which were "held down to 1 cent per ton for Japan through an agreement between MITI [Ministry of International Trade and Industry] and the industry, while U.S. firms paid up to 35 cents per ton" (p. 190). Borrus, Tyson, and Zysman provide examples from the microelectronics industry in the 1960s and early 1970s of Japanese government use of its monopsonist power to extract technology transfers from U.S. firms. Most recently, the dispute over the FSX fighter agreement could be interpreted as an attempt by the U.S. government to use its market power to counterbalance the Japanese government's monopsony position vis-à-vis McDonnell Douglas. Common to these cases has been a pattern of selective protection, strict regulation of inward foreign direct investment and technology transfer, and preferential tax treatment and access to capital until the industry achieves international competitiveness. Rosovsky (1985) has called this pattern "the denial of the profits of innovation."

Impact of Industrial Policy Measures on Trade Specialization

To investigate the impact of industrial policy on Japan's trade pattern, industry exports were regressed against the industry ERP, the total (loan plus tax) capital subsidy, and government R&D subsidies.[12] The regressions were estimated for the largest set of industries for which a complete data set could be assembled.[13] The ordinary least squares cross-section regressions were estimated for five years (1968, 1972, 1976, 1980, 1984). Breusch-Pagan (1979) Lagrange multiplier tests revealed no evidence of heteroscedasticity. The regression results are reported in table 12.4.

The policy variables appear to explain a surprisingly large share of cross-sectional variance in exports. The coefficients of the capital subsidy variable (*CAPSUB*) and R&D subsidy variable (*R&DSUB*) were significant with the expected signs in two and four cases, respectively. The coefficients of the capital

Table 12.4 Regression Results for Contemporaneous Relationship Between Exports and Industrial Policy Measures in Japan, Selected Years

Year	Dependent variable	Constant	ERP	CAPSUB	R&DSUB	RBAR**2
1968	X	141.09 (0.53)	-0.17 (-0.48)	1.80 (3.67)[a]	0.58 (2.37)[b]	.64
1972	X	678.14 (0.98)	-0.14 (-0.53)	1.70 (1.72)	0.29 (1.86)	.70
1976	X	-490.13 (-0.34)	-0.03 (-0.17)	4.06 (2.93)[b]	0.91 (4.15)[a]	.86
1980	X	-2697.47 (0.65)	0.05 (0.30)	0.11 (0.03)	1.36 (4.55)[a]	.68
1984	X	2247.73 (0.53)	0.03 (0.21)	0.15 (0.03)	1.35 (7.13)[a]	.81

Note: X = exports (millions of current dollars); *ERP* = effective rate of protection multiplied by domestic sales (100 million current yen); *CAPSUB* = accumulated value of capital subsidy (100 million current yen); *R&DSUB* = R&D subsidy (100 million current yen). The superscript a indicates a coefficient significantly different from zero at the 1-percent level; b indicates significance at the 5-percent level. Coefficients on *CAPSUB* and *ERP* have been scaled by a factor of 10 for purposes of presentation.

subsidy variable were significant in 1968 and 1976, while the coefficients of the R&D subsidy variable were significant in 1968, 1976, 1980, and 1984. In contrast, the coefficients of the ERPs are statistically insignificant in all five regressions. The values of the estimated coefficients vary considerably from regression to regression. This is not surprising since the regressions were estimated in current values, and price levels and exchange rates changed substantially over the sample period. It is consequently difficult to summarize with any degree of precision the impact of subsidies on exports, although the impact is statistically significant.[14]

A related topic of interest in the industrial policy debate is the degree to which policy interventions have been forward-looking. This was investigated by regressing the industrial policy variables on exports eight years later. (Alternatively, these regressions could be interpreted as tests of the extent to which policy interventions have had long-lasting, or persistent, effects.) These results, reported in table 12.5, are even more compelling than those reported in table 12.4. Industrial policy variables from 1968 explain a greater share of variance and take larger and statistically more significant coefficients when regressed against 1976 exports than the contemporaneous policy variables did. Similarly, the 1976 explanatory variables explain more of the variance of 1984 net exports than the contemporaneous variables did. The R&D subsidy variable is statistically significant in all three regressions reported in table 12.5, while the capital subsidy variable is significant in one of the three cases.

**Table 12.5 Regression Results for Eight-Year
Leading Relationship Between Japanese Exports
and Industrial Policy Measures, Selected Years**

Dependent variable	Independent variables				RBAR**2
	Constant	ERP	CAPSUB	R&DSUB	
X1976	-1422.85 (-1.87)	-1.37 (-1.38)	1.54 (11.09)[a]	4.44 (6.41)[a]	.95
X1980	2598.57 (0.87)	-0.71 (-0.60)	0.88 (1.88)	1.66 (2.53)[b]	.79
X1984	3791.41 (0.96)	0.02 (-0.04)	0.08 (0.22)	3.90 (6.55)[a]	.87

Note: X = exports (millions of current dollars); *ERP* = effective rate of protection multiplied by domestic sales (100 million current yen); *CAPSUB* = accumulated value of capital subsidy (100 million current yen); *R&DSUB* = R&D subsidy (100 million current yen). The superscript a indicates a coefficient significantly different from zero at the 1-percent level; b indicates significance at the 5-percent level. Coefficients on *CAPSUB* and *ERP* have been scaled by a factor of 10 for purposes of presentation.

Alternative Hypotheses

The results reported in tables 12.4 and 12.5 reveal a strong statistical relationship between industrial policy variables and pattern of exports. The results could be interpreted as indicating the direct impact of industrial policy on the trade pattern. They do not, however, establish a causal relationship between policy interventions and observed outcomes, nor do they prove that Japanese policymakers were able to "pick winners." At least two other hypotheses are consistent with these results.

First, the pattern of statistical significance obtained in table 12.4 (the capital subsidy variable is significant in the earlier periods, the R&D subsidy variable in the later periods) is consistent with the results reported by Balassa and Noland (1989), who analyzed the evolution of Japanese comparative advantage without reference to policy variables. That is, the explanatory variables in table 12.4 may be instruments that are picking up the "natural" evolution of Japanese comparative advantage. In particular, the ability of firms to exploit many of the special tax provisions will be positively associated with profitability and investment. Thus the use of special depreciations, for example, may be a response to emerging comparative advantage in a particular sector rather than a leading indicator of it. Likewise, increases in capacity through investment may be a prelude to exporting. Consequently, causality may run from emerging comparative advantage to investment and interest subsidies to exports, rather than from subsidies to investment to comparative advantage and exports.

A second explanation consistent with the reported results is presented by Saxonhouse (1983). He argues that Japan's generally low and relatively evenly distributed subsidies (reported in tables 12.2 and 12.3) make it doubtful that these industrial policy measures could be driving changes in Japan's trade pattern. Rather, industrial policy has historically acted as a substitute for a well-developed equity market.[15] In his view, industrial policy is essentially a signaling device, identifying sectors of future promise. This could thus be interpreted as a variant of "picking winners."

One can test the hypothesis that policy interventions have driven the changes in Japan's trade pattern against the alternative hypothesis that the changes are attributable to the "natural" evolution of comparative advantage. This can be done by using a well-specified model to generate counterfactual data on "natural" comparative advantage and then analyzing the extent to which deviations of the observed trade pattern from the counterfactual predicted trade pattern are associated with industrial policy. This is an obvious extension of this research. The other alternative hypothesis, that industrial policy acts as a substitute for the equity market, appears to be essentially untestable.

To test the former hypothesis, the starting point is a Helpman-Krugman model of differentiated products by country of origin. A country's output (Q), is produced from a factor-use matrix (A) and a set of endowments (V):

(3) $$Q = A^{-1}V.$$

World output can be described similarly:

(4)
$$Q_w = A^{-1}V_w.$$

Under the assumption of identical homothetic utility functions and factor price equalization, each country consumes each variety of the commodities in the same proportion:

(5)
$$C = sQ_w,$$

where s is the country's share of world output, and C is its consumption vector.

Trade balance implies that the value of production is equal to the value of consumption, so that

(6)
$$p'Q = p'C = sp'Q_w,$$

where p is the price vector. Thus, if trade is balanced, the consumption share is the production share of world output:

(7)
$$s = p'Q / p'Q_w.$$

The vector of imports is the difference between the country's production and consumption shares:

(8)
$$M = s(Q - Q_w).$$

Exports are the excess of domestic production over domestic consumption (including imports):

(9)
$$X = Q - sQ_w.$$

Substituting equation 5 into equation 9 and dividing through by national income, yields:

(10)
$$X / p'Q = (Q / p'Q) - (Q_w / p'Q_w) = (A^{-1}V / p'Q) - (Q_w / p'Q_w),$$

that is, the commodity export share of national income is a function of national income, world income, technology, and factor endowments. This model, applied to commodity import shares, has been previously estimated by Saxonhouse (1988). The following equation is estimated for each commodity group:

(11)
$$X_{ij} = a + \Sigma b_{ik}V_{kj} + u_{ij},$$

where X_{ij} is the exports of commodity i as a share of national income of country j; a is the industry share of world income (a constant term); V_{kj} is the endowments of resource k of country j as a share of national income; b_{ik} is the coefficient indicating the impact on export share of commodity i of an increase in the kth endowment; and u_{ij} is the disturbance term.[16]

Equation 11 was estimated for a cross-section of twenty-nine countries (excluding Japan), the largest sample for which complete trade and endowment data sets could be constructed for 1968, 1972, 1976, 1980, and 1984.[17] Japan was excluded from the sample so as not to "contaminate" with industrial policy effects the parameter estimates used to construct the projected Japanese trade data described below. (Data definitions and sources are described in greater detail in the appendix.) The explanatory variables consisted of the constant term, nine factor endowments (labor, physical capital, human capital, arable land, pasture land, forest land, coal, oil, and minerals), and the cif / fob ratio, which was used as a proxy for transport costs.[18] Since the variable X_{ij} is truncated at zero, a Tobit estimator was used to estimate equation 11.[19]

The estimated coefficients from these regressions and data on Japanese factor endowments were used to construct predicted values of Japanese export shares. The deviations between the actual values of Japanese export shares and these predicted values were then regressed against the policy variables. If Japanese industrial policy measures have had no impact on the trade structure, then the policy variables should be uncorrelated with the dependent variables.

The counterfactual data were pooled to construct a panel data set, and regressions, on both the contemporaneous and lagged explanatory variables, were estimated using the appropriate random effects estimator.

The results, reported in table 12.6, are quite interesting in light of the results obtained earlier. There is no evidence that the subsidies had an impact on exports distinct from what could be attributed to Japan's factor endowment. This suggests that the correlation between the subsidies and Japanese exports reported earlier may have been due to the "market conforming" character of the policy interventions, rather than to any causal relationship. In contrast, the coefficient on the ERP is negative and statistically significant in both regressions. This could be interpreted as indicating that, on average, protection discouraged exports, presumably by raising the relative rate of return on domestic sales. This result, though quite plausible, appears to weigh against the emphasis in much of the industrial policy literature on the role of protection in fostering infant industries.

It must be reiterated, however, that these results rest on the adequacy of the model used to generate the underlying counterfactual data. In particular, Noland (1989), using a Heckscher-Ohlin-Vanek model, reports results that suggest that the capital and R&D subsidies have had a significant impact on the cross-commodity pattern of Japanese net exports, while the impact of protection has been negligible. This underlines the provisional nature of the results reported in this section.

**Table 12.6   Regression Result for Relationship Between
Deviations from Predicted Exports and
Industrial Policy Variables**

Dependent variable	Independent variables				RBAR**2
	Constant	ERP	CAPSUB	R&DSUB	
Contemporaneous Relationship					
X -FITTED X	0.04	-0.74	-0.10	0.02	0.61
	(0.63)	(-7.35)[a]	(-0.95)	(1.26)	
Eight-Year Lagged Relationship					
X -FITTED X	-0.15	-0.97	-0.05	0.02	0.15
	(-1.16)	(-2.29)[b]	(-0.11)	(0.41)	

Note: X = exports (millions of current dollars); *ERP* = effective rate of protection multiplied by domestic sales (100 million current yen); *CAPSUB* = accumulated value of capital subsidy (100 million current yen); *R&DSUB* = R&D subsidy (100 million current yen). The superscript a indicates a coefficient significantly different from zero at the 1-percent level; b indicates significance at the 5-percent level. Coefficients on *CAPSUB* and *ERP* have been scaled by a factor of 10 for purposes of presentation.

Conclusion

Few issues in trade policy have been as contentious as that of the impact of industrial policy on Japan's trade structure. This study has reviewed the evidence on a variety of policy tools such as protection, direct and indirect subsidies, and special tax treatment.

Regressions of these quantifiable industrial policy tools on Japanese exports indicate that capital and R&D subsidies are significantly correlated with actual sectoral exports. The causal relationship between the subsidies and export performance is unclear, however, and several hypotheses were advanced to explain the observed statistical relationship. One possibility is that the subsidies were "market conforming" and merely mimicked the natural evolution of Japanese comparative advantage. To explore this possibility, a cross-national factor endowment model was estimated to generate counterfactual data on Japanese exports in the absence of industrial policy interventions. Deviations between actual and predicted exports were then regressed against the policy measures. The results indicated that the subsidies were completely uncorrelated with the pattern of exports, once factor endowments were taken into account, while protection discouraged exports.

These conclusions are tempered by three major qualifications. First, the level of sectoral aggregation imposed by data constraints is far higher than is desirable. Second, the test of industrial policy effects, controlling for factor endowments, may be quite sensitive to the specification of the model used to generate the counterfactual trade data. And third, the issue of less formal or quantifiable forms of industrial policy intervention has not been addressed. These policies, including formal and informal restrictions on inward foreign direct investment and monopsony bargaining for technological transfer, may have played and may continue to play an important role in Japan's industrial development. They will certainly be an important issue for future research.

Appendix

Data on exports, imports, and factor endowments were collected for the years 1968, 1972, 1980, and 1984 for the twenty-nine countries listed in footnote 17 of the text, plus Japan. This country sample was determined by data availability.

The trade data originate from General Agreement on Tariffs and Trade (GATT) tapes. The labor endowment is defined as the economically active population; the data come from the International Labor Organization *Yearbook of Labor Statistics*. The capital stock was calculated by summing and depreciating the purchasing power adjusted gross fixed investment series found in Summers and Heston (1984). The asset life of capital was assumed to be eighteen years and the depreciation rate 13 percent.

Human capital is calculated by multiplying the economically active labor force by the Psacharopoulos index of the per capita educational capital. The Psacharopoulos index is defined as the average per capita expenditure on education embodied in the labor force calculated from data on highest level of educational achievement, years of schooling at each level, and expenditures per year at each level normalized by the amount of expenditure for one year of primary school education. Data on educational achievement and schooling duration are from the United Nations Educational Social and Cultural Organization (UNESCO) *Statistical Yearbook*. Expenditure weights come from Psacharopoulos (1973).

Data on land endowments come from the Food and Agricultural Organization (FAO) *Production Yearbook*.

The coal endowment was measured by domestic production in thousands of metric tons and comes from the U.S. Bureau of Mines *Minerals Yearbook*. (Data on coal mining capacity or reserves were unavailable for most countries.) The minerals index is the value of domestic production of thirteen minerals; the production data are from the *Minerals Yearbook*, and the price data are from the International Monetary Fund (IMF) *International Financial Statistics (IFS)*. The composition of this index was determined by taking the top twenty minerals (excluding oil, natural gas, and coal) in terms of the value of world output in 1984 and then dropping those for which price data could not be found. The oil endowment in proven reserves was taken from the American Petroleum Institute *Oil and Gas Yearbook*.

The cif / fob data come from the IMF, *IFS Trade Supplement*.

Where data for Taiwan were unavailable from these sources, data were taken from *Taiwan Statistical Data Book*, Council for Economic Planning and Development, Executive Yuan Republic of China.

Notes

1. Eads and Yamamura (1987) contains an exhaustive bibliography of Japanese and English language sources. See also the volume edited by Komiya, Okuno, and Suzumura (1988).
2. The ERPs for the primary products sectors are misleading because they do not take into account quotas (in agriculture) and subsidies (in agriculture and mining).
3. This was calculated as follows. Interest and discounts paid to the public financial intermediaries for each of the industries were deducted from total interest payments and discounts as presented in the Ministry of Finance, *Corporate Enterprise Statistics* (Hojin Kigyo Tokei), and the resulting figure was divided by industry borrowing from private financial institutions to get a figure for the nominal rate of interest charged by these organizations. This was then converted into the effective rate of interest by adjusting for bank deposits by industry from the *Corporate Enterprise Statistics*, and the rate of return on deposits from Bank of Japan, *Economic Statistics Annual*.
4. This discussion follows Ogura and Yoshino (1988).
5. Prior to 1951, a system of accelerated depreciation for important machinery was in effect, which allowed an additional 50-percent write-off over and above the normal depreciation for certain types of machinery and equipment. In 1951 this accelerated depreciation system was expanded to cover machinery acquired for the "rationalization of industry" (50-percent write-off of the purchase price in the first year), and "experimental equipment" (50-percent write-off in the first year, 20-percent in the second and third years). These provisions were so generous that in the 1950s, 50 percent of the cost of a new automobile factory could be written off in the factory's first year in operation (Saxonhouse 1983).
   Over time, the designation of machinery and equipment eligible for these provisions became increasingly more specific and complex, and in 1961 the system was reformed. The three-year "experimental equipment" system was scrapped, and items formerly covered under this scheme were incorporated into the general depreciation system. The first-year depreciation on "rationalization" machinery was reduced to 33 percent of acquisition cost. At the same time, however, stipulated asset lives of machinery and equipment were reduced by an average of 20 percent. In 1964, the first-year write-off for "rationalization" machinery was reduced to 25 percent, but stipulated asset lives were further reduced in 1966. The importance of the special tax provisions declined through the 1960s, with a slight reversal in the early 1970s when the definition of "rationalization" machinery was broadened.
6. This system permitted a firm with rising exports to claim a special depreciation equal to the product of the increase in its export-sales ratio and the amount of normal depreciation. The multiplier was reduced to 80 percent of the increase in the export-sales ratio in 1964, increased to 100 percent in 1966, and reverted to 80 percent in 1971. Additional special increases in depreciation, depending on export product, were introduced in 1968, but withdrawn in 1971. The whole system of export-based special depreciations was abandoned in 1972, but much of it was allegedly absorbed into the "rationalization" machinery provisions.
7. Data on the amount of the special depreciation, average life of fixed assets, and the corporate tax rate come from the Ministry of Finance, *Fiscal and Monetary Statistics Monthly*. See Ogura and Yoshino (1985) for further details on this calculation.
8. Japanese policymakers also have access to off-budget funds for industrial promotion through the revenues of quasi-public organizations such as the Motor Boat Racing Association and the Japan Bicycle Rehabilitation Association (Prestowitz 1988). The amounts of these funds do not appear particularly large, however. Saxonhouse (1983)

cites *The Wall Street Journal* to the effect that no more than $500,000 a year from these sources was made available to the Japan Machine Tool Builders Association.

9. The tax benefits are not dependent on the origin of the purchased software or equipment, so the impact of these provisions has been to expand the Japanese market for these products, not to assist Japanese manufacturers *per se*. Likewise, special provisions that allow computer manufacturers to deduct expected losses on the return of equipment offered to users on a trial basis do not discriminate by origin and thus in principle could be used by domestic manufacturers, local subsidiaries of foreign manufacturers, or importers.

10. The first tax preference scheme was the previously mentioned special depreciation allowances on machinery for experimental R&D of new technology introduced in the 1950s. In 1966, tax deductions on experimental research expenditures were introduced to allow firms to deduct a fixed proportion (currently 20 percent) of their experimental research expenditures in the current year over and above the highest expenditures in previous years, up to 10 percent of the firm's total corporate tax payments. Firms are also allowed to deduct the purchase value of the fixed assets of officially sanctioned research cooperatives from taxable income entirely in the year of acquisition. Other tax provisions have allowed firms to offset some of the costs of acquiring foreign technology.

11. The Small Business Finance Corporation has been particularly active in providing finance to small and medium-size businesses for the development and commercialization of new technologies. The government-funded Center for the Promotion of R&D-Oriented Firms guarantees up to 80 percent of private lending to small and medium-size firms for R&D on new technology.

12. Since the capital subsidy will have an impact not only in the current period, but for the lifetime of capital, the flow series were deflated by an investment goods price series, summed, and depreciated to get an estimate of the implicit capital subsidy stock.

13. These were mining, food processing, textiles, pulp and paper, chemicals, petroleum and coal products, nonmetallic products, iron and steel, nonferrous metals, metal products, general machinery, electric machinery, transportation machinery, and precision machinery. The high degree of industry aggregation is necessitated by data availability constraints, and caution is warranted in assessing the subsequent results.

14. The small number of data points could potentially be made larger by constructing a pooled time-series cross-section panel data set. The variability in the underlying exchange rates and price levels and the large variability in coefficients across equations imply that it would be difficult to obtain unbiased coefficient estimates from a pooled regression in this application. This approach is pursued, however, in a somewhat different context in the next section.

15. Some skepticism about this argument with regard to current reality is understandable since the Tokyo stock market has the highest capitalization rate in the world.

16. Saxonhouse also includes a country-specific factor quality parameter in his regressions.

17. The countries are Argentina, Austria, Brazil, Canada, Denmark, Finland, France, Federal Republic of Germany, Greece, Hong Kong, Indonesia, Israel, Italy, Republic of Korea, Malaysia, Mexico, Norway, Pakistan, Peru, the Philippines, Singapore, Spain, Sweden, Taiwan, Thailand, Tunisia, Turkey, United Kingdom, and the United States.

18. Alternatively, one could think of locational proximity as an endowment.

19. Detailed results are available from the author.

References

Balassa, B., and M. Noland. 1988. *Japan in the World Economy*. Washington, D.C.: Institute for International Economics.

Balassa, B., and M. Noland. 1989. "The Changing Comparative Advantage of Japan and the United States." *Journal of Japanese and International Economies* 3: 174-88.

Baldwin, R., and P.R. Krugman. 1986. *Market Access and International Competition: A Simulation Study of 16K Random Access Memories*. NBER Working Paper 1936. Cambridge, Mass.: National Bureau of Economic Research.

Bank of Japan. Various years. *Economic Statistics Annual*. Tokyo.

Borrus, M., L. D'Andrea Tyson, and J. Zysman. 1986. "Creating Advantage: How Government Policies Shape International Trade in the Semiconductor Industry." In P. R. Krugman, ed., *Strategic Trade Policy and the New International Economics*. Cambridge, Mass.; MIT Press.

Breusch, T.S., and A.R. Pagan. 1979. "A Simple Test for Heteroscedasticity and Random Coefficient Variation." *Econometrica* 47: 1287-94.

Council for Economic Planning and Development, Executive Yuan Republic of China. Various years. *Taiwan Statistical Data Book*. Taipei.

Eads, G.C., and K. Yamamura. 1987. "The Future of Japanese Industrial Policy." In K. Yamamura and Y. Yasuba, eds, *The Political Economy of Japan*. Vol. 1, *The Domestic Transformation*. Stanford, Calif.: Stanford University Press.

Food and Agricultural Organization (FAO). Various years. *Production Yearbook*. Rome.

Goto, A., and R. Wakasugi. 1988. "Technology Policy." In R. Komiya, M. Okuno, and K. Suzumura, eds, *Industrial Policy of Japan*. San Diego, Calif.: Academic Press.

International Labor Organization. Various years. *Yearbook of Labor Statistics*. Geneva.

International Monetary Fund (IMF). Various years. *International Financial Statistics*. Washington, D.C.

Itoh, M., and K. Kiyono. 1987. "Welfare-Enhancing Export Subsidies." *Journal of Political Economy* 95: 115-37.

Komiya, R. 1988. "Introduction." In R. Komiya, M. Okuno, and K. Suzumura, eds, *Industrial Policy of Japan*. San Diego, Calif.: Academic Press.

Komiya, R., M. Okuno, and K. Suzumura, eds 1988. *Industrial Policy of Japan*. San Diego, Calif.: Academic Press.

Leamer, E.E. 1989a. "The Structure and Effect of Nontariff Barriers in 1983." Department of Economics, University of California, Los Angeles.

Leamer, E.E. 1989b. "Latin America as a Target of Trade Barriers Erected by the Major Developed Countries in 1983." Department of Economics, University of California, Los Angeles.

Ministry of Finance, Government of Japan. Various years. *Corporate Enterprise Statistics*. Tokyo.

Ministry of Finance, Government of Japan. Various years. *Fiscal and Monetary Statistics Monthly*. Tokyo.

Noland, M. 1989. "The Impact of Industrial Policy on Japan's Trade Specialization." Institute for International Economics, Washington, D.C.

Ogura, S., and N. Yoshino. 1985. "Tokubetsu Shokyaku, Zaisei Toyushi to Nihon no Sangyo Kozo" ["Impacts of Accelerated Depreciation and Government Loan Programs on Japanese Industrial Structure"]. *Nihon Keizai Kenkyu* 36 (April): 110-20.

Ogura, S., and N. Yoshino. 1988. "The Tax System and the Fiscal Investment and Loan Program." In R. Komiya, M. Okuno, and K. Suzumura, eds, *Industrial Policy of Japan*. San Diego, Calif.: Academic Press.

Okuno-Fujiwara, M. 1988. "Interdependence of Industries, Coordination Failure and Strategic Promotion of Industry." *Journal of International Economics* 25: 25-43.

Prestowitz, C.V., Jr. 1988. *Trading Places*. New York: Basic Books.

Psacharopoulos, G. 1973. *Returns to Education*. San Francisco: Jossey-Bass.

Rosovsky, H. 1985. "Trade, Japan, and the Year 2000." *New York Times*, 6 September 1985.

Saxonhouse, G.R. 1983. "What Is All This About 'Industrial Targeting' in Japan?" *The World Economy* 6 (September): 253-74.

Saxonhouse, G.R. 1988. *Differentiated Products, Economies of Scale, and Access to the Japanese Market*. Seminar Discussion Paper No. 228. Ann Arbor: Research Seminar in International Economics, University of Michigan.

Schultze, C.R. 1983. "Industrial Policy: A Dissent." *Brookings Review* (Fall): 3-12.

Shouda, Y. 1982. "Effective Rates of Protection in Japan." *Nihon Keizai Kenkyu* 11 (March): 68-70.

Shinohara, M. 1982. *Industrial Growth, Trade, and Dynamic Patterns in the Japanese Economy*. Tokyo: University of Tokyo Press.

Summers, R., and A. Heston. 1984. "Improved International Comparisons of Real Product and Its Composition, 1950-80." *Review of Income and Wealth* 30 (June): 207-62.

Trezise, P.H. 1983. "Industrial Policy is Not the Major Reason for Japan's Success." *Brookings Review* 1 (spring): 13-18.

Tyson, L. D'Andrea, and J. Zysman. 1989. "Preface: The Argument Outlined." In C. Johnson, L. D'Andrea Tyson, and J. Zysman, eds, *Politics and Productivity*. Cambridge, Mass.: Ballinger.

United Nations Educational Social and Cultural Organization (UNESCO). Various years. *Statistical Yearbook*. New York.

United States Bureau of Mines, Department of the Interior. Various years. *Minerals Yearbook*. Washington, D.C.

United States Trade Representative (USTR). 1989. "'Super 301' Trade Liberalization Priorities." USTR, Washington, D.C.

Yamamura, K. 1986. "Caveat Emptor: The Industrial Policy of Japan." In P. R. Krugman, ed., *Strategic Trade Policy and the New International Economics*. Cambridge, Mass.: MIT Press.

South

13

Development Economics and the General Agreement on Tariffs and Trade

J. Michael Finger

What trade policies best support economic development? Over the past forty years, developing countries have tried many different approaches and recorded many different outcomes. Their experiences have been analyzed for policy lessons by many scholars, among whom Béla Balassa has been one of the leaders. Also, the international community has developed a system of rules, the General Agreement on Tariffs and Trade (the GATT) that attempts to guide countries toward certain policy choices and away from others. One might presume that the parts of the GATT relating to developing countries reflect the knowledge these scholars have sorted out of experience. That presumption would be incorrect, however. The process of rules making or institution building, it seems, has a momentum quite separate from the emergence of knowledge about what works. Nobel laureate James M. Buchanan (1984, 5) makes the point as follows: "Institutions do matter — over the long run perhaps far more than the adoption of this or that policy option or the election of this or that politician or party."

In this essay, I compare the evolution of GATT rules about what policy choices a developing country should take with the growth of knowledge about what trade policies are effective. The first section, which reviews this growth of knowledge, is brief because its content is familiar. Balassa's and others' studies of developing countries' actual experiences tended to show that countries did well when they followed what classical economics would prescribe as reasonable trade and exchange rate policies. The thrust of the GATT toward developing countries, a less familiar matter, occupies the next three sections. In these sections, I explain how the GATT has come to institutionalize a set of economic presumptions shown to be inappropriate by the work reviewed in the first section.

The institutional structure, having been established without incorporating the "new" ideas and facts about trade and development, now serves to keep these concepts out. Developing countries, although very active at the Uruguay Round, have been reluctant to bring forward proposals based on economic concepts other than those embodied in the present rules. Thus proposals based on the experiences of the successful developing countries are excluded from consideration. This neglect is a significant loss to the international community. The experiences of successful developing countries have considerable potential to guide the improvement of international rules — rules that could not only pass the lessons of experience from one developing country to another but could also help *developed* country governments resist growing internal pressures for import restrictions. Such matters are taken up in the fifth section of this essay.

The Growth of Knowledge: Developing Countries' Experiences as Validation of Classical Economics

Perhaps the problem was a simple matter of timing. The important decisions that determined the economics of the GATT were made in the 1950s and 1960s, whereas the "new" research on the role of trade in development gained momentum later — its arrival perhaps best signaled by the almost simultaneous publication in 1970-71 of Balassa's *The Structure of Protection in Developing Countries* and of Little, Scitovsky, and Scott's *Industry and Trade in Some Developing Countries.*

I have put the word "new" in quotation marks because even in the 1950s there were strong and clear applications of classical economics to the problems of development, particularly by Jacob Viner (1953) and Gottfried Haberler (1959)[1] — applications arguing that developing countries should avoid direct trade controls and impose at most a modest tariff. Although the "new" economics came wrapped in a new technology, these ideas are close to its central policy conclusions. In essence, what Viner and Haberler took as postulates the new research formulated and tested as hypotheses, then presented as conclusions.

Such thinking was, however, a long way from mainstream development thinking in the 1950s. Ian Little refers to Haberler and Viner as "rebels," and adds that "their opponents would have referred to them as orthodox neoclassicists" (Little 1982, 75). But, Little explains, they were not "orthodox" in the sense that their views coincided with those of policymakers or even with those of economists who wrote mostly about development. "Certainly, United Nations officials were not in this camp, and almost no developing country policymakers would have endorsed such views" (p. 75).

It is interesting to see the orthodox view of development through the eyes of one of the rebels. Viner, in the third of his National University of Brazil lectures of 1950, stated:

All that I find in Prebisch's study and in the other literature along similar lines emanating from the United Nations and elsewhere is the dogmatic identification of agriculture with poverty, and the explanation of agricultural poverty by inherent natural historical laws by virtue of which agricultural products tend to exchange on ever-deteriorating terms for manufactures, technological progress tends to confine its blessings to manufacturing industry, and agricultural populations do not get the benefit of technological progress in manufactures even as purchasers, because the prices of manufactured products do not fall with the decline in their real costs (1953, 44).

Popular development thinking separated itself not only from conventional economic thinking but from conventional economic history as well. Compare, for example, the following two statements. The first is from Viner:

No country except the United States has attained a high level of per capita income which has not maintained a high ratio of imports to total national product, and no country, except possibly Russia, can in this respect make the United States its model without courting perpetual poverty. The high degree of self-sufficiency of the United States was due in part to a deliberate national policy of high tariff protection. But it was the continental character of the United States ... as well as the technical skills of its people, which enabled the American [economy] to dispense with foreign products ... [and] to achieve economic prosperity despite its commercial policy and its low ratio of foreign to domestic trade (1953, 116-17).

The second is from Prebisch:

Development [in the nineteenth century and the initial decades of the twentieth] in the periphery was a spontaneous phenomenon of limited scope and social depth; it came about under the dynamic influence of a unique combination of external factors which have since ceased to exist (1964, 6).

History and economic theory were irrelevant, and thus everything had to be *planned* anew. Little (1982, chapters 3 and 4) explains that "planning" was an important element of popular development thinking in the 1950s. This belief was complementary to several other precepts. One was the presumption that "industrialization" and "development" were the same thing. Manufacturing made for good jobs and rich countries; agriculture provided bad jobs and kept countries poor. To raise wages, a less developed country had to establish the industries that had the higher wages in the industrial countries. And, because commodity earnings would inexorably decline and capital goods imports would inexorably be required, less developed countries would have a persistent tendency toward balance of payments problems. There was "the absolute necessity of building up trade in industrial exports" (Prebisch 1964, 20).

Every industrial sector was presumed to be linked to every other one in an "external" way — thus, for example, the ceramics industry could not be world class unless the steel industry was likewise world class. But nothing was linked through profits or prices. Price movements created "monopoly" if prices went up and "poverty" if they went down, but they did not provide "resource allocation" or "efficiency." Efficiency had to be planned in, and because industrialization had to change everything simultaneously if it were to succeed, planning, particularly investment planning, had to be based on the shadow prices that would prevail *after* the plan was achieved. The importance of "structural" rather than price links meant that all-at-one-time or "big bang" changes were necessary. A less developed country could be competitive in manufactured goods *across the board* or not at all. The planned-for big bang would transform a country from an exporter of materials and importer of manufactures to the opposite.

What changed? First Japan changed into an industrial power. Then other Asian-Pacific countries that followed Japan's policy experience began to register similar successes. At the level of public perception, this was the beginning of what Staffan Burenstam Linder calls the "demonstration effect," which eventually engendered among the Asian newly industrialized countries a rising regional confidence in their own development model. A scholarly look could perceive across countries varying degrees of mix of import-substitution versus open trade policies, and for a trained observer, the existence of "varying degrees of" allows identification of "the effects of." In 1970-71 came the Little, Scitovsky, and Scott study and the initial World Bank studies, in which Béla Balassa was the leading researcher (Balassa and associates 1971). These were followed by studies at the Kiel Institute led by Jurgen Donges (1976); the 1978 Bhagwati and Krueger studies for the National Bureau of Economic Research; and, eventually, many others.[2]

Balassa also played a leading role in two related lines of research. For one, his research on the European Economic Community showed that the effects of removing trade barriers was to a large degree an expansion of *intraindustry* trade. There were no major displacements of industries in one country by exports from another. Comparative costs, in general, were not so different, and competition tended to be on a product-variety rather than industry basis. This work (Balassa 1963, 1966) helped to put aside the "big bang" presumption of the 1950s that trade in industrial goods was an "all or nothing" proposition.

Second, Balassa initiated work after the 1974 oil shock to investigate how well developing countries had coped with such external shocks.[3] This work compared again the performances of countries with import-substitution strategies and countries that had export-oriented or open-trade strategies or had shifted signifi-cantly toward open-trade strategies when hit by severe external shocks. Balassa found that countries that continued or shifted to open-trade strategies were significantly more successful in maintaining investment and growth. The popular presumption that less developed countries are hit by relatively large terms of trade shocks was found to be correct. But the research showed that forced import substitution was not the best policy response. The absence of policies to *force* import substitution did not mean that there would be no import substitution, however. Balassa's work showed that neutral policies that allowed relative price changes to work through the economy would induce significant substitution of domestic production for imports of products whose relative prices had increased.

Perhaps the key shift in development thinking came with the realization that less developed countries *could* export manufactured goods and that they could move into such export production a bit at a time. At the level of the mechanics of development thinking, this change involved (or allowed) two significant simplifications. First, observable world prices, not almost-impossible-to-calculate shadow prices, are the relevant measure of alternatives. "For the individual country, world prices are the pivot on which all scarcities turn" (Bell 1987, 824). Second, the project replaces the plan as the intrinsic unit of analysis. These changes did not make enemies of the technocrats. Indeed, the technocrats saw them as a new challenge: finding ways to see, through the mess of country policies, incentives, and disincentives, how far the signals that influenced domestic decisions were from the real scarcities that lay below.

The content of this change of thinking is well-reviewed elsewhere (see, espe-cially, Little 1982), so I will not extend this discussion. In closing this section, however, I want to note the timing of that change. Almost all the rest of the "new" empirical research on trade and development was published in 1970 or later. As I explain below, the economics of the GATT was mostly in place by 1970.

The Initial GATT Negotiations

Kenneth W. Dam, in his well-known study on the GATT, describes it as "a product of U.S. planning and a reflection of certain views that dominated the thinking on trade matters of U.S. diplomats in the 1940s" (1970, 11). Freedom of international commerce had been the third of President Woodrow Wilson's Fourteen Points. To Cordell Hull, Secretary of State for President Franklin D. Roosevelt, the link was straightforward: "[U]nhampered trade dovetailed with peace; high tariffs, trade barriers and unfair economic competition with war."[4] Keeping trade unrestricted was, in the bigger scheme of things, a means to maintain global peace and stability.

As to *how*, the U.S. proposal came down to asking each member country to accept three basic obligations: that it use only approved instruments of trade control, that is, tariffs only; that it apply these instruments in a nondiscriminatory way; and that it submit them to a long-term process of binding and reduction through multilateral negotiation (Hudec 1987, 133).

The mechanics were drawn from the U.S. Reciprocal Trade Agreements Program. Under the Reciprocal Trade Agreements Act of 1934 and its extensions, the United States by 1947 had negotiated and implemented thirty trade-liberalizing agreements, sixteen of them with a developing country. Each agreement contained a provision for a reciprocal exchange of tariff reductions and a framework of other obligations to protect the commercial value of the tariff reductions. There were some specific exceptions from the general framework of obligations, but there was no pattern of special exceptions for developing countries. Indeed, Hudec reports, "the sixteen developing country agreements ... tended to contain fewer special derogations than did the agreements with developed countries" (1987, 7). The United States, in its presentations to the International Trade Organization negotiations in 1946-47, actively opposed special commercial policy conditions for developing countries. The United States held that development was primarily a matter of private capital investment and that special measures to deal with this belonged elsewhere, not in the commercial policy rules of the international system.

Neither the United Kingdom nor France fully supported this position. Both wanted to retain preferential tariff regimes of the traditional "metropol versus former colony" sort, and both wanted to retain the power to protect their own economies from imports in order to promote the reconstruction and eventual growth of their economies. Also behind their reluctance to accept nondiscrimination as a universal principle was the worry that they would never catch up to the United States as exporters of industrial goods. And both of these countries accepted to a much greater degree than did the United States that infant industry protection was an effective way to promote industrialization.

Developing countries argued that import quotas were essential to implementation of other development plans and that preferences for developing countries (that is, discrimination against imports from developed countries) were necessary to promote their own industrialization. At the level of principle, they wanted the international community to recognize explicitly that protection in developing countries would, in the long run, increase trade (Little 1982, 60, 61). Developing country proposals at the International Trade Organization negotiations displayed two major concerns: the desire for a commitment from the developed countries to provide significant resource transfers and the desire for freedom from the general idea of discipline that the arrangement was trying to impose among the other members. Behind developing countries' unwillingness to accept any international discipline over their trade policies, Little sees the following presumptions:

- *First, and this was a grave mistake, they never expected to be able to export manufactures to the industrialized countries; but they might export a little to their [ethnic and geographic] neighbors....*
- *Second, they assumed that the industrialized countries would not protect against raw materials.*
- *Third, on competing farm products (sugar being the most important) the case was probably lost anyway, for the United States itself proposed to exempt farm products from the ban on quotas (1982, 61).*

At a more direct level of concern, developing countries wanted to preserve the manufacturing firms that had grown up during World War II.

As no doubt the reader knows, agreement was never reached on the International Trade Organization. The international rules for commercial policy that were agreed are contained in the GATT. The International Trade Organization draft charter had more tightly circumscribed exceptions for developing than for developed countries. In the GATT, the opposite is true. The draft International Trade Organization charter recognized the right of a country to provide infant industry protection by raising bound tariffs or imposing quotas, but prior approval of the organization was necessary (Hudec 1987, 14). In contrast, no prior approval was required for what might be described as developed country exceptions, such as import restrictions for balance of payments or safeguards reasons.

Article XVIII was the principal provision of the original GATT dealing with the trade problems of developing countries. According to Dam, "The theory of the article is quite simply that less developed countries should be freer than developed countries to impose quantitative and other restrictions in order to protect infant industries and to combat payments imbalances" (1970, 227). Section A of Article XVIII allows protection "to promote the establishment of a particular industry" (para. 7a). Section B allows a developing country to establish restrictions "to safeguard its external financial position and to ensure a level of reserves adequate for ... development" (para. 9). Section B of Article XVIII parallels Article XII, which allows balance of payments restrictions by developed countries, but the Article XVIII criteria are less stringent. For example, consultations are required of developing countries only every second year rather than every year.[5] In sum, the GATT exceptions for developing countries were **circumscribed by** procedural requirements, but the international community, in ratifying the GATT, explicitly acknowledged that the special position of developing countries justified some dispensation from the legal discipline other countries must accept (Hudec 1987, 15).

Why, at the time of organizing the GATT, did the United States allow the position it had negotiated into the draft International Trade Organization charter to be significantly compromised? A major reason seems to be the nature of the negotiations themselves. The overall structure of the negotiations was that the community of nations would agree to a program of discipline on the behavior of individual countries. The underlying conceptualization recognized this discipline as a "cost" to an individual country, but a cost that would be borne in pursuit of a common good. So the acceptance of *individual costs* for the *common good* was the basic trade-off each participant was asked to make — the basic form of the negotiations. In such a context, it is very difficult to ask the weaker members of the community to make the same sacrifice as the stronger. Protestations that commercial policy rules are not the appropriate way to provide for the less fortunate sound like excuses for greed.

Hudec, in his interpretation of the role of developing countries in the GATT, brings out this factor — what one might describe as the influence of Max Corden's conservative social welfare function on relations between rich and poor states. "It is very difficult to convene an enterprise involving rich and poor without having some welfare dimension to the work.... [The] inability to resist this need to give 'something' has been a constant factor in the dynamics of GATT legal policy" (1987, 16).

A second factor pushing toward U.S. agreement on exceptions for developing countries was its desire for some exceptions of its own: for its restrictions on agriculture, its existing safeguards, and antidumping and countervailing duty laws. A third reason was that the United States had no clearly articulated economic argument for the economic benefits each country would receive by participating in an open economic system.[6] The articulated "pro" arguments tended to be political arguments based on strategic considerations and the idea of building a political relationship among the free world countries.

Another point against imposing equal discipline on developing countries was that once these countries had taken a position of asking for this kind of "benefit," granting it began to have immediate political value but no immediate economic or budgetary cost. And finally, the GATT itself was not the forum in which the rules of the international trading game were negotiated. The initial GATT was merely the paperwork used to quickly put in place an already agreed round of tariff cuts. If the agreed tariff cuts were not implemented quickly, pressures to renegotiate would build. Besides, everything but the tariff cuts was considered "provisional" and was expected to be superseded by the International Trade Organization. From the U.S. perspective, the GATT was the bird in the hand of trade liberalization for which it might perhaps be worth letting go a few birds in the bush of exceptions — compromises to the idea of discipline. A nice pragmatic solution — get what you most want now and fix the problems that come with it later.

In the conclusion to the first chapter, Hudec provides a less pragmatic interpretation — indeed, an ominous one:

> *Once it had been conceded, as a matter of principle, that legal freedom constitutes "help" to developing countries, the future was virtually fixed.... When other kinds of "help" were not enough there was always the possibility of doing something more on the legal side. Granting legal freedom to other countries is an easy concession to give, for it requires neither domestic legislation nor the use of other legal powers by the grantor countries. It is possible to "give" merely by doing nothing (1987, 18).*

The Haberler Report and the GATT Action Program

For the first seven or eight years, the GATT system operated more or less by the book.[7] The GATT became, in use, the legal code that the International Trade Organization charter had been intended (at least by the United States) to be. The "contracting parties" (the official GATT language for "member" is "contracting party") overcame the absence of an institutional existence by referring to themselves as the CONTRACTING PARTIES (in all capital letters) when they acted collectively and officially — for example, to determine whether the agreed code had been violated. There were tight reviews of exceptions to the general idea of discipline against import restrictions. "Resort to the infant industry exception in Article XVIII was limited, but what activity there was was treated with some importance.... Balance of payments reviews were carried out with careful scrutiny" (Hudec 1987, 26). In practice, conditions were imposed on the development exceptions, and when developing countries acceded to the GATT they were required to make substantial tariff concessions.

The period 1954-60 saw a considerable shift in the momentum of the GATT. Developing countries pressed for more freedom for infant industry measures and for less reciprocity in the trade-liberalization negotiations. The United States became more concerned with strategic-block issues: the Cold War made the building of a political relationship more important and the United States therefore more willing to give ground on the details of the economic relationship. Consequently, at the 1954-55 review, the GATT was modified to include in its text a statement that the infant industry argument was consistent with its principles.

From that point, the infant industry justification for protection was written in as consistent with the GATT rather than being treated as an excuse for an exception to the GATT. "In the same spirit, the draftsmen deleted a tough-minded sentence in the original text warning that unwise use of such measures would harm both the applicant country and others" (Hudec 1987, 27). In sum, the review session presented an almost enthusiastic endorsement of the principle that freedom from the sort of constraints that the GATT attempted to impose on individual country behavior *helped* the developing countries. So the GATT in the late 1950s was rapidly losing interest in the enforcement of legal discipline on developing countries (although a formalistic compliance was maintained) and was developing an enthusiasm for an infant industry ideology of growth.

At the same time, the trade performance of developing countries began to worry the international community. The trade of developing countries was expanding less rapidly than the trade of the industrial countries, and the industrial countries were also posting better overall economic growth rates. This lagging economic performance of the developing countries spurred the CONTRACTING PARTIES in November 1957 to ask a Panel of Experts to study the matter. The panel was made up of Roberto de Oliveira Campos, Gottfried Haberler (Chairman), James Meade, and Jan Tinbergen. The panel's report, commonly called "the Haberler Report," is described by Kenneth Dam as "perhaps the turning point in the GATT's relations with less-developed countries" (1970, 228).

The terms of reference of the panel begins with an expression of concern "regarding certain trends in international trade, in particular the failure of the trade of less developed countries to develop as rapidly as that of industrialized countries, excessive short-term fluctuations in prices of primary products, and widespread resort to agricultural protection." The panel is charged to provide "an expert examination of past and current international trade trends and their implications, with special reference to the factors referred to above; [and] an assessment of medium-term prospects for international trade in the light of the facts and trends as [the panel] sees them" (Campos et al. 1958, 1).

The report is concerned mostly with trade in primary products and with policies relating to this trade. Of the fifty-seven summary points listed in the first chapter, only one is about manufactured exports. Some twenty concern fluctuations in export earnings or commodity stabilization policies; some twenty more are about the agricultural policies of the industrial countries, including the formation of the European Economic Community (EEC). If the reader interprets as realities the concerns the report expresses about what EEC agricultural policies might become, the discussion of agricultural policies sounds very much like a 1989, rather than a 1957, review.[8]

The report provides a comprehensive response to its terms of reference and does so mostly within the (then) mainstream of development thinking implicit in the terms of reference. For example (the numbers preceding these statements are the paragraph numbers in the report):

22. *It is impossible, upon the evidence now available, to conclude whether or not there has been an increase in agricultural protection in industrial countries in recent years.*

24. *The terms of trade in the post-war period were more favorable to non-industrial countries than in 1938, but recently turned against them ....*

25. *The import requirements of the non-industrial countries are likely to increase more quickly than the rest of world trade....*

26. *The exports of the non-industrial countries are very sensitive to internal policies of industrial countries....*

44. *A number of underdeveloped countries are now exporting low-priced manufactures, the markets for which depend upon moderation in industrial protectionism in the highly industrialized countries.*

The report's conclusions, however, as summarized in the first chapter, demonstrate much broader thinking:

61. *The issues which we have considered in detail in our report affect primarily the policies of the highly industrialized countries; but we consider that they, as well as the primary producing countries, would gain by the proposed changes.*

62. *We think that there is some substance in the feeling of disquiet among primary producing countries that the present rules and conventions about commercial policies are relatively unfavorable to them.*

63. *While the underdeveloped primary producing countries have valid reasons for making a rather freer use of trade controls than the highly industrialized countries, in a number of cases protective policies have been carried too far by these countries; and these countries also have used for the protection of their industries a number of special weapons which are not normally the subject of negotiation with other countries. We have not examined in any detail these problems of protectionism in the non-industrial countries.*

64. *Further progress depends upon the willingness of the industrial and the non-industrial countries to negotiate on a wide range of their economic and financial policies.*

Thus the report concludes that existing arrangements are relatively unfavorable to primary producing countries. While it also concludes that there are valid economic reasons for a developing country to restrict imports, it points out that they have done so to excess and that progress depends on both developed and developing countries reducing their restrictions.[9] The conclusion the report puts first is the crux of the classical economic view of trade policy: a country's import policy reform will have a positive effect on its own economy, not just on the economies of exporting trade partners.

To the diplomatic community, the Haberler report made one point: it verified that developing countries were losing ground under the GATT. Hudec (1975, 209) captures the tone well: "[T]he Haberler Report exploded a good deal of the developed country righteousness by showing that the developing country trade was actually losing ground under GATT." Kenneth Dam, another legal scholar not known for taking a soft line on the matter of GATT discipline for developing countries, argues that "The substance of the report was that the predicament of the underdeveloped countries was due in no small measure to the trade policies of the developed countries" (1970, 229). Thus, in the political world the report's warning about developing countries' own policies was ignored.[10] In effect, the international community overlooked the report's analysis and conclusions.

The thinking implicit in the reports' terms of reference, not the thinking explicit in its conclusions, became the basis for policy actions. The CONTRACTING PARTIES responded with a resolution "to initiate immediate consideration of a coordinated program of action" to embrace three topics: a new tariff round, nontariff protection of agriculture, and other obstacles, particularly to the expansion of developing country exports. "Committee III," which was created to take up the third topic, prepared a number of tabulations of developed countries' import restrictions on a long list of "products of export interest" to developing countries. Later, the CONTRACTING PARTIES created an Action Committee to examine submissions by developed countries of such information and to consult the developed countries "with a view to removing" these trade barriers.

The international community saw the matter as a direct one: developing country exports are lagging; therefore, developed country restrictions are the cause.[11] Only a few maverick intellectuals considered the possibility that the lagging trade performance of developing countries might be explained in significant part by their own policies.

The Haberler Report, the Action Program, and the Action Committee added a new *affirmative action* dimension to the developed-developing country relationship within the GATT. Beyond the developed countries' obligation to exempt developing countries from GATT's normal discipline — that is, to allow them to impose trade restrictions — the developed countries also had an obligation to unilaterally remove their import restrictions on products of export interest to the developing countries. In other words, developed countries were to extend the concessions they agreed to at any further tariff rounds beyond the scope of products traded principally among themselves.

Several other factors also contributed to the changes within the GATT that weakened the belief in the need for policy discipline for developing countries and strengthened the belief that developed countries had an obligation to do something for them. One was a simple matter of numbers. From 1960 until 1970, GATT membership increased from twenty-one developed and sixteen developing countries to twenty-five developed and fifty-two developing countries. Twenty-eight of the thirty-six new developing country members came in under special procedures for newly independent territories; only eight got in by negotiating tariff concessions (Hudec 1987, 24).

Another factor was the competition between the U.N. Conference on Trade and Development (UNCTAD) and GATT to be the institution through which relations between developing and developed countries were managed. That rivalry is the topic of the next section.

The GATT-UNCTAD Rivalry

What is the best trade policy for development? One alternative is the harsh "tariffs only" conclusion derived from classical economics, as explained, say, in Haberler's Cairo Lectures (Haberler 1959). The idea of "GATT discipline" as it prevailed in the period 1947-54 is the institutional representation of this viewpoint. But the alternative to which the international community turned in the late 1950s and in the 1960s suggested a kinder, gentler attitude toward developing countries. As the poorer members of the trading community, developing countries ought not to be asked to assume the same burden of discipline as the richer members. And, since the facts showed that they were slipping further behind, a kinder, gentler attitude should include an affirmative action program by the richer members, to create new opportunities for the poorer countries to export to the richer. The rivalry between GATT and UNCTAD to "staff out" this concern to promote developing country exports became, in the 1960s, an important influence on the economics of the GATT. Within this rivalry, UNCTAD achieved three significant victories.

First, the UNCTAD view captured the facts: not only the lagging trade performance of developing countries, but also the growing awareness that all was not well with import-substitution policies. As Prebisch phrased it, "Industrialization encounters growing difficulties in the countries where it is pursued furthest" (1964, 9). Extreme capital intensity and very high costs were becoming apparent. The problem, Prebisch explained, is another "vicious circle."[12] Costs are high because exports are low (economies of scale are not achieved), and exports are low because costs are high (1964, 22). Developed countries must therefore provide the needed export opportunities — the developing world requires affirmative action from the developed. UNCTAD's particular twist on the matter was that this access should be preferential, that developing country exporters should not be required to compete with, say, established German exporters for sales in the United States.

The political attractiveness of preferences for developing countries acted synergistically with two technical victories for UNCTAD. These technical victories allowed UNCTAD's concepts rather than the GATT's to provide the scale used by the international community to "keep score" on the amount of affirmative action provided.

One of these victories concerned the attachment of negative connotations to the way in which the normal GATT mode of reducing trade barriers would provide improved access for developing country exporters — even when the improved access was granted unilaterally. Let me give an example. In negotiations with each other through the GATT, Australia and New Zealand agree that each will reduce its tariff on $1000 of imports from the other and that each will also reduce its tariff on $500 of imports from a developing country. The latter action is obviously a unilateral extension of access to the developing country.[13] The case is much the same if Australia and New Zealand exchange concessions on products that each imports two-thirds from the other, one-third from a developing country. In both cases each developed country (Australia and New Zealand) has reduced its tariff on $500 of imports from a developing country, and has done so without receiving a reciprocal concession.

Yet, as UNCTAD taught the world to keep score, Australia and New Zealand would receive no credit for affirmative action. UNCTAD'S calculations compared the amount of developed country exports covered by the agreed concessions ($2000 in the example) with the amount of developing country exports covered ($1000 in the example).

Are Australia and New Zealand therefore "good citizens" because the $1000 is something, or "bad citizens" because the $1000 is less than the $2000? UNCTAD's evaluation of the Kennedy Round used the second standard; for example, "the products in which the developing countries had expressed particular interest, and in which they have already established some trade, received on average significantly smaller tariff reductions than did other products. This result reflects the fact that those product groups for which industrialized countries are the main suppliers received deeper and more widespread cuts" (UNCTAD 1968, 4).

By emphasizing that developed countries reduced tariffs on a larger share of their imports from each other than from developing countries, UNCTAD suppressed the idea that such tariff cuts provided a unilateral concession and assigned guilt to the developed countries because the concessions they exchanged among themselves were larger than those they provided without compensation to the developing countries. In so doing, UNCTAD detached the traditional GATT mode of going at trade liberalization — reciprocal most-favored nation concessions — from the earning of any affirmative action credits.[14] The international community (even the GATT, as the following paragraphs show) accepted the UNCTAD way of evaluating the morality of tariff reductions.

The other UNCTAD tactical victory was to build up the idea that tariff preferences (particularly the Generalized System of Preferences, which UNCTAD administered) were the only true indicator of a country's affirmative action.

A concern for expressing the growing belief that developed countries had positive obligations toward the developing countries led also to the adoption in 1965 of Part IV of the GATT. Part IV uses the "shall" language of legal obligation but then adds other specific language that undercuts the sense of *legal* obligation. For example, Article XXXVII, titled "Commitments," begins: "The developed contracting parties shall to the fullest extent possible — that is, except when compelling reasons, which may include legal reasons, make it impossible...."

The strength of the old test of good faith — exempting developing countries from normal GATT discipline — did not wane as that of the new test — affirmative action — ascended. Consider, for example, a pamphlet published in 1964 by the GATT Secretariat titled *The Role of GATT in Relation to Trade and Development*. According to Hudec's review, the pamphlet accurately described the GATT's legal discipline for developing countries. "What was interesting was its effort to portray the absence of legal obligations as a virtue. This is perhaps the clearest demonstration ... of the link during this time between the GATT legal policy towards developing countries and its very strong desire to attract and hold developing country members" (1987, 60).

As this analysis implies, the GATT rules were being shaped by an our-organization-versus-their-organization competition for membership, and not by any concern to guide or push countries to choose the most effective trade policies. UNCTAD for its part was doing the same. Raul Prebisch, UNCTAD's first Secretary-General in 1961, actively recruited developed and developing countries' loyalty to UNCTAD:

> [GATT represents] the classic pattern of exchanging manufactured goods for primary commodities (Prebisch 1964, 7).
> GATT has brought about considerable reductions in ... tariffs and other restrictions [but they] ... have been of benefit mainly to the industrial countries (p. 27).

> *[In GATT,] problems of international trade are dealt with in a fragmentary fashion, and not as part of a general problem of development.... GATT has not proved effective in coping with trade between the developing and the industrial countries nor has it promoted trade relations among the developing countries themselves (p. 99).*

By the time of the Tokyo Round of negotiations, the developed countries had returned (at least in form) to the idea of discipline. The focus was shifting from tariffs to nontariff trade restrictions, and the Tokyo Round codes attempted to expand and interpret agreed rules about the use of such restrictions. However, each code included a provision for special and differential treatment of developing countries. Only the United States went so far as to threaten to limit extension of the codes' privileges to developing countries that accepted the codes' disciplines, although it pulled back from its threat whenever practical politics intervened.[15]

At the end of the Tokyo Round, the GATT Secretariat prepared a report on the outcome of the round. Hudec interprets the report as follows:

> *It was written quickly (but very thoroughly) in order to preempt the kind of negative evaluation that UNCTAD had made after the Kennedy Round .... It celebrated all the "victories" achieved by the Group of 77.... [A] central element of the "victories" was all the new legal freedoms developing countries had won, especially those which involved discriminatory special and differential treatment.... The year was 1979. Here was the GATT, still thoroughly preoccupied with holding the allegiance of developing countries and still making a virtue of the fact that GATT rules do not apply to developing countries (1987, 91).*

If the Kennedy and Tokyo Rounds were the two halves of a GATT-UNCTAD soccer match, we would say that the score was UNCTAD 2, GATT 0, the second goal being an "own-goal." Put another way, the GATT church pretty much took on the theological position of UNCTAD concerning developing-developed country relations and the role of trade in economic development.

Neither the score nor the theology has changed. The subtitle of Hudec's chapter on developments in the 1980s is "form without substance," and this seems to be the mainstream interpretation of developing countries' obligations under the GATT. Another noted legal scholar, John H. Jackson, concludes that "many developing countries are able to take advantage of either explicit or implicit exceptions in the GATT so as to pursue almost at will any form of trade policy they wish" (1989, 277).

If "individual sacrifice for the common good" accurately reflected the economics of the GATT and if the GATT were supposed to serve a social welfare function, then the position of developing countries in GATT might be considered appropriate. But if we look at GATT from a public choice perspective — as an institution designed to nudge countries toward the best choice of trade policy — then we would give it a lower score.

The Uruguay Round

That things in the GATT have not changed in the 1980s does not mean that things have not changed. Concern is growing about the increased use of trade restrictions by developed countries. While some of these restrictions are GATT-questionable, a significant fraction of them, including antidumping and counter-vailing duty measures, are arguably GATT-legal.[16] Another matter of concern is that major movements by the developed countries to remove trade restrictions have been bilateral or regional, for example, the Australia-New Zealand and Canada-United States trade agreements and the European Community's "1992" program.

Trade policy changes in developing countries have been equally significant. There have been major reforms in some countries — Chile and Mexico are examples — and continuing liberalization in many others, particularly Korea and other newly industrialized countries in Asia. There have been some new restrictions as well.[17]

Several developing countries took an active role in getting the Uruguay Round under way. In early 1986, achieving agreement to undertake the round seemed impossible. Preparations were stuck, and agendas for the Punta del Este meeting were reviewed several times without progress. Quietly, however, officials from a group of middle-size developing and developed countries began to discuss matters among themselves. They shaped perspectives, forged operational ideas, and calculated relevant balances. Much more, they discussed ideas with other delegations, patiently modifying and extending their proposals as they went along. One of the positive effects of this behind-the-scenes leadership was the sense of the value of the GATT system that it conveyed to smaller countries and the development of a perspective that gave expression to their concerns.

The contribution of the developing countries to the politics of getting the new GATT round under way raised hopes that these countries would make an equally important contribution to GATT's economics. Most decisions by developing countries to remove trade restrictions have been unilateral decisions, based on an appreciation of the own-country benefits of such reforms versus the costs.

For developed countries, the removal of trade restrictions has been shaped by a strong vision of an open international trading system and of that system's collective benefits to the community of nations. A concern to promote and maintain peace and stability through economic means has perhaps been a clearer objective than have the economic benefits likely to accrue to a particular nation. The focus has been systemic and the approach multilateral. This systemic focus has characterized not just the GATT, but other important vehicles for the reduction of developed countries' trade barriers as well, such as negotiations to remove trade and exchange restrictions in Europe and to form the European Economic Community and the European Free Trade Association. Within the multilateral approach, trade liberalization means an exchange of concessions. Reductions of import restrictions increase the imports of the country granting the concessions and are viewed as a cost. But in the multilateral process, such costs buy increased exports and help build the system from which all will benefit.

For developing countries, the perspective on trade policy reform has been different. The focus has been national and the approach unilateral. This perspective may underestimate the value and fragility of a coherent international trading system, but it includes a fuller appreciation of the classical perspective, particularly of benefits that openness to international competition can convey to an individual economy. Like the multilateral decisions of the developed countries, unilateral decisions for reform reflect an appreciation of the economic benefits that export expansion allows. High-cost inputs are a burden to exports, and lower restrictions on imported inputs are a stimulus to export expansion.

Export expansion is a valid reason for import liberalization, but not the only one. Many developing countries have built on the other reasons. They recognize that economic development requires the improvement of human resources and the acquisition of modern technology. They also recognize that close communication with other economies, through the competitive process, is an important stimulus to the upgrading of domestic resources and domestic forms of economic organization.[18] The experience of these countries provides many lessons on how an individual economy can benefit from the removal of restrictions that isolate it from the international economy.

Looking at increased international trade from the perspective of the gains to an individual economy offers many possibilities, particularly for controlling the spread of new trade restrictions. The current GATT technology attempts to limit the use of import restrictions by specifying when a country may impose them. A country is not asked to weigh the domestic gains from an instance of import competition against the domestic costs. The GATT technology looks only at the domestic costs and authorizes import restrictions when these costs take a certain form or reach a certain degree. By so doing, the GATT system reinforces the idea that the importer bears the costs of trade while the exporter enjoys the gains.

Despite the promise of a new perspective on the benefits of trade, things seem to have gone the wrong way. The urge to get more exports and suffer fewer imports has dulled the developed countries' sense of the value of the system. Asking developing countries to examine trade liberalization in a multilateral context brings them to the instinctive view that exports are the gains from trade and imports the costs. At GATT, things are done the GATT way.

My pessimism that the potential discussed above will not be realized is based on two observations. The first concerns the developing countries' positions and proposals at the Uruguay Round. At the highest level of visibility, the developing country position is the Brazil-India position, which is the traditional GATT position of developing countries: against any compromise of developing country freedom from stated GATT obligations and for unilateral affirmative actions by the developed countries to help the developing countries. The implicit definition of what will "help" is (as always) the mercantilist one. At a lower level of visibility, developing countries have offered technical suggestions to limit the scope of allowable trade restrictions, for example, on the determination of "dumping" or "injury." These are, *in the traditional GATT sense*, good and responsible proposals. But (and I have emphasized "in the traditional GATT sense" for this reason) the traditional GATT sense of how to discipline the use of trade restrictions no longer works very well.

The other reason for my pessimism comes from the responses I have received when I have challenged researchers and academics on these matters. For example, at a symposium in South America I suggested that the developing countries had missed a chance to contribute to the international community from their own experiences. I asked: What did the government of Mexico or Chile take into account when it decided on its own trade reforms? What is there in such thought processes that might contribute to the Uruguay Round?

I offered two suggestions: (1) a proposal in the safeguards negotiations to give the costs of protection equal standing with the gains; perhaps even introduction of a "reverse safeguards" procedure through which a domestic interest could petition for removal of a trade restriction that caused it harm (for example, machinery producers for removal of restrictions on steel imports); and (2) a proposal to make the "protection balance sheet" (a concept elaborated in the GATT "Wise Men's Report" of 1985) the focus of the trade policy review mechanism.

There were three responses to my suggestion that developing countries prepare and present nonmercantilist proposals: (1) the United States would not accept nonmercantilist proposals, so it would be futile to make them; (2) the current GATT builds on mercantilist economics, and since developing countries want to improve the GATT not overthrow it, they must work within its mercantilist confines; (3) within the mercantilist conception of access to foreign markets as a country's right and discipline over its own use of import restrictions as the obligation, it is easy to define special and differential treatment for developing countries — unrequited access and less discipline. If this perception of costs and benefits is put aside, it is not immediately clear how special and differential treatment for developing countries might be defined.

There is perhaps a reply to each of these objections, but a reply is not my point. My point is this: We think about the GATT only in the GATT way.

Conclusions

At the beginning of this essay, I posited rhetorically that the institutionalized bad economics of the GATT might be just a matter of bad timing: the rules were written one day, but the appropriate economics were not uncovered until the next. It is time to take the question on directly: Is the problem simply a matter of unfortunate timing?

The answer is "no."

The work of Haberler and Viner shows that the "new" ideas about trade and development were around from the beginning. The supporting evidence reviewed at the beginning of this essay came later, but its emergence did overlap some of the events that shaped the GATT's perspective on trade and development, such as the UNCTAD-GATT rivalry throughout the 1970s and the GATT's Tokyo Round report, which was published in 1979. Finally, at no time did more of the evidence favor the economics that was built into the GATT than favored the economics that was left out.

In any case, given the way the choices were made, such evidence was irrelevant. The formative decisions came out of an adversarial process that focused first the emotions and then the intellect on the issue of more versus less of whatever sense of discipline the rules happened to contain.[19] The evidence is relevant mostly to the issue of determining what is the most effective form of discipline. But as the decision process came into being, that was not the focal issue.

As the Uruguay Round unfolds, it is becoming even clearer that the institutional structure of the GATT, having initially left out the "new" ideas and evidence about trade and development, now serves to keep them out. Building the "old" economics into the institutional decision structure of the GATT preserved a developed-developing country division that would have disappeared had the only influence been a strictly intellectual one.

In summary, my conclusions are these three:

- There is a GATT way of thinking about the role of trade in development.
- The economics of the GATT way is different from what is considered good economics by much of the profession.
- When we — policymakers and academics alike — put on our "GATT hats," we tend to put on our "GATT minds" as well.

Notes

1. Both Viner and Haberler refer to their work as applications of "classical" economics. Haberler, in his exposition, often talks about what the "old-fashioned economist" would conclude.
2. The World Bank's *World Development Report* 1987 reviews and extends what has been learned about the topic "industrialization and foreign trade." It also provides an extensive bibliography.
3. See, for example, Balassa (1981, 1985, part II). Balassa's method became the basis for a significant part of the World Bank's *World Development Report 1981*.
4. Quoted by Cooper (1987, 299) from Cordell Hull's *Memoirs*. Cooper provides similar quotations from Presidents Franklin D. Roosevelt and Harry S. Truman.
5. Dam (1970, 227ff) provides a more extensive comparison.
6. As explained in the first section above, there was no trade and development literature on which to draw.
7. Hudec (1975) provides a useful history and analysis.
8. The other summary points concern capital flows, monetary reserves, and macroeconomic stabilization policies.
9. The statement quoted above includes the words "to negotiate" but the text of the report (p. 127) is more specific: "a negotiated settlement involving a gradual shift away from undesirable policies on both sides."

10. Less than a year later, Haberler (1959), in his Fiftieth Anniversary Commemoration Lectures at the National Bank of Egypt, elaborated on these points: "My overall conclusion is that international trade has made a tremendous contribution to the development of less-developed countries in the 19th and 20th centuries and can be expected to make an equally big contribution in the future, if it is allowed to proceed freely" (p. 5). "[D]evelopment policies should be such as to work through and with the help of the powerful forces of the price mechanism instead of opposing and counteracting the market forces" (p. 36). Haberler accepted the infant industry argument and suggested a uniform tariff of 20-30 percent as the only allowable interference with free trade. But he added, "I am fully aware of the fact that practically all underdeveloped countries (and developed countries for that matter) pursue policies that are almost the exact opposite of those sketched above [highly differentiated tariffs, exchange controls, and the like]. It is my contention that this type of policy hurts the underdeveloped countries" (p. 36).

11. Had the community been trained to see the matter as an application of effective protection or domestic resource cost concepts, things might have been different. But such concepts were yet to come in popular usage.

12. Little (1982, chapters 3 and 4) points out that during the period 1943-60, "vicious circles" were a popular form of explanation among development theories of why poverty persists. "Big push" was the complementary concept in policy advice.

13. The concessions are extended on a most-favored nation basis. We assume, for simplicity, that each good is imported only from the country with which the concession was negotiated or only from the developing country.

14. My own work contributed a footnote on this matter. In 1971, while on the UNCTAD staff, I set out to examine the effect of the GATT rounds on developing country exports. My intent was to demonstrate the need for preferences. My hypothesis was that with most-favored nation tariff cuts, even when they covered developing country exports, developing country exporters were left at the starting gate. I found the opposite to be the case. Where the Dillon and Kennedy Round cuts had touched developing country exports, the response was much faster growth of developing than of developed country exports. These findings are published in Finger (1974 and 1976). Like many of the relevant facts, these were dug out long after decisions had institutionalized the wrong economics.

15. In the 1980s, Section 301 of the U.S. Trade Act has emerged as an important policy instrument of the United States. Section 301 borrows some of the external features of legalism, but its application of a unilateral interpretation of what is legal and its availability to any U.S. interest that argues that its foreign competition is "unreasonable" (though not necessarily "illegal") suggest that it is grounded not in "legalism" but in old-fashioned mercantilism. Section 301 is not reviewed here.

16. Finger and Messerlin (1989) provide a review of these restrictions.

17. World Bank (1988) and Whalley (1989) provide lists of countries in both categories — those implementing new trade restrictions and those removing old ones.

18. The "old-fashioned" or classical view of Viner (1953), Haberler (1959), and Keesing (1976) emphasized the importance of the market process as communication.

19. I have taken this idea so much to heart that I am no longer willing to ask if it is Robert Hudec's idea or mine.

References

Balassa, B. 1963. "European Integration: Problems and Issues." *American Economic Review Papers and Proceedings* 53 (May): 175-84.

Balassa, B. 1966. "Tariff Reductions and Trade in Manufactures Among Industrial Countries." *American Economic Review Papers and Proceedings* 56 (June): 466-73.

Balassa, B. 1981. "Policy Response to External Shocks in Selected Latin American Countries." In M. Gillis and W. Baer, eds, *Export Diversification and the New Protectionism*. Urbana: University of Illinois Press for the National Bureau of Economic Research.

Balassa, B. 1985. *Change and Challenge in the World Economy*. London: Macmillan.

Balassa, B., and associates. 1971. *The Structure of Protection in Developing Countries*. Baltimore, Md.: Johns Hopkins University Press.

Balassa, B., and associates. 1982. *Development Strategies in Semi-Industrial Economies*. Baltimore, Md.: Johns Hopkins University Press.

Bell, C. 1987. "Development Economics." In J. Eatwell, M. Milgate, and P. Newman, eds, *The New Palgrave, A Dictionary of Economics*. London: Macmillan; New York: Stockton; Tokyo: Maruzen.

Bhagwati, J. 1978. *Anatomy and Consequences of Exchange Control Regimes*. Cambridge, Mass.: Ballinger.

Buchanan, J. M. 1984. "Alternative Perspectives on Economics and Public Policy." (Cato Institute) *Policy Report* 6: 1-5.

Burenstam Linder, S. 1986. *The Pacific Century: Economic and Political Consequences of Asia-Pacific Dynamism*. Stanford, Calif.: Stanford University Press.

Campos, R. de Oliveira, G. Haberler, J. Meade, and J. Tinbergen. 1958. *Trends in International Trade*. Geneva: GATT.

Cooper, R.N. 1987. "Trade Policy as Foreign Policy." In Robert M. Stern. ed., *U.S. Trade Policies in a Changing World Economy*. Cambridge, Mass.: MIT Press.

Dam, K. 1970. *The GATT: Law and International Economic Organization*. Chicago: University of Chicago Press. (Midway Reprint 1977).

Donges, J. B. 1976. "A Comparative Survey of Industrialization Policies in Fifteen Semi-Industrial Countries." *Weltwirtschaftliches Archiv*. Band 112 (Heft 4): 626-59.

Finger, J.M. 1974. "GATT Tariff Concessions and the Exports of Developing Countries." *Economic Journal* 84 (September): 566-75.

Finger, J.M. 1976. "Effects of the Kennedy Round Tariff Concessions on the Exports of Developing Countries." *Economic Journal* 86 (March): 87-95.

Finger, J.M., and P.A. Messerlin. 1989. *The Effects of Industrial Countries' Policies on Developing Countries*. Policy and Research Series No. 3. Washington, D.C.: World Bank.

GATT. 1979. *The Tokyo Round of Multilateral Trade Negotiations*. Geneva.

GATT. 1985. *Trade Policies for a Better Future*. (The Leutwiler Report). Geneva.

Haberler, G. 1959. *International Trade and Economic Development*. Cairo: National Bank of Egypt.

Hudec, R.E. 1975. *The GATT Legal System and World Trade Diplomacy*. New York: Praeger.

Hudec, R.E. 1987. *Developing Countries in the GATT Legal System*. London: Gower, for the Trade Policy Research Center.

Jackson, J. H. 1989. *The World Trading System: Law and Policy of International Economic Relations*. Cambridge, Mass., and London: MIT Press.

Keesing, D. B. 1976. "Outward Looking Policies and Economic Development." *Economic Journal* 77 (June): 303-20.

Krueger, A. O. 1978. *Liberalization Attempts and Consequences*. Cambridge, Mass.: Ballinger.

Little, I.M.D. 1982. *Economic Development: Theory, Policy and International Relations*. New York: Basic Books.

Little, I.M.D., T. Scitovsky, and M. F. Scott. 1970. *Industry and Trade in Some Developing Countries: A Comparative Study*. London and New York: Oxford University Press for the Development Centre of the Organization for Economic Cooperation and Development.

Prebisch, R. 1964. *Towards a New Trade Policy for Development*. New York: United Nations.

United Nations Conference on Trade and Development. 1968. *The Kennedy Round: Estimated Effects on Tariff Barriers*. New York: United Nations.

Viner, J. 1953. *International Trade and Economic Development*. London: Oxford University Press.

Whalley, J., coordinator. 1989. *The Uruguay Round and Beyond*. London: Macmillan.

World Bank. 1988. *Adjustment Lending: An Evaluation of Ten Years of Experience*. Policy and Research Series No. 1. Washington, D.C.

14

Exchange Rate Policy in Developing Countries

W. Max Corden

This paper distinguishes between two approaches to exchange rate policy in developing countries: the "real targets" and the "nominal anchor" approaches. It also looks at whether the exchange rate follows other policies and private sector price and wage setting or leads them. The real-targets approach, which is now the orthodox policy, assumes that nominal exchange rate changes have prolonged real effects and that the exchange rate should adapt to other policies. The nominal-anchor approach uses the exchange rate as an instrument of anti-inflation policy, as a way of constraining domestic policies and influencing private sector reactions. In examining the implications of the nominal-anchor approach, the paper considers to what extent it might explain the low inflation experiences of the many countries in which exchange rates have been (more or less) fixed for long periods. The implications of increasing capital mobility for exchange rate policy are also examined, and some conclusions for policy are presented. The analysis draws on examples of exchange rate policies and experiences of a group of seventeen developing countries that are being studied as part of a World Bank project on macroeconomic policies and growth over a longer period.[1]

This paper is written in honor of Béla Balassa, an economist who has had an enormous influence on the developing country policy debate and, above all, on the movement toward more open policies. For many years, his incredible productivity has filled me and many others with awe. His work is always thoroughly down to earth and highly policy-relevant. In this respect, the present paper is an attempt at emulation.

On the subject matter itself, Béla's most comprehensive contribution is Balassa (1987), although he has touched on some of the issues in many other writings. It is interesting to look at his several collected volumes (Balassa 1977, 1981, 1985a, 1989a, b) from this point of view. It is clear that he is a "real targets" man, praising countries for adjusting their nominal exchange rates to bring about desirable real exchange rate changes (in response to external shocks, for example) or to avoid undesirable ones, and criticizing countries for failures on this front. A principal theme of Balassa (1987) — backed typically by a compact presentation of the relevant empirical evidence from many studies by himself and others — is that elasticity pessimism with regard to the real exchange rate is not justified. In *Change and Challenge in the World Economy* (1985a), he examines in detail the

Turkish experience of 1979-83, in which a reversal of a 22-percent real appreciation led to a doubling of exports between 1980 and 1983.

On the basis of all this evidence, it will be assumed here that changes in the real exchange rate — provided they are expected to last for some time — do have significant switching effects, increasing exports, reducing imports, and normally raising the demand for domestic output. But this leaves open the issues to be discussed in the paper: to what extent do changes in the nominal exchange rate lead to long-term changes and to what extent do they influence domestic macroeconomic policies?

Two Approaches to Exchange Rate Policy

The real-targets approach uses the nominal exchange rate, together with other policy instruments, to attain real objectives such as an appropriate (noninflationary) level of demand for home-produced goods and services (internal balance) and a desired current account target. In its assumption that a nominal policy instrument can achieve a real objective, this approach is essentially Keynesian. Furthermore, it assumes that the government can be trusted to make sensible use of the exchange rate and other instruments, that is, it does not need to be constrained. In addition, this approach assumes that the nominal exchange rate is a policy instrument that is distinct from domestic monetary and fiscal policies, although it must be applied together with these policies. These are all conventional assumptions in a great deal of World Bank and International Monetary Fund (IMF) policy advice and, I think, in the policy advice implicit or explicit in much of Béla Balassa's writings.

The assumption that the exchange rate is a policy instrument separate from domestic monetary policy is particularly important to the discussion. It means that a nominal exchange rate objective can be attained by sterilized intervention. It is thus assumed that effective exchange controls or other measures are used to ensure that international capital mobility is not high for the country.

The approach implies that a nominal devaluation has real effects that are sufficiently long lasting to be worth pursuing, at least provided expenditure policy avoids excess demand at the same time. Domestic prices and wages are assumed to be imperfectly flexible downward (in the simplest models, they are actually held constant). There is now strong evidence that, except in the chronic-inflation countries of Latin America, devaluations do have real effects that last for several years, provided appropriate credit policies are also followed. Thus the evidence seems to justify one of the key assumptions, at least for a period of, say, two to four years. Even in the case of high-inflation countries, continuous nominal depreciations may have real effects in the sense of preventing the real appreciations that would otherwise take place.[2]

The alternative, nominal-anchor approach is a version of monetarism and used to be known as "international monetarism." The exchange rate is used to anchor the domestic inflation rate (broadly) to the inflation rate of trading partner countries. Possibly the exchange rate is adjusted on the basis of some predetermined scale to affect the inflation differential with trading partner countries. It constrains domestic monetary policy (and hence possibly fiscal policy), making it endogenous. The exchange rate leads rather than follows other nominal variables, such as domestic price and wage inflation, in order to attain real objectives, such as maintenance of competitiveness. Apart from restraining governments, this approach is meant to send out clear and credible signals to private agents about prospects for inflation. The implication is that if the signals are clear and credible, the real economy will adjust appropriately to various shocks, including anti-inflationary exchange rate policy.

The approach — which focuses both on the need to restrain government inflationary tendencies through some kind of commitment and on the influence of the credibility of government monetary policies on private agents' expectations — is very much in tune with recent macroeconomic theorizing. For that reason, it is surprising that the current policy orthodoxy with regard to developing countries takes little account of it. Hence I discuss it at some length here.

Exchange Rate Policy Targeted on Real Variables

This section presents a systematic analysis of certain issues related to the real-targets approach. How should the nominal exchange rate move in response to various "real" shocks or objectives, such as fiscal expansion or trade liberalization? What is the meaning of exchange rate "overvaluation" or "misalignment"?

The Basic Model: Switching and Expenditure Adjustment

Figure 14.1 is the familiar "Swan diagram" (Swan 1963), but it calls for careful interpretation here. It is assumed that the country is small in world markets, so that any changes in the terms of trade are exogenous.

The vertical axis shows the relative price of traded to nontraded goods in domestic currency terms, allowing also for the effects of tariffs, quantitative restrictions, and so on, that affect this relative price ratio. This is the S ratio, the S standing for either "Salter" or "switching."[3] It is sometimes called the "real exchange rate," a movement upward being a real depreciation.[4] The horizontal axis shows real expenditure or absorption (E), which can increase as a result of monetary or fiscal expansion or various other factors, such as higher incomes yielded by a terms of trade improvement. The curve Y_0 shows varying combinations of S and E that yield constant real income Y_0 resulting from constant demand for home-produced goods. Curve Y_1 represents a higher level of demand and income. Similarly, curve C_0 represents a constant current account balance, and curve C_1 a current account that is more in deficit.

Let us now look at the three crucial prices, namely the prices of nontraded goods, imports, and exports.

First, there is a large category of nontraded goods N, with price p_n. This category contains two subclasses: (1) pure nontradables, which would be priced

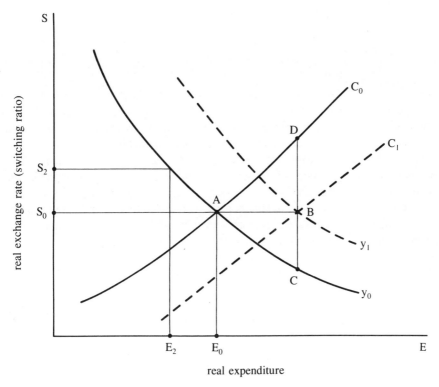

Figure 14.1   The Real-Targets Approach

on the basis of domestic demand and supply even if there were free trade, and (2) goods that might have been imported under free trade but, because of prohibitive quantitative import restrictions, are priced on the basis of domestic demand and supply rather than the prices of competitive imports. The latter goods are the quantitative restriction-propelled nontraded goods — importables that have been converted into nontraded goods.

Second, there are imports M, whose domestic price is $e(1+t)p_m$, where p_m is the border price of imports in foreign currency terms, e is the nominal exchange rate defined as units of domestic currency per unit of foreign currency (an increase being a depreciation), and t is the tariff rate, whether explicit or implicit (quantitative restrictions), whichever effectively determines price. If import restrictions are tightened or their range is expanded within the broad category of M, t will rise.

Finally, there are exports X, where p_x is the foreign price of X, and ep_x is the domestic price.

Since there are two kinds of traded goods, weights must be attached to the two prices to get an average price of traded goods. The weights are a and $1 - a$. We thus get an expression for S, the relative price of traded to nontraded goods, taking into account trade restrictions and allowing for the possibility that the terms of trade (p_x / p_m) may change:

(1) $$S = e \, [a(1+t)p_m + (1-a)p_x] / p_n .$$

When the weights are held constant, S can change because of changes in the exchange rate, in protection, in one or two foreign prices, or in domestic (non-traded) prices, the last possibly because of a change in the nominal wage level. If there is a nominal depreciation, that is, if e rises, and with p_n, t, p_m, and p_x given, S will increase. In that case, we can equate a change in S with a change in e, a movement upward in figure 14.1 (positive switching) being a real depreciation or devaluation. An increase in p_n would lower S (negative switching). If p_n rises more than e (and with p_m, p_x, and t still constant), one might say that there has been real appreciation. When p_m, p_x, and t are constant, and only e and p_n vary, it seems appropriate in terms of conventional usage to use the real exchange rate concept, with positive switching resulting from real depreciation (e rising more than p_n). But a problem with this concept arises when p_x, p_m, or t changes.

A Fiscal Expansion: How Should the Exchange Rate Move?

Let us now consider a common situation in developing countries. A fiscal expansion is financed by borrowing, domestic or foreign. We take this as given. We also hold protection (t), and world prices (p_x, p_m) constant. Which way does S have to move? Should the exchange rate appreciate or depreciate?

It is not difficult to show that if the deficit is domestically financed and there is initial excess capacity and unemployment, the exchange rate needs to depreciate. In figure 14.1, at a constant e and p_n, the movement would initially be from A to B, the net result of the fiscal expansion itself and possibly of some crowding out of private spending (as a result of a higher interest rate or of credit rationing brought about by the domestic financing). The current account worsens to C_1 and demand for nontraded goods rises, bringing demand for home-produced goods to Y_1. Clearly, a depreciation could restore the initial current account situation provided it were possible to sustain higher domestic output. The system would go to D.

The more interesting case is that in which the deficit is foreign financed and the initial situation is one of full capacity or full employment (internal balance). In this case, the system cannot stay above Y_0, although it may move there initially, so S must fall to bring the country to C. This could be brought about by a rise in p_n, yielding a real appreciation. If a domestic price rise (temporary inflation) is to be avoided, nominal appreciation is required. The current account, of course, worsens. This negative switching reduces the profitability of export industries (and of any import-competing industries) and so yields the familiar Dutch disease effect. It is caused by a fiscal expansion that is foreign financed or financed, at least temporarily, out of reserves when the starting point is one of internal balance.

(Given such a starting point, any transfer into the country, whether in the form of loans or aid, would have the same effect.)

It follows that the fiscal expansion may have to be associated with either a depreciation or an appreciation, depending on the extent to which the output of home-produced goods can be increased and the extent to which the deficit can be financed by foreign borrowing or the use of reserves.

Now suppose the country is at the last situation, at point C, with a current account deficit and internal balance. Reserves are running out or foreign borrowing is becoming difficult. Can one say that the exchange rate is "misaligned" or "overvalued"? We still hold p_x, p_m, and t constant. Should the country be advised to devalue?

If fiscal policy remained unchanged, a devaluation might temporarily bring the country back to B (or even to D), creating excess demand at home. But p_n would rise until S were back at C. *Given the fiscal policy*, the appreciated e is the correct one and is not overvalued. The fiscal expansion has to be reversed if the current account is to be improved. If it is impossible to reverse the fiscal expansion, there is no point in depreciating since this would only cause temporary inflation. This point is often forgotten. It is wrong in this situation to advocate devaluation without the assurance that adequate fiscal contraction will also take place. But it would also be wrong to advocate fiscal contraction alone, leaving the exchange rate unaltered and p_n inflexible downward, since a recession would result. Given that the current account has to be improved, it is really the *package* of fiscal policy and exchange rate that is misaligned. A reversal of the fiscal expansion should be accompanied by a devaluation so as to undo the earlier appreciation of the currency.

Import Restrictions and Exchange Rate Misalignment

Protection — realistically, quantitative import restrictions — can now be introduced as a variable. To simplify, we hold p_n, p_m, and p_x constant. The two policy instruments are e and t, a rise in t representing a tightening or extension of restrictions. According to equation 1, a given S can be obtained with varying combinations of e and t. Suppose we start at the desired level of S, namely S_0 (in figure 14.1), obtained by combining a particular level of e, namely e_0, with a positive level of t, namely t_0. Is the exchange rate then "misaligned"? The answer depends on whether the exchange rate *leads* or *follows*.

It is certainly possible that it follows. The level of protection may have been set at t_0 because this was desired as a long-term protectionist strategy or because tariffs are used to raise revenue. In that case, protection leads, and e_0 is then the equilibrium rate to ratify t_0, given the target S_0.

The currently more familiar story is that of trade liberalization. Again, the exchange rate is meant to follow. The much repeated message is that trade liberalization requires devaluation to maintain both internal balance and the initial current account balance (see Corden 1971 and Krueger 1978). This is an important example of the real-targets approach. If the devaluation does not take place, trade liberalization cannot be sustained. In due course, import restrictions, although not necessarily the same ones as before, will be reimposed to deal with a current account problem that may have been caused by the earlier liberalization. In fact, this is the explanation for many failed liberalization attempts. The exchange rate is meant to follow but fails to do so (Krueger 1978).[5]

A common experience in developing countries has been creeping overvaluation followed by increasing trade restrictions. A country starts at its desired internal and external position (point A in figure 14.1) and with a low level of trade restrictions, say zero. But then because of domestic monetary expansion, domestic prices (p_n) rise faster than world prices. Therefore S would fall unless e were increased *pari passu*. Continuous nominal depreciation is needed to compensate for the excess of domestic inflation over world inflation. But the country fails to depreciate sufficiently for a variety of reasons, perhaps primarily to discourage further inflation. Therefore restrictions have to be continually intensified to maintain S_0 and hence equilibrium at A in figure 14.1. This is a case in which the exchange rate leads when, from the point of view of the real-targets approach, it should have followed. Restriction of imports turns out to be the residual policy, and it is not optimal.

Because of the increasing import restrictions imposed as a result of the continuous overvaluation of the real exchange rate, export industries are continuously squeezed.[6] Eventually, however, the limit of import restrictions will be attained: the country will be down to its bedrock level of imports. Then either S must fall below S_0, producing a current account deficit or an internal balance problem (depending on whether real expenditure, E, is raised or reduced), or the exchange rate must start depreciating.

Numerous examples of this pattern could be given. Indeed, there is hardly a country in our group of seventeen that has not at some time gone through an episode like this, where rigidity of the nominal exchange rate leads to increasing import restrictions.[7] That this is an undesirable outcome is, of course, a constant theme in the literature, in the writings of Béla Balassa, and in World Bank policy recommendations. The exchange rate should be adjusted appropriately. That is the essence of the real-targets approach.

Nigeria presents a rather dramatic example of this kind of story. Inflation (consumer price index) was about 23 percent in 1983 and 40 percent in 1984, and yet the exchange rate stayed fixed. From the end of 1982 to the end of 1984, the real exchange rate (calculated by the IMF) increased by 64 percent (appreciated). Import restrictions were increasingly tightened. In 1985, the exchange rate was allowed to depreciate substantially so that by mid-1986 the earlier real appreciation was more than fully reversed. But it was still far too high in real terms, mainly because of the precipitous fall in the price of oil in 1986. By that time, imports were certainly down to bedrock. A structural adjustment program was adopted in 1986 and implemented through 1987. Import licensing was abolished and the exchange rate was floated. There was a massive nominal and real devaluation: the IMF index (in which a real depreciation is a decline) went from

114 in mid-1986 to 25 at the beginning of 1989 (which may also give some indication of the tariff equivalent of the import restrictions just before they were abolished).

Wage Indexation: What Difference Does It Make?

The implications of wage indexation for the real-targets approach need to be considered. Wage indexation, explicit or implicit, has been a factor at certain times in all the Latin American countries, above all in Brazil, but much less so in the other countries of our group. At the same time, however, one cannot help noting the big drops in real wages that have taken place since 1981 in Argentina, Mexico (both countries with influential and centralized trade union movements) and Chile (which had wage indexation from 1976 to 1981). Turkey has also seen a big decline in real wages since 1980, but in many of the other countries, wage indexation has not been a factor at all. Of course one cannot conclude that just because real wages have fallen substantially over some period, they can fall indefinitely. For example, in Mexico since 1988 there has been some degree of indexation as part of a social pact.

If there is formal or informal wage indexation, p_n will tend to rise, usually with a lag, when e rises. In the extreme case, a devaluation cannot bring about a change in S. How does this possibility affect the orthodox real-targets model?

With the economy starting at internal balance (Y_0 in figure 14.1), a devaluation in the absence of indexation would lead to an endogenous rise in p_n until internal balance was restored. This rise in p_n could be avoided by a simultaneous reduction in E. So, if a current account improvement is desired, E must fall; if internal balance is also to be maintained, then e must rise. There is a role for devaluation, but only as part of a policy package. By contrast, when there is indexation, p_n rises when e rises and would do so even if E were reduced. There is no role for devaluation at all, not even as part of a policy package. A reduction in E would be needed to improve the current account, but supplementing it with a devaluation would not affect S and thus could not maintain internal balance.

Suppose we observe that devaluations have been followed by increases in p_n, possibly causing the whole effect on S to be eroded after a while. There can be two explanations, and from a policy point of view, it is important to know which is correct. One possible explanation is that E was not reduced sufficiently, so p_n rose because of excess demand. The conclusion then follows that a policy package that included contractionary aggregate demand policy should have been implemented or implemented more strongly. The second explanation could be that there was some tendency to indexation, formal or informal. In that case, a reduction in E would not have allowed S to rise, that is, would not have brought about positive switching, even though it was still required for a current account improvement. The policy implication in that case may be to try to end indexation.

There is some useful evidence about which explanation is likely to be more important. Edwards (1989, 264-69) analyzed the erosion of the real effects of nominal devaluations for a large group of developing countries (twenty-nine "stepwise" devaluations) and found that the rate of growth of domestic credit played a crucial role. In terms of our model, that would mean that a failure to reduce E would tend to lead to failure of devaluation to have a sustained real effect. This suggests that indexation is relatively less important than is adoption of the full policy package.

The Exchange Rate as Nominal Anchor

We now consider the alternative approach to exchange rate policy, in which the exchange rate is used as a nominal anchor, restraining government inflationary policies and sending out clear, credible signals to private agents about prospects for inflation. In this approach, the exchange rate leads. In terms of the model presented so far, p_n is no longer given: it becomes endogenous and depends on what happens — and what is expected to happen — to e. In this view, a readiness to devalue to achieve short-term real objectives means that this anchor is abandoned, and in the long run more inflation results. And when expectations are also allowed for, the long run may not be very long. Furthermore, the argument is that in the long run real output would not be affected by the exchange rate or the level of nominal expenditure.

The Exchange Rate as Anchor: Domestic Policies and Private Agents' Reactions

One can decompose the nominal-anchor approach into three steps. (We continue to assume low capital mobility owing to effective exchange controls or other reasons.) First, the government makes a nominal exchange rate commitment. Second, the government is presumed to adjust its domestic monetary policies to this commitment as well. Since, to a great extent, monetary policy in developing countries is determined by fiscal policy (deficits tend to be monetized to varying extents), this means that fiscal policy must adjust to exchange rate policy. To reduce the rate of money supply growth, a fiscal deficit will have to be reduced. Phrased in somewhat oversimplified form, in the nominal-anchor approach the exchange rate leads and fiscal policy (insofar as deficits are monetized) must follow.[8] (This is in contrast to the real-targets approach, in which fiscal policy leads and the exchange rate follows.)

Governments have two temporary ways of evading the constraint on monetary policies that a nominal exchange rate commitment is meant to provide. One way is to impose increasingly tight import restrictions to deal with the consequences of the incompatibility of monetary and exchange rate policies. The other way is to run down reserves and finance the growing current account deficit with foreign borrowing. The constraint imposed by the exchange rate can be — and often has been — evaded in these ways with severely adverse effects. An example from Nigeria was given earlier, and many other examples could be given as well.

If the constraint is effective, however, then the third step is that private agents in due course adjust their price and wage setting to the fiscal, monetary, and exchange rate policies. If government commitment to the exchange rate itself and to any needed adjustment in domestic monetary policy has sufficient credibility and is clearly perceived by private agents, their price and wage setting may adjust quickly and without much loss of output when policy is designed to reduce the rate of inflation.

This nominal-anchor approach thus hinges on both government and private behavior. It can fail, or work badly, either because domestic monetary policy (implying, usually, fiscal policy) is slow to adjust or evades the constraint completely or because private price- and wage-setting agents are slow to adjust and so devaluation has real effects for some time.

One might take the view that government does not need to be constrained, that it might have a genuine commitment to reducing inflation or maintaining price stability. It could achieve these goals either through an exchange rate policy to which domestic monetary policy is adjusted — as in the approach just discussed — or through a noninflationary or anti-inflationary domestic monetary policy to which the exchange rate is adjusted. Thus, again, the exchange rate could lead or follow, but this time the choice is between two ways of achieving the same nominal objective, that is, between two forms of monetarism — exchange rate and money supply (or nominal income) targeting.

The case in favor of using the exchange rate as the nominal anchor is that it is a very visible, very well-defined anchor, which increases the likelihood that private agents will adjust quickly. It is much more visible, and so more credible, than a money supply or nominal expenditure target or a more general anti-inflation commitment. Its visibility is strengthened when the exchange rate is fixed to a particular currency, such as the dollar, rather than to a basket of currencies. The case against using the exchange rate as a nominal anchor is that exchange rate targeting is more likely to produce a balance of payments problem.

The last point is illustrated in figure 14.2. Assume the country starts at point A with a steady rate of inflation, nominal expenditure growth, and depreciation yielding a constant S and constant E at point A. To reduce the rate of inflation, one approach is to reduce the rate of depreciation. If the nominal expenditure reduction comes with a lag, the movement is thus first from A to B, with S falling and E constant (or even rising). The current account deteriorates from C_0 to C_1. In addition, output falls. Then real expenditure is reduced (the rate of growth of nominal expenditure is reduced) to restore the current account, and the system moves to D. Output falls further. Eventually the domestic rate of inflation declines and the system returns gradually to A, with output recovering. The movement from B to D represents the government monetary policy reaction and the movement from D to A the private agents' reaction. Of course, in the final equilibrium the inflation tax will have had to be replaced by some other tax or government expenditure will have had to fall.

Now contrast this with the case in which domestic expenditure reduction leads rather than follows. First the rate of growth of expenditure falls, while the exchange rate is not yet adjusted. The system moves to F, with the current

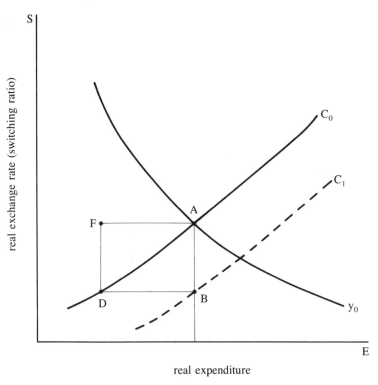

Figure 14.2   The Nominal-Anchor Approach

account improving. Then, with the improvement in the current account, the real exchange rate appreciates (the rate of depreciation declines), bringing the country to D and restoring the original current account situation. The third stage — the move from D to A — is the same as in the case in which the exchange rate leads. The main point to notice here is that, when the exchange rate leads (as it does in the nominal-anchor approach), domestic policy adjustment might lag behind, resulting in a temporary balance of payments problem.[9] This possibility is avoided when domestic expenditure policy leads in the disinflationary process.

Experiences in Five Asian Countries and Turkey: Have Exchange Rate Policies Actually Constrained Domestic Policies?

The exchange rate experiences of the five Asian countries in our group may shed light on the relevance of the nominal-anchor approach. At some stage between 1975 and 1984, these countries switched from a fixed exchange rate (tied to sterling or the dollar) to pegging to a basket, with some exchange rates more flexible than others. In general, these countries have had low inflation (with exceptions in some periods). To what extent have their exchange rate policies constrained domestic policies and provided nominal anchors? (Of course, a fully documented answer can hardly be given here, nor can their exchange rate policies be described in detail.)

Let us begin with the extreme case. Thailand's rate was fixed to the dollar from 1955 until 1984, with just one small devaluation (9 percent in 1981) during that period and a 15-percent devaluation at the end. Thailand did not even adjust its nominal exchange rate to its two severe adverse terms of trade shocks (the two oil shocks). The baht has tended to move with the dollar even after formal pegging to the dollar ended.

India's rupee was fixed to sterling until 1975, with just one major devaluation (36 percent in 1966) during the postwar period up to 1975. In 1975, India switched to a flexible peg, with the peg being to a trade-weighted basket. Since then, overt devaluations have been avoided, and there have been various movements in nominal and real rates. At times there seems to have been some tendency to rigidity (but not actual fixing) in terms of the dollar; the real rate depreciated from late 1985 to 1988, reflecting dollar depreciation.

Pakistan's rate was unified in 1972, then devalued sharply (130 percent) because of the secession of Bangladesh. The rate was then pegged to the dollar until 1982. Since 1982 it has depreciated in terms of the dollar and in real terms.

In Indonesia, the nominal exchange rate was fixed to the dollar from 1970 to 1978, but there was substantial real appreciation owing to higher domestic inflation. This was made possible by the oil boom, which generated the Dutch Disease effect. In 1978 there was a 33-percent devaluation. Since then, the rupiah-dollar rate has been kept fairly constant, apart from devaluations in 1983 (33 percent) and 1986 (31 percent).

Sri Lanka's exchange rate was fixed to sterling from 1952 to 1976 (with some devaluations after 1972). In 1977, the rate was unified, many exchange controls were removed, and there was a large (81 percent) depreciation. The rupee depreciated against the dollar until 1985 but stayed almost constant in trade-weighted nominal terms. During that period of 1977 to 1985, Sri Lanka's experience was somewhat similar to Indonesia's from 1970 to 1978, with real appreciation resulting from some degree of rigidity of the (trade-weighted) nominal exchange rate.

So what can be said about the experience of these countries in which, for fairly long periods of time, the exchange rate was fixed in nominal terms, whether formally so or effectively so, sometimes to the dollar or sterling and at other times to a currency basket? Since 1973, the floating of the major currencies has clearly presented a problem — especially since 1981, when the dollar started appreciating and later depreciating. With the currency relationships among major trading partners changing so much, the concept of a clear nominal anchor became difficult to maintain and abandonment of the various pegs became inevitable — late though this was in many cases relative to the 1973 watershed year when the Bretton Woods system finally collapsed. One can sense that some of the Asian governments have wanted to maintain the credibility of a peg by moving with the dollar rather than firmly pegging to a basket, even after the formal peg to the dollar was ended. But this created problems by leading to unintended real appreciations or depreciations as the dollar moved up and down.[10]

Thailand, India, Pakistan, and Sri Lanka have been low inflation countries, and even Indonesia (from 1969) could be categorized that way (certainly compared with the Latin American experience).[11] Did their exchange rate policies compel these countries to follow low inflation fiscal and monetary policies in order to avoid balance of payments and competitiveness problems? Can one explain their low inflation records in terms of the exchange rate functioning as a nominal anchor? The real commitment, I suspect, was not to the exchange rate as such, but to low inflation, and hence to conservative domestic monetary and fiscal policies.[12]

What kept these countries off the South American road? What was the nature of their exchange rate commitment, especially up to 1981? Clearly, the commitment has not been absolute. There were devaluations before 1981 (and there have been significant real and nominal depreciations since 1982). In focusing on the pre-1982 period, it seems to me that the explanation for a considerable degree of the rigidity of nominal exchange rates lies in certain well-established beliefs.

One was a concern with prestige: devaluation was thought to represent an admission of failure. More generally, views about the desirability of fixed exchange rates remained widely held in these Asian countries even after the 1973 collapse of the Bretton Woods system. A second important factor was the thoroughly justified belief that devaluation was inflationary. In Sri Lanka's first macroeconomic crisis of 1968-70, devaluation was ruled out as an appropriate policy instrument because of concern with the adverse effect of a devaluation on newly established industries that were heavily dependent on imported inputs. Other countries have also had this concern.

When exchange rate pegging to a single currency came to an end, all five of these countries continued to follow low inflation policies. Looking back with hindsight, it may be that the spell of the fixed exchange rate backed up the anti-inflation commitment, so that there was some element of a nominal exchange rate anchor. But with substantial devaluations by some countries since 1973, and with large changes in bilateral nominal rates compelled by the fluctuations in the dollar, the spell has no doubt been broken by now.

Similar issues arise for various other countries in our group that maintained more-or-less fixed rates (sometimes with occasional devaluations) for long periods, namely Costa Rica until 1980 (with a devaluation in 1974), Kenya, Mexico until 1976, Morocco, Nigeria (to 1984), and Turkey. In all these cases, there have been long periods with fixed or near-fixed rates lasting well after the 1973 breakdown of the Bretton Woods system. Some of these countries — Costa Rica (briefly), Mexico, Nigeria, and Turkey — have gone through high inflation episodes, while Kenya and Morocco have not. All have used quantitative restrictions for balance of payments purposes at various times. Only the two countries in our group that are part of the franc zone — Côte d'Ivoire and Cameroon — have had a true fixed exchange rate commitment, leading inevitably both to low inflation and to real depreciations and appreciations that reflected movements in the franc-dollar rate.

The case of Turkey is particularly interesting. Since about 1977 the economy has moved from relatively low inflation to high inflation, a transformation associated with a switch in exchange rate regime from a fixed rate to a crawling peg.[13] From the point of view of the real-targets approach, a very simple story can be told. For reasons that need not be discussed here, Turkey had its debt crisis from 1977 to 1979. The need to drastically improve the current account and to reverse the appreciation of the real exchange rate that occurred between 1974 and 1979 called for substantial real depreciation. As part of a major stabilization program, the nominal exchange rate was depreciated by about 70 percent in 1980. From 1981 on, the rate was adjusted daily. The net result was a substantial real depreciation of about 30 percent by 1984, followed quickly by a remarkable export boom. This episode was regarded by Balassa (1983) and others as a striking and praiseworthy example of the success of exchange rate policy and, above all, as evidence that export supply and demand elasticities were high.

How does this episode look from the point of view of the nominal-anchor approach? The exchange rate was fixed to the U.S. dollar up to 1973, and during the period 1960-70 inflation averaged less than 5 percent. From 1971 to 1977 it averaged 18 percent. In 1980, an exceptional year, inflation was over 100 percent, reflecting the effects of the stabilization program, principally the big devaluation and large price adjustments by state enterprises. Inflation averaged 37.5 percent from 1981 to 1986 and has increased since then, reaching 75 percent in 1988 and 1989.

One could argue that such a high rate of inflation sustained now for nine years after a drastic stabilization program can only be explained by the removal of the nominal anchor in 1980. If that is the case, one would have to say that Turkey faced a trade-off between the benefits of maintaining a more appropriate real exchange rate for some time and the longer-term costs of higher inflation. This could be described as an "exchange rate-adjusted Phillips curve" trade-off. It is the trade-off that is implied if one concedes the validity of both the real-targets and the nominal-anchor approaches. But against the view that the change in the exchange rate regime explains (or helps to explain) the relatively high inflation rate since 1981, it can be pointed out that the inflation rate was already beginning to increase in 1971 and had reached 44 percent by 1978.

A reasonable conclusion is that by 1980 substantial devaluation was essential and indeed inevitable. But a government more committed to low inflation might have tried to fix the exchange rate firmly at a new, more depreciated level. Yet this would only have worked if there had been a genuine long-term commitment to a noninflationary monetary policy (and hence fiscal policy) in support of the nominal anchor at its new level. This commitment would have required strong public support, including a willingness to accept the transitional costs.

Inflation and Exchange Rates in the Latin American Chronic-Inflation Countries

Any discussion of the exchange rate as a nominal anchor must refer to the much-discussed experiences of the four chronic-inflation countries of South America in our group, as well as Mexico. Brazil and Colombia have practiced crawling peg policies over long periods, but it is clear in these cases that the exchange rate followed rather than led.[14] The aim of continuous nominal exchange rate adjustment was to avoid real appreciations — a clear example of the real-targets approach in an inflationary context — not to slow up inflation by constraining government or sending signals to private agents. This "passive crawling peg" policy, as Williamson (1981) has called it, has also been practiced in Argentina, Chile, and Mexico since 1982.[15] Finally, Argentina and Chile had each experienced an earlier brief, but much discussed, nominal-anchor episode.[16]

The Argentine episode of 1976-80 (under Finance Minister Martinez de Hoz) is now viewed as a classic case. A crawling peg exchange rate, with advance announcement of the devaluation rate (a *tablita*), operated for two years from 1979. In Williamson's (1981) classification, this was an "active crawling peg." A real appreciation resulted, and there was massive capital outflow. Domestic inflation failed to decline much because of continued high fiscal deficits. The failure of domestic inflation to decline sufficiently brought about the real appreciation. The failure was thus in the accompanying domestic policy, which led directly to a balance of payments problem and indirectly, because of the lack of credibility of the policies, to a slow reaction by private agents.

In the case of Chile, the exchange rate was fixed to the dollar for a brief period from the end of 1979 to 1981 in order to bring inflation down from 33 percent. The policy succeeded, since inflation was 7 percent by the end of 1981. But there was still high unemployment and a large real appreciation (the U.S. dollar was appreciating during that period relative to other currencies and Chilean inflation was still higher than U.S. inflation). Domestic monetary and fiscal policies were not out of line. To some extent, domestic prices and wages were slow to adjust to reduced inflation because of lagged wage indexation. But such slow adjustments in prices and wages in response to disinflationary policies could be expected even if there had been no formal wage indexation. In addition, some degree of real appreciation was also to be expected because of massive capital inflow. In my view, this much-analyzed episode cannot really be considered a failure. Chile's subsequent problems arose because of excessive private borrowing during that brief period as well as a decline in the terms of trade and a rise in real interest rates.

The two-year Chilean exchange rate commitment was a nominal anchor only insofar as the government chose to adhere to it. The fundamental commitment in Chile was to the objective of reducing inflation, just as in the five Asian countries the commitment has been to the objective of keeping inflation low.[17] The true anchor is the policymakers' conviction — usually rooted in and backed by widespread community conviction — that inflation is undesirable. Perhaps a fixed exchange rate has a role in signaling the government's anti-inflationary commit-ment to private agents. But they will always be alert — as they were in Argentina — to the possibility that the signal is a false one. If they are rational, they will look for the underlying commitment.

Capital Mobility: What Difference Does It Make?

Finally, in considering exchange rate policy, one cannot ignore the increase in capital mobility. Without going into the issue in detail, the judgment may be made that in many of the countries in our group — including Indonesia, Pakistan, Thailand, Morocco, Turkey, and all the Latin American countries — international capital mobility is now high and has been steadily increasing through the 1970s and 1980s.[18] What is the implication of this finding for exchange rate policy?

In general, the appropriate model is still one in which sterilized intervention is possible — that is, in which domestic interest rate policy is distinct from foreign exchange rate intervention policy. Hence the model is one of imperfect capital mobility, whether owing to partially effective exchange controls or imperfect substitutability of domestic-currency-denominated and foreign (usually dollar) assets.

The implication is that it is no longer possible to maintain for any length of time a nominal exchange rate that the market considers seriously overvalued. Such expectations would lead to capital outflow and thus to a balance of payments problem unless domestic interest rates rose sufficiently. And the tightening of domestic monetary policy to sustain an exchange rate may have to be so severe that there are limits to this instrument. While the exchange rate does not have to float, the rate must be quickly adjusted when market expectations turn signifi-cantly against it.

Some countries' policies of maintaining an exchange rate have been so consis-tent and hence so credible that market pressures against it hardly take place. Perhaps Thailand is the best example. But for most developing countries, the days of the Bretton Woods "fixed but occasionally adjustable" system are over. This consideration explains why many countries in our group have moved in the direction of more flexibility since 1982 — usually, so far, to flexible pegs rather than floating rates (with the exception of Nigeria, which has had a floating rate since 1986).

The Bretton Woods system broke down in 1973 largely because of increasing capital mobility and the failure of the United States and perhaps others to pursue credible domestic policies to sustain particular rates. Thus the developed world moved into the floating rate stage. By contrast, the developing countries (other than the four chronic-inflation countries of South America) generally tried until around 1982 to maintain either fixed rates or a fairly inflexible peg, with inter-mittent adjustments. But capital mobility increased for them as well, although with a lag, and many of these economies became destabilized as a result of the recession and debt crisis of 1980-82. With a few exceptions, their exchange rate regimes have now become much more flexible, and it seems unlikely that they could go back to the fixed but adjustable regimes of the earlier period.

This has implications for both the real-targets approach and the nominal-anchor approach. Both approaches call, at any point in time, for a policy-determined nominal rate. It might be an active crawling peg, but this still means that it is fixed at a point in time. Yet such a rate cannot be sustained unless the market is convinced it will be sustained. It is true that expectations of depreciation can be offset by sufficiently high domestic interest rates. But the need to target domestic monetary policy on sustaining the exchange rate when the market expects substantial depreciation is itself a constraint on the attempt to fix the exchange rate.[19]

It follows that the whole package of policies that goes with an exchange rate commitment — whether to achieve a real target or a nominal anchor — must be thoroughly credible if an exchange rate is to be maintained. This is conceivable when a country has been following consistent policies in the past (like Thailand or like Mexico up to 1973) and is perhaps keeping the rate constant or crawling on some steady basis. In the absence of such credibility, the actual rate would have to follow the direction in which the market expects it to move.

The policy implication is that, when there is high capital mobility, it is no longer possible to have extensive discussions about the appropriate real exchange rate and what this implies for the nominal rate, and then to make a major adjustment, perhaps as part of a stabilization program. Changes have to be made quickly, and normally they must be small and more frequent. This is the direction in which countries have been moving. When large changes are expected — and it is rare for a large change to be unexpected[20] — the market will force an early adjustment. If particular changes are desired in order to achieve real targets, the domestic policies that go with them must be in place or credibility about policy intentions must first be established. If there is a change in the fundamentals, such as a change in the terms of trade or a major trade liberalization, a nominal exchange rate change will be expected and cannot be delayed. If quick policy action does not bring it about, the market will force it.

While all the issues connected with the two approaches remain relevant when there is capital mobility, and the basic trade-offs remain the same, credibility now becomes crucial. If either approach calls for a particular nominal exchange rate and the market does not believe it will be sustained, two steps will need to be taken quickly. First, domestic monetary policy will need to be tightened sufficiently to maintain the rate immediately. Second, signals will need to be sent out — for example, through fiscal policy decisions — that will convince the market that the rate will be sustained. The short Argentinean episode of 1979-80 under Martinez de Hoz clearly shows what happens when this is not done.

Conclusion

Can one conclude with some simple policy recommendations? I would suggest four propositions which, although simple, have important repercussions. First, in general, the real-targets approach to exchange rate policy is the right one. The exchange rate should follow rather than lead, taking into account the various shocks or changes in other variables — notably fiscal policy, trade policy, and terms of trade changes.

Second, exchange rate policy should be associated with an appropriate noninflationary monetary policy. Normally, there has to be a direct commitment to the anti-inflation objective if inflation is to be avoided. In the absence of such a commitment — with monetary policies being inflationary — exchange rate policy must still be aimed at the real target (the real exchange rate) unless there is reason to believe that this would actually affect the commitment itself to a significant extent.

Third, because of capital mobility, delayed exchange rate adjustments must be avoided: if the rate needs to be changed, it should be done quickly.

Fourth, there is some role for the nominal-anchor approach for two groups of countries, which are at opposite extremes of the inflation scale. One group includes countries that have long-established fixed exchange rate systems (with occasional devaluations) and relatively noninflationary records. These countries may be well advised to stay with such a system, since their commitment will be credible. One thinks here especially of Thailand (and possibly Indonesia) and, of course, of the African countries in the franc zone. But only a few countries in our group could fall into this category now, although many more would have in 1973.[21]

At the other extreme are countries with a history of high inflation that are ready to stabilize by radically shifting their policies and making the necessary commitment. These countries may find a fixed exchange rate (or an active crawling peg) a valuable anchor in helping to constrain government monetary policies and in achieving credibility with the markets (including the labor market). Possibly Argentina, Brazil, and Mexico are in this category. But whenever a fixed-rate regime or an active crawl is chosen, there is likely to be some cost because of the real exchange rate misalignment (the exchange rate-adjusted Phillips curve trade-off), at least for a limited period.

Notes

The analysis in this paper draws on some of the findings of a World Bank research project entitled "macroeconomic policies, crisis and growth in the long run." The views expressed here are those of the author and should not be attributed to the World Bank. The author is indebted to Premachandra Athukorala for valuable comments on an earlier version of this paper.

1. All references to developing countries are to this group or to individual members of the group. The countries include two that are members of the franc zone — *Cameroon* and *Côte d'Ivoire* — and so their exchange rates have been completely fixed; four — *Argentina, Brazil, Chile,* and *Colombia* — that were "chronic inflation" countries before 1973, when they had quite high inflation rates and crawling peg or variable exchange rates even when most other countries had fixed rates and low inflation; and finally,

eleven others — *Costa Rica, Mexico, Morocco, Turkey, Kenya, Nigeria, India, Indonesia, Pakistan, Sri Lanka,* and *Thailand.*

2. On the basis of the real exchange rate indices calculated by the IMF, it seems clear that, for many of the countries in our group, real and nominal (trade-weighted) exchange rates have moved together closely since 1981. For earlier years, there is strong evidence in Edwards (1989). But the effects do tend to get eroded, as evidenced both in Edwards (1989) and, for example for Indonesia, in Warr (1984).

3. The reference is to Salter (1959), who presented the first systematic, diagrammatic model with traded and nontraded goods.

4. The assumption is made here that imports and domestically produced importables are perfect substitutes — an assumption which is clearly unrealistic in a world of product differentiation. Hence it should be regarded as no more than a simplifying assumption. It should be noted that the real exchange rate, as well as being defined as the relative price of domestically produced tradables to nontradables, as here, could be defined as an index of "competitiveness," that is, as the price of traded goods in foreign countries, adjusted for the nominal exchange rate, relative to their prices in the domestic economy. This definition, which is favored in Balassa (1987), hinges on the realistic assumption that foreign and domestic tradables are imperfect substitutes, so their prices, adjusted for the exchange rate, can indeed differ. The main arguments in this paper — especially in the comparison between the real-targets and the nominal-anchor approaches — apply fully when imports and domestically produced import-competing goods are imperfect substitutes; the latter, in terms of the (Salter) model of this paper, are, in effect, nontradables.

5. The point is also made in many papers by Béla Balassa.

6. The term "real exchange rate" is used here in a particular way, namely to refer to the movement of ep_m / p_n or ep_x / p_n, that is, excluding the effect of the change in t. Alternatively, one might follow Edwards and van Wijnbergen (1987) and define the real exchange rate as S (equation 1 in this paper), in which case there would not necessarily be any real appreciation when a fall in ep_m / p_n leads to a sufficient rise in t.

7. It might be argued that the chronic-inflation countries of Latin America in our group have never been reluctant to depreciate. In particular, Brazil has been most ready to depreciate, with the nominal exchange rate tracking domestic inflation with the aim of roughly maintaining the real rate over considerable periods. Nevertheless, Brazil has made much use of quantitative import restrictions. Wage indexation has often limited the ability of Brazilian nominal exchange rate depreciation to bring about sufficient real depreciation. In the case of the other chronic-inflation countries in our group — Argentina, Colombia, and (at an earlier stage) Chile — there was also often a reluctance to depreciate enough or quickly enough. Colombia has usually had a crawling peg, although, from the point of view of optimal switching and avoidance of restrictions, it has not always crawled fast enough.

8. This simplification does not apply when a fiscal deficit is financed by issuing domestic bonds or by foreign borrowing. One must then refer specifically to monetary, not fiscal, policy. As the experience of Côte d'Ivoire shows, a fixed exchange rate is compatible with a big budget deficit provided foreign finance is available.

9. When expectations and capital mobility are introduced, a foreign exchange crisis can occur at this point.

10. This problem has been central to the literature on exchange rate policies for developing countries. How should developing countries fix their rates in a world where the major currencies are themselves floating? See Black (1976), Williamson (1982), and Joshi (1990).

11. The average annual inflation rates (consumer price index) for the period 1965-88 have been 8.7 percent for Pakistan, 8.4 percent for Sri Lanka, 8.2 percent for India, and 6 percent for Thailand. For Indonesia, the inflation rates in each year during the period 1962-68 were well over 100 percent, but the average for 1969-88 was 14 percent. Figures for 1982-88 were 10.3 percent (Sri Lanka), 8.6 percent (India), 8.5 percent (Indonesia), 5.9 percent (Pakistan), and 3 percent (Thailand) — rather remarkable when seen from the Latin American perspective or, in the case of Thailand, from any perspective.

12. It must also be noted that all these countries used quantitative import restrictions and exchange controls for short-term balance of payments purposes (strongly so in the case of India, Pakistan, and Sri Lanka). So all had available a switching instrument that could substitute for devaluation — although not, of course, for continuous devaluation.

13. This discussion draws on the study on Turkey by Ziya Onis and James Riedel (to be published) conducted for the World Bank project.

14. See Urrutia on Colombia and Fendt on Brazil, both in Williamson (1981).

15. With respect to Mexico it should be added that, after six years of depreciation necessitated by high inflation, the Mexican peso was fixed to the dollar in 1988 and was adjusted on the basis of an active crawling peg policy in 1989. Both episodes were part of the Mexican stabilization plan which, among other things, required wage increases to be limited. But one cannot really say in this case that the exchange rate was the nominal anchor: the anchor was (and is, at the time of writing) the commitment to the whole stabilization plan.

16. On Argentina see Calvo (1986); on Chile, Balassa (1985b), Corbo (1985), and Edwards and Edwards (1987); and on both countries, Corbo, de Melo, and Tybout (1986) and Corbo and de Melo (1987).

17. A critique of the nominal-anchor approach as applied to Chile can be found in Balassa (1985b, 203-08).

18. Measurement of capital mobility is difficult (see Cumby and Obstfeld 1983, Cuddington 1986, various papers in Lessard and Williamson 1987, and Haque and Montiel 1989). It is not sufficient to look at actual capital movements. There have been dramatic episodes of capital flight from Argentina and Mexico, so clearly mobility is high in those cases. But capital mobility may also be high in the case of a country such as Brazil where, until recently, incentives for capital outflow were not as strong because the flexibility of the nominal exchange rate was designed to maintain the real rate. In other countries, interest rates are raised quickly when there is a tendency to capital outflow; in still other countries, notably Pakistan and Turkey, the flow of remittances from citizens working abroad is likely to vary to some extent in response to exchange rate expectations.

19. The problem arises only when expected depreciation substantially exceeds expected domestic inflation, so that a high real rate of interest is required to sustain the current nominal exchange rate. A high real exchange rate has adverse effects both for private investment and for the budget. This problem is intensified when inflationary expectations are excessive (when actual inflation falls below expected inflation). In addition, in many developing countries the domestic free market rate exceeds the international (U.S.) rate by a substantial risk factor. The net effect of all these factors can be shown by the Mexican example. In 1989, when Mexico practiced an active crawling peg policy, its real rate of interest as usually calculated was around 30 percent while the U.S. rate was closer to 4 percent. The usual calculation assumes that the expected rate of inflation is equal to the current one, but there is little doubt that in this case the expected rate of inflation in Mexico exceeded the remarkably low current one, so that the true real rate of interest must have been less than 30 percent.

20. The one example from our group of countries of a large unexpected devaluation is the 33-percent Indonesian devaluation of 1978, the motive for which was "exchange rate protection" of the tradables sectors, not a balance of payments problem (see Warr 1984). It appears from the low forward premium that the 15-percent Thai devaluation of 1984 was also unanticipated.

21. One might even wonder about the franc zone countries. As a result of a public spending boom in Côte d'Ivoire in 1976-80, inflation increased, causing a real appreciation, which led to increased tariff and nontariff import restrictions. Latin American-style inflation has certainly been avoided in spite of a prolonged fiscal crisis, but import restrictions and a severely reduced growth rate have not.

References

Balassa, B. 1977. *Policy Reform in Developing Countries.* Oxford: Pergamon Press.

Balassa, B. 1981. *The Newly Industrializing Countries in the World Economy.* Oxford: Pergamon Press.

Balassa, B. 1983. "Outward Orientation and Exchange Rate Policy in Developing Countries: The Turkish Experience." In B. Balassa, *Change and Challenge in the World Economy.* London: Macmillan.

Balassa, B. 1985a. *Change and Challenge in the World Economy.* London: Macmillan.

Balassa, B. 1985b. "Policy Experiments in Chile, 1973-83." In Gary M. Walton, ed., *The National Economic Policies of Chile.* Greenwich, Conn.: JAI Press.

Balassa, B. 1987. "Effects of Exchange Rate Changes in Developing Countries." DRD Discussion Paper No. 201. Washington, D.C.: Development Research Department, World Bank.

Balassa, B. 1989a. *New Directions in the World Economy.* London: Macmillan.

Balassa, B. 1989b. *Comparative Advantage, Trade Policy, and Economic Development.* New York: Harvester Wheatsheaf.

Black, S.W. 1976. *Exchange Rate Policies for Less Developed Countries in a World of Floating Rates.* Princeton Essays in International Finance No. 119. Princeton, N.J.: Princeton University.

Calvo, G. 1986. "Fractured Liberalism: Argentina Under Martinez de Hoz." *Economic Development and Cultural Change* 34 (April): 511-33.

Corbo, V. 1985. "Reforms and Macroadjustment in Chile during 1974-84." *World Development* 13: 893-916.

Corbo, V., and J. de Melo. 1987. "Lessons from the Southern Cone Policy Reforms." *The World Bank Research Observer* 2 (July): 111-42.

Corbo, V., J. de Melo, and J. Tybout. 1986. "What Went Wrong with the Recent Policy Reforms in the Southern Cone?" *Economic Development and Cultural Change* 34 (April): 607-40.

Corden, W.M. 1971. *The Theory of Protection.* Oxford: Oxford University Press.

Cuddington, J. 1986. "Capital Flight: Estimates, Issues and Explanations." Princeton Studies in International Finance No. 58. Princeton, N.J.: Princeton University.

Cumby, R.E., and M. Obstfeld. 1983. "Capital Mobility and the Scope for Sterilization: Mexico in the 1970s." In P. Aspe et al., eds, *Financial Policies and the World Capital Market.* Chicago: University of Chicago Press.

Edwards, S. 1989. *Real Exchange Rates, Devaluation, and Adjustment: Exchange Rate Policy in Developing Countries.* Cambridge: MIT Press.

Edwards, S., and A. Cox Edwards. 1987. *Monetarism and Liberalization: The Chilean Experience.* Cambridge, Mass.: Ballinger.

Edwards, S., and S. van Wijnbergen. 1987. "Tariffs, Real Exchange Rate, and the Terms of Trade: On Two Popular Propositions in International Economics." *Oxford Economic Papers* 39 (September): 458-64.

Haque, N., and P. Montiel. 1989. "Capital Mobility in Developing Countries: Some Empirical Tests." International Monetary Fund, Washington, D.C.

Joshi, V. 1990. "Exchange Rate Regimes in Developing Countries." In M. Scott and D. Lal, eds, *Public Policy and Economic Development: Essays in Honour of Ian Little*. Oxford: Oxford University Press.

Krueger, A. 1978. *Foreign Trade Regimes and Economic Development: Liberalization Attempts and Consequences*. Cambridge, Mass.: Ballinger.

Lessard, D.R. and J. Williamson. 1987. *Capital Flight and Third World Debt*. Washington, D.C.: Institute for International Economics.

Salter, W.E.G. 1959. "Internal and External Balance: The Role of Price and Expenditure Effects." *Economic Record* 35 (August): 226-38.

Swan, T.W. 1963. "Longer Run Problems of the Balance of Payments." In W.M. Corden and H.W. Arndt, eds, *The Australian Economy: A Volume of Reading*. Melbourne: Cheshire.

Warr, P.G. 1984. "Exchange Rate Protection in Indonesia." *Bulletin of Indonesian Economic Studies* 20 (August): 53-89.

Williamson, J., ed. 1981. *Exchange Rate Rules*. New York: St Martin's Press.

Williamson, J. 1982. "A Survey of the Literature on the Optimal Peg." *Journal of Development Economics* 11: 39-61.

15

Trade Policy, Market Orientation, and Productivity Change in Industry

Mieko Nishimizu and John M. Page, Jr.

On the supply side, economic growth is determined by the expansion of productive resources and by improvements in their use. Total factor productivity (TFP) is a measure of the efficiency with which all inputs are combined and utilized in the production of goods and services.

Two questions concerning productivity growth are particularly relevant for the design of economic policy. Both questions are empirical in nature. First, what is the nature and magnitude of productivity growth? Second, does the character of the productive environment matter; that is, do stages of development or the nature of the policy regime make a difference to productivity change?

We address the first question by examining the historical experience of productivity growth in manufacturing industries of a diverse group of countries. A major objective of our analysis is to determine whether the role of productivity change in growth differs between developing economies, which are in the process of structural transformation, and developed economies, which have already passed through this process. We then address the second question by exploring a number of the important hypotheses about the role of economic policy in affecting industrial growth and efficiency over time.[1] Do policies designed to protect producers from import competition weaken incentives to improve productivity, and do market allocation systems result in improved productivity performance?

In its research design, this inquiry follows closely the framework of comparative empirical analysis pioneered by Béla Balassa and his associates (1971, 1982) in examining the structure of protection in developing countries. Balassa made major contributions to the understanding of commercial policy in developing countries by drawing generalizations ("stylized facts") from a broad sample of carefully executed country studies of effective protection and by linking the empirical results to the design of public policy.

Interpretations of Total Factor Productivity Change

The analytical framework for measuring TFP is founded on the economic theory of production and cost, and the relevant literature is well known.[2] The theory of production and cost depicts technology to represent the maximum feasible limit to production, with changes in TFP as the shift in that frontier. Technology summarizes know-how applied to production. The framework is based on a simple stylization of production and markets that ignores a number of issues that may be important. Among these are the technological relationship between inputs and outputs, the behavioral objectives of producers, and the competitive conditions of markets. In presenting our empirical results, we first discuss limitations of the framework that are important in understanding what estimated TFP changes (or differences) mean and in interpreting these estimates to ascertain their implications for economic policy.[3]

Traditionally, TFP change has been interpreted as efficiency gains due to implementation of new generations of technical knowledge. This interpretation is appropriate for TFP growth trends in the long term, where technological information has been disseminated widely; new technology has been learned by managers, workers, and engineers alike; new investments have been made; and inefficient firms have been weeded out in a competitive production environment. TFP changes are then the result of changes in this broadly interpreted technology applied to production.

In the short to medium term, however, the environment within which production takes place may make it infeasible for a firm to choose input-output combinations on the production frontier. If capacity is constrained, fixed inputs will restrict the firm's ability to vary output continuously at constant marginal cost. Thus, shorter-term TFP measures often fluctuate because they partly reflect changes in capacity-utilization.[4]

Other constraints may also prevent firms from choosing frontier production points. Firms may require explicit resource allocation — for training workers and engineers, learning practices, and generally mastering new technology — to reach a technological frontier. These conditions were originally investigated by Farrell (1957), who defined the amount by which measured TFP is less than its potential as "technical inefficiency." Nishimizu and Page (1982) have combined these two concepts using a methodology to decompose TFP change into technological progress and changes in technical efficiency.

Even if firms are free of constraints and can produce at the frontier, however, they may still choose to do otherwise because of behavioral objectives other than profit maximization. The loss in potential output due to a lower allocation of work effort than needed to maximize profits was called "X-inefficiency" by Leibenstein (1976). For managers, workers, or both, it may be important to make satisfactory trade-offs between leisure and work. Such trade-offs may not be simply a matter of taste, but may be motivated by public policies. Martin and Page (1983), for example, investigated managerial effort-leisure decisions and concluded that "public policies designed to alter output and input prices, or to promote the development of 'desirable' enterprises through direct grants, can engender economic costs by allowing managers to indulge their preferences for a quiet life and / or encouraging them to engage in 'rent-seeking,'... leading to a reduction in X-efficiency" (p. 616).

Industrial Productivity Growth: Does "Environment" Matter?

The production environment is defined by the nature of markets for inputs and outputs and by market and nonmarket constraints including public policies. Large changes in production environments alter prices, quantities, or qualities of inputs and outputs and may thus have important short- to medium-term impacts on productivity growth during the process of adjustment to new conditions. Different production environments sustained over a long period of time may have differential impacts on long-term productivity growth by offering different stimuli to managers to improve productivity and cost discipline.

Exploring the empirical relationship between the environment and productivity performance calls for a multicountry comparison to delineate systematic patterns of productivity growth in manufacturing industries of developing and developed countries. For most developing countries, economic growth has been based on shifts of resources from less productive to more productive activities, along with changes in tastes and in the composition of demand as income rises. The rate at which this structural transformation takes place is likely to be greater under conditions of significant market disequilibria. Economies with pronounced market disequilibria (particularly in factor markets) are more likely to experience rapid expansion or contraction of output, inputs, and productivity than developed ones. If productivity is increasing faster in growing activities than in contracting ones, so much the better since this variance in productivity growth should help accelerate growth for the economy as a whole. Markets of mature industrialized economies are better characterized by competitive equilibria, which tend to equate the productivities of different resources at the margin. Therefore growth in mature economies is more likely to be the outcome of a long-run process of resource accumulation and technological change.

The proposition that industries may differ significantly across countries in their productivity performance has a longstanding place in the economics of growth. The infant industry argument rests on the proposition that although *levels* of productivity may be lower in new industrial activities or newly industrializing economies, *rates* of productivity change will be higher, thereby permitting these industries or economies to catch up with their competitors.[5] Despite a wide use of the infant industry argument to provide a rationale for industrial promotion in developing countries, little evidence exists on the relationship between income levels and productivity change in industry (see Westphal 1981 and the literature cited therein).

Our TFP database on manufacturing industries contains seventeen countries (see table 15.1). The estimation periods for these countries vary somewhat between the late 1950s and early 1980s, but the measurement methodologies are reasonably comparable among our data sources. The coverage of industrial activities and the level of disaggregation also differ among countries, but we were able to maintain twenty-one industries (at roughly the two-digit level in the International Standard Industrial Classification, the ISIC) as the common denominator among the different

Table 15.1 Countries in the Industrial
Total Factor Productivity Database

Country	Income per capita (1981 US$)	Time period	Source
Sweden	14,870	1963-80	Wyatt (1983)
United States	12,820	1960-79	Gallop and Jorgenson (1984)
Finland	10,679	1960-80	Wyatt (1983)
Japan	10,085	1960-79	Jorgenson et al. (1985)
Yugoslavia	2,794	1965-78	Nishimizu and Robinson (1984)
Argentina	2,560	1956-73	Delfino (1984)
Chile	2,559	1960-81	Mierau (1986)
Mexico	2,250	1970-80	World Bank (1986c)
Hungary	2,100	1976-83	World Bank (1986a)
Korea	1,700	1960-77	Nishimizu and Robinson (1984)
Turkey	1,542	1963-76	Nishimizu and Robinson (1984)
Philippines	787	1956-80	Hooley (1982)
Thailand	679	1963-77	Bateman (1986)
Egypt	651	1973-79	Handoussa et al. (1986)
Zambia	597	1965-80	World Bank (1984)
Indonesia	524	1975-82	Nehru et al. (1985)
India	256	1959-79	World Bank (1986b)

Note: Per capita income figures are from World Bank *World Development Report 1985*.

estimates. (The basic data on industrial output and TFP growth are provided in an annex table, available on request, which also gives the industrial classification.)

To find systematic patterns in data that have country and industry dimensions, we conducted a two-way analysis of variance on the distributions of TFP growth rates.[6] The results indicate that one cannot reject the hypothesis that all industrial TFP growth rates are drawn from the same distribution within each country but that one can reject the hypothesis that country TFP growth rates are drawn from the same distribution within each industry. Thus significant intercountry variations exist for each industry with a largely common technology and rate of technological change, suggesting that differences in productivity performance among countries are influenced by country-specific as opposed to industry-specific factors.

Figure 15.1 shows the relationship between the average rate of TFP growth in the industrial sector of each country and its per capita income (see table 15.1 for per capita income data). The most striking feature of the figure is the extreme difference between the TFP performance of the high-income countries and all others. For the four economies with incomes above $10,000 per person, the average rate of TFP growth appears to be roughly independent of the level of per capita income. In these economies, there is very little variance around the average rate of approximately 1 percent a year. One percent a year may in fact represent what the mature industrial economies should expect as the long-term rate of technological change in industry.

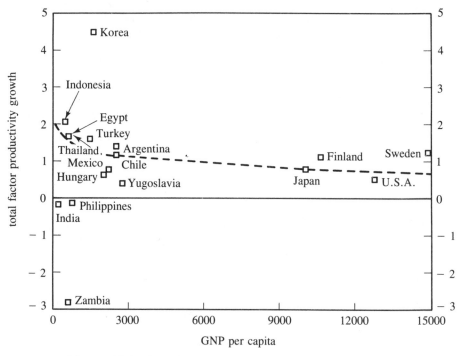

Figure 15.1 Relationship between Total Factor Productivity Growth and GNP per Capita

It is more difficult to find regularities among developing countries in the per capita income range up to $3,000. If all observations are included, the relationship may be curvelinear in income, with low-income countries (less than $1,000 per person) associated with low or negative productivity change on average, and middle-income countries ($1,000-3,000 per person) showing rates of TFP change above those of developed countries. We were unable, however, to find any non-linear relationships that are statistically significant.

An alternative interpretation is also possible. Three countries in figure 15.1 (India, Philippines, and Zambia) have negative rates of TFP growth. Negative productivity performance in the medium to long term is incompatible with the process of structural transformation. These countries, however, appear to have sustained such performance, on average, for more than two decades. Thus, long run negative productivity change may reflect irregularities attributable to the sustained use of inappropriate economic policies or errors in measurement. If we exclude these countries, average rates of productivity growth appear to fall with the rising level of per capita income. Statistically, this relationship can be log-linear in per capita income:

$$TFPG = 4.29 - 0.37 \ln y,$$
$$(1.93)\ (0.24) \qquad\qquad R^2 = 0.16,$$

where the variables *TFPG* and *y* are TFP growth rates and per capita income, respectively, and standard errors are given in parentheses.

Similar relationships exist between TFP growth rates and per capita income in individual industries as well. Simple regression results on the log-linear relationship are given in table 15.2. The fall in average rates of TFP growth with increasing income appears to be more pronounced for such industries as food, beverages, and tobacco; chemicals; transport equipment; and, to a lesser extent, wood and furniture; paper and printing; and nonmetallic minerals. In petroleum and coal products and ferrous and nonferrous metals, the average rates of TFP growth are exceptionally low or negative for mature industrial economies, leading to a relatively sharp fall in the rates of productivity change with rising income.

Table 15.2 Total Factor Productivity
Change and Per Capita Income,
Regression Results for Twelve Industries

Industry	Intercept	Slope	R^2
Food, beverages, and tobacco	12.69 [a]	-1.34 [a]	0.44
Textiles, apparel, and leather products	4.03 [b]	-0.30	0.06
Wood products and furniture	6.55 [c]	-0.55	0.12
Paper and printing	5.39 [a]	-0.50 [c]	0.13
Rubber products	3.78	-0.15	0.01
Chemical products	8.83 [a]	-0.82 [b]	0.33
Petroleum and coal products	8.92 [c]	-1.08 [c]	0.34
Nonmetallic mineral products	5.32 [c]	-0.45 [c]	0.12
Ferrous and nonferrous metal products	13.73 [a]	-1.46 [b]	0.30
Metal products and nonelectrical machinery	2.64	-0.09	0.02
Electrical machinery and precision instruments	5.47 [c]	-0.36	0.04
Transport equipment	8.54 [b]	-0.75 [c]	0.20

Note: The estimated relationship is $TFPG = a + b \ln y$.
a. Significant at the 99-percent level.
b. Significant at the 95-percent level.
c. Significant at the 90-percent level.

These results suggest an empirical regularity that supports the infant industry argument. On average, the rate of TFP growth falls with rising income, reaching a stationary-state rate of approximately 1 percent a year at high levels of per capita income. This relationship also carries over into a wide range of individual industries. Apparently, developing countries can sustain rates of productivity growth in excess of those in the developed countries of sufficient magnitude and duration to permit them to catch up, and so the infant industry argument can therefore be empirically viable. However, the presence of a subset of countries with different patterns of productivity growth — including Korea's spectacular performance as a positive outlier — also suggests that productivity growth may be susceptible to variations in the economic policy regime chosen to promote industry.

There is another pattern in the TFP growth rates across different countries that raises interesting questions and speculations. There is a significantly positive rank correlation between the standard deviation of the productivity distributions and the per capita income level of different countries (Kendall's tau is 0.758, significant at the 95-percent level).[7] The association between the variance of TFP growth rates and the level of incomes is most striking when the four industrial countries (Sweden, United States, Finland, and Japan) are contrasted with all others.[8]

Theoretically, long-run competitive equilibrium should minimize differences in TFP growth rates (or levels) among different industries. Because high rates of TFP growth permit producers to increase more rapidly the compensation of production factors, resources should be pulled toward high productivity growth industries until differentials in growth rates (and levels) of productivity are eliminated. (Similar patterns appear for both output and input growth.) Thus, increasing variance in TFP growth with declining per capita income is consistent with the view that structural impediments to resource mobility (including lack of information and incomplete markets) are significant determinants of the pattern of productivity growth in developing countries.[9]

Trade Policy, Market Orientation, and Productivity Performance

If the variance in output, resource, and productivity growth among different activities is greater for developing countries, policies that affect resource allocation may have higher risk than they do in industrial economies. Misallocation of resources to low productivity industries may persist longer than in developed market economies, and the penalties associated with low productivity growth are greater. In the extreme case, inappropriate policies for resource allocation may result in negative productivity change, offsetting the contributions of faster accumulation to output growth.

Hypotheses on the Relationships Between Policies, Growth, and Productivity

Many hypotheses have been advanced concerning the relationships between development policies, growth, and productivity change. Prominent among them are hypotheses addressing the appropriate use of trade policy in increasing growth and productivity, which now constitute a substantial body of literature. Although the focus of Balassa's research was on the allocative costs of high and variable protection, it is noteworthy that his early work on the structure of protection (1971) also argued that trade policy could have an important impact on productivity change. Perhaps equal attention to that received by trade policy has been given to the role of market mechanisms in guiding the allocation of resources and providing incentives for cost discipline and productivity improvement.

One obvious linkage between trade policy and productivity performance is related to the assumed positive association between output growth and productivity change — an association that has been named Verdoorn's Law. Kaldor (1967) noted that Verdoorn's Law is most prominently observed in manufacturing and other secondary industrial activities and argued that the fundamental explanation for this law is scale economies. In developing countries, market size has long been viewed as an important determinant of growth and structural transformation. The existence of economies of scale, or of any other reason for the Verdoorn-Kaldor hypothesis, implies that a widening of the market through trade should lead to reductions in real production costs. In the context of an outward-oriented development strategy, this argument is usually cast in terms of the benefits of increased demand through export expansion, but it applies equally to rapid import substitution in large domestic markets.[10]

The literature on foreign exchange constraints offers another possible link between trade policy and productivity performance. This link derives from the observation that in many developing countries, imported intermediate and capital goods are not highly substitutable with domestically produced goods. Policies that limit the availability of these imports reduce the potential of domestic producers to utilize capacity and therefore reduce productivity in the short to medium term. Increased availability of foreign exchange, on the other hand, can raise capacity utilization and lead to short-term increases in TFP.[11]

A different trade policy argument has to do with the effects of international competition on the efficiency of domestic producers. It is possible that the challenge implied by international trade forces domestic industries to respond by adopting new technologies to improve efficiency and generally reducing costs wherever possible. This theme has been developed by Balassa and widely discussed in his writings on commercial policy (see, for example, Balassa 1989). According to this argument, both export rivalry and import competition are beneficial to productivity performance. Although an import liberalization policy may restrict the demand for domestic goods, such a policy also increases competition and therefore improves production efficiency. The converse argument is also widely asserted: protectionist policies designed to promote import substitution can have dynamic efficiency costs (beyond the allocative losses) arising from reductions in competitiveness and increased inefficiency in production.[12]

On the efficiency costs of protectionist policies, however, there is logical clarity on one issue: the *instruments* by which protection is afforded to domestic industries can affect productivity performance quite apart from the *levels* of protection granted. Thus, for example, quantitative restrictions on imports break the link between domestic and international prices, thereby insulating domestic producers from *movements* in international prices. Such an import regime will permit rising costs to be passed forward in a fashion that is not possible under equivalent tariff protection. Changes in international prices convey substantial information on productivity trends in the rest of the world; instruments that interfere with the transmission of these prices can make the productivity performance of competitors irrelevant and lead to deteriorations in comparative advantage over time.[13]

Arguments similar to those on the efficacy of international competition also apply to domestic competition. Ultimately, it is the force of competition — whether external or internal — that challenges firms and induces the response of technical change, innovation, and sustained efforts to increase productivity and reduce cost. It is often the case that this challenge-response mechanism is largely absent in economies in which nonmarket allocation of resources dominates, whether in the form of planning or market regulation.

Moreover, the relationship between resource allocation and productivity performance depends on the planning and regulatory rules applied in such economies. Theoretically, it is possible for planners or regulators to "simulate the market," so enabling distributions of TFP growth rates very like those of market economies to develop. In practice, however, it is impossible for planners or regulators to have ideal models and information that replicate market solutions continuously, particularly in large and complex economies. As a result, planned or highly regulated economies tend to generate incentives that equate averages, which are easily observed, as opposed to marginals, which are more difficult to see. Thus, nonmarket economies may differ significantly from market economies in both their levels and distributions of TFP growth rates.

The hypotheses discussed above are not mutually exclusive. Neither are the postulated effects of policy choices on productivity performance independent of each other. It is likely that one observes the net effect of a combination of these phenomena simultaneously, so that discriminating among policies and their consequences is difficult. In addition, one must always be cautious in implying the direction of causality from a statistical association.

Analysis of the Association between Policies and Productivity Growth

The Verdoorn-Kaldor Law provides us with a starting point in exploring associations between policies and productivity change. Suppose we take the Verdoorn-Kaldor Law as an expression of some technological axiom. Given the rapid industrial growth made possible by structural disequilibrium, productivity growth in developing economies should be more varied among industrial activities, but faster on average for the sector as a whole in the medium to long term, compared with developed economies. Hence a strong association between output growth and productivity growth should be regularly observed in newly industrializing economies, as long as policies meant to promote industrialization do not attenuate it.

Since productivity growth is a measure of supply-side response, we focus on the demand-side of industrial growth. We take the growth of export demand and the growth of total domestic demand less import demand as the exogenous components of demand-side growth (or as components determined by exogenous policy regimes). We can also interpret the latter as representing the degree of import penetration in the domestic market of each industry.

In addition, we consider two aspects of economic policies. The first is the instruments used to protect domestic producers from import competition. More specifically, we evaluate the extent to which different countries have applied quantitative restrictions on industrial imports, through trade plans, quotas, and import licensing. The second aspect is the market orientation of different policy regimes, that is, the degree to which the regimes permit resource allocation to occur through competitive markets in the industrial sector. We evaluate the extent to which different countries have used planning, direct government investments, investment licensing, and other distortionary measures (such as price and wage controls, product portfolio regulations, and firm size limitations) in the industrial sector.

The single equation model we estimate is of the following form:

$$TFPG = a_0 + a_1 \, QR + a_2 \, NM + b_0 \, e + b_1 \, e \, QR + b_2 \, e \, NM + c_0 \, (m\text{-}d)$$
$$+ \, c_1 \, (m\text{-}d) \, QR + c_2 \, (m\text{-}d) \, NM + u,$$

where $TFPG$, e, m, and d, are the growth rates of total factor productivity, export demand, import demand, and total domestic demand, respectively. QR and NM are dummy variables that take, respectively, the value of unity for policy regimes in which quantitative import restrictions and nonmarket allocation of resources dominate. Because all nonmarket economies in our sample also use quantitative import controls, the variables are defined to be mutually exclusive. A random disturbance term, u, is added and assumed to be distributed normally around zero.

We estimate the model on our country and industry panel of data for the entire time period in the sample and for two important subperiods, the period prior to the first oil shock (through 1973) and the period following 1973 up to the early 1980s. Broadly speaking, the first period can be thought of as an era of steady growth in industrial output and trade for the world economy. The second was one of adjustment to a series of major disturbances following the initial rise in petroleum prices, including rising protectionism, a fall in the world prices of many primary products, rising interest rates in international financial markets, and further fluctuations in oil prices.

For some countries, major changes in policy regime are observed between these two periods, and so the structure of the dummy variables differs between the periods (see table 15.3). Because we were unable to find a direct measure of growth in total domestic demand (or of domestic deliveries) that is consistent among all industries and countries in our sample, we had to resort to the surrogate measure of gross output growth rates. Thus, we assume that the rate of growth in total domestic demand is correlated with that of gross output at the level of aggregation of manufacturing industries in our data. Under these assumptions, we applied an ordinary least squares regression to the cross-section data. The results are presented in table 15.3. The regressions explain between 7 and 11 percent of the variance in TFP growth rates, and omnibus F-statistics are significant in all cases.

Table 15.3 Policy Regimes and Change in Total Factor Productivity Growth: Regression Results

	Intercept			Export growth			Import penetration		
	a_0	QR	NM	b_0	QR	NM	c_0	QR	NM
Whole period	1.07 [a]	-0.89 [c]	-0.36	0.01 [b]	-0.01	-0.04	-0.08 [a]	0.05 [c]	0.06
(1956-1983) [d]	(0.29)	(0.46)	(0.56)	(0.00)	(0.01)	(0.04)	(0.02)	(0.02)	(0.04)

$R^2 = .072$ F = 5.23 (563 observations)

Before 1973	0.89 [b]	-0.00	-1.00	0.02 [a]	-0.02 [c]	-0.01	-0.00	0.03	-0.02
	(0.37)	(0.57)	(0.97)	(0.00)	(0.01)	(0.07)	(0.03)	(0.04)	(0.05)

$R^2 = .079$ F = 2.72 (262 observations)

After 1973	0.84 [c]	-1.42 [b]	0.02	0.02 [c]	-0.01	-0.05	-0.13 [a]	0.09 [b]	0.10 [c]
	(0.44)	(0.69)	(0.72)	(0.00)	(0.01)	(0.04)	(0.03)	(0.03)	(0.05)

$R^2 = .113$ F = 4.57 (301 observations)

Summary by policy regime	Intercept	Export growth	Import penetration
Whole period			
Market-oriented, no QRs	1.07 [a]	0.01 [b]	-0.08 [a]
Quantitative restrictions	0.18	0.00	-0.03 [b]
Nonmarket-oriented	0.71 [a]	-0.03	-0.03
Before 1973			
Market-oriented, no QRs	0.89 [b]	0.02 [b]	-0.00
Quantitative restrictions	0.89 [a]	0.00	0.03
Nonmarket-oriented	-0.11	0.01	-0.02
After 1973			
Market-oriented, no QRs	0.84 [c]	0.02 [c]	-0.13 [a]
Quantitative restrictions	-0.58	0.01	-0.04 [b]
Nonmarket-oriented	0.87 [a]	-0.03	-0.03

Note: Policy regimes of countries are as follows:
Quantitative restrictions (QRs)
   Before 1973 - Argentina, Chile, Mexico, Philippines, Turkey
   After 1973 - Indonesia, Mexico, Philippines, Turkey, Zambia
Nonmarket-oriented
   Before 1973 - India, Yugoslavia
   After 1973 - Egypt, Hungary, India, Yugoslavia
a. Significant at the 99-percent level.
b. Significant at the 95-percent level.
c. Significant at the 90-percent level.
d. See table 15.1 for the time period relevant for each country.

Our first important result concerns exports. Export growth is positively correlated with TFP growth in the industrial sector, but only in economies that follow market-oriented policies in general and that do not resort extensively to quantitative import restrictions in particular. This result is present in both periods but is stronger in the period before 1973. For the other economies, there is no association between export growth and productivity growth. Non-market-oriented policy regimes tend to subsidize exports and to view them as a means of raising foreign exchange to finance necessary imports; little regard seems to be given to the economic efficiency of such exports. Similarly, quota-constrained market economies often have incentive regimes that favor the development of small quantities of high-cost exports to provide foreign exchange for inputs into import-substitution industries. The results therefore appear to be consistent with the tendencies of these policy regimes.

These results on exports do not provide insight into the direction of causation, however. It is plausible to assert that rapid productivity growth (derived perhaps from exogenous factors) leads to cost advantages, which are translated into increased exports. It is equally plausible, however, to assert that the competitive pressure of export markets induces more rapid productivity change in industry. In any case, however, the significant and positive association between TFP growth and export success provides some empirical justification on a broad range of issues: the efficacy of export-oriented development strategies (of Korea and Japan, for example), the increasing popularity of export-promotion policies among developing countries, and even the current concerns in some industrial countries (notably the United States) about the need to improve "international competitiveness" in manufacturing, in addition to relying on the exchange rate to improve export performance.

A second result to be noted concerns the role of import penetration. Significant relationships emerge between import penetration and TFP performance during the post-1973 period of adjustment, but the effect is quite different depending on the character of the policy regime. After 1973, open market economies have a significantly negative association between increased rates of import penetration and TFP growth. This could be interpreted as reflecting the nature of industrial adjustment in the post-1973 period. Industries in open economies have had to adjust to substantially altered relative prices in order to establish or regain international competitiveness. In industries where adjustment through productivity growth was slow or did not occur, imports would have captured an increasing share of the domestic market. This may imply that under conditions of adjustment with relatively low barriers to imports, low rates of TFP growth are a source of increased import penetration, as imports expand due to their competitive advantage.

Similar results hold for economies in which industries are protected by quantitative measures. In these economies, however, the negative association between import penetration and TFP growth is strongly attenuated. This result is consistent with the fact that price disadvantages arising from poor productivity performance are not fully reflected in increased imports since imports are exogenously fixed in the short to medium term in a restrictive trade regime. In addition, because domestic demand expansion does not spill over into imports when quantitative restrictions are applied, rapid increases in capacity utilization arising from expansionary demand management will result in falling unit costs. Whatever the cause, however, the offsetting effect is not large enough to eliminate the significantly negative net coefficient on import penetration in the post-1973 period.

Among countries that guide industry with nonmarket policies, however, the attenuating effect with respect to import penetration was sufficiently strong to completely offset the negative association. This is consistent with the fact that these countries pursued expansionary demand management policies throughout the 1970s while shielding their industries from external shocks and competition. In other words, industries in these economies have substantially delayed the needed adjustment to the new economic environment.

In the steady growth period before 1973, there is no apparent relationship between TFP change and import penetration. This may indicate that after an initial short-run period of adjustment, import competition results in a "recovery" of TFP performance in the longer run. Ultimately, rates of domestic productivity change will approximate international price (and exchange rate) movements, which should give rise to long-run independence between the two variables.

A third result of some consequence has to do with the rate of TFP growth that is independent of the impact of export expansion and import penetration. Among open market economies, these rates of TFP change are significantly positive regardless of the period in question. During the growth years before 1973, economies with quantitative import restrictions also show an average TFP growth rate similar to that of open market economies. After 1973, however, closed economies exhibit significantly lower TFP growth rates — in fact, the average rate, controlled for trade effects, becomes essentially zero. In the case of nonmarket-oriented economies, average TFP growth is statistically zero during the pre-oil shock period. After 1973, average productivity growth, net of trade effects, becomes similar to that of open market economies.

Taken together, the three sets of results build a case for the medium- to long-term benefits of a market-oriented policy environment that is more open to international trade.[14] In such economies, export expansion is strongly and positively associated with productivity growth, and this relationship holds consistently during the period of adjustment to major external shocks as well as during the years of steady growth. While import penetration into slower productivity growth industries does occur after 1973, the average rate of TFP growth (controlling for the effect of export expansion and import penetration) remains positive. Industries in these economies seem to be adjusting to establish or regain their competitive advantage. In the long run, import competition results in a recovery of TFP performance, as evidenced by the lack of association between productivity growth and import penetration in the steady growth period before 1973.

During the rapid growth period prior to 1973, the industrial productivity performance of economies resorting to quantitative trade barriers appears similar to that of more open market economies, with the exception, of course, of the absence of the positive export effect. When confronted with major external shocks, however, industries protected by quantitative restrictions seem to have difficulty adjusting. While import penetration was less strongly associated with negative productivity growth, average productivity performance collapsed.

Among nonmarket-oriented economies, industrial productivity performance is significantly lower than in others during the steady growth years — TFP growth was essentially nil before 1973. After 1973, there is no evidence of a significant correlation between TFP growth and import penetration, and in fact productivity growth behavior becomes similar to the pre-1973 behavior of economies protected under quantitative restrictions. In nonmarket economies, all of which shielded their industries from external shocks, the results substantiate the view that major delays occurred in industrial adjustment.

Conclusion

The results that we have presented tend to raise as many questions as they answer. Broadly, however, the results suggest that productivity growth is not an exogenously determined variable that proceeds independently of the character of the production environment — be it stages of development or nature of the policy regime.

In industry, the role of productivity change in growth differs between mature economies, which have passed through the process of structural transformation, and developing economies. For developed economies, the contribution of productivity change to growth seems to derive primarily from long-run technological change, which tends to limit the magnitude of TFP growth rates. Nevertheless, productivity growth represents a substantial share of economic growth, given the relatively low rates of factor accumulation in these economies. Among developing countries, the potential for exploiting sectoral productivity differentials in the process of structural transformation presents an opportunity for achieving higher medium-term rates of productivity growth than in the developed economies.

One relationship of particular interest that emerges from the data provides an empirical verification of the infant industry argument. Rates of industrial productivity growth decline from about 3.5 percent a year (on a gross-output basis) at low levels of income to an asymptotic value of approximately 1 percent a year for countries at high levels of income. However, three major outliers in the low-income range (India, Zambia, and the Philippines) exhibit sustained negative rates of productivity change. These observations are clearly inconsistent with the infant industry argument as well as with sustainable growth of the industrial sector in the medium to long term. We have interpreted the negative industrial productivity growth in these countries as examples of policy-induced deviations from the longer-run structural relationship between income and productivity change.

Our analysis shows that the variance of TFP, output, and input growth rates generally increases with declining per capita incomes. We have interpreted this phenomenon as reflecting the greater structural impediments to resource allocation in developing economies. The structural characteristics present both an increased potential for productivity gains through reallocation from low to high productivity growth industries and a significant risk because of the lack of "automaticity" in correcting allocative errors.

Our analysis of patterns of productivity change indicates that although structural characteristics are important in explaining TFP change in industry, policy regimes can create major changes in the production environment that result in "atypical"

TFP performance. We were able to examine only one subset of variables related to the policy environment for industry — that related to foreign trade performance, commercial policy, and market orientation. Although these variables do not define the whole policy set for industry, they provide several important insights into the relationship between the policy regime and productivity change.

First, export growth in industry is positively associated with TFP performance, in periods both of long-term growth and of shorter-term adjustment. This positive export effect, however, is absent under import regimes that use quantitative restrictions and under industrial policy regimes that interfere with resource allocation through competitive markets. Second, during the adjustment period following the 1973 oil shock, poor productivity performance was associated with increased import penetration, albeit more strongly in regimes that relied on nonquantitative instruments of commercial policy. In the steady growth period before 1973, however, there is no such relationship. Import competition appears to result in a recovery of TFP performance in the long run. Third, industries protected primarily by quantitative barriers to trade seem to have difficulty adjusting to external shocks, unlike industries subject to a more open trading environment. For nonmarket-oriented economies that shielded their industries from external shocks, our results support the view that industrial adjustment was greatly delayed. Taken together, these results demonstrate that dynamic gains can accompany superior productivity performance in more open and market-oriented policy environments. This, in turn, suggests a case for the medium- to long-term benefits of such policy environments.

Our results substantiate the view that the production environment can profoundly affect productivity, particularly in developing countries. The structural characteristics of these economies create the potential for accelerated productivity growth through the expansion of industries having substantial scope for mastery of technology and improvements in technical efficiency. At the same time, however, there is a risk that policy actions that affect resource allocations may prevent the realization of these productivity gains.

Notes

This paper stems from a World Bank Research Project: Productivity Change in Infant Industry. The authors wish to thank Deborah Bateman for her advice and constructive discussions, Sujin Hur for excellent research assistance, and Barbara Mierau Klein for providing us with her unpublished data on Chile.

1. See Nishimizu and Robinson (1984) for an empirical investigation of similar questions regarding four semi-industrialized economies. See Balassa (1981), Bhagwati (1987), and Westphal (1981) for clear discussions and examination of the relevant policy issues.
2. For a historical perspective on productivity research, see Fabricant (1973). The concept of TFP was first introduced by Tinbergen (1942) and Stigler (1947), independently of each other. The economic theory of production was proposed as the explicit analytical framework for TFP measurement by Solow (1957). He defined TFP growth as the shift

in an aggregate production function, and measured TFP growth for the U.S. economy over the period 1909-49. In recent decades, advances in closely related areas of economic theory and measurement have strengthened the theoretical foundations of TFP measurement. Particularly important were advances in duality theory, including the work by Shephard (1953, 1970), Uzawa (1964), and McFadden (1966, 1978). Advances have also been made in the basic measurement problem of aggregation in defining appropriate quantity and price indices of output, input, and TFP. These contributions include those of Diewert (1976, 1978). A concise summary of the relevant theoretical literature and references is given in Caves, Christensen, and Diewert (1982a,b). See also Gollop and Jorgenson (1980).

3. See introductory remarks by Solow (1957), which offer a pragmatic view on these limitations. See also Nelson's (1981) critical survey of the productivity literature.

4. Important contributions to improvements in TFP measurement include Kendrick (1954, 1956, 1961), Denison (1962, 1967, 1969, 1972, 1974), Griliches and Jorgenson (1966), Christensen and Jorgenson (1969), among others.

5. For public intervention to be justified, the normative infant industry argument adds that the eventual excess profits in the industry must yield a present value higher than the present value of the net losses due to initial excess costs, when discounted at the social discount rate. In addition, a market failure or imperfection must exist to justify public underwriting of a portion of the initial costs.

6. The two-way analysis of variance yields the following:

	Degree of freedom	Sum of squares	Mean square	F statistic
Countries	18	796.5	44.2	6.73
Industries	21	251.5	2.0	1.82
Error	348	2285.7	6.6	
Total	366	3333.6		

7. There is also a positive rank correlation between the per capital income level and the coefficient of variation of the TFP growth distributions, with Kendall's tau equal to 0.691 at the 90 percent level of significance.

8. The average coefficient of the four industrial countries in the sample is 1.22, compared with a mean value of 2.95 for developing countries.

9. It is also possible that errors in measurement are greater in developing countries than in developed ones.

10. See Bhagwati (1987) for a comprehensive discussion of outward-oriented strategy and related trade policy issues.

11. See Handoussa, Nishimizu, and Page (1986) for a demonstration of this proposition in Egypt after the "opening."

12. Care must be taken, however, not to overstate the arguments regarding the benefits of outward orientation. Excessive export promotion policies, for example, will distort incentives and lead to rising inefficiency in export production. Also, the infant industry argument calls for according protection to high-cost industries that cannot compete immediately but are expected to become internationally competitive.

13. Nishimizu and Page (1986) present a formal analysis of this argument and some supporting empirical evidence.

14. See, for example, Balassa (1981) for a comprehensive analysis of adjustment policies.

References

Abramovitz, M. 1956. "Resource and Output Trends in the United States Since 1870." *American Economic Review* 46 (May): 5-23.

Balassa, B. 1981. *Adjustment to External Shocks in Developing Economies.* World Bank Staff Working Paper No. 449. Washington, D.C.

Balassa, B. 1989.*Comparative Advantage, Trade Policy and Economic Development.* New York: Harvester Wheatsheaf.

Balassa, B., and associates. 1971. *The Structure of Protection in Developing Countries.* Baltimore, Md.: The Johns Hopkins University Press.

Balassa, B., and associates. 1982. *Development Strategies in Semi-Industrial Economies.* Baltimore, Md.: The Johns Hopkins University Press.

Bateman, D. 1986. "The Role of Productivity Growth in Thailand's First 20 Years of Industrialization: An Analysis of the Manufacturing Sector." World Bank, Industry Department, Washington, D.C.

Berndt, E.R., and M.A. Fuss. 1981. "Productivity Measurement Using Capital Asset Valuation to Adjust for Variations in Utilization." Paper Presented at the Econometric Society Summer Meetings, San Diego, California (June).

Bhagwati, J. 1987. "Outward Orientation: Trade Issues." Paper presented at the World Bank-International Monetary Fund Symposium on Growth-Oriented Adjustment Programs, Washington, D.C.

Cassels, J.M. 1937. "Excess Capacity and Monopolistic Competition." *Quarterly Journal of Economics* 51 (May): 426-42.

Caves, D.W., L.R. Christensen, and W.E. Diewert. 1982a. "Multilateral Comparisons of Output, Input, and Productivity Using Superlative Index Numbers." *The Economic Journal* 92 (March): 73-86.

Caves, D.W., L.R. Christensen, and W. E. Diewert. 1982b. "The Economic Theory of Index Numbers and the Measurement of Input, Output, and Productivity." *Econometrica* 50 (November): 1393-1414.

Chenery, H.B. 1986. "Growth and Transformation." In H. Chenery, S. Robinson, and M. Syrquin, eds, *Industrialization and Growth: A Comparative Study.* London: Oxford University Press.

Christensen, L.R., and D.W. Jorgenson. 1969. "Measurement of U.S. Real Capital Input, 1929-1967." *Review of Income and Wealth* 15: 293-320.

Cowing, T.G., and R.E. Stevenson, eds. 1981. *Productivity Measurement in Regulated Industries.* New York: Academic Press.

Delfino, J.A. 1984. "La Productividad En Argentina." Universidad Nacional de Cordoba.

Denison, E.F. 1962. *Sources of Economic Growth in the United States and the Alternatives Before Us.* Supplementary Paper No. 13. New York: Committee for Economic Development.

Denison, E.F. 1967. *Why Growth Rates Differ.* Washington, D.C.: The Brookings Institution.

Denison, E.F. 1969. "Some Major Issues in Productivity Analysis: An Examination of Estimates by Jorgenson and Griliches." *Survey of Current Business* 49 (May): 1-27.

Denison, E.F. 1972. "Final Comments." *Survey of Current Business* 52 (May): 95-110.

Denison, E.F. 1974. *Accounting for United States Economic Growth 1929-1969.* Washington, D.C.: The Brookings Institution.

Diewert, W.E. 1976. "Exact and Superlative Index Numbers." *Journal of Econometrics* 4: 115-145.

Diewert, W.E. 1979. *The Economic Theory of Index Numbers.* Discussion Paper 79-09. Vancouver: Department of Economics, University of British Colombia.

Fabricant, S. 1973. "Perspective on Productivity Research." In *Conference on an Agenda for Economic Research on Productivity*. Washington, D.C.: National Commission on Productivity.

Farrell, M.J. 1957. "The Measurement of Productive Efficiency." *Journal of the Royal Statistical Society* series A, vol. 120, part III: 253-81.

Gollop, F.M., and D.W. Jorgenson. 1980. "U.S. Productivity Growth by Industry, 1947-1973." In J.W. Kendrick and B.N. Vaccara, eds, *New Developments in Productivity Measurement and Analysis*. Chicago: University of Chicago Press.

Gollop, F.M., and D.W. Jorgenson. 1984. *U.S. Economic Growth: 1948-1979*. Cambridge, Mass.: Harvard University Press.

Griliches, Z., and D.W. Jorgenson. 1966. "Sources of Measured Productivity Change: Capital Input." *American Economic Review* 56 (May): 50-61.

Handoussa, H., M. Nishimizu, and J.M. Page, Jr. 1986. "Productivity Change in Egyptian Public Sector Industry After 'The Opening,' 1973-1979." *Journal of Development Economics* 20 (January / February): 53-73.

Hooley, R. 1982. *Productivity and Growth in Philippine Manufacturing: Retrospect and Future Prospects*. Manila: Philippine Institute for Development Studies.

Jorgenson, D., W.M. Kuroda, and M. Nishimizu. 1985. "Japan-U.S. Industry Level Productivity Comparison, 1960-1979." Paper prepared for the U.S.-Japan Productivity Conference, Cambridge, Mass., August 26-28.

Kaldor, N. 1967. *Strategic Factors in Economic Development*. New York: W. F. Humphrey.

Kendrick, J.W. 1954. "National Productivity and Its Long-Term Projection." *Studies in Income and Wealth*, vol. 16. New York: National Bureau of Economic Research.

Kendrick, J.W. 1956. "Productivity Trends: Capital and Labor." *Review of Economics and Statistics* 38 (August): 248-57.

Kendrick, J. W. 1961. *Productivity Trends in the United States*. Princeton, N.J.: Princeton University Press.

Klein, L.R. 1960. "Some Theoretical Issues in the Measurement of Capacity." *Econometrica* 28 (April): 272-86.

Leibenstein, H. 1976. *Beyond Economic Man*. Cambridge, Mass.: Harvard University Press.

Martin, J.P., and J.M. Page, Jr. 1983. "The Impact of Subsidies on X- Efficiency in LDC Industry: Theory and an Empirical Test." *The Review of Economics and Statistics* 65 (November): 608-17.

McFadden, D. 1966. *Cost, Revenue and Profit Functions: A Cursory Review*. Institute for Business and Economic Research Working Paper No. 86. University of California, Berkeley.

McFadden, D. 1978. "Cost, Revenue, and Profit Functions." In M. Fuss and D. McFadden, eds, *Production Economics: A Dual Approach to Theory and Applications*. Amsterdam: North-Holland.

Mierau, B. 1986. "The Impact of Trade Policies on Productivity Performance in the Chilean Manufacturing Sector." Ph.D. Diss., Department of Economics, Georgetown University, Washington, D.C.

Nadiri, M.I. 1970. "Some Approaches to the Theory and Measurement of Total Factor Productivity: A Survey." *Journal of Economic Literature* 8 (December): 1137-77.

Nadiri, M.I. 1972. "International Studies of Factor Inputs and Total Factor Productivity: A Brief Survey." *Review of Income and Wealth* 18 (June): 129-54.

Nehru, V., Ho-Shik Kim, and D. Bateman. 1985. "The Structure and Performance of Indonesian Manufacturing." World Bank, Washington, D.C.

Nelson, R.R. 1981. "Research on Productivity Growth and Differences: Dead Ends and New Departures." *Journal of Economic Literature* 19 (September): 1029-64.

Nishimizu, M., and J.M. Page, Jr. 1982. "Total Factor Productivity Growth, Technological Progress and Technical Efficiency Change: Dimensions of Productivity Change in Yugoslavia, 1965-78." *The Economic Journal* 92 (December): 920-36.

Nishimizu, M., and J.M. Page, Jr. 1986. "Productivity Change and Dynamic Comparative Advantage." *Review of Economics and Statistics* 68 (May): 241-47.

Nishimizu, M., and S. Robinson. 1984. "Trade Policies and Productivity Change in Semi-Industrialized Countries." *Journal of Development Economics* 16 (September / October): 117-206.

Shephard, R.W. 1953. *Cost and Production Functions*. Princeton, N.J.: Princeton University Press.

Shephard, R.W. 1970. *Theory of Cost and Production Functions*. Princeton, N.J.: Princeton University Press.

Smith, A. 1937 (1776). In E. Cannan, ed., *An Inquiry into the Nature and Causes of the Wealth of Nations*. New York: Random House.

Solow, R.M. 1957. "Technical Change and the Aggregate Production Function." *Review of Economics and Statistics* 39 (August): 312-20.

Stigler, G.J. 1947. *Trends in Output and Employment*. New York: National Bureau of Economic Research.

Tinbergen, J. 1942. "Zur Theorie der Langfristigen Wirtschafts-entwicklung." *Weltwirtschaftliches Archiv* band 55, no. 1; English translation (1959). "On the theory of Trend Movements." In L.H. Klassen, L.M. Koyck, and H.J. Witteveen, eds, *Jan Tinbergen, Selected Papers*. Amsterdam: North-Holland.

Uzawa, H. 1964. "Duality Principles in the Theory of Cost and Production." *International Economic Review* 5 (May): 216-20.

Verdoorn, P.J. 1949. "Fattori che Regolano lo Sviluppo della Productivia del Lavoro." *L'Industria*: 3-11.

Westphal, L. E. 1981. *Empirical Justification for the Infant Industry Argument*. World Bank Staff Working Paper No. 445. Washington, D.C.

World Bank. 1982. "Portugal: Policies for Restructuring." (Restricted Distribution).

World Bank. 1984. "Zambia: Industrial Policy and Performance." (Restricted Distribution).

World Bank. 1985. *World Development Report 1985*. Washington, D.C.

World Bank. 1986a. "Hungary: Industrial Policy, Performance, and Prospects for Adjustment." (Restricted Distribution).

World Bank. 1986b. "India: Industrial Regulatory Policy Study." (Restricted Distribution).

World Bank. 1986c. "Mexico: Trade Policy, Industrial Performance, and Adjustment." (Restricted Distribution).

Wyatt, G. 1983. "Multifactor Productivity Change in Finnish and Swedish Industries, 1960 to 1980." ETLA Elinkeinoelaman Tutkimuslaitos B 38. Helsinki.

16

Adjustment Under Different Trade Strategies: A Mean-Variance Analysis with a CGE Model of the Yugoslav Economy

Irma Adelman, Dušan Vujovic, Peter Berck, and Miroljub Labus

A major focus of Béla Balassa's research since the mid-1970s has been on the comparative performance of economies pursuing different trade strategies under external shocks. Using data from different economies over various periods (see, for example, Balassa 1984, 1986, and 1987), he has demonstrated that, on the average, economies that have engaged in export-oriented growth have adjusted better to the two oil shocks than economies that have engaged in import-substitution policies. He has therefore argued that the proper policy response by developing countries to the more variable and slower-growing international environment of the 1970s and 1980s is to shift to open development strategies and export their way out of the debt crisis. In his later writings (for example, Balassa 1989), he has emphasized that this shift requires institutional reform within developing countries to make them more flexible and more responsive to price signals.

Introduction: Commercial Policies Under Uncertainty

The analytic literature on trade under uncertainty does not offer unequivocal results concerning optimal commercial policies. Some models of trade under uncertainty indicate that uncertainty in international markets may make it optimal for a risk-averse country to move toward autarky (Ruffin 1974, Sarris 1985, and Cheng 1987). This line of research suggests that, under conditions of uncertainty, import substitution may well be superior to export-led growth. However, the literature on trade under uncertainty also indicates that optimal adjustment policies differ with the structure of the model (for example, how much substitution has been built in); the timing of decisions (for example, whether decisions must be taken before the uncertainty is revealed or can be postponed until after the uncertainty has manifested itself); the objectives of the adjustment (for example, whether the aim of adjustment is to achieve stability, growth, or better income distribution); and the modeling of the shocks (for example, whether uncertainty is additive or multiplicative, and whether the shock is a price or a quantity shock). Theoretical conclusions thus tend to be model- and situation-specific and to offer no general guidelines concerning optimal development and adjustment strategies under uncertainty (see Adelman et al. 1989).

Actual adjustments to the oil shocks of 1973 and 1979 and to the debt shocks of the 1980s have varied greatly among countries. And the variety in adjustment patterns has been more complex than a simple dichotomy of export orientation or import substitution (see Corbo and de Melo 1989 for adjustment in Latin American countries, and Lin 1986 for East Asian countries). In particular, countries have differed not only in commercial policies but also in their degree of liberalization of domestic commodity and credit markets, efforts to reduce total absorption, inflation rates and measures to control them, and extent of debt-led growth. The sequencing of different policy measures has also varied substantially among countries, as have the conditions prevailing before adjustment began. While some clusters of policies can be labeled import substitutionist and others export expansionist, the adjustment policies of individual countries do not correlate perfectly with either trade regime. Furthermore, countries have switched among trade regimes with sufficient rapidity that the full effects of neither policy regime can be fully captured by following given countries' actual experiences.

Some economies have clearly adjusted more successfully to shocks arising in the external sector than others. But it is hard to disentangle from cross-country evidence just how much of the relative success of particular countries was due to differences in policies (for example, with respect to protection), how much to differences in economic structure, and how much to the differing impacts of the same external shocks on economies that have been pursuing different development strategies in the past and are of different sizes.

In this paper, we investigate the transition from import-substitution to an export-oriented strategy in the context of a single economy, Yugoslavia. Yugoslavia has followed different trade policies during the past two decades. The year 1980 saw the culmination of a long period of import substitution and growing foreign debt. In 1984, Yugoslavia experienced a strong short-term external adjustment based on an International Monetary Fund (IMF) standby arrangement that was regarded as a first step toward an export-oriented strategy. The year 1984 was characterized by substantial government pressures to export and continued import rationing, but without neutral tariff policies or an increase in the economic flexibility of the domestic economy. The economy in 1987 reflected a relaxation of government pressures to export, gradual reduction in import quotas, and greater, although still incomplete, flexibility and openness of the trade regime.

None of the years portrays a "fully open" trade regime, in the Balassa-Bhagwati sense; however, both 1984 and 1987 reflect attempts to embark on export-oriented growth. And both 1984 and 1987 reflect trade-offs between external and internal adjustment relative to 1980. We study the characteristics of these trade-offs, as well as the robustness of the economy to shocks arising in international markets under these different trade regimes.

Methodology

Our methodology is to develop three separate computable general equilibrium (CGE) models (one each for 1980, 1984, and 1987) based on the social accounting matrix (SAM) appropriate for each of these years. The model solutions are used to study the economic characteristics of these three different periods. To study the stability of the economy in response to external perturbations, we construct a set of random international shocks on most of the exogenous variables in the model. The distribution of these shocks is based on an empirically derived variance-covariance matrix among shocks. We then expose each CGE model to the same set of one hundred random shocks drawn from this distribution and compute the expected values and variances of the equilibrium values of the endogenous variables for each of the three years.

We thus standardize the shocks to which the model economy is exposed. By comparing the means and variances of the endogenous CGE variables in response to the same exogenous shocks under three trade regimes, we can compare the robustness of the economy to shocks under different strategies.[1] Furthermore, since our comparison is based on comparative statics, our results reflect how the economy reacts to shocks in the long run, after enough time has elapsed to allow the economy to reach a new equilibrium. Unlike experiments produced by nature, our simulations are standardized for the type of shock and the basic structure of the economy, except for differences induced by the effects of trade regimes. Our simulations also reflect equilibrium responses.

Our results support Balassa's thesis concerning the stability of export-oriented development and the crucial role of institutional adjustment. The results also offer additional insights into the trade-offs between debt servicing and debt repayment and domestic welfare, and the dependence of preferred trade-strategy choices on the degree of risk aversion of policymakers.

The remainder of this section describes (1) the construction of the international shocks; (2) the CGE model used to transform the probability distribution of these shocks into a probability distribution of prices, incomes, domestic production, and imports and exports; and (3) the indicators of domestic welfare.

The Shocks

In this model, we analyze shocks to the domestic economy arising from international sources: dollar world prices of imports and exports in each of four traded sectors (agriculture, industry, energy, and services); workers' remittances in dollars; and the convertible exchange rate. (Independent shocks to the exchange rate are justified on the grounds that the exchange rate was controlled by the government but nevertheless was a potential source of shock since the government followed different adjustment rules during the period under review.) Our method of modeling the shocks was to consider as shocks the deviations from the values of the variables that could be predicted one year ahead. The values of the variables were first normalized so that their 1972 values were unity. The normalized values were then regressed over the period 1972 to 1987 on their lagged values and a constant.[2] The deviations from these regressions were then taken as the values of the shocks.

The equations fit with R-squares varying between .400 and .867; all had significant coefficients. Most of the variance in industrial export prices was systematic, and most of the variance in agricultural import prices was random. Table 16.1 gives the correlation matrix and the coefficients of variation of the shocks. The standard errors are substantial, yielding coefficients of variation between 11 percent and 35 percent. Energy prices had the highest variance, and the exchange rate had the lowest coefficient of variation over the sample period. The off-diagonal elements in the matrix indicate that the correlations among shocks are significant. In particular, worker remittances have a correlation of unity with the world price of energy exports and .82 with the world price of energy imports; worker remittances thus tend to mitigate the effects of high import prices. Except for energy prices, the correlation between the world price of Yugoslav imports and exports is not all that high. The correlation matrix also suggests some tendency for the world price of tourism to counteract the effects of high exchange rates.

Table 16.1 Correlation Matrix and Standard Errors of International Shocks

| | | | World price indexes | | | | | | Workers' |
| | | | Imports | | | Exports | | | |
	Exchange rate	Serv-ices	Agri-culture	Indus-try	Ener-gy	Agri-culture	Indus-try	Ener-gy	remit-tances
				Correlations					
Exchange rate	1.00	-0.58	-0.39	-0.29	-0.08	-0.30	0.18	-0.06	-0.06
World price indexes:									
Services	-0.58	1.00	0.61	0.26	-0.24	0.53	-0.38	-0.28	-0.28
Agriculture imports	-0.39	0.61	1.00	0.11	-0.21	0.34	-0.23	-0.40	-0.40
Industry imports	-0.29	0.26	0.11	1.00	0.47	0.01	0.21	0.31	0.31
Energy imports	-0.08	-0.24	-0.21	0.47	1.00	-0.32	0.62	0.82	0.82
Agriculture exports	-0.30	0.53	0.34	0.01	-0.32	1.00	-0.27	-0.13	-0.13
Industry exports	0.18	-0.38	-0.23	0.21	0.62	-0.27	1.00	0.61	0.61
Energy exports	-0.06	-0.28	-0.40	0.31	0.82	-0.13	0.61	1.00	1.00
Workers'remittances	-0.06	-0.28	-0.40	0.31	0.82	-0.13	0.61	1.00	1.00
			Coefficients of variation (in %)						
	10.66	13.15	35.21	25.51	32.83	21.29	14.20	19.98	19.98

Source: Computed from data for 1972-87 derived from *International Trade Statistics Yearbook* (various years), *International Financial Statistics Yearbook* (various years), and data published by the Federal Statistical Office and the National Bank of Yugoslavia.

The shocks themselves were constructed by drawing one hundred nine-tuples of shocks from a multivariate t-distribution with the estimated variance-covariance matrix and three degrees of freedom. A t-distribution was used because it has relatively fat tails, and our sample period included the two oil shocks and the grain price shock of 1973-74, which could not be adequately represented with a multivariate normal distribution.

Mapping of External Shocks into Domestic Activity Incomes and Prices
We used CGE models to map the random external shocks into variances of imports, exports, GDP, and consumer group incomes and prices. Three CGE models — for 1980, 1984, and 1987 — were used to translate the same distribution of external shocks into distributions of the endogenous variables. The models were identical in analytic structure, but each was based on a social accounting matrix for the appropriate year. The basic CGE has six sectors (agriculture, energy, industry, construction, productive services, and nonproductive services) and eight institutions (three household types [rural, urban, and mixed], enterprises, general government, collective consumption, and two rest-of-the-world accounts [clearing and convertible]). Both micro and macro closures in the model are Keynesian. Sector-specific wages are fixed, reflecting persistent wage differentials across sectors, and savings adjust to exogenously set investment.

We discuss here only the departures from the standard specification of CGE models.[3] Not surprisingly, these departures are in three areas: the specification of factor markets, the specification of firm behavior, and the specification of international trade.

The model has two sector-specific factors of production (labor and capital) reflecting the lack of factor markets in the Yugoslav economy. Capital is fully employed in each period and its rate of return varies. Labor has exogenously set sectoral wages, leading to adjustments in the effective use of labor by sector and to sector-specific unemployment. Value added is a constant elasticity of substitution aggregation of the factors of production, with elasticities of substitution ranging between 0.3 in agriculture and 1.2 in services. Gross domestic production is a Leontief aggregation of value added and intermediates.

The Yugoslav economy is organized in a collection of self-managed firms.[4] However, employment and wage distribution are regulated by a complex system of legislation which circumscribes the behavior of firms.[5] Specifically, the legal environment for self-managed firms in the sample period included such features as exogenously set minimum employment rates by sector, constraints on the use of retained profits for wages or exogenously set "proportions in enterprise income distribution," minimum and maximum wage controls, and discretionary tax exemptions for poorly performing enterprises and other subsidies. Since the Yugoslav CGE model was built as an applied model, we adopted a specification of firm-behavior that could accommodate most of these features. This was accomplished by splitting the factor demand relationships in the model from the determination of factor incomes. Factor demands follow the marginal-value-product rule. In dynamic (sequential) runs this rule is subject to minimum-employment constraints. If the labor demand derived from the marginal-value-product rule is overridden by the exogenously set minimum employment constraint, then the factor-specific efficiency parameter adjusts downward. Factor incomes are computed subject to additional government-set sector-specific constraints on enterprise income distribution (see Vujovic et al. 1985 and 1986 and Vujovic and Labus forthcoming).[6]

The third peculiar feature of the Yugoslav economy (and of other socialist economies) that needs to be modeled is the presence of two different trade and current accounts: convertible and clearing. Convertible trade consists of trade in which companies import and export in response to market signals subject to trade restrictions, and in which commodity and financial flows need to be in equilibrium. A convertible current account surplus (deficit) results in lower (higher) foreign debt or increased (decreased) foreign exchange reserves.

Clearing trade is determined on a long-term (five-year) contractual basis at the state level (commodity lists), with little or no reference to world-market prices. Clearing trade occurs only within the Eastern block and need not balance ex post. Imbalances can occur because of unanticipated changes in commodity prices or the clearing exchange rate or because of a failure to deliver contractually agreed-on quantities. A clearing trade surplus translates into an involuntary, zero-interest, open-ended-grace-period loan that can be "repaid" only by running a trade deficit with the same country in subsequent periods. But this might be very difficult to achieve since commodity lists are determined years in advance and the deficit-running country has no incentive to remedy the problem. Needless to say, a current account surplus within a clearing account area has a strong inflationary impact in the surplus country.

Clearing trade was modeled separately from convertible trade and convertible balance of payments because of its size (between 20 and 30 percent of total foreign trade) and different behavior. To enable the modeling of shocks in the convertible exchange rate, a fixed convertible exchange rate version of the model was used, and the clearing exchange rate was allowed to adjust. Both clearing and convertible exports followed the Powell and Gruen (1968) constant elasticity of transformation (CET) specification, but clearing exports had a very low elasticity of transformation. Similarly, both export demands were modeled with constant elasticities, but clearing export demands were very inelastic. Both clearing and convertible imports were modeled with fixed quantities and gave rise to import rents that clear the markets and accrue to importing enterprises. Armington functions were used to determine the changes in the composition of total domestic supply.

Equilibrium in convertible trade is achieved through an adjustment of exports to the exogenous random changes in the exchange rate and export prices, and through changes in the current account balance. Equilibrium in clearing trade is achieved primarily through an adjustment in the clearing exchange rate since export adjustments are constrained by low elasticities. It should be noted that the value of imports is not constant, despite quantity controls on imports, because of random changes in import prices and exchange rate.

The database for the three CGE models consisted of independently estimated social accounting matrices[7] for 1980, 1984, and 1987. Model parameters for 1984 (elasticities, consumption shares, level and shift parameters, and so on) were estimated from time-series data for 1965-84.[8] Parameters for 1980 and 1987 were kept at their 1984 values except for the trade and the trade-related elasticities. Specifically, changes from 1984 values were made for the elasticities of export demand, the elasticities of substitution between imported and domestic commodities, and the elasticities of transformation between supply to domestic markets and supply to world markets. These changes were introduced to reflect the impact of changes in trade regimes on the trade-related elasticities.

In 1980, import substitution was the dominant trade orientation. The elasticities of export demand, the elasticities of substitution between imported and domestic commodities, and the elasticities of transformation between supply to domestic markets and supply to world markets were all low. World demand for Yugoslav exports was rather inelastic because there were binding import restrictions in Organization for Economic Cooperation and Development (OECD) countries for major Yugoslav exports. Substitution between domestic and imported commodities was low, at the margin, since the domestic market was flooded with imported goods. There was little flexibility in shifting supply from domestic markets to exports because production was oriented mostly toward satisfying domestic market needs. To reflect these different conditions in 1980, we lowered the respective 1980 elasticities by 20 percent relative to 1984.

By contrast, in 1987 substantial trade and current account surpluses were achieved and a partial move toward export trade orientation was accomplished. World demand for Yugoslav exports was more elastic because the composition of exports had changed and a smaller fraction of exports was subject to import restrictions in OECD countries. After years of import restrictions, substitution possibilities between domestic and imported commodities had increased, particularly in consumer and capital goods. Finally, the elasticity of transformation between domestic and export supply had increased since firms had become more competitive; had increased the efficiency of input use, especially of energy and imported intermediates; and had improved their ability to move into foreign markets by producing goods more suitable for export. These new conditions in 1987 were reflected by increasing the respective trade-related elasticities by 20 percent relative to 1984.

In our experiments, the model structures were identical for the three years, as were all the non-trade-related parameters. The shocks were also the same, in percentage terms. The only differences among periods were in the social accounting matrices used and in the trade-related elasticities. These differences presumably reflect the changes in economic structure and the changes in behavior induced by the different trade regimes.

The Evaluation of Robustness and Welfare Changes

To provide information on the robustness of the economy under different trade regimes, the three CGE models were each run one hundred times, once for each of the previously computed combinations of shocks.

Welfare losses were generated by the economy's adjustment from the debt-supported import-substitution policies followed up to 1980 toward the export-oriented adjustment and debt-service policies of the 1980s. Since the representative consumer in each group (rural, mixed, and urban) is assumed to be risk averse, the instability in real incomes generated additional welfare losses. To evaluate the magnitude of these losses, we computed the expected equivalent variation for the consumer with the mean income of the group. The equivalent variation is the amount of money one would have to pay to make a consumer as well off as he or she would have been in the comparison-base in the absence of shocks. The expected equivalent variations for each year relative to the base in that year represent the welfare costs of instability. The expected equivalent variations with respect to 1980 reflect both the cost of adjustment and the costs of instability relative to the 1980 base.

The CGE model uses a linear expenditure system to represent consumers. The ordinal indirect utility function associated with that demand system is given by $v(y,p)$, where y is the income of the average consumer and p is the vector of prices facing the consumer. For a linear expenditure system, $v = (y - m'p) \prod p_i^{\alpha_i}$, where m is the "subsistence" vector, and α_i is the marginal share of income spent on good i. Let the expected utility for class i EU_i be

$$EU_i = E\left[\frac{v_i^{1-\beta}}{1-\beta}\right],$$

where the expectation is taken over the one hundred replicates. This utility function has decreasing absolute risk aversion and increasing, asymptotically constant relative risk aversion. It also has positive and diminishing marginal utility. We chose a value of β equal to 0.3. This value is in the range of values estimated for β in other countries and our results are not sensitive to this value. To estimate the equivalent variations we also need the minimum consumption bundle, $m'p$. We assumed that the values of $m'p$ are 60 percent of income for urban groups, 50 percent of income for mixed rural-urban groups, and 40 percent of income for rural groups.[9]

Results

Tables 16.2 through 16.4 summarize the behavior of the model Yugoslav economy under international shocks in our three model years. Table 16.2 summarizes the macroeconomic variables for the income, activity, and trade flows. It indicates the base solution values for the major variables in the CGE models and, under the one hundred replicates of random shocks, the expected values of the solution values of the variables, the standard deviations of the solution values, and the

Table 16.2 Macroeconomic Variables for the CGE Model of the Yugoslav Economy under International Shocks

Variable	1980				1984				1987			
	Base	Mean	Stand. dev.	Range	Base	Mean	Stand. dev.	Range	Base	Mean	Stand. dev.	Range
	(in billions of 1980 dinars)											
GDP at factor cost[a]	1704	1704	40	1591 1835	1753	1747	52	1533 1900	1805	1805	38	1631 1930
Institution/factor income												
Enterprise[bc]	494	495	40	382 622	464	459	45	273 591	493	492	41	310 625
Wages[de]	1027	1026	2	1023 1032	788	788	1	786 790	974	974	1	972 976
Disposable income[df]												
Rural households	87	85	6	73 106	76	74	7	61 97	72	71	4	63 84
Mixed households	318	317	4	308 332	236	235	5	226 251	272	271	3	266 281
Urban households	732	729	8	714 757	536	533	8	518 561	657	656	5	646 672
Consumption[d]												
Rural households	80	78	6	67 97	84	82	6	71 101	63	62	2	57 71
Mixed households	303	302	4	293 316	250	248	4	240 263	240	239	2	235 247
Urban households	700	697	8	682 723	503	501	7	486 527	554	553	4	545 567
Collective consumption[g]	132	131	0	131 133	171	170	1	169 172	231	231	0	230 232
Domestic supply[b]												
Agriculture	433	432	4	423 446	480	479	5	467 497	464	463	3	452 472
Energy	424	422	6	408 443	474	472	11	447 508	400	399	5	387 417
Industry	2169	2162	24	2115 2244	2025	2019	22	1972 2094	2253	2249	14	2210 2296
Construction	484	483	3	477 492	312	311	2	306 318	319	319	2	313 324
Productive services[h]	872	869	10	849 903	695	692	9	673 724	894	892	7	876 915
Nonproductive services[i]	589	588	2	584 595	314	313	2	310 319	591	590	1	587 595

Table 16.2 Macroeconomic Variables for the CGE Model of the Yugoslav Economy under International Shocks (cont.)

(in millions of dollars)[j]

Variable	1980				1984				1987			
	Base	Mean	Stand. dev.	Range	Base	Mean	Stand. dev.	Range	Base	Mean	Stand. dev.	Range
Exports	14930	15073	497	13359 15983	13637	13755	397	12399 14702	15814	15877	235	15049 16402
Of which convertible	9211	9094	748	5213 10541	8955	8835	793	4735 10377	12237	12147	946	7440 14087
Imports goods and services	18016	17909	1528	13255 22371	13431	13513	1250	9826 18784	14492	14475	1266	10363 19989
Of which convertible	16492	16433	198	16080 17165	10117	10080	133	9833 10557	12344	12322	87	12104 12626
Balance goods and services	-3087	-2836	-1390	-6618 1239	207	243	1326	-5775 3847	1322	1402	1294	-4313 5370
Terms of trade effect[k]	0	294	1346	-2872 4963	0	102	1226	-3090 4802	0	210	1408	-3360 6078
Import-control rents[l]	0	44	1587	-4575 5073	0	-135	1355	-5573 4015	0	-8	1319	-5804 4321

a. Converted to constant prices using the implicit gross material product deflator.
b. Converted to constant prices using the producer price index.
c. Equivalent to net retained profits before taxes. Excludes wage and interest payments.
d. Converted to constant prices using the consumer price index.
e. Gross wages, net of income in kind, before taxes and contributions, subsidies, and transfers.
f. Household income after taxes, including remittances and private transfers.
g. Consists of health care, social security, education, and the like.
h. Includes transport, wholesale and retail trade, tourism and catering, business services, and crafts.
i. Includes banking, insurance, housing, government, education, and health.
j. Converted into dollars using the dinar per dollar exchange rates of 24.64 for 1980, 125.67 for 1984, and 725.0 for 1987.
k. Computed as the change in the terms of trade times the volume of exports.
l. Rents are the difference between the world prices and the solution prices under the quota times the import quota quantity.

Source: Computed from one hundred replicates of random shocks to the Yugoslav CGE models for each of the analyzed years.

minimum and maximum solution values. Since variances give the same weight to positive and negative deviations from the base solution, and since very risk-averse policymakers care primarily about the relative frequency of adverse outcomes, these are summarized in table 16.3. The welfare evaluation of these outcomes is presented in table 16.4.

The first point to emerge from table 16.2 is that, for most of the income and activity flows, the expected values are close to the base solutions and the standard deviations of the solutions are small. Even though the shocks themselves have coefficients of variation averaging 22 percent and ranging from 10.7 percent (on the exchange rate) to 35 percent (on agricultural import prices), the coefficients of variation of the endogenous income and activity flows average only 2.2 percent. Only enterprise income and rural household income and consumption have coefficients of variation exceeding 5 percent.

Thus, on the average, the economy operates so as to considerably dampen the amplitudes of the fluctuations of domestic activities and incomes in response to external shocks. The mapping of external shocks on the domestic economy is very contractionary, despite the many non-neoclassical rigidities built into the model which constrain its substitution possibilities. The model allows for substitution possibilities between domestic and foreign goods in production and consumption through the Armington composite good in intermediate and final demand and through the CET specification in domestic supply. Substitution possibilities are also present in the sectoral composition of consumption and gross production. These substitution effects through international trade and through changes in the structure and levels of domestic production and consumption result in substantial smoothing of domestic fluctuations regardless of trade regime.

The second point to emerge from table 16.2 is that, despite small coefficients of variation, the range in outcomes is nevertheless substantial. For example, the minimum value of GDP at factor cost, averaged over all experiments for the three years, was 10 percent below the respective base solutions, and the equivalent minimal rural household incomes were 14.3 percent below their base values.

The third point to emerge from table 16.2 is that the shift from the import-substitution policies of the 1970s toward export-oriented adjustment has had different effects on domestic activity than on international disequilibria. Our solutions indicate that adjustment to international disequilibrium has been very substantial, while economic growth has been sluggish and real household incomes first declined substantially and then recovered somewhat although remaining significantly below the 1980 base.

Base Solutions

The results obtained for the base solutions are due to the differences in the SAM among periods. The differences in trade elasticities do not affect the base equilibrium solutions since for each solution-year the model was calibrated to reproduce the base-year SAM. There were no differences in model specification, nontrade exogenously specified model parameters, or in the distribution of shocks.

Table 16.2 indicates that GDP at factor cost continued to grow throughout 1980-87, but very slowly (0.6 percent annually between 1980 and 1984 and 1.1 percent between 1984 and 1987). Enterprise incomes declined less (7 percent) than wages (23 percent) between 1980 and 1984 and recovered relatively more than wages between 1984 and 1987, almost reaching the 1980 level in 1987 while wages were still 5 percent less than in 1980. Household real incomes declined substantially between 1980 and 1984 (by 26 percent), with urban incomes declining the most and rural household incomes the least. Between 1984 and 1987, household incomes recovered but remained 12 percent below their 1980 base.

Our results show that the functional distribution of income (rows 2-3 in table 16.2) changed quite significantly between periods. The distribution of household incomes also changed (rows 4-6 in table 16.2): the share of rural household income rose by 20 percent between 1984 and 1987 and then fell by 23 percent, ending up 7 percent below its 1980 share. Consumption expenditures (rows 7-10 in table 16.2) were relatively more constant than incomes, with continually increasing collective consumption, and with real household savings bearing the brunt of the adjustment burden.[1] Domestic supply (rows 11-16 in table 16.2) declined more than household incomes in 1984, so in 1984 the availability of goods and services was tight. The reverse happened in 1987: domestic supply increased 75 percent more than domestic incomes, leading to a relaxation of shortages. The composition of domestic supply changed substantially, especially in 1984: a higher share of agriculture and industry and a substantially smaller share for services, especially nonproductive services.

The extent and nature of external adjustment are described in the last 7 rows of table 16.2. External adjustment was very substantial and occurred initially mostly through cuts in imports despite strong export pressures. In 1980, the foreign trade deficit on goods and services was $2.8 billion. The strong export pressures coupled with stringent import quotas imposed in 1984 turned the deficit into a surplus of $240 million. By 1987, the surplus was $1.4 billion, achieved through export expansion with some relaxation of import quotas. The 1987 surplus was achieved not only on goods and services but also on current account. The current account surplus resulted from the surplus on the balance of goods and services, from the continued strong inflow of remittances, and from the somewhat lower interest payments on foreign debt (both interest rates and the debt outstanding declined in 1984 and 1987).

The base solutions thus indicate that between 1980 and 1984 external adjustment was achieved at the cost of stagnant GDP, large declines in household incomes (25 percent), and substantial contraction in domestic supply (13.5 percent). By contrast, external adjustment between 1984 and 1987 was achieved through the growth of exports (16 percent) and GDP (3 percent), with rising household incomes (18.2 percent) and domestic supply (2.8 percent). Thus, the real domestic cost of external adjustment was considerably less in the export promotion period, between 1984 and 1987, than in the austerity period, between 1984 and 1980. This confirms Balassa's findings that adjustment under export-orientation is less costly than adjustment through import restraint.

Stability under Shocks

The variances under shock had a systematic pattern. The systematic variation in variances across variables reflects the direct and indirect adjustment elasticities and substitution possibilities through trade at the sectoral level. The macro variances also reflect the sectoral composition of the relevant aggregates. Across years then, the variances under shock reflect not only the differences in trade elasticities, but also the differences stemming from the changed economic structures portrayed in the respective SAMs. As before, model specifications remained unchanged and the same distribution of shocks was imposed on the model economy in 1980, 1984, and 1987.

Table 16.2 indicates that the trade flows are considerably more variable than the income and activity flows, although their amplitudes are still much below those of the shocks. The coefficients of variation of exports and imports average 4.4 percent, roughly twice those of the income and activity flows. Fluctuations are more pronounced in convertible trade than in total trade and in exports than in imports. Imports are not constant, despite physical quantity constraints, because imports also depend on the random import prices, the random convertible exchange rate, and the model solution for the clearing exchange rate.

The greater variability in trade flows is to be expected since the shocks come from foreign trade and foreign trade represents a relatively small portion of domestic activity at the sectoral level. The greater variability in trade flows also results from model features that impose the major burden of adjustment on trade. The model features constraining the impact of shocks on activity and income flows, in a given solution period, are exogenously fixed sector-specific capital, aggregate investment, and total government consumption; lack of substitution possibilities in the use of intermediates; and distribution rules that stabilize household incomes and consumption. By contrast, trade was shocked directly, through shocks on world prices and exchange rates; no offsetting changes in import quantities were allowed; the 1984 Armington substitution parameters were low (0.9 on the average), resulting in a relatively stable domestic supply; and the 1984 Powell-Gruen transformation parameters were elastic (1.1 on the average), allowing relatively easy shift of domestic supply to exports.

Under the export-oriented IMF-supported adjustment of 1984, the vulnerability of the economy to shocks generally increased relative to 1980, especially in the income and activity flows. There were some exceptions, which indicate the bias of policy: wages, consumption flows, and the domestic supplies of industry, construction, and productive and nonproductive services had lower standard deviations in 1984 than in 1980. Supply was stabilized through greater dependence on domestic production and lower variance of domestic production. Even though substitution between labor and capital was possible in the model and there were fluctuations in employment, wages had a lower variance under shocks in

1984. Consumption was more stable in 1984, despite greater fluctuations in incomes, because the volatility of household incomes was passed on to household savings. But only wages and rural household consumption had lower coefficients of variation in 1984 than in 1987. On the trade side, the picture was more complex: total exports, total imports, and the total trade balance on goods and services were more stable in 1984 than in 1980, but the greater stability of the totals on the export side was achieved through greater variability in the components.

In 1987, the variances of the income and activity flows were all smaller than in 1980. On the trade side, the picture was again more mixed. The main convertible exports (industry, construction, and services), which represent 74.4 percent of total exports, were all more variable in 1987 than in either 1984 or 1980. However, the variability of total exports decreased continuously between 1980 and 1987, and total convertible exports and total and convertible imports were less variable in 1987 than in 1984. The variances in total individual exports were greater than in 1980 and generally greater than in 1984 as well.

Discussion of Results

These results make sense in view of the characteristics of the Yugoslav economy in 1984 and 1987. In 1984, the economy was more constrained and more rigid than in 1980 because no significant change in the institutional structure of the economy had accompanied the trade reorientation. This resulted in greater variances of activity and income flows in response to exogenous shocks in 1984 than in 1980. Furthermore, the export orientation was accomplished by measures that effectively forced the economy to continue exporting and to cut imports. Although the dollar value of exports declined (by 9 percent) between 1980 and 1984, the real dinar equivalent of foreign exchange proceeds retained by enterprises rose, and the ratio of exports to imports increased. Exports were not simply a response to price incentives, such as devaluation, but also a result of the foreign exchange retention scheme adopted in 1983. Before the foreign debt crisis of 1982-83, companies were allowed to keep a large portion of their foreign exchange earnings, and the supply of foreign exchange on the black market was ample. As the debt crisis grew, the federal government increased the mandatory surrender rate on foreign exchange earnings to provide sufficient foreign exchange for debt servicing and energy imports. In addition, regional governments also claimed a larger share of foreign exchange earnings for imports of intermediates for non-tradable activities. As a result, the supply of foreign exchange on the black market fell considerably, and many companies had to export to achieve a reliable inflow of foreign exchange for imports (spare parts and intermediates) needed to maintain production. Expenditure switching and production switching under rigidities led to the significant fall in domestic supplies observed in the 1984 base solution. This fall in domestic supplies could only be validated by a large fall in household incomes.

By 1987, firms had partially adapted to the export orientation. The output mix was more export-oriented, production was less dependent on imported interme- diates, and firms had become more efficient in using their intermediate inputs. Some expenditure-switching between imports and domestic production had taken place on the final demand side as well. The increase in exports was more incentive-driven, because of a series of very substantial and abrupt currency deva- luations combined with continuous exchange rate adjustments following differential inflation rules. Import quotas were somewhat relaxed and substitution of domestic intermediate and domestic final demand in domestic supply made the quotas less onerous. Some institutional changes were introduced: price controls were largely abolished, official foreign exchange markets were established, accounting rules were changed to reflect market valuation of assets and replacement cost deprecia- tion, nominal interest rates were continuously adjusted to yield positive real interest rates, credit expansion was strictly controlled, and more stringent financial discipline was imposed on companies and banks.

The end result was a more flexible economy, more driven by market calculus and better able to respond to changing signals from world markets. The lower variances in income and activity flows observed in our experimental results for 1987 are consistent with these characteristics of the 1987 Yugoslav economy. So is the adjustment through export and income growth found in our calculated 1987 base solution.

The Mean-Variance Frontier

Rational individuals and rational policymakers would prefer outcomes on the mean-variance frontier. That is, they would choose only among outcomes that are low-mean and low-variance, moderate-mean and moderate-variance, and high-mean and high-variance. They would eschew low-mean, high-variance outcomes. Table 16.2 shows that, with the very few exceptions noted in our discussion of variances above, the income and activity flows for 1984 are low-mean and high-variance and are therefore dominated by either 1987 or 1980. For total exports, 1987 dominates 1980 and 1984 and is a moderate-mean, moderate-variance year. With respect to total convertible exports, 1984 is dominated by either 1980 or 1987. For industrial exports, service exports, convertible industrial exports, convertible service exports, and total imports, all three years are on the mean-variance frontier. However, for the overall trade balance on goods and services, both 1980 and 1984 are dominat- ed by 1987.

Examination of the mean-variance frontier thus shows that, except for exports and rural household consumption, 1984, the year of transition to export orienta- tion without significant domestic structural adjustment, is dominated by either 1980, the year of import substitution, or by 1987, the year of substantial adjust- ment to export orientation. Which trade situation is preferred by policymakers on mean-variance grounds depends on whether independent value is attached to exports and rural consumption, over and above total household consumption and the overall trade balance. Generally, one would tend to conclude from the mean-variance analysis that the partial-transition situation of 1984 is dominated in mean-variance terms by either 1980, the high-mean, high-variance year for most variables, or by 1987, the low-mean, low-variance year for all but exports and the trade balance.

Feasibility apart, mean-variance considerations suggest that the basic policy choices are between import substitution and substantial adjustment of the economy to export orientation. Partial adjustment to export orientation leads to inferior outcomes. Which strategy choice is preferred depends on the risk aversion of policymakers and on the weight they attach to international adjustment versus domestic adjustment. For domestic outcomes, the low risk-aversion choice is import substitution and the high risk-aversion choice appears to be export-expansion with substantial domestic structural and institutional adjustment to export orientation. If primary weight is attached to external adjustment and the trade balance on goods and services is taken as the major indicator of the extent of external adjustment, export orientation with substantial adaptation (reflected by 1987 in our results) is the only solution on the mean-variance frontier.

Frequency of Adverse Outcomes

Not all variability is unwelcome. In particular, risk-averse individuals and policymakers want to avoid outcomes below the mean and to enjoy outcomes above the mean. This asymmetric view of variability is not reflected in the variance. It is reflected in table 16.3, which lists the relative frequency of adverse outcomes in our one hundred replicates. We chose three different comparison standards: 3 and 10 percent below the own-mean, and 10 percent below the 1980 mean.

Table 16.3 indicates that the sample probability of GDP at factor cost being 3 percent below its own mean is 7 percent in 1980, as much as 15 percent in 1984, and only 4 percent in 1987. However, the sample probability of GDP at factor cost falling as much as 10 percent below the 1980 base is negligible in all years. Enterprise incomes had a high probability of adverse outcomes in all years. For example, in 1984, there was a 31-percent probability of enterprise incomes being 10 percent below the 1980 mean. By contrast, wages had a negligible probability of adverse outcomes except in 1984, when there was a sample probability of unity of wages falling more than 10 percent below the 1980 mean. All household incomes had high probabilities of being 10 percent below the 1980 mean.

Total exports had a 25-percent probability and convertible exports had a 10-percent probability of having values less than 10 percent below the 1980 mean in 1984. Convertible exports had a higher relative frequency of adverse outcomes than total exports, both overall and in individual sectors. Imports were declining, so that the probability of being 10 percent below the 1980 mean was quite high in both 1984 and 1987. Perhaps most significant, the trade balance on goods and services had a probability of about 50 percent of being as much as 10 percent below its own mean, but only a 1-percent probability of falling 10 percent below the 1980 mean. Both the terms of trade effect and the import-control rents were, by definition, centered on a zero mean in all years. Since rents absorb the effects

Table 16.3 Frequency of Adverse Outcomes in One Hundred Replicates of Random International Shocks to the CGE Model Yugoslav Economy, 1980, 1984, 1987

(percentages)

Variable	1980			1984			1987		
	Own base		1980 base	Own base		1980 base	Own base		1980 base
	-3%	-10%	-10%	-3%	-10%	-10%	-3%	-10%	-10%
GDP at factor cost	7	0	0	15	0	1	4	0	0
Institution / factor income									
Enterprise	35	7	7	31	14	31	29	7	9
Wages	0	0	0	0	0	100	0	0	0
Disposable income									
Rural households	36	2	2	37	13	66	32	0	94
Mixed households	0	0	0	1	0	100	0	0	100
Urban households	0	0	0	0	0	100	0	0	58
Exports goods and services									
Total	16	1	1	12	1	25	3	0	0
Of which convertible	20	7	7	22	7	10	19	4	1
Industry	12	0	0	12	0	0	9	3	2
Of which convertible	26	8	8	26	10	8	29	9	5
Services	29	4	4	33	4	96	27	4	0
Of which convertible	6	0	0	6	0	88	5	0	0
Imports goods and services									
Total	35	9	9	35	10	98	28	11	96
Of which convertible	0	0	0	0	0	100	0	0	100
Trade balance goods and services	52	47	47	53	52	1	58	49	1
Terms of trade effect[a]	55	55	55	59	59	64	62	62	65
Import-control rents[b]	58	57	57	53	53	64	58	58	62

a. Computed as the change in the terms of trade times the volume of exports.
b. Rents are computed as the difference between the world prices and the solution prices under the quota times the import quota quantity.
Source: Computed from one hundred replicates of random shocks to the Yugoslav CGE models for each of the analyzed years.

of import quantity quotas, they were quite variable; the probability of all types of adverse outcomes was therefore large.

The Welfare Evaluation

Table 16.4 summarizes our calculations for expected utility and equivalent variations. Of course, the utility numbers in the table are only ordinal; any monotone transformation of these numbers would be equally valid. The table indicates that external adjustment was achieved at the cost of a steady decline in household utility between 1980 and 1987 for all household groups. For example, the expected utility of rural households declined by 31 percent between 1980 and 1987 and that of urban households declined by 27 percent over that period. The cost of adjustment was thus quite substantial. But except for rural households, welfare was diminishing at a declining rate.

Table 16.4 Household Utilities and Equivalent Variations: Welfare Effects of International Shocks to the CGE Model Yugoslav Economy, 1980, 1984, 1987

	Rural			*Mixed*			*Urban*		
Household type	*1980*	*1984*	*1987*	*1980*	*1984*	*1987*	*1980*	*1984*	*1987*
Base utility	22.8	20.1	15.7	49.7	39.2	35.0	76.1	59.4	55.6
Expected utility									
Mean	22.4	19.8	15.5	49.5	39.0	35.0	75.9	59.2	55.5
Variance	1.3	1.5	0.4	0.2	0.3	0.1	0.3	0.4	0.1
Minimum	20.5	17.6	14.4	48.7	38.1	34.5	74.9	58.2	55.0
Maximum	26.6	24.2	17.7	51.3	41.0	35.9	78.1	61.5	56.6
Equivalent variations (%)[a]									
Relative to own base	2.18	2.69	1.46	0.41	0.57	0.26	0.32	0.45	0.19
Relative to 1980 base	2.18	18.54	42.39	0.41	29.22	39.39	0.32	30.11	36.31

a. Numbers are percentages of base income required as compensation to keep households at the same utility level as in the respective base.
Source: Computed from one hundred replicates of random shocks to the Yugoslav CGE models for each of the analyzed years.

The equivalent variations with respect to their own bases (next to last row of table 16.4) represent the percentage increase in base income that would be required to compensate individuals for the variability in their utility induced by the distribution of external shocks. The equivalent variations rise between 1980 and 1984 and then decline in 1987, winding up lower than in 1980. They are largest for rural groups and smallest for urban groups. The largest equivalent variation indicates that a compensation of 2.69 percent of base income would be required to keep rural households at the same utility level as they had in the 1984 base. The smallest equivalent variation indicates that a compensation of 0.19 percent would be needed to restore urban households to the same utility level as in the 1987 base.

One way to look at these equivalent variations is to compare them with the rate of growth of GDP. On the average, about eight months of growth of income at the average rate of growth of GDP between 1980 and 1987 would be required to compensate the average Yugoslav household for the shock-induced variance in their household income.

The equivalent variations relative to the 1980 base (last line of table 16.4) indicate the magnitudes of compensation required to restore household utilities to the 1980 base as well as to compensate households for the variability in their incomes. These compensations are very large. For example, a transfer of 42.4

percent of 1980 income would be required to restore rural households in 1987 to their 1980 base utility; for urban households, the analogous number is 36.3 percent. The lion's share of the calculated compensation is for the reduction in expected utility. Since the marginal utility of income is declining, and our linear expenditure system utility function applies only to above-subsistence income, the equivalent variation is larger than the ratio of incomes and larger than the ratio of expected utilities. For example, for rural households, our calculations indicate that for 1987 the required compensation is 35 percent larger than the decline in the ratio of utilities between 1987 and 1980. The order of magnitude of the equivalent variation is not sensitive to the values of $1 - \beta$, but it is sensitive to the ratio of subsistence income in total income. The higher that ratio, the higher the ratio of the equivalent variation to the ratio of utilities.

These calculations indicate that the cost of adjustment to Yugoslav households has been enormous. For example, assuming an average rate of growth of income equivalent to the average rate of growth of real gross material product between 1975 and 1987, it would take about twelve years of income growth to compensate rural households for their loss in utility during the period of external adjustment. Our equivalent-variation calculations also indicate that, in relative terms, rural households have borne a larger share of the burden of adjustment. In absolute terms, however, the transfer required to restore urban households to their 1980 utility levels would be close to five times as large as the transfer required to compensate rural households. The total economywide equivalent variation required in 1987 to restore all households to their utility levels of 1980 would amount to 23.6 percent of 1987 GDP at factor cost. The cumulative compensation required to maintain the utility of all households at the 1980 level throughout the entire 1980-87 period is an astronomical 111 percent of 1987 GDP at factor cost.

Conclusion

Our calculations fully support the contention of Béla Balassa concerning the greater robustness to external shocks of economies following open, export-oriented trade strategies, once the structure of the economy, its institutions, and its efficiency have adjusted to the shift from import substitution to an export orientation. They also underscore the crucial importance of the structural adaptation of the economy to export-oriented growth for minimizing the costs of adjustment and reducing the vulnerability of the economy to shocks. Year 1984, which reflects very partial adjustment of the Yugoslav economy to export orientation, is dominated in the mean-variance sense by either 1980 or 1987. It reflects the worst of all possible worlds, achieving less of a current-account surplus than 1987 and imposing much larger welfare losses than either 1980 or 1987. Once the economy has adapted its economic and institutional structure and its behavior patterns are more fully suited to export orientation, adjustment to external imbalance is better and the costs of adjustment to debt servicing and debt repayment are smaller.

In a mean-variance sense, the choices appear to be between the high-mean, high-variance import-substitution year of 1980 and the low-mean, low-variance export-orientation year of 1987. As Balassa has emphasized in his writings, high risk aversion on the part of a country or its leaders would lead the country to prefer the low-variance export orientation to the high-variance import-substitution policies, once the country had successfully adjusted to the shift in trade orientation. In utility terms, all households would have preferred 1980 to 1987 by a large margin, were the debt-led import-substitution policies of the previous decade sustainable. But since continuation of these policies has become infeasible, export orientation with structural and institutional adjustment appears to provide a better, though not easy, answer.

Notes

We are indebted to the Fulbright Program for providing a fellowship to Dusan Vujovic, enabling this research, and to Jaime de Melo for insightful comments.

1. The methodology is based on that used by Adelman and Berck (forthcoming) to study food security.
2. Data for the regressions came from various sources. For the world price variables, the price data for Yugoslav imports and exports were constructed from the three-digit Standard Industrial Trade Classification (SITC) in the United Nations' *International Trade Statistics Yearbook* for various years. Prices for imports and exports at the three-digit level were computed from the value and weight information in tables 16.4 and 16.5 and then aggregated to the two-digit level by using value shares. The world price index for services, which represent mostly tourism and transport, was constructed from a weighted average of the "transport" and "hotel and restaurant" GNP deflators in the national accounts of the Federal Republic of Germany and the United States. This index was used for both service imports and exports. Information on worker remittances and exchange rates was taken from the IMF's *Financial Statistics Yearbook* for various years.
3. For detailed descriptions of the standard CGE model, see Adelman and Robinson (1978) and Dervis, de Melo, and Robinson (1982).
4. In theory, self-management simply implies a different maximand for the firm — the maximization of value added per worker — than for a profit-maximizing firm. Traditional labor-management theory has demonstrated that a prototypical self-managed firm following this maximand under *ceteris paribus* conditions generates lower employment and output than a comparable profit-maximizing firm. The self-managed firm also has a negatively sloped supply curve which gives rise to the notorious Ward paradox (the firm responds to higher prices with a contraction of output and employment; see Ward 1958, Vanek 1970, and Domar 1966). These presumed theoretical responses are under challenge, however (see, for example, Kahana 1989 and Bonin and Fukuda 1986), and cannot easily be reconciled with the empirical Yugoslav evidence (see, for example, Sapir 1980, Nishimizu and Page 1982, and Bateman, Nishimizu, and Page 1988).
5. The legislative definition of the socialist labor-managed firm bears only a limited resemblance to the theory of the labor-managed economy developed around the work of Ward and Vanek. The legislative definition of socialist self-management is heavily affected by noneconomic (ideological, political, national, and other social) concepts.

Moreover, the real socialist self-management system is an outcome of selective implementation of the legislation, decided upon through an extremely complex and often obscure regionalized political process, and operating under specific institutional arrangements (including excessive economic regulation).

6. For an alternative approach to modeling self-managed firm behavior and labor-market-clearing procedures in the context of the first Yugoslav CGE model, see Robinson and Tyson (1985). Their model is in the same spirit as ours. However, they reflect the employment constraints by disaggregating labor into two categories (fixed and variable) and determine variable employment through constrained profit maximization guided by an accounting wage.

7. The Yugoslav Federal Statistical Office has a long tradition of producing input-output tables. It produced twelve tables between 1955 and 1980, and two more (for 1983 and 1987) are in the process of being completed. While the idea of integrated national accounts had been highly praised by Yugoslav statisticians and economists since early 1950s, inconsistencies between data sets collected and processed by different government agencies prevailed. An elaborate attempt to integrate the accounts following the official Material Product System (MPS) concept was undertaken as an independent research project within the Federal Statistical Office (see Stjepanovic 1984). It later served as a base for producing a full-fledged social accounting matrix for 1984 (see Stjepanovic 1986) and for developing the social accounting matrices for 1980 and 1987 used in the CGE models for the respective years.

8. A detailed account of the procedures used in estimating the 1984 social accounting matrix and the 1984 CGE parameters is given in Vujovic et al. (1986) and Vujovic and Labus (forthcoming).

9. The value chosen for the income share of the subsistence bundle for urban households corresponds to the relative income level at which the Yugoslav government authorizes the use of the federal development fund, subsidizes consumption and intervenes through transfers, grants an income tax exemption, or authorizes minimum guaranteed wages. For rural households, the subsistence share is lower because of auto-consumption.

10. Total household savings were computed in a two-tier process. In the first step, local currency savings were a fixed proportion of domestic household income before taxes, foreign transfers, and domestic nontaxable transfers. In the second step, foreign exchange household savings, which in recent years have constituted 80 percent of total private savings, were computed as a fixed proportion of private foreign exchange transfers.

References

Adelman, I., and P. Berck. Forthcoming. "Food Security in a Stochastic World." *Journal of Development Economics.*

Adelman, I., and S. Robinson. 1978. *Income Distribution Policies in Developing Countries: A Case Study of Korea.* Stanford: Stanford University Press.

Adelman, I., E. Yeldan, A. Sarris, and D.W. Roland-Holst. 1989. "Optimal Adjustment to Trade Shocks Under Alternative Development Strategies." *Journal of Policy Modelling* 11: 1-54.

Balassa, B. 1984. *Adjusting to External Shocks: The Newly Industrializing Developing Economies in 1974-76 and 1979-81.* DRD Discussion Paper No. 89. Washington, D.C.: World Bank.

Balassa, B. 1986. "Policy Responses to Exogenous Shocks in Developing Countries." *American Economic Review* 76 (May): 75-8.

Balassa, B. 1987. "The Importance of Trade for Developing Countries." *Banca Nazionale del Lavoro Quarterly Review* no. 163 (December):437-69.

Balassa, B. 1989. *A Conceptual Framework For Adjustment Policies.* PPR Working Paper No. 139. Washington, D.C.: World Bank.

Bateman, D.A., M. Nishimizu, and J.M. Page. 1988. "Regional Productivity Differentials and Development Policy in Yugoslavia, 1965-1978." *Journal of Comparative Economics* 12 (March):24-42.

Bonin, J.P., and W. Fukuda. 1986. "The Multifactor Illyrian Firm Revisited." *Journal of Comparative Economics* 10 (June): 171-80.

Cheng, L. 1987. "Uncertainty and Economic Self-Sufficiency." *Journal of International Economics* 23: 167-78.

Corbo, V., and J. de Melo. 1989. *External Shocks and Policy Reforms in the Southern Cone: A Reassessment.* In G. Calvo et al. eds, *Debt, Stabilization and Development: Essays in Memory of Carlos Diaz Alejandro.* Oxford: Basil Blackwell.

Dervis, K., J. de Melo, and S. Robinson. 1982. *General Equilibrium Models For Development Policy.* Cambridge: Cambridge University Press.

Domar, E.D. 1966. "The Soviet Collective Farm as a Producer Cooperative." *American Economic Review* 16 (September): 734-57.

International Monetary Fund. Various years. *Financial Statistics Yearbook.* Washington, D.C.

Kahana, N. 1989. "The Duality Approach in the Case of Labor-Managed Firms." *Oxford Economic Papers* 41: 567-72.

Lin, C.Y. 1986. "East Asia and Latin America as Contrasting Models." Paper presented at a conference at Vanderbilt University.

Nishimizu, M., and J.M. Page. 1982. "Total Factor Productivity, Technological Progress and Technical Efficiency Change: Dimensions of Productivity Change in Yugoslavia, 1965-1978." *Economic Journal* 92 (December):920-36.

Powell, A.A., and F.H. Gruen. 1968. "The Constant Elasticity of Transformation Production Frontier and Linear Supply System." *International Economic Review* 9: 315-28.

Robinson, S., and L. Tyson. 1985. "Foreign Trade, Resource Allocation, and Structural Adjustment in Yugoslavia: 1976-1980." *Journal of Comparative Economics* 9 (March): 46-70.

Ruffin, R.J. 1974. "International Trade Under Uncertainty." *Journal of International Economics* 4: 243-59.

Sapir, A. 1980. "Economic Growth and Factor Substitution: What Happened to the Yugoslav Miracle?" *Economic Journal* 90: 294-313.

Sarris, A. 1985. "Food Security and Agricultural Production Strategies Under Risk in Egypt." *Journal of Development Economics* 19: 85-112.

Stjepanovic, L. 1984. *System of National Accounts as a Base for Planning and Information* (in Serbo-Croatian: Sistem privrednih bilanca kao analiticko-dokumentaciona osnova planiranja i informisanja). Zagreb, Yugoslavia: Informator.

Stjepanovic, L. 1986. *System of Integrated National Accounts as a Base for the Yugoslav Structural Economywide Model* (in Serbo-Croatian: Sistem integrisanih privrednih bilansa kao informaciona osnova globalnog strukturnog modela jugoslovenske privrede). Belgrade, Yugoslavia: Federal Statistical Office.

United Nations. Various years. *International Trade Statistics Yearbook.* New York.

Vanek, J. 1970. *The General Theory of Labor-Managed Market Economies.* Ithaca: Cornell University Press.

Vujovic, D., and M. Labus. Forthcoming. *General Equilibrium Models of the Yugoslav Economy* (in Serbo-Croatian: Modeli opste ravnoteze jugoslovenske privrede). Belgrade, Yugoslavia: BIGZ Press, Federal Statistical Office.

Vujovic, D., M. Labus, and G. Biocic. 1985. *General Equilibrium Model of the Yugoslav Economy Based on the Social Accounting Matrix* (in Serbo-Croatian: Model opste ravnoteze jugoslovenske privrede zasnovan na matrici drustvenih racuna). Belgrade, Yugoslavia: Federal Statistical Office.

Vujovic, D., M. Labus, G. Biocic, and L. Stjepanovic. 1986. *A SAM-Based Approach to Checking the Consistency of Policy Measures in Yugoslavia.* Institute for Statistics Working Paper No.9. Belgrade, Yugoslavia: Federal Statistical Office.

Ward, B. 1958. "The Firm in Illyria: Market Syndicalism." *American Economic Review* 18 (September): 566-89.

17

Taxes, Tariffs, and Trade in an Industrializing Low-Income Country: Simulating Policy Choices in India, 1973-74 to 1983-84

Henrik Dahl and Pradeep K. Mitra

Two of Béla Balassa's most important contributions to the study of trade and development have been to demonstrate the value of an outward orientation in development strategy and to emphasize the pursuit of trade policy rules that, while not optimal in the theoretical sense, are both administratively simple and acceptable in terms of their implications for efficiency and equity.

This paper explores these two themes in the case of India, a country that began to liberalize its trade regime in the 1970s after nearly twenty-five years of import substitution-based industrialization. During that decade, exports increased by 8 percent and imports by more than 6 percent annually in real terms. While this performance was impressive compared with India's previous record, it was relatively modest compared with performance in a number of newly industrializing countries.

The paper addresses two complementary questions. First, what would have been the domestic implications had India followed a more liberal trade regime in the 1970s? Second, could other configurations of tariff and tax policy instruments have improved welfare while remaining compatible with a strategy of increased outward orientation?

Answers to these questions have two aspects. The lowering of tariffs and (absent the offsetting lump-sum taxes of classical trade theory) their replacement by domestic taxes to enable the government to meet its expenditure commitments can be expected (although not guaranteed) to have positive welfare effects. This is also true of attempts to partially optimize the tariff structure even if protection to some sectors is not reduced. The framework of this paper is designed to capture these effects and to quantify their magnitudes as well as the available data will allow. There is, however, a second aspect to a strategy of increased outward orientation. An increase in imports, especially of intermediate and capital goods that embody new technology, is likely to lead to an upgrading of technology in the industrial sector and ultimately to improved export performance. Indeed, this has been a significant element in industrial policy thinking since the 1979-80 round of petroleum price increases. However, the direct technological gains from such a policy are difficult to quantify.

In examining these issues for the case of India, we first briefly describe a moderately disaggregated applied general equilibrium model for India. We use the model to calculate the effects of gradual trade liberalization and to analyze tariff rationalization schemes. A final section summarizes the main findings.

A Model for India

A six-sector general equilibrium model of India is used to simulate the consequences of alternative trade policies.[1]

Model Specification

The *production* side of the model distinguishes six sectors, which follow agriculture-industry-services lines: agriculture, consumer goods, capital goods (including construction), intermediates, public infrastructure, and services. Industry is disaggregated into use-based categories (consumer, capital, and intermediate goods) to capture the differential impact of policies on different parts of the industrial sector.

The model distinguishes four categories of production-related *income* (income from self-employment, wage income, land / capital income, and income from implicit government subsidies on publicly provided infrastructure) as well as non-production-related income. The latter category comprises such items as interest on the national debt, domestic current transfers, net factor income from abroad, and net current transfers from the rest of the world. Incomes are mapped according to fixed rules into a single rural and a single urban household.

Final demand comprises private consumption, public consumption, exports, and investment. Household incomes are mapped into private consumption via a savings function. Private consumption demand for the output of the six production sectors is generated by separate rural and urban linear expenditure systems. Public consumption of each sector's output is exogenous. Export demand is a function of income in the rest of the world and of the ratio of export prices to those of substitutes in international markets. Investment demand is directed almost entirely at the capital goods sector, which includes construction.

The *trade* side incorporates price-responsive export and import relationships. Derived demand for both intermediate and final imports depends on the level of output and the import price to the user relative to that of the domestically produced variety, where appropriate.[2] Final imports in the agriculture, consumer goods, and public infrastructure sectors (principally food, edible oils, and petroleum, respectively) are policy-determined rather than price-responsive. The country is small in the relevant market, so import prices are given. Exports depend on the state of demand in the rest of the world (world income) and on export prices relative to the prices of substitutes. Thus, the country is able to vary its export sales by changing its export prices. Export elasticities are set at a value of -5 across the board — higher than that suggested by available econometric estimates (Lucas 1988).[3] This implies that export taxes will be levied at an optimum. However, since export taxes are negligible in India, these are set to zero. For this reason, the optimal import tariffs in the experiments reported below attempt at least partially to mimic the incidence of export taxes.

Gross output in each sector must equal the sum of final demand, intermediate demand, and changes in stocks, less imports. Since each of these components is either exogenous or price-responsive, the *market clearance* conditions determine prices. In factor markets, employment of hired labor is rationed at a fixed real wage; self-employed labor is a residual category whose returns vary to clear the labor market. Because of its insignificant size in India, there is no rural-urban migration, so rural and urban labor markets are not linked on the supply side.

The amount of land in the agricultural sector and the stock of capital in each of the other sectors are fixed within periods but augmented across periods as investment takes place.

The relation between household incomes and consumption determines *household savings. Government savings* are the difference between government income and expenditure. More precisely, government savings equal the sum of tax and tariff revenue, the return on public infrastructure net of subsidies and other income, less the value of government consumption. *Foreign savings* are exogenously specified. The sum of these three sources of savings equals *investment*. Investment is exogenously specified in the experiments reported here, and government savings must adjust via changes in revenue to satisfy the savings-investment equality. The breakdown of investment by sector of origin is given by base year input-output data; investment typically comes entirely from the capital goods sector. Its breakdown by sector of destination is taken from national accounts data, when available. Otherwise, it is chosen to reproduce base year proportions or to move in response to differences in sectoral rates of return to capital, or a combination of both.

The Historical Run

The model is calibrated on a consistent data set for 1973-74 (details are provided in Mitra and Tendulkar 1986). Data on indirect taxes by sector are presented in tables 17.1 and 17.2. In interpreting the subsequent experiments, it is useful to bear in mind that in 1973-74 exports accounted for 4 percent of GDP and imports for 6 percent and that tariffs brought in 7 percent of total revenue.

The model is then used to reproduce the growth of the principal macroeconomic aggregates in the Indian economy between 1973-74 and 1983-84. This simulation of historical developments provides a benchmark for comparison with the results of the counterfactual policy experiments presented in the next two sections of the paper.

The tracking procedure is as follows.[4] First, the exogenous variables for which time-series data are available (unit value indices for imports and exports, government consumption and the like) are set at their given values throughout the period.

**Table 17.1 Sector-Specific Rates of Indirect Taxes
by Types of Taxes, 1973-74**

Sector	Import duties	Excise duties	Other indirect taxes	Subsidies
Agriculture	0.046	0.005	0.006	-0.013
Consumer goods	0.334	0.101	0.028	-0.004
Capital goods	0.512	0.014	0.023	0.0
Intermediate goods	0.478	0.144	0.044	-0.003
Public infrastructure	0.0	0.0	0.117	0.008
Services	0.0	0.0	0.027	0.008

Source: Mitra and Tendulkar (1986, app. 4).

**Table 17.2 Sector-Specific Rates of Indirect Taxes on
Domestically Produced and Imported
Intermediate Inputs and Final Demand, 1973-74**

Sector	Intermediate inputs		Final demand	
	Domestic	Imported	Domestic	Imported
Agriculture	0.021	0.313	-0.003	0.073
Consumer goods	0.087	0.163	0.250	-0.673
Capital goods	0.097	0.425	0.029	0.378
Intermediate goods	0.121	0.279	0.247	0.724
Public infrastructure	0.127	0.846	0.0	0.0
Services	0.106	0.672	0.0	0.0

Source: Mitra and Tendulkar (1986, app. 4).

Second, certain parameters (called tracking parameters) for which empirical information is not available for years other than the base year (for example, rates of productivity growth by sector and savings propensities of rural and urban households) are varied in order to minimize the sum of squared deviations from year to year between the data-specified growth rates of tracking indicators (GDP, consumption, investment, exports, and imports at constant prices) and those generated by the model.[5] Comparisons of the actual growth rates and those generated by the model to produce the historical run are presented in figures 17.1 to 17.5.

Tariff Reduction Over Time

The Experiment
This section looks at the implications for India of following a policy of gradual tariff reduction from 1973-74 to 1982-83. For this experiment, all tariff rates are

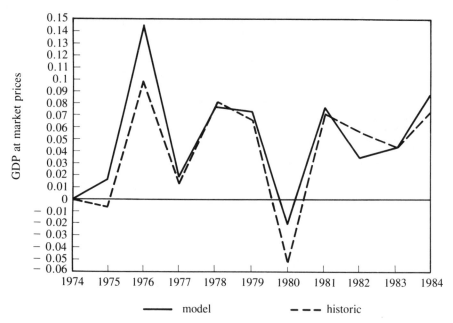

Figure 17.1   GDP at Market Prices: Model and Historic Growth Rates, FY 1974-84

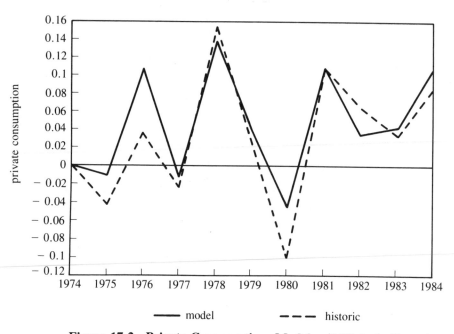

Figure 17.2   Private Consumption: Model and Historic Growth Rates, FY 1974-84

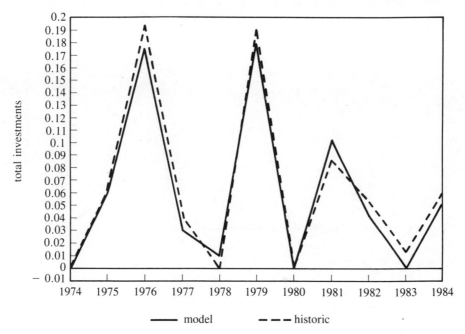

Figure 17.3   Total Investment: Model and Historic Growth Rates, FY 1974-84

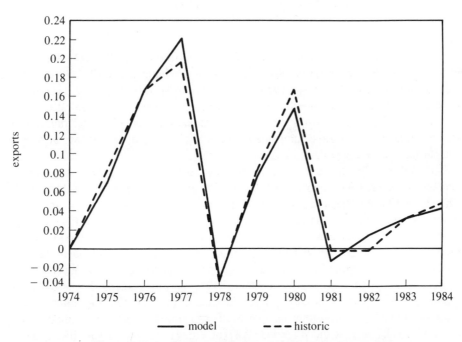

Figure 17.4   Exports: Model and Historic Growth Rates, FY 1974-84

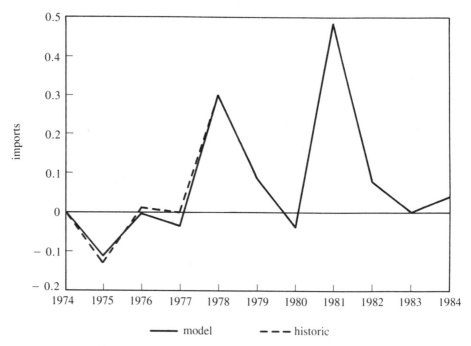

**Figure 17.5   Imports: Model and Historic Growth Rates,
FY 1974-84**

proportionally reduced in steps so that by 1983-84 their overall level is half that of 1973-74 while their relative structure remains unchanged (in 1974-75 all tariff rates are multiplied by 0.95, in 1975-76 by 0.9, and so on). To allow the government to meet its commitments and thus preserve expenditure neutrality, total investment and foreign savings are forced to remain at their historical run values, with revenue losses, if any, being made up by scaling all domestic tax rates by a suitable (endogenous) scalar.

It is not possible to tell a priori whether domestic taxes will need to be increased or decreased when tariff rates are lowered. This depends on the relative general equilibrium elasticities of export and import demand with respect to landed import prices. Lowering tariff rates will, *ceteris paribus*, lead to an increase in imports, but also to a reduction in domestic prices, thus increasing exports. If the import price elasticity is higher than the export price elasticity, a domestic tax rate reduction may be required to lower domestic prices further and so to boost exports in order to keep foreign savings constant. The experiment keeps the partial price elasticities of exports constant across the board (at -5). On the import side, however, there is a constant elasticity of substitution between domestic and imported goods, so that the price elasticity of import demand is variable, depending on the levels of the import ratio and relative prices. For that reason, the sign of the domestic tax change depends on the state of the economy.

Results

The results of the tariff reduction experiment are summarized in table 17.3, which shows the required change in domestic tax rates, the change in terms of trade, and the change in private welfare compared to the historical run.[6]

Table 17.3 Results of the Gradual
Tariff Reduction Experiment
(percentage deviation from historical run)

Year	Tariff rates	Domestic taxes	Terms of trade	Welfare
1973-74	--	--	--	--
1974-75	- 5	-1.07	-0.28	0.01
1975-76	-10	0.29	-0.30	0.00
1976-77	-15	1.42	-0.44	0.01
1977-78	-20	1.87	-0.91	-0.02
1978-79	-25	1.69	-1.18	-0.01
1979-80	-30	-0.21	-1.30	0.02
1980-81	-35	-14.90	-3.21	1.69
1981-82	-40	-1.96	-2.65	-0.06
1982-83	-45	1.21	-3.03	0.03

Reducing tariffs requires small offsetting domestic tax changes in all but one year. The exception is 1980-81, which evidently exhibits the "elasticity trap" discussed above, and requires a 15-percent cut in all domestic taxes to preserve expenditure neutrality. For all years, the required changes in terms of trade, given an export elasticity of -5, are small.

The results show that the welfare impact of trade liberalization is low and is dominated by the changes in domestic taxes: the welfare change usually has the opposite sign of that of the tax change. These results can be explained by the low share of trade in India[7] and by the greater importance in public revenue over much of this period of domestic indirect taxes (80 percent) compared to tariffs (20 percent). Therefore, the welfare effect of large changes in tariff rates can easily be offset by small changes in domestic tax rates. Above all, these findings underline the moderating impact on welfare of domestic tax increases that are necessary to allow the government to meet its expenditure commitments. Finally, it may be noted that changes in the ratio of rural to urban cost of living are also low, which means that the policy of gradual tariff reduction has no noticeable intersectoral consequences.

The results presented here refer to trade liberalization undertaken through tariff reductions alone. They do not include the impact of relaxing the widespread non-tariff barrier of licensing restrictions on imports. One reason for the exclusion of such barriers is the difficulty of matching the licensing categories with commodities at the six-sector level of aggregation used in the model. That exercise is currently being undertaken with a more disaggregated model (Mitra and Go, forthcoming), but available evidence (quoted in Kishor 1989) suggests that the premium on import replenishment licenses for exporters fell from about 25 percent in 1973-74 to about 5 percent in the early 1980s, due largely to the shift to a more active exchange rate policy and higher tariffs on imports. This implies that attempts to simulate such policies would find the welfare gains of the liberalization of licensing barriers to be moderated by the negative impact of complementary measures, such as increased tariffs, undertaken for balance of payments management.

The welfare gains from tariff and nontariff adjustments are not, however, the only expected benefits of a policy of liberalization. Imports of certain kinds of intermediate and capital goods that embody new technology can also be expected to boost technology and X-efficiency within the industrial sector. The framework used here does not model technological change in an endogenous manner, but other experiments with the model (Mitra and Tendulkar 1986) suggest that, for example, a 5-percent across-the-board increase in total factor productivity in manufacturing sectors would lead to a roughly 0.25-percent increase in private consumption and, with fixed foreign savings, to a 6-percent increase in investment. This translates into a somewhat less than 0.25-percent increase in welfare for consumption and, depending on the relative premium on investment, into a higher figure for the increase in investment. Empirical evidence (Ahluwalia 1986) indicates a 0.6-percent annual *decline* in total factor productivity from 1966-67 to 1979-80 in India. Thus, depending on one's judgment on the behavior of total factor productivity following trade liberalization, it would be possible to use the figures illustrated above to adjust the estimates of table 17.3 upward to account for the welfare gains from increased technical efficiency.

Policy discussions of technological improvement through import liberalization often focus on the need to increase foreign savings both to boost investment and to help finance the process until exports have had an opportunity to respond. To examine this issue, the model could be run with higher investment and foreign savings rates and the resulting (higher) consumption gains could be modified using a valuation of the increased foreign savings-induced terminal stock of debt.[8] That particular extension is straightforward and is not pursued here.

Tariff Rationalization

Constraints to Tariff Rationalization
Although the gradual reduction of tariffs seems a feasible policy option, the resulting welfare gains and losses are slight enough to make it tempting to look for other tariff policies that may have superior welfare effects. This section examines the welfare changes resulting from following revenue-neutral alternatives that include both optimal and administratively simpler policies, such as uniform

nominal tariffs. These changes are compared with the 1983-84 historical run solution displayed in table 17.4.

Table 17.4 Historical Run Tariff Rates, 1983-84

Sector	Tariff on intermediate goods	Tariff on final goods
Agriculture	0.3134	0.0731
Consumer goods	0.1629	0.6728
Capital goods	0.4247	0.3781
Intermediate goods	0.2790	--
Public infrastructure	--	--

Tariffs on intermediate and final goods are distinguished in this experiment. Since domestically produced and imported intermediates are (imperfect) substitutes, changes in tariffs on intermediate goods directly affect protection. Protection is also affected by changes in final goods tariffs in the capital goods sector, since the imported good can substitute for the domestically produced variety (with an elasticity of 0.9). That is not the case for final imports in agriculture, consumer goods, and public infrastructure sectors (food, edible oils, and petroleum, respectively). Since the government releases those imports in the domestic market at domestic prices, tariffs on those imports have no direct impact on protection.

One additional feature of the Indian economy is also important to an understanding of the results discussed here. The relatively closed nature of the economy implies that imported intermediate consumer and capital goods are not very important to domestic production, so very large changes in tariffs on those intermediates are consistent with little change in final goods prices. Thus, in the absence of any further constraints, attempts to optimize the tariff structure can lead to seemingly unreasonable values for tariffs on imports of consumer and capital goods for intermediate use. The way in which this problem is handled in the experiments is described below.

Any reorganization or optimization of the tariff structure must recognize the dual function of tariffs: to protect domestic producers from imports and to raise public revenue. It is therefore necessary to specify the constraints to reform that arise from these two objectives.

Protection in developing countries is typically recommended on infant industry grounds. It is argued that protection, by permitting an increase in the volume of gross output, confers "learning by doing" type benefits. These eventually lower the costs of production and allow the industry to become competitive. The argument is therefore intertemporal: society incurs the costs of protection today in return for benefits in the form of higher productivity tomorrow.

However, as is well known, domestic policies directed toward factor markets are to be preferred to trade restrictions (Baldwin 1969), so the argument for interference with trade may be traced to constraints on administrative capacity, especially in developing countries. The optimal degree of protection can be derived from an assessment of intertemporal costs and benefits (see Mitra 1990a). However, it is frequently the case that protection, though an *objective* ultimately derivable from such an intertemporal calculation, is thought of as a noneconomic *constraint*.

In that spirit, we assume that consumer, capital, and intermediate goods (sectors 2, 3, and 4), which comprise mainly tradable manufacturing goods, are covered by a protection constraint of the type

(1)
$$\sum_{i=2,3,4} P^*_{v_i} V_i = \eta \sum_{i=1}^{6} P^*_{v_i} V_i \, ,$$

where $P^*_{v_i}$ is the international (value added) price for sector i and the V_i terms are value added quantities in any experiment. This requires that the sum of value added (at international prices) in a subset of priority sectors (in this case, manufacturing) account for no less than some prespecified proportion η of total value added (again at international prices).[9]

The constant η is calibrated as follows.

First, all trade taxes are removed in the base solution, but all domestic taxes are scaled to ensure that, with investment and foreign savings fixed at base run values, the government can meet its expenditure commitments. The value added prices in each sector in such an "expenditure-neutral" free trade run, denoted P^*_v, are taken to be the international prices at which value added quantities are to be evaluated.

Second, the sum of value added in sectors 2, 3, and 4 in the base period,

$$\sum_{i=2,3,4} P^*_{v_i} V_i \, ,$$

is compared with total value added in all six sectors,

$$\sum_{i=1}^{6} P^*_{v_i} V_i \, ,$$

where everything is evaluated at the international prices derived above. This yields the parameter η (equaling 0.1497).

Third, for all subsequent experiments, the protection constraint in equation 1 is written with η fixed at its calculated value.

The Experiment

The theory of an optimal structure of tariffs given specific revenue and protection objectives and different assumptions about the availability of domestic tax instruments has been developed at some length elsewhere (Heady and Mitra 1987, Mitra 1990a). Here, we calculate optimal tariffs (those that maximize the social welfare function as defined in footnote 6), assuming a fixed domestic tax structure and the revenue and protection objectives described below. We also examine the welfare losses from following the administratively simple rule of uniform, across-the-board tariffs.

The experiments of this section calculate uniform and optimal tariffs for three cases:

- a pure revenue-raising case, which drops the protection constraint but requires that enough revenue be raised to meet the expenditure and investment levels of the historical run;
- a pure protective case, in which tax and tariff revenue must equal revenue in the base run, with the difference being adjusted through lump sum transfers to the private sector;[10]
- a protective-with-revenue-raising case, in which the protection constraint is reintroduced and revenue is not rebated to the private sector.

Results

Results of the tariff rationalization experiments are summarized in table 17.5, which shows the resulting tariff structures, and table 17.6, which shows the corresponding changes in welfare and foreign savings, and the levels of protection and lump-sum transfers to the private sector.

In calculating optimal tariffs for each of the three cases, we hold the tariffs on intermediate imports of consumer and capital goods, for the reasons explained earlier, at the levels corresponding to the uniform level for each case. The other tariffs are variable.

The results show that the optimal tariff structure is very far from the historical run structure shown in table 17.4 and far from the uniform tariff rate structure. While the uniform tariff rate is almost the same in all three cases, the picture is more varied with respect to the optimal tariffs. The revenue-raising optimum has a higher tariff on final capital goods and on intermediate imports entering agriculture and the intermediate-goods-producing sectors than does the protection optimum. On all counts, protective tariffs are lower than revenue-raising tariffs because nondistortionary lump-sum taxes are available. Protective-with-revenue-raising tariffs are a compromise between purely revenue-raising and purely protective tariffs.

The purely revenue-raising tariffs imply a somewhat greater share of value added at world prices in manufacturing (0.1503) compared to the historical run (0.1497). The manufacturing sectors are also the major import users, so increasing their share of production raises the tax base for tariffs.

Finally, the results for purely protective tariffs show that, in the optimal state, much higher lump-sum taxes are levied on households than under uniform tariffs. Once again, this is due to the nondistortionary nature of lump-sum taxes and the distortionary costs associated with tariffs.

The welfare effects of all the tariff rationalization schemes are negligible (table 17.6). As mentioned before, the semi-closed nature of the Indian economy partly

**Table 17.5 Result of Tariff Rationalization Experiment:
Uniform Rate versus Optimal Rate with Different
Revenue and Protection Objectives, 1983-84**

	Objective		
Tariff policy	*Revenue raising*	*Protection*	*Protection and revenue raising*
Uniform rate	0.2992	0.2877	0.2878
Optimal rates			
Final imports			
Agriculture	0.9386	0.8753	0.9312
Consumer goods	-	-	-
Capital goods	0.3413	- 0.0552	0.1160
Public infrastructure	- 0.3327	- 0.3593	- 0.3377
Intermediate imports			
Agriculture	- 0.1833	- 0.2256	- 0.0630
Consumer goods[a]	0.2992	0.2877	0.2878
Capital goods[a]	0.2992	0.2877	0.2878
Intermediate goods	0.2314	0.0781	0.1701

a. Rates are held at the uniform-rate level because imports in these categories constitute such a small part of domestic production that very large changes in their tariffs lead to little change in final goods prices. Attempts to optimize the tariff structure can lead to seemingly unreasonable values for these tariffs.

explains this finding. However, analogous experiments done for more open economies, such as Cameroon, yield only somewhat higher welfare gains (Dahl, Devarajan, and van Wijnbergen 1986). The results could be altered if protection or revenue-neutral reorganization of tariffs led to a reduction in resource-wasting and rent-seeking behavior, a consideration that is not modeled here. Notice, however, that unlike the experiments with progressive tariff reductions over time, which were reported earlier, the present set of exercises reorganizes existing tariff structures *without* moving toward trade liberalization. Hence the benefits of technological and X-efficiency gains and of reductions in rent-seeking cannot be expected to be significant.[11]

Conclusion

This paper asked whether policy changes in the direction of greater trade liberalization or a different configuration of tariff and tax policy instruments would have led to welfare improvements. In both cases, the change would have been negligible. First, a policy of reducing tariffs over a ten-year period to half their original level while keeping investment and foreign savings at their historical levels and

**Table 17.6 Summary Measures of the Tariff
Rationalization Experiment, 1983-84**

Tariff policy	Objective		
	Revenue raising	*Protection*	*Protection and revenue raising*
	Percentage deviation from historical run		
Private welfare			
Uniform rates	-0.002	0	0
Optimal rates	0.08	0.11	0.09
Foreign savings	0	-3.81	0
	Levels		
Share of manufacturing in value added $(\eta)^a$			
Uniform rates	0.1497	0.1497	0.1497
Optimal rates	0.1503	0.1497	0.1497
Lump sum transfers			
Uniform rates	0	-0.78	0
Optimal rates	0	-26.54	0

a. For an explanation of how η is calibrated, see the text.

levels and meeting the government's expenditure commitments by scaling domestic tax instruments as needed, makes no significant difference in terms of overall welfare gains or losses or of their rural-urban distribution. Second, a revenue- or protection-neutral reorganization of tariffs either to maximize welfare or to implement administratively simple rules such as uniformity, while keeping the domestic tax structure fixed, has a negligible impact on welfare. Similar results pertaining to standard welfare gains of the classical Harberger type have emerged from a number of other studies (see, for example, Srinivasan and Whalley 1986).

The paper also suggests that, given the results of earlier experiments with the same model showing the responsiveness of welfare to technical progress, these estimates of welfare gains could be adjusted upward. However, empirical work on technology transfer in India (Desai 1985), although richly suggestive of such processes, has not as yet provided quantitative measures of the efficiency benefits arising from increased exposure to international competition. Hence the extent to which the modest welfare gains derived from a model such as the one used here must be adjusted upward to accommodate the gains from technological advances remains an important and open question.

Notes

We thank Jaime de Melo for helpful comments on an earlier draft.

1. See Mitra and Tendulkar (1986) for a detailed and formal description of the model and the database used for calibration.
2. For imported goods that have no domestically produced substitute, import demand depends only on the level of output.
3. However, the overestimate is unlikely to be significant, given a general downward bias in most estimates of price elasticities of export demand (Gelb and Condon 1985).
4. Details of the procedure are described in Dahl (1987) and Mitra and Go (forthcoming). Since the model is calibrated to reproduce base year (1973-74) data, the tracking refers to the years 1974-75 onwards.
5. While such intertemporal calibration is standard practice among applied general equilibrium modelers, we have formalized the exercise by resorting to an explicit minimization. Although such a procedure shares certain similarities with econometric estimation, it is less systematic than the latter in allowing year-by-year variations in the tracking parameters. Some of those variations are necessarily substantial in order to reproduce annual fluctuations of the macroeconomy within an equilibrium methodology. They may be interpreted as the result of some exogenous shocks or of certain policy instruments which are not explicitly incorporated in the model.
6. The separately estimated linear expenditure systems for the rural and urban household are represented by the utility function

$$u = \prod_{i=1}^{6} (c_i - \gamma_i)^{\beta_i} \, ,$$

   where c_i, γ_i, and β_i correspond to consumption, subsistence consumption, and marginal budget share of good i, respectively. Social welfare is taken to be the sum of rural and urban utilities.
7. However, modest gains have also been recorded in trade liberalization experiments with numerical general equilibrium models in more open economies (see Srinivasan and Whalley 1986).
8. The model incorporates a debt module that keeps track of the effect of foreign borrowing on the stock of debt and debt service payments (amortization and interest) corresponding to medium- and long-term (official and private) and short-term debt (see Mitra and Tendulkar 1986).
9. This approach has been used in the literature on effective protection (Bertrand 1972).
10. In this experiment, we examine uniform and optimal tariffs when protection alone is the objective of policy, that is, when we do not postulate a revenue constraint. This latter notion is not easily interpreted in general equilibrium, for the following reason. Since government expenditures — consumption and transfers — are fixed in real terms, they must be met by any solution. Thus, a postulate of revenue neutrality does not add very much to the analysis. Moreover, it may be noted that foreign savings are allowed to vary slightly in this case.
11. The welfare effects of relaxing the constraint on intersectoral capital mobility (a short-run assumption) are very small. This is partly because a reallocation of capital in accordance with relative sectoral returns results in a more import-intensive production structure, which is incompatible with constant foreign savings. For more details on investment reallocation arising from such rules, see Mitra and Tendulkar (1986).

References

Ahluwalia, I. 1986. "Industrial Growth in India: Performance and Prospects." *Journal of Development Economics* 23:1-18.

Baldwin, R. 1969. "The Case Against Infant Industry Protection." *Journal of Political Economy* 68:295-305.

Bertrand, T. 1972. "Decision Rules for Effective Protection in Less-Developed Economies." *American Economic Review* 62:743-46.

Dahl, H. 1987. "Ganges: A Computable General Equilibrium Model for India." Country Policy Department, World Bank, Washington, D.C.

Dahl, H., S. Devarajan, and S. van Wijnbergen. 1986. *Revenue-Neutral Tariff Reform: Theory and an Application to Cameroon.* Country Policy Department Discussion Paper No. 1986-25. Washington, D.C.: World Bank.

Desai, A. 1985. "Indigenous and Foreign Determinants of Technological Change in Indian Industry." *Economic and Political Weekly* 20, (November): 2081-94.

Gelb, A., and T. Condon. 1985. "Béla on Simultaneous Equations Bias in the Measurement of Structural Trade Elasticities." Development Research Department, World Bank, Washington, D.C.

Heady, C., and P. Mitra. 1987. "Distributional and Revenue-Raising Arguments for Tariffs." *Journal of Development Economics* 26:77-101.

Kishor, N. 1989. "Movements in Real Effective Exchange Rates, India: 1973-1988." Country Economics Department, World Bank, Washington, D.C.

Lucas, R.E.B. 1988. "Demand for India's Manufactured Exports." *Journal of Development Economics* 29:63-75.

Mitra, P. 1990a. "Tariff Design and Reform in a Revenue-Constrained Economy: Theory and an Illustration from India." Paper presented to the International Seminar in Public Economics, Delhi, January.

Mitra, P. 1990b. "Adjustment in Oil Importing Countries." Country Economics Department, World Bank, Washington, D.C.

Mitra, P., and D. Go. Forthcoming. "The Reform of the Indian Trade Regime." World Bank, Washington, D.C.

Mitra, P., and S. Tendulkar. 1986. *Coping with Internal and External Exogenous Shocks: India, 1973-74 to 1983-84.* Country Policy Department Discussion Paper No. 21. Washington, D.C.: World Bank.

Srinivasan, T. N., and J. Whalley, eds. 1986. *General Equilibrium Trade Policy Modeling.* Cambridge, Mass.: MIT Press.

East

18

Stabilization and Economic Transition in Hungary: The Next Two Years

János Kornai

Béla Balassa's interest in economic developments in his native Hungary has never waned. In an article written in 1983 (Balassa 1983),[1] he stressed the relationship between Hungary's internal economic reform and its openness to the world economy. In this paper,[2] along Balassa's line of thinking, I emphasize the interconnections among all the essential elements of a policy program aimed at the fundamental economic transformation of the Hungarian economy. I also make certain assumptions about the actors in this transformation. I assume that a new government will be formed as a result of free elections and that the government will enjoy the confidence of parliament and the majority of voters.

I am confident that the core of ideas presented here is applicable not only in Hungary, but also in other socialist countries in transition to a free economy. Despite considerable differences in history, culture, and present political and economic conditions, the socialist countries in Eastern Europe have important features in common, and they will share similar difficulties in the coming years.

In all of them, the public sector plays an dominating role. Although these economies display sporadic elements of a genuine market system, they do not yet have the institutions, legal support, and cultural attitudes needed for a well-functioning free market. Prices, interest rates, and exchange rates are distorted. These small open economies need to integrate themselves fully with the world economy, and yet the composition and quality of their production are inappropriate to the demands of the world market. A huge bureaucracy penetrates every aspect of these economies, and similar malaises weaken them: recession or stagnation of real output and consumption, open or repressed inflation, chronic shortages and, in most cases, a heavy external debt burden. Workers are unhappy with the protracted sacrifices asked for the sake of stabilization, and large strata of the population sink deeper into poverty, while technocrats, bureaucrats, and managers fear any changing of the guard.

Given these circumstances, and taking the example of Hungary, what economic policy should be pursued in the next two or three years? In addition to presenting my recommendations, I argue that implementation of the required tasks should not be prolonged and that stabilization cannot be accomplished in a series of small steps. This stabilization "surgery" must be performed cleanly in one stroke, that is, it should begin on a stated date and should be completed within no more than a year. Certain elements of the program must be made known to the public in advance; others will emerge clearly only during the course of the operation. But the public must be kept informed at all stages.

My aim here is not to present all the details of the stabilization program that Hungary must undertake; that will require the work of many experts over a period of several months. My aim is far more modest. I wish to formulate a few key principles as clearly as possible in the context of the following practical question: what should be the tasks of the new government? The principles laid down here may be open to question, but none of these issues can be dodged. Although I discuss them individually, these measures must be implemented simultaneously.

Policy Reform Proposals

Stopping Inflation

Inflation is a grave problem. While this seems self-evident, it is not so to everyone. A number of government officials and economists downplay the dangers of inflation, believing fatalistically that inflation has been ordained for Hungary. Quite conspicuously, neither the opposition parties nor the governing party has promised to eliminate inflation. Minister of Finance László Békesi has said: "Regrettably, it is not possible to do away with inflation in the coming years. On the one hand, it is the legacy of the earlier voluntaristic economic policy and thus the manifestation of the existing imbalances and inefficiencies. On the other hand, inflation is but the natural fever that accompanies restructuring."[3]

Inflation is not a natural disaster. It exists because the financial authorities have allowed it to exist. It is created by governments or the political powers behind them, and only they can end it. This is not to say, however, that many other groups are not also involved. Inflation is a game for many players: all those who have a role in shaping financial processes or in determining prices and wages and all those whose expectations of inflation help to keep inflation going.[4] Nonetheless, the government remains the leading player, and nowhere is this more evident than in the strongly centralized socialist economy, where government influence on prices and wages, credit, investment, and other economic processes is incomparably stronger than elsewhere.[5] Ultimately, the government controls the banknote press, printing new money to cover the gap between expenditures and revenues.

Assuming for the moment that the current annual rate of inflation is indeed only 15-20 percent, as official calculations claim,[6] inflation is still a grave problem, for at least two reasons. First, inflation descends mercilessly on the population, leading to perpetual unrest as people see their hard-earned savings melt away. Inflation implements a special kind of permanent redistribution, affecting primarily the poor, salary-earners, and pensioners. In the tug-of-war between prices and nominal wages, the losers are those who lack the organizational support and political influence to extract the wage hikes needed to catch up with price rises. Reducing inflation should be a primary part of any welfare policy designed to help the poor, and yet it almost never is.

Second, inflation makes rational economic calculations impossible. Prices cease to fulfill their signaling function, as the effects of relative shifts in prices are blurred by the general rise in the price level. Inflation also undermines the central process governing the efficiency of resource allocation. In a market economy, the efficiency of production becomes manifest in the profit of the producer: inefficient production leads to losses, and the loss-making producer is eventually ousted from the market. But within an inflationary context, this process is subverted as both efficient and inefficient production are "vindicated." Inefficient firms can cover their costs through price increases, hiding their failure behind an inflation-justified argument of rising costs. As long as bureaucratic state-owned firms remain the dominant sector in the economy, hard budget constraints will be impossible to enforce, and an already soft budget constraint is further softened by inflation. It becomes impossible to determine whether the state-owned firm operates efficiently or to identify the reasons behind rising costs.

To terminate the inflationary process, supply and demand must be balanced at the macro-level. With a given supply facing a given demand, an equilibrium will come about at some price level if prices are allowed free play. Let us examine the three variables of this relationship more closely.

Expected *supply* cannot be estimated in advance with any real precision. The process of restructuring will lower production in certain sectors, while increasing it elsewhere. This adjustment process affords the opportunity to reallocate labor and other material resources to the private sector. None of the stabilization measures should have an adverse effect on the private sector's readiness to produce. So we start from the assumption that, at the macro-level, supply will remain unchanged during the first year or two of stabilization. As for *demand*, it must remain unchanged during stabilization, although a light increase might be unavoidable during a short transition period. But soon after the beginning of the program, demand must be firmly controlled.

With supply and demand given, then, what will be the average *price level* at which supply and demand will reach equilibrium? There is no way to calculate in advance precisely what the overall effect of the complicated, circular price and cost spillovers will be.[7] In all likelihood, however, the new average price level will be much higher than the current level. Provided that the government sticks steadfastly to an anti-inflationary policy, the price rises accompanying stabilization need not lead to inflation. Inflation is a dynamic process, involving spiralling increases in prices, wages, and other cost factors. If this spiral is cut and excess demand is done away with, inflation can be eliminated.

Restoring Budgetary Equilibrium

As with inflation, fatalism pervades discussion of fiscal disequilibrium: the problem is viewed as irremediable. I believe, however, that in the course of stabilization, budgetary balance can, indeed must, be fully restored through certain drastic measures.

Revenue. The need to cut public expenditure is clear, but even with a drastic cutback in certain types of expenditures — especially the elimination of subsidies — we are still left with the essential costs of state administration and the armed forces, service on the foreign debt, and critical welfare programs. The core of my proposal is simple: we should set taxes to cover this given annual expenditure. Although expenditure cuts are politically more palatable than higher taxes, we must not delude ourselves with the belief that expenditure cuts will be higher than expected.

This plan requires a radical reshaping of the tax system, which is now a troubled brew of the paternalistic redistribution promises of a socialist economy, the fiscal impotence of a destitute third world country, and the refined progressive tax system of a Scandinavian welfare state. Those who elaborated Hungary's new tax regulations managed to sell them to the economic leadership, to parliament, and to some of the public by suggesting that Hungary play at being a little Sweden. As a bitter joke has it in Budapest, we are now paid Hungarian wages minus Swedish taxes.

In drafting a new tax system, we need to start, at least conceptually, with a clean slate and systematically to reconsider the underlying principles.[8] The following suggestions for reform do not strive for completeness but rather emphasize the principles that are most important to the stabilization program.[9]

First, taxes should be collected where they are "seizable," with preference given to the technically simplest forms of taxation. This point, seemingly technocratic and devoid of ethical significance, actually implies serious ethical and political requirements. We are dealing with Hungary, not Scandinavia. The sad legacy of the official propaganda declaring that the state belongs to the people is that no one believes it. People now consider it a laudable act to defraud the state, appropriate its wealth, or shun their own obligations. Those who refrain from this kind of behavior are viewed as dupes. This conduct will not change overnight, no matter how great the political change. While no one can predict how long it will take to turn around the public spirit, we can safely assume that the change will not occur in the next two or three years, which is the time-horizon of the present study. Consequently, in estimating budget revenue, we must be prepared for the fact that a considerable number of people will try to dodge taxes by understating their incomes. In addition, much of the private sector still belongs to the shadow economy, and it will take time and supportive government measures before it voluntarily emerges into the light.

Under these conditions, what are the implications of a tax system that relies heavily on voluntary compliance? There are at least three, and none is pleasant to contemplate. One, the government is deceiving itself by counting on revenue it will never collect. Two, the government builds into the system the likelihood that citizens will try to cheat, a highly dishonest stance on its own part. This means that the deputies in parliament who pass the tax laws and the officials who execute them in effect say to the defrauders: "We know that all the decent dupes will pay their taxes, and we do not expect to collect taxes from those of you who are determined to shirk them." Or third, the government determines resolutely to collect personal income taxes. But in a country where tax morality is very low, the government will have to spy on taxpayers, investigating income sources and spending patterns and encouraging people to denounce suspected tax evaders to the police.

Thus, the principle of simplicity is more than a technical one. Hungary needs a tax system that avoids the dilemmas described above. The tax system should not test citizens' loyalty, nor should it force the legislators and the bureaucrats to decide whether to spy on households. The tax categories should be as impersonal as possible. Later, as democracy becomes consolidated and the private sector begins to flourish, most Hungarian citizens will regain their sense of civic responsibility and attachment to the state. Only then can we begin to consider a general personal income tax.

A second principle is that the tax system should be as neutral as possible. With rare exceptions, the state should not use taxes for reward or punishment. We must put an end to demands for arbitrary tax exemptions for certain products, services, activities, or social groups. If the legislature decides that a subsidy is needed for welfare, cultural, or other social considerations, the item should show up on the expenditure side of the budget, not as a tax reduction on the revenue side achieved through a manipulation of tax rates. The expenditure process is transparent and avoids the temptations of a system in which subsidies can become lost in the mists of reduced tax rates. Thus whatever the tax category (consumption tax, payroll tax), the tax rate should be rigorously uniform, and all politicians should declare unequivocally that they will not yield to any lobbying or threats or depart from the principle of uniform rates.[10]

The third principle is likely to shock many Hungarians: the tax system need not be progressive. Although income distribution is primarily an ethical issue, some people attach an intrinsic value to equality of income and welfare. But there can be no "correct" income distribution on purely rational grounds. "Equality" is a complex moral value of several dimensions. I can fully identify with several of its aspects (equality before the law, equal entitlement to basic human rights) while rejecting the call for the equalization of material incomes.[11]

At the same time, I agree with the principle of social justice in distribution,[12] and I believe that a distribution system is fair only if it ensures continuous improvement for the least well-off members of society in the *long run*.[13] This is a dynamic requirement. It does not inquire about the precise share the least well-off members of society receive from a given national income at a given moment. Thus, it is not a redistributive requirement. Rather, it compares the situation of the poor today with their condition tomorrow, holding out the promise that their financial circumstances will improve perceptibly in the foreseeable future. Any society that does not guarantee this is unjust.

The requirement of social justice is inseparable from the requirement of incentive. Income distribution should give the strongest possible incentive to the increase of the total income of society, as this is the *sine qua non* of a steady increase in the income of the poorest. (By contrast, improvement of the lot of the poorest through redistributive means offers only finite prospects.) This leads to the last general requirement for the tax system: it should contain no counter-incentives to improving economic performance and increasing investment. Among other things, this means no progressive tax that penalizes those who work more than others and no tax penalties on savings deposits. Numerous studies on the relationships between tax rates and revenues have shown the detrimental effect of a high tax rate on a stagnating or sluggish GNP. By avoiding the counterincentive created by excessively high tax rates, the government will be much more successful in increasing revenue; once it clears the way for the rapid growth of national income, it will be able to collect more in taxes even at lower rates.

Having briefly identified the main principles of the tax system, I will quickly mention the principal tax categories needed to put this system into practice:

- A linear *consumption tax* or, more precisely, a value added tax.[14] This tax would differ from the present system in that uniformity would be firmly enforced. Every type of consumption, without exception, should be subject to the same tax rate.
- A single linear (nonprogressive) *payroll tax*. All employers who pursue their activity legally should be subject to payroll taxes for any kind of remuneration of their employees.
- A single linear (nonprogressive) *profit tax*. This tax rate should be strictly uniform and should be applied to the profits of all legally registered firms, irrespective of ownership (state or private, Hungarian or foreign).[15]
- Although not a tax in the technical sense, I include *customs duties* here. If they are required for revenue purposes, the rates should be so small and uniform as to minimize any price distortion. With few justified exceptions, there should be no differentiation among customs tariffs on various products.[16]

I have not aimed at completeness in this enumeration of revenue sources.[17] However, when the details are worked out, it is essential that the main sources of revenue (consumption tax, payroll tax, profit tax, and import duty) cover actual expenditures. Despite some disingenuous remarks made during budget debates suggesting that the whole issue boils down to the question of who foots the bill, the budget or the people, it is of course the people who bear all the costs. The issue under consideration is never a choice between the budget and the people. Rather, the question always concerns the distribution of the burdens among the various strata of the population and between present and future generations. Since there is no getting away from this reality, I suggest that tax procedures be executed in the simplest and most efficient way possible.

Expenditure. Expenditure must be considered as a given sum during stabilization, except for the elimination of price and production subsidies. Subsidized prices help not only those in need but others as well. While the state must act humanely to assist those in acute need, it must do so through welfare expenditures commensurate to the country's potential, not through price subsidies. In particular, there is no justification for the general subsidization of foodstuffs in Hungary. For those people who can hardly make ends meet even at today's subsidized food prices, we need to introduce direct support measures that do not create price distortions.

Production subsidies must also be eliminated. This is the right moment to put an end to two decades of argument about loss-making state-owned firms and large agricultural cooperatives. Two temporary exceptions might be made: transitional support to help industries over the worst of the poststabilization shock and initial support to infant industries.

Managing Demand

In this section, I discuss only a few aspects of demand management, emphasizing in particular credit and wages. Above all, I highlight the dangers that might jeopardize the success of the stabilization program.

With respect to the *private sector*, fixed quotas must be established on credit from the state banking sector. It is important to ensure both that this credit reaches the private sector on demand (the state sector must be prevented from siphoning it off) and that the private sector does not overstep these limits during the critical first phase of stabilization. Once the private sector is on its feet, the supply of credit may be increased in proportion to the growth of its credit demand.

With respect to the *state sector*, we will assume, as discussed above, that the demand manifested in the state budget is strictly restrained. The real danger lies in the possibility of run-away demand in state-owned firms. Legal spending curbs are needed for these firms, and the real test of these curbs will be the stabilization program itself.

In the past few decades, the financial authorities have pursued a restrictive monetary policy,[18] an effort that has been only partly successful. This policy managed to prevent run-away demand and the outbreak of hyperinflation, as occurred in Yugoslavia and Poland, but it was accompanied by undesirable side-effects. Often it prevented expansion in production and investment in areas where this would have been profitable. Given that real interest rates have been unrealistically low, it has not been possible to develop a rational restrictive monetary policy. Therefore, one of the first and most important instruments of a more prudent and well-grounded policy is high positive real interest rates on loans.

In particular, two issues related to the restriction of demand require careful attention. One concerns the *granting of credit among state-owned firms*. In the classical socialist command economies, credit supply was the monopoly of the state banking system, and "commercial credit" was strictly forbidden. However, in the wake of "market socialism"-type reforms and the partial liberalization of state-owned firms, interfirm credit has sprung up suddenly and spread widely. But this practice is really only a form of pseudo-credit. The purchasing firm simply refuses to pay the selling firm, forcing it to sell its shipment on credit. The forced creditor then frequently becomes insolvent itself, and in turn refuses to pay its suppliers. Eventually, a liquidity crisis occurs, prompting the banking system to bail out those in direst straits.

This is but one distorted manifestation of Hungary's pseudo-credit system, pseudo-banking system, and pseudo-capital market. Nonetheless, this interfirm commercial credit is a part of the "money creation" process and must be included on the money supply side of the balance during quantitative planning of the stabilization program. At the same time, the current distorted system must be abandoned and replaced by the legal forms and institutions of commercial credit characteristic of market economies.

The second issue concerns *wages* and is the most difficult, and politically sensitive, part of the stabilization operation. Total wages paid by state-owned firms must not exceed the limit established for the stabilization program. Precisely what this limit should be relative to the nominal wage level of the prestabilization period is difficult to say. For a short time, it may be that a measure of surplus purchasing power will need to be released and that this will be accompanied by a wave of price increases — a transitional corrective price-level increase — in order to absorb a portion of unspent forced savings and liquidate the "monetary overhang." It is also possible that this will be unnecessary; further analysis is needed.[19]

Once this average wage level is determined, various tools can be used to stabilize it, such as limiting the total wage fund of the firm. This will, of course, reduce the independence of enterprise managers and will make it difficult to achieve the optimal combination of factors of production. But if we fail to take this step, the managers of state-owned firms will continue to raise wages indiscriminately. This situation cannot be controlled by indirect means, and it is self-deception to expect managers to restrain wages voluntarily under a system of bureaucratic state ownership.

While wage control through administrative means prejudices efficiency in several respects, the only way to alter this situation is by replacing state ownership with private ownership. Only private ownership can pit a natural "antagonist" — the owner, who pays the wages out of his own pocket — against the employee who demands a wage increase. This genuine and natural conflict is impossible to simulate through pseudo-ownership reforms, and as long as state ownership remains dominant, only bureaucratic means can be applied to counter the pressure from below for wage increases.

Ever since the concept of market reform of state ownership emerged a couple of decades ago, the issue of administrative restraint of wages has been shirked.[20] It is high time to face this bitter fact. The maintenance of wage discipline is the Achilles' heel of the entire stabilization operation: if we fail in this, the whole operation will come to naught.

Rationalizing Prices

Stabilization will be successful if it ultimately replaces the current arbitrary and irrational price system with a rational market-determined system, in which prices carry meaningful economic information. Achieving this change requires that several conditions be met. Some of them are self-evident and relatively easy to fulfill. Others are not.

I will begin with the self-evident part of the task. The prices of all private-sector transactions should be allowed to move freely. This in itself will not guarantee that the private price system will be fully rationalized since numerous units in the private sector have contacts with the state sector either as sellers or as buyers. Consequently, the prices of the state sector spill over into the costs and prices of the private sector. Nonetheless, the input-output flow within the private sector is comparatively high in a number of products and services, so for quite a number of them, private prices could be the standard against which state prices are measured.

Prices in the state sector are a much tougher nut to crack. The goal is to develop market-clearing prices. Thus, apart from a few exceptions, *total liberalization of prices* is necessary in this sector as well. But while stabilization must lead to price liberalization, I can only offer conditional suggestions regarding the road leading to this end.

When considering the price system, the state of supply and the size of the reserves of essential consumer goods, energy, and raw materials must be taken into account. If a serious shortage appears likely, two options are available: allowing the prices of essential products and services to rise sky-high right at the outset of stabilization, or restricting prices for a short transitional period while simultaneously acting to quickly increase supply (for example through imports) and *then* proceeding with price liberalization. With the exception of a very few permanently regulated prices (public services, monopoly output), every incidence of price regulation must be viewed as a transitional evil to be ended as quickly as possible. The sooner imports, including private imports, are freed up and the greater the opportunity for the private sector to fill the gaps left by the state sector, the sooner it will be possible to end such regulation.

In the beginning of the stabilization process, state-owned firms may have difficulty determining initial prices. A few rules of thumb may prove useful in that respect until market forces can take over to determine prices.

For tradable products, there should be no dramatic difference between foreign and domestic price levels. This should render most shopping excursions abroad superfluous and so limit "shopping tourism." Achieving this correspondence of domestic and international prices implies implementation of all the recommendations made in this paper: strict uniformity of consumption tax rates and customs tariffs, and the elimination of consumer and producer subsidies.

To establish initial relative prices, firms could take present-day Austrian or West German prices as their starting point. Among market economies, Hungary's ties are the strongest with these countries. While their prices are also distorted by a number of factors and their demand-supply situation and cost structure are different from Hungary's, their prices are at least genuine prices. Relative prices in the Hungarian private sector present state firms with another basis for fixing the initial prices at the beginning of stabilization. Genuine market prices have already emerged in the private markets for foodstuffs and real estate and in a significant part of the service sector and other areas. These prices should guide state-owned firms.

While the methods discussed above might provide orientation in determining the relative prices of various products and services, the general price level is a different matter. It will depend on numerous other macroeconomic factors (supply of credit, wage level, aggregate supply and demand, and so on). When the state firm makes its calculations, it takes into account the *exchange rate* determined by the state financial authorities and used by the state banking system (see the following section). The firm should also take into account positive *real interest rates*. These rates, which should apply for at least the initial period of stabilization, must be announced in advance. They can be modified later, in accordance with the real credit market situation.

Even with these guidelines, however, when the firm finally enters the market, it will to some degree be making a leap in the dark with respect to its initial price. What happens next should be determined by the free play of demand and supply. It is important to liberate all prices quickly. It will take time for demand and supply to reach equilibrium and for a market-clearing price to emerge. If the initial selling price ensures high profitability, the market will attract imports, which will eventually bring the price down; in the contrary situation, the processes will move in the opposite direction to achieve equilibrium.

In the final analysis, liberalization leads to basically uniform prices. Although in the case of imperfect competition (characteristic of most sectors of a developed market economy), prices are somewhat dispersed, this is a natural dispersion. What the stabilization operation must bring to an end is the artificial dispersion of prices on the basis of other criteria, such as "white" versus "gray" or "black" market prices, prices dictated by the authorities versus free-market prices, prices determined by state firms versus those determined by the private sector. The tearing down of these price walls will permit the evolution of a basically uniform price system.

No one can tell how long the emergence of uniform market-clearing prices will take. Surely, it will take more than a year or two. Price fluctuations are a natural part of this process, as are occasional dazzling profits or losses. Let us not be afraid of the "anarchy" of the market. While public sentiment in Hungary has already reconciled itself to the losses, envy and disapproval too often greet the making of tremendous profits. Yet this is the engine of adaptation. The promise of making money hand over fist, even if only a few share directly in this wealth, might move thousands or hundreds of thousands to take chances and embark on genuine business enterprises.

Today the structure of the Hungarian economy is riddled with disproportion and disharmony, an environment that is strongly attractive to entrepreneurs in a free enterprise system. The greater the disproportion between demand and supply, the more money that can be made from any activity that restores equilibrium. (By contrast, where the economic structure is stable, the only way to earn extra income is to introduce technical innovations or important new products.) This situation also calls for changes in attitudes and moral judgments. According to the economic theory that has prevailed for decades in Hungary, the only ethically acceptable form of income is that earned by labor. "Profiteering" or "speculation" are condemned, as is taking advantage of shortages in order to make a profit. Price, however, is not a moral but an economic category. Shortages will not disappear if we ask sellers to practice self-restraint and to kindly refrain from price hikes. Rather, we must put an end to the position of superiority that sellers occupy in a sellers' market.

A final issue with respect to the new price system concerns the loss-making state-owned firms. We are very much in the dark about which firms show a genuine loss and which only a pseudo-loss. While the calculation is relatively easy in the case of, say, the mining industry (relatively few factors, and the value of output is easy to gauge using world market prices), it is practically impossible for the manufacturing industry. Here, costs are affected by the spillover of a myriad of input prices, which in turn are influenced by a maze of subsidies and tax exemptions. It would not be surprising if a number of state-owned firms which are considered loss-makers today turn out to be profitable after stabilization. Nor would the opposite case be surprising.

Introducing a Uniform Exchange Rate and Convertibility

Three closely related reforms of the exchange rate would be required during stabilization: application of a uniform exchange rate, full convertibility of the forint, and liberalization of all import and export activities, for state-owned firms as well as private sector firms.

The first task cannot be performed by coercion, that is, by banning private currency transactions and declaring the private exchange rate illegal. Uniformity of the exchange rate will develop without administrative coercion provided currency can be bought without restriction from the state bank at a price no higher and sold at a price no lower than the private exchange rate. To prevent the exchange rate applied by the state banking system from causing serious disproportions on the Hungarian currency market, a market-clearing exchange rate is required. Exactly what that rate will be depends largely on how the other parts of the stabilization program progress and on what happens with inflation before stabilization begins. One basis for deciding the rate could be today's gray market private exchange rate. If the private currency market is legalized before the stabilization program begins, as I recommend, a more accurate gauge might be tomorrow's "white" private exchange rate.

Stabilization is likely to require devaluation of the forint. The extent of the devaluation will depend on the factors already mentioned and on the movement of the official exchange rate in the period up to the start of stabilization.

Before the state banking sector can ensure convertibility, numerous conditions must be fulfilled. I will mention two of them. The most important is control of the demand for hard currency. The most problematic area is the state sector. State-owned firms under a soft budget constraint have had an almost insatiable hunger for Western imports and hard currency. This hunger must be curbed by ensuring that firms are short of forints (and that a realistic, market-clearing exchange rate applies). If a tight monetary policy and a hard constraint on credit to the state sector can be achieved, convertibility will be sustainable without gravely endangering the country's foreign exchange balance. If not, the problems will start all over again, and the only solution will be the rationing of hard currency to state-owned firms.

A second requirement for stabilizing the exchange rate at a realistic level and ensuring convertibility is that the state have adequate foreign currency reserves to meet excess demand for hard currency without suspending the free sale of foreign currency. (Of course, further measures must also be taken to restore equilibrium between supply and demand, such as reducing demand expressed in domestic currency or devaluing the forint again.)

Once a uniform, realistic, market-clearing exchange rate and convertibility have been established, comprehensive import liberalization can occur. But if the conditions for a uniform rate and full convertibility remain unfulfilled, only private imports can be freed without running a major risk. It is a dangerous game to give state-owned firms full freedom to import while state-sector demand is still not under an effective constraint or adequate control.

All these changes might do more than help to restore the country's short-term external and internal financial equilibrium: they might also contribute to lasting expansion of production and improvement of quality standards. Unrestrained import is indispensable to competition among sellers, which is itself one of the strongest incentives for ensuring that the public is better supplied, that shortages are eliminated, and that technological improvement occurs.

Eliminating the Shortage Economy

Inflation and shortage coexist in Hungary today. The economic policy outlined here offers an opportunity to eliminate both of these closely linked phenomena.

The shortage syndrome is complex and has its roots in both micro- and macro-level problems. Among its causes are the socialist system's property relations and methods of control and its financial and price systems. Shortages are not going to disappear once the stabilization program is initiated. For quite some time, the market will operate with greater friction and weaker adaptive features than older, well-established markets. But liberalization of the private sector and introduction of the stabilization program should eliminate the main factors leading to the chronic, general-shortage economy. Here I will summarize only the most important conditions for eliminating the shortage economy.

If the stabilization program succeeds in achieving and maintaining equilibrium in supply and demand, it will have eliminated one of the fundamental causes of shortage: excess demand. If, however, demand is allowed to get out of control again, inflationary pressures and shortages will reemerge. More precisely, if the government prevents prices from rising to counteract excess demand, repressed inflation will inevitably occur, along with the concomitant shortage syndrome. As mentioned before, an important aspect of demand management is keeping a tight hold on demand in the state sector. It is foolhardy to expect internally motivated hard budget constraints to prevail in state-owned firms since the development of a genuine profit incentive in these firms is quite unlikely. Investment hunger and wage drift are bound to prove irresistible. Thus the state sector's propensity toward spending needs to be controlled from outside — as political change continues, by a legislature, acting independently of the bureaucracy and able to impose restrictions on the spending of state-owned firms.

A second basic aspect of eliminating the shortage economy is expansion of the private sector. Already, formal and informal private sector activity has been able to satisfy several kinds of demand that the state sector cannot meet. The fact that shortages have been much less characteristic of Hungary than of many other socialist countries can be ascribed, in part, to the scope of this second economy, which has filled some of the gaps left by the state sector. Unlike the state sector, the private sector faces a hard budget constraint: its spending is strictly restrained by the simple fact that the private owner has to pay from his own pocket. Consequently, there is no intrinsic mechanism reproducing excess demand, as in the state sector.

We must allow the private sector to prosper, and the public must be educated to understand the logic of private initiative and the market. It is precisely shortage that attracts entrepreneurs, provided they are allowed to profit from the situation. Once solvent demand appears where supply is insufficient, mobile capital will rush to capture any prospective business. The private sector's flexibility, initiative, and ability to recognize and exploit opportunities quickly, together with freedom of entry and competition, can remedy thousands of microshortages.

Finally, as already discussed, free prices are indispensable for maintaining macroequilibrium between demand and supply and for ensuring quick adjustment between demand and supply at the micro-level.

Other Aspects of the Stabilization Program

Simultaneity of Reform

None of the measures so far described is unfamiliar, and many of them have already been partially implemented. The problem is that implementation has been inconsistent and sluggish. The ambiguity that prevails in one set of measures reduces the efficiency of others. The sum total of ten different kinds of half measures is not five full successes but five full fiascos. All the measures discussed here are conditional on one another. Stopping inflation requires a balanced budget. Balancing the budget can be achieved only after a radical change in the tax system. Ending subsidies to loss-making firms is conditional on the introduction of a new tax system and the ability to identify loss-making firms through the workings of market-clearing equilibrium prices. Genuine market prices cannot emerge, however, amid accelerating inflation. And partial price adjustments, rather than converging in a rational system of relative prices, only speed up the inflationary spiral. The list of these concentric and interdependent measures is very long; taken together, they provide an economic explanation for the need to execute the stabilization operation at one stroke.

For the sake of emphasis, it is worth making the negative statement: most of the measures beneficial as parts of the stabilization package would be dangerous and damaging if introduced without implementing the other measures. For instance, a total freeing of prices can cause grave damage in the absence of wage discipline. Harm can come of full currency convertibility if demand from the state sector is not firmly controlled. The stabilization measures already introduced have failed one after the other because the authorities tried to introduce them hastily, aiming at targets torn out of their economic context.

I would like to add two further arguments to these economic reasons.

The first is an economic-psychological one. If we want to stop inflation, we must radically alter inflationary expectations. The more each employer and employee, business person, and moneyholder counts on a 20-percent rise in the rate of inflation, the more likely it is that they will adjust to this expectation by adding at least 20 percent to the prices and wages asked and offered on the market. A credible stabilization operation could sever the vicious self-fulfilling circle of inflationary expectations.

The second argument is primarily a humanitarian one. The Hungarian people suffer considerably as a result of the current economic ills. It is the prime obligation of political organizations and governmental institutions to alleviate people's misery. The rehabilitation of the economy entails deep sacrifices, but the sacrificial period should not drag on endlessly. István Széchenyi, the great nineteenth-century reform politician and one of the first Hungarian economists, used the metaphor of a tooth extraction in his volume *Credit*: "The tooth extractor or operator is cruel if he keeps pulling slowly and faintly on account of senseless soft-heartedness, and performs his job with only minor cuts and for a long time."[21] I firmly believe that people would prefer by far to face a single, radical shock and the ensuing trauma if they were convinced that the situation would improve, rather than to suffer the slow but steady economic deterioration and social spasms we are now undergoing.

Humanitarian and Economic Reserves

Society must prepare for stabilization by maintaining appropriate reserves. Four kinds of reserves are indispensable.

The most important is a humanitarian reserve for extending emergency grants to those in dire straits. Eventually, everyone will have to adapt to the new market situation after stabilization. Those who prove permanently unable to accommodate to the new conditions should be assisted by means of an adequate welfare policy. Here, however, I refer not to the permanent safety net that every humanitarian society requires, but rather to the extraordinary and temporary relief aid needed in the first year or two of stabilization.

Second, there must be a reserve of goods and capacities to ensure the availability of vital consumer goods, fuel and other energy sources, and other essential goods. If the initial adjustment is convulsive, serious disorders can be avoided through adequate state reserves.

Third, the state should dispose of enough convertible hard currency reserves to pay for extraordinary imports in case of temporary troubles and to enable the state banking system to ensure convertibility. Should excess demand for foreign currency appear, it should be met first by reserves. (It is another matter to decide what means to use after the first reaction to restore equilibrium on the foreign currency market.)

Last, there should be a credit reserve for extending transitional loans to firms facing an unexpected liquidity crisis during stabilization. These should be hard credits, not soft bailout money. Any firm that fails even with the help of such loans must be forbidden to reschedule the original credit or obtain a new one. Stabilization as a whole should result in the acceleration of the harsh natural selection process, and these transitional loans should be the last chance for organizations that consider themselves strong enough to survive.

Funding for all four kinds of reserves must be included in the stabilization plan and set aside in advance. Stabilization is doomed to failure if the economic balance equations are more or less in equilibrium, but it then turns out that, to live through the crisis, additional funding is needed in one or more of these areas, which will disrupt the precarious equilibria.

The International Context

The stabilization program must rely basically on Hungarian resources and capacity. The drafters of the plan should take into account foreign assistance only to the extent that it can be counted on with certainty. In this sense, the plan should be overcautious. At the same time, however, I am convinced that liberalization of the private sector, as well as the stabilization program itself, will considerably widen the scope for foreign assistance. Let us examine the most important tasks in this context.

The government must reshape Hungary's ties with the Comecon countries. The longer-term foreign trade aims are complex. Hungary needs to reduce its dependence on both the export and import sides while also promoting a more advantageous structure for its foreign trade. The most important drawback of Hungary's export ties with the Comecon countries is the low quality standards in these markets. Remarkably, this lack of standards is precisely what makes these commercial ties so attractive to state-owned firms. Hungary must shift its sphere of interest to markets with higher standards, but while doing so must take special care to maintain business continuity, even in the wake of political change. A business contract must not be violated unilaterally: this is the basic law of honest trading. Hungary's reliability must in no way be compromised.

With respect to Hungary's ties with the Western economies, an important issue is private foreign capital. The attitude of Western governments and international organizations toward Hungary receives disproportionate emphasis in public debate. While their behavior matters, the attitude of Western businessmen and entrepreneurs is of even greater significance. There is no "Capitalist International"; the capitalists of the world did not unite. They do not dance to the tune of a piper in some world center, be it Washington, Bonn, or Tokyo. Businessmen do, however, pay close attention to experiences recounted by fellow businessmen concerning their experiences in Hungary (and elsewhere). One bitter story about a multitude of bureaucratic obstacles is enough to spoil a hundred government guarantees.

We need to remember the link that Béla Balassa has pointed out between domestic adjustment and external economic relations. Indeed, a socioeconomic system cannot have two faces: an ugly one toward its citizens and a charming one toward the outside world. We cannot keep building Potemkin villages: running elegantly furnished Western-style banks in downtown Budapest while clients in provincial towns have to line up for hours for a simple banking transaction. Sensible Western capitalists who cannot be easily cheated have no confidence in the *exceptional* conditions granted to them: special tax exemptions, special convertibility terms, and special customs duties applicable only to foreigners. They will trust, however, conditions that are granted routinely to all Hungarians.

None of these comments is meant to play down the importance of the assistance Hungary could obtain from Western governments and international financial institutions. The stabilization program is the best occasion for mobilizing Western assistance. Many governments and commercial bankers in the West feel that they were burned by the experience of unbridled lending in the 1970s, when their loans melted away in the hands of borrowing governments. In the case of Hungary, the governments in power have presented new reform schemes each year, while the debts have continued to mount and economic ills have worsened. This time, a unique opportunity presents itself. Chances are good that Hungary will have a freely elected parliament and a new government that enjoys its support. This new government will have the opportunity to present a clearly articulated stabilization program. Foreign governments could well be won over to this cause. They might be convinced to provide extraordinary loans under better than average terms and to reconsider our existing debts as well.

The new government should pledge its word to the Hungarian nation to renegotiate the country's debts, but it should abstain from announcing a rescheduling in the conventional sense of the term. Such a move would only undermine Hungary's reputation in the financial world. The country may be able to avoid rescheduling under the pressure of an emergency. This does not mean, however, that Hungary must acquiesce unquestioningly to the size of the debt-service burden to be borne by the present generation. The people have already suffered too much. They cannot be expected to accept further suffering in exchange for promises of a better world sometime in the distant future. The debt burden borne by the Hungarian people must be eased now, within the next couple of years.

This is a controversial problem among Western economists and policymakers, since several countries are struggling to pay off their debts. The leaders of the national central banks behave in a very similar way with respect to the foreign debt burden. Their main criterion is a negative one: "Take care not to annoy the creditor banks!" In addition, those at the political helm are usually ignorant of international financial matters and trust their own bankers unreservedly. If their bankers frighten them with dire predictions — "We will come to a bad end if we do not pay now!" — they will readily opt for more belt tightening.

The debtor is at the mercy of his creditor, but the creditor is exposed to the debtor as well. Parallel to the announcement of its stabilization program, the new government of Hungary should also pledge its determination to reduce the debt-service burden. There is no need to act precipitously, nor should the government violate any credit contract arbitrarily. But there must be separate negotiations with each group of creditors, who must be made to understand through calm but emphatic arguments that Hungary cannot repay its debts according to the original schedule. The country needs a judicious renegotiation of its obligations, not a spectacular, dangerous, and humiliating collective rescheduling. As many of these revisions as possible should be negotiated during the period leading up to stabilization; the stabilization program itself will provide occasion for continued negotiations. The restructuring of the debt is vital for ensuring that stabilization does not place intolerable burdens on the public.

Conclusion

Two tasks will have to be addressed simultaneously by all countries in transition from socialism to a market economy, namely the development of a large private sector and the introduction of fundamental stabilization measures. This combination makes the task extremely difficult. First, stabilization will be required even in countries that are not now experiencing hyperinflation, because the previous regime has left a host of financial imbalances demanding radical surgery. Second, stabilization itself will not restore a genuine private sector, which can be achieved only through a long, organic process. Although the tasks are daunting, I believe that the Hungarian population is approaching the point at which it can tolerate this effort. People are fed up with the perpetual tinkering and the concomitant sense of uncertainty. They are ready to take on the risks of a radical operation. And for all the temporary trauma and pain it will cause, the operation at least holds out the promise of a better order.

Notes

1. Among his earlier writings on Hungary, see also Balassa (1959, 1978).
2. This piece summarizes chapter 2 in my book, *The Road to a Free Economy, Shifting from a Socialist System: The Case of Hungary*, published by W.W. Norton & Company in April 1990. The book, a translation from the Hungarian, is a revised and expanded version of the Hungarian text, *Indulatos röpirat a gazdasági átmenet ügyében (A*

Passionate Pamphlet in the Cause of Economic Transition). The author gratefully acknowledges the help of Meta de Coquereaumont and Carla Krüger in the formulation and editing of the present text.

3. L. Békesi (1989, 19) was interviewed by I. Wiesel.

4. A profound analysis of inflationary expectation and other constituents of inflation can be found in Vissi's article (1989). From among the works on inflation in Hungary, I would mention the articles of Csoór and Mohácsi (1985), Petschnig (1986), and Erdős (1989).

5. The participants in this drama are the following: the Price Control Office, which fixes the official price; the state-owned firm, which determines the prices of products that can be sold at free prices; the commercial bank, which hands out state money; the National Bank, which puts money in circulation and is supposed to regulate its allotment; the Ministry of Finance, which is in charge of the budget and whose expenses constantly exceed revenues; and finally, the government itself and the political powers behind it. Each performer points a finger at the others, and each takes the opportunity during its "inflationary" act to blame the others for their similar role. Yet far from being independent of one another, they together constitute the "governmental sector."

6. I believe that the inflation rate in Hungary is considerably higher than official statistics indicate. The official calculation does not assign sufficient weight to private sector prices, especially prices in the unregistered shadow economy, where prices increase much faster than in the state sector. The products and services provided by the private sector account for a large and ever increasing part of total consumption. The official report contains other distortions as well. What is needed is a research team that would be able to calculate inflation independently of the Central Statistical Office, which is a governmental body.

7. Meanwhile, however, we must still do our best to predict the processes that can be expected during and after the stabilization program by applying current scientific means, such as modern macroeconomic models.

8. This study does not consider how these proposals, if accepted, should be translated into the language of the tax laws. For purposes of conceptualization, however, it is expedient to start with a clean slate.

9. For a general survey of the basic principles of taxation, see, for example, Musgrave and Musgrave (1980) and Stiglitz (1986).

10. This principle is critical from the perspective of the market economy as well. There can be no genuine market without genuine prices. Biased tax exemptions become incorporated in the price system and prevent us from having a clear idea of the real cost of each product. And since all elements of the price system are interdependent, each price will appear in the form of costs in the overall set of prices and wages. Ultimately, differentiated and chaotic taxes distort the price system.

11. My approach treats the question of what should be done for the good of the poor, the handicapped, the destitute, and the disabled separately from the problem of whether those who are more prosperous should be deprived of a greater part of their earnings and properties.

12. Of course, this still leaves open the question of how "social justice" is to be defined. Basically, I accept the criterion of justice suggested by Rawls (1971), which is presented here in a simplified version. For those interested in the details of the problem, see, for example, Rawls (1971), Nozick (1974), Sen (1988), and Kis (1986).

13. This is a necessary, but not sufficient condition of social justice.

14. The proposed tax system levies taxes primarily on the consumption of income. Nonconsumed income remains tax-exempt in this respect, thereby indirectly inducing

saving and investment. The idea that an income tax puts savers at a disadvantage has its roots in the works of John Stuart Mill. The same idea has since been argued strongly by Irwing Fisher (1942). For the advantages and disadvantages of a consumption tax, especially a value-added tax, see Musgrave and Musgrave (1980).

15. One may well be concerned that this category and the previous one fail to tax incomes generated outside officially registered firms. I would distinguish two types of "invisible" income. The first is that of individuals who make money by engaging in diverse forms of moonlighting: some might market fruit grown in their gardens, a secretary might do some extra typing, a translator some extra translations, the schoolgirl some babysitting, and so on. The whole society benefits since these activities add to the national income. I think we need to resign ourselves to the prospect that this kind of income will remain untaxed. However, my proposals are not meant to exempt plant-size private enterprises from paying the profit tax. With new laws protecting private enterprise, we would be able to offer the private entrepreneur an "exchange deal": legal protection and guaranteed enforcement of private contracts in return for paying taxes. The more successful the country becomes in ensuring the security of private property, the more worthwhile it will be for private firms to come out of the dark and accept the obligation of paying taxes.

16. The support of domestic infant industries may require protective tariffs.

17. This study leaves open several problems of the tax system, such as the issue of the property tax, the taxation of the self-employed and so on. Of course, a new tax system must solve these problems as well.

18. In this connection, see Várhegyi (1989).

19. In the case of the Polish stabilization program, this kind of "corrective nominal wage increase" seemed unavoidable. It is not clear whether it will be necessary in Hungary as well.

20. The exceptions deserve respect. See, for example, the works of Gábor (1988) and Gábor and Kővári (1987).

21. Széchenyi (1979, 214). The quote was brought to my attention by Katalin Szabó.

References

Balassa, B. 1959. *The Hungarian Experience in Economic Planning.* New Haven: Yale University Press.

Balassa, B. 1978. "The Economic Reform in Hungary: Ten Years After." *European Economic Review* 11: 245-68.

Balassa, B. 1983. "Reforming the New Economic Mechanism in Hungary." *Journal of Comparative Economics* 7: 253-76.

Békesi, L. 1989. "Jövedelni reform — elosztási igéretek nélkül" (Income Reform Without Promise of Distribution). Conversation between I. Wiesel and L. Békesi. *Társadalmi Szemle* 44: 16-23.

Csoór, K., and P. Mohácsi. 1985. "Az infláció tényezöi, 1980-1984" (The Main Factors of Inflation, 1980-1984). *Gazdaság* 19: 21-39.

Erdös, T. 1989. "Átgondolt gazdaságpolitikát: A külsö és a belsö egyensuly, a gazdasági növekedés és az infláció problémái" (A Well-Considered Economic Policy: The Problems of External and Internal Equilibrium, Economic Growth and Inflation). *Közgazdasági Szemle* 36: 545-57.

Fisher, I. 1942. *Constructive Income Taxation*. New York: Harper.

Gábor, I.R. 1988. "Lépéskényszerek és kényszerlépések: Jegyzetek két évtized kormányzati munkaerö-és bérpolitikájáról" (Being Forced to Take Steps and the Forced Steps: Notes on Governmental Labor and Wage Policy Over Two Decades). *Közgazdasági Szemle* 35: 803-7.

Gábor, I.R., and G. Kövári. 1987. "A munkaeröpiac állami koordinációja és a bérszabályozás" (The State Coordination of the Labor Market and Wage Regulation). *Gazdaság* 21: 48-58.

Kis, J. 1986. *Vannak-e emberi jogaink?* (Do We Have Human Rights?). Budapest: Független Kiadó.

Musgrave, R.A., and P.B. Musgrave. 1980. *Public Finance in Theory and Practice*. New York: McGraw-Hill.

Nozick, R. 1974. *Anarchy, State and Utopia*. New York: Basic Books.

Petschnig, Z.M. 1986. "Inflációs feszültségek és megoldásaik" (Inflationary Tensions and Their Solutions). *Gazdaság* 20: 38-51.

Rawls, J. 1971. *A Theory of Justice*. Cambridge, Mass.: Harvard University Press.

Sen, A. 1988. "Freedom of Choice: Concept and Content." *European Economic Review* 32: 269-94.

Stiglitz, J. 1986. *Economics of the Public Sector*. New York and London: W.W. Norton and Company.

Széchenyi, I. 1979. *Hitel* (Credit). Budapest: Közgazdasági és Jogi Könyvkiadó.

Várhegyi, É. 1989. "Results and Failures of Monetary Restriction." Budapest: Pénzügykutató Rt.

Vissi, F. 1989. "Infláció a gazdaság stabilizálásának idöszakában" (Inflation During the Stabilization of the Economy). *Gazdaság* 23: 5-28.

19

Township, Village, and Private Industry in China's Economic Reform

William Byrd and Alan Gelb

For most economists, seventeen articles and a book on comparative economic systems and reform would constitute a sizable volume of output. In the case of Béla Balassa, this work is dwarfed by his prodigious output in other areas. Nevertheless, his deep interest in this topic is only natural. From its early stages, he has analyzed the Chinese economic reform process, comparing it with developments in Eastern Europe, especially his native Hungary. A notable characteristic of Balassa's analysis, for example, in "China's Economic Reforms in a Comparative Perspective (1987)", is a strong focus on the incentive structures linking performance and rewards. This emphasis, natural to one so involved in analyzing trade (and other) regulatory regimes, provides a unifying thread for analysis of the spread of "responsibility systems" in agriculture and industry and of the evolving balance between planning and markets for both products and factors that characterizes the reform process.

Next to the decollectivization of agriculture, the most striking economic transformation in China since 1978 has been the rapid growth of rural nonstate industry. Firms in this sector are owned by a hierarchy of local government units below the county level — towns (or townships), villages, and in some areas production teams — and to a lesser extent by private individuals and groups. Reflecting their mix of ownership, these firms are referred to here as TVPs,[1] while that part of the TVP sector that is owned by township and village community governments (that is, not privately owned) will be referred to as township and village community enterprises (TVCEs).

China had attained a certain degree of rural industrialization by the late 1970s, but this occurred within the confines of an administrative straitjacket. This earlier industrialization has been dwarfed by the burst of activity that followed the easing of ideological and political prohibitions against rural nonagricultural activities after 1978. Private industrial and other nonagricultural ("sideline") activities came to be permitted, even encouraged. In 1987, limits on the size of private firms, which had been only sporadically enforced, were lifted. Following several years of spectacular growth, by 1987 TVPs accounted for some 23 percent of total industrial output value of Chinese industry. Some rural areas that only a few years back had relied almost entirely on agriculture have become overwhelmingly industrial communities, with agriculture continuing as a marginal activity subsidized out of industrial income.

What does the growth of the TVP sector mean for China's overall reform? To what extent does it represent a broadening of the market mechanism outside agriculture and a potential source of competition for state industry? How compatible with a market economy are the patterns of incentives for TVP owners, managers, and workers? What are the regional implications of TVP development? We examine these questions here, drawing on the results of a recent collaborative research project between the World Bank and the Institute of Economics of the Chinese Academy of Social Sciences.[2]

The extent and characteristics of rural industrial development differ greatly among China's many counties. The project therefore involved in-depth fieldwork in four counties selected for their diversity in development stages and organizational features.[3]

As suggested by table 19.1, two of the counties, Wuxi and Nanhai, are relatively industrialized. Wuxi, in Jiangsu Province near Shanghai, has for a long time been the most industrialized rural county in China and offers a good example of a "traditional" system of tightly integrated local government-owned firms. Neither labor nor land markets have developed in Wuxi, although there are elements of a capital market. Nanhai County, situated in the booming coastal province of Guangdong with its more freewheeling economy, has also industrialized rapidly and has benefited from expanding links with foreign business, especially through Hong Kong. Labor markets are relatively open, and a laissez-faire attitude prevails concerning private versus local-government ownership of firms. Jieshou County in Anhui Province represents a more-or-less average level of TVP development for China, but its policies toward the sector are unusual in that private enterprises have been encouraged and even sponsored by local governments. An active land market has developed, as have "specialized villages," a new mode of rural industrial development. Shangrao County in Jiangxi Province represents a level of TVP development below the national average, with "traditional," and unsuccessful, management of the sector.

This examination of the TVP sector looks briefly at the rise of the sector, its relationship with agricultural reform, and the patterns of labor absorption in the sample counties. Next it considers the market environment for TVPs — the extent to which these firms compete on an equal basis in free product and factor markets — and summarizes what is known about the efficiency of different ownership types. A look at the incentives for owners of TVPs follows this discussion. As the owners are mainly various levels of local governments, an important question in judging the significance of the TVP sector is the extent to which such firms will behave differently from those owned by the state.[4] The research indicates some important differences between state ownership and ownership by "small" units of government, which suggests that looking at the TVP sector as simply another form of state enterprise is misleading. This examination ends with a consideration of the incentives for labor and patterns of labor payments in the TVP sector.

Table 19.1 TVP Ownership Structure in Four
Counties of China, 1985
(percentage of total gross industrial output value of TVPs)

Type of TVP	Wuxi	Nanhai[a]	Jieshou	Shangrao	China
Township firms	48	43	36	43	45
Village firms	47	31	13	22	38
Team firms	2	16	-	-	9
Private firms	3	10	51	35	8
Total (millions of yuan)	3,705	1,421	127	31	175,008

Note: TVPs are firms owned by township or village governments or by private individuals or groups.
a. Shares in gross revenues of industrial TVPs.
Source: Fieldwork of World Bank / Institute of Economics of the Chinese Academy of Social Sciences research project.

The Rise of the TVP Sector

The development of China's TVP sector during the past thirty years can be divided into several phases. The Great Leap Forward of the late 1950s led local governments to establish numerous rural small-scale industrial firms, but most of them turned out to be unsustainable. As a result, the TVP sector shrank drastically in the early 1960s. A new wave of TVP development began in 1970, based on the government's desire to promote production of key inputs for the mechanization of agriculture (agricultural tools and implements, tractors, other agricultural machinery, chemical fertilizer, and the like). But this development spread beyond the limits set by government, and a few parts of the country, like southern Jiangsu Province, achieved rural industrialization on a self-sustaining basis. In its third phase, TVP development has been an integral part of rural and agricultural reforms since 1978.

The Production Responsibility System
Agricultural reforms have had a major impact on the TVP sector. Prices of farm products were raised substantially, improving agriculture's terms of trade. Mandatory quotas for areas planted, output, and compulsory procurement were eliminated or reduced. Most important, in the early 1980s the commune system gave way to the production responsibility system, under which most communal land was divided equally on per capita or per worker terms.[5] The obligations of households were limited to tax payments, procurement quotas at set prices, and contributions to social funds. As noted by Balassa (1987), quotas were often set in absolute terms, providing a strong incentive for increasing production.

The response to these reforms is well-documented. Although acreage shifted away from grain production, per capita grain output rose and overall per capita gross agricultural output grew by two-thirds. About half the increased output between 1978 and 1984 could be attributed to increased inputs and half to growth of total factor productivity (Johnson 1986 as presented in Balassa 1987). Lin (1986) found that growth of output was correlated with the extent to which the production responsibility system was introduced.

China's rural communities were profoundly affected by the production responsibility system. A major consequence was to make apparent the extent of surplus rural labor and so to generate pressures to address the employment problem. With continuing controls on mobility (forestalling a major population shift to urban areas), job creation in rural areas was needed not only for social stability but to enable the potential productivity gains of the production responsibility system to be fully realized. At the same time, increased rural incomes boosted the demand for consumer goods and housing, creating markets for products suitable for production by smaller firms, while rural savings, deposited in the local banking system, offered a growing source of capital to finance industrial investment. Demand and supply factors thus combined to impel rural industrialization.

Incentives for labor and potential owners of industrial firms also changed markedly after 1978. Many TVPs had previously paid wages directly to worker production teams, and the workers had then participated in year-end collective income distributions. This greatly diluted incentives. Even in enterprises that paid workers directly, fixed-time wages were usual. Under the production responsibility system, however, firms could shift to direct, performance-related pay in a variety of forms (although, as described below, the income of a community still has an important influence in setting the terms of these payments). For local governments, the benefits of owning successful industrial firms were boosted by progressive decentralization of the fiscal system. In areas like Wuxi County, the response to this confluence of forces was to further promote existing local-government-owned industry; other localities like Nanhai sought a mix of government and private initiative; and still other places turned to primarily private enterprise-based rural industrialization.

Output Growth in the TVP Sector

Between 1978 and 1987 the value of rural gross industrial output is estimated to have increased by about 26 percent annually (table 19.2). During this time the price level, as measured by the consumer price index, increased by 5 percent a year. Gross fixed assets of TVCEs rose at over 20 percent a year and bank loans to TVCEs at the remarkable rate of 44 percent. Fieldwork suggests that early profit opportunities, which were clearly very high, were progressively whittled away by increased competition within the TVP sector. This is confirmed by aggregate data, which show profits rising more slowly than output, assets, and wage payments.

**Table 19.2   Selected Indicators of Growth in the TVP Sector
in China, 1978-83 and 1983-87**

(average annual percentage change)

Indicator	1978-83	1983-87	1978-87
Rural industrial output	19.7	41.5	26.4
Rural industrial labor force	3.1	15.9	7.4
Fixed assets[a]	15.7	26.7	20.5
Bank loans[a]	34.7	55.4	43.8
Profits before tax[a]	7.4	14.1	10.3
Employment	2.7	9.8	5.8
Wage bill	15.2	24.9	19.4
Average wage	12.1	13.7	12.9
Memorandum items			
Average wage, state firms	6.1	15.6	10.2
Inflation (CPI)	3.1	7.6	5.1

Note: TVPs are firms owned by township or village governments or by private individuals or groups.
[a] TVCEs only. (TVCEs are town- and village-government-owned TVPs.)
Source: State Statistical Bureau of China (various years); *China Rural Statistical Yearbook* (various years).

Employment in rural nonagricultural activities rose sharply in this period, from 22 million in 1978 to 77 million by 1986 (including seasonal and part-time workers). Much of this increase was due to service activities, however, and the industrial TVP sector posted more modest increases. In the more advanced localities, in particular, rural industrialization has accompanied declines in the agricultural labor force. For example, in Wuxi County during 1978-85 the industrial labor force grew by 19 percent a year while the agricultural force declined by 13 percent a year. Average wages paid by TVPs, which were initially well below state-firm levels, rose rapidly but then moderated to slightly below the rate of increase in the state sector. In 1978-87, the average real TVP wage rose by almost 8 percent a year.

As a result of rapid TVP growth, the ownership structure of China's industry as a whole has changed markedly (see table 19.3). The share of the TVP sector has increased sharply, from only 3 percent in 1971 to over 23 percent by 1987, while the share of state enterprises has declined considerably. All types of TVPs have seen an increase in their share, but growth has been most marked for private firms. There has been a corresponding shift in the composition of rural gross output. Whereas in 1978 crop cultivation represented 53 percent and industry only 19 percent of output, by 1987 the share of crop cultivation had fallen to 30 percent while that of industry had risen to 35 percent. Smaller gains were posted by other farming activities and by construction, transport, and commerce.

Table 19.3 Ownership Structure of Chinese Industry, Selected Years

(percentage of total industrial output value)

Category	1971	1978	1983	1987
State	85.9	77.6	72.6	59.7
Urban collective	10.9	13.7	14.4	14.6
Urban individual[a]	-	-	0.1	0.6
Urban other	-	-	0.8	2.0
Rural nonstate (TVP)	3.2	8.7	12.1	23.1
Township	1.6	4.8	6.3	9.3
Village				8.4
Below village	1.6	3.9	5.8	5.4
Individual firms				3.3

Note: TVPs are firms owned by township or village governments or by private individuals or groups.
a. Includes partnerships.
Source: State Statistical Bureau of China (various years), *China Rural Statistical Yearbook, Statistical Materials on China's Industrial Materials*.

The share of TVPs in the output of specific product groups varied greatly, although they were active in virtually all broad product groups by 1985. Considering only TVCEs shows that in 1985 they accounted for 26 percent of the gross value of industrial production in machine building, 19 percent in construction materials, and 13 percent in textiles. They produced some 80 percent of all bricks, almost 20 percent of cement, and nearly 25 percent of paper and cardboard made in China.

Markets and Administrative Structure

Market Environment

Does the rise of the TVP sector represent a strengthening of market forces? Or do TVPs, like their state counterparts, operate largely according to mandatory or "guidance" plans? Insofar as they are market based, are their markets fragmented by "local protectionism" policies implemented by local governments, or are their markets regional or national?

The answers to these questions differ for product and factor markets. Surveys provide ample evidence that planned output as a share of total output is minimal for most TVPs. Furthermore, they are "outward oriented" with respect to their home communities, as might be expected given the very small size of their home markets. For example, in Wuxi only 4 percent of sales of industrial TVCEs occurred within the home township in 1985. Large majorities of sampled firms in all four counties sold at least 40 percent of their output outside the home province.

In any case, communal governments have little scope for protecting their enterprises from outside competition. TVPs also rely heavily on the market mechanism for intermediate inputs, with the partial exception of electric power.

On the factor side, however, the TVP sector is heavily community oriented. All firms (including private enterprises) must obtain land and financial capital (usually in the form of bank loans) through the good offices of their local governments.[6] Although a labor market is emerging in some areas, labor allocation still takes place in many localities. In particular, technically skilled labor tends to be allocated by governments, rather than bid for by potential employers. Except for labor in some areas, TVPs in different localities do not generally compete for factors on the basis of price.

The efficiency of the TVP sector therefore depends both on the efficiency of factor allocation *within* individual localities and on the degree to which locking productive factors into small administrative units induces misallocation of resources *between* localities. The first issue is related to the incentives faced by TVP owners, managers, and employees. Extensive treatment of the second issue is beyond the scope of this brief coverage of TVPs, but it appears that decisions on location and scale of TVPs are seriously, and sometimes adversely, affected by the dispersion of ownership across communities and by the limited scope of joint ventures between communities. Small communities also face increased risk from concentration of their resources in one or two large firms.

Overall, there is considerable anecdotal and statistical evidence that the TVP sector's market environment and orientation lead to efficient performance by Chinese standards. In many industries, TVPs outcompete state enterprises or at least hold their own. Production function estimates (both Cobb-Douglas and translog) for sample enterprises suggest that TVPs have experienced rapid technical progress (or improvement in X-efficiency) over time and that they operate under increasing returns to scale. Interestingly, productive efficiency does not seem to vary systematically with type of ownership (Svejnar forthcoming), which suggests that the general market orientation and the community ties common to nearly all TVPs dominate any impact of different forms of ownership.

Local Government and Enterprise Hierarchies
With property rights still undeveloped in China, some degree of association between the bureaucratic status of the owners of an enterprise and the status of the firm is not surprising. By and large, there is little discrimination against local TVCEs by county governments, as they have a strong interest in promoting local industrialization. At higher levels of government, however, unfavorable policies such as abrupt curtailment of credit have sometimes been imposed.[7] Within the hierarchy of local governments, there is often some degree of favoritism for enterprises owned by the corresponding government unit, because of the strength of fiscal and other ties. Considerable rivalry may exist between local governments at similar levels.

Lowest on the bureaucratic totem pole are, of course, the private enterprises. Competition for technically and administratively skilled personnel is normally the most severe source of conflict between private firms and local TVCEs, especially where, as in Wuxi, local governments seek to closely regulate firms and their pay scales. The formation of private firms and their entry into specified lines of activity can be restricted in many ways, such as through regulations on energy use and zoning or sanctions on skilled workers wanting to leave TVCEs for private firms. The extent to which private firms are encouraged or discouraged varies widely among localities, reflecting differences in the extent to which traditional community-owned firms are protected from private sector competition. But even in areas supportive of private enterprise, such as Jieshou, the weakness of property rights can lead to numerous problems. These may include "collectivization" of private firms under pressure from workers and local authorities and more voluntary changes of ownership based on improved administrative status and security for the original proprietors.

Incentives for TVP Owners

Spatial Inequality
Most of China's rural population is rooted in small communities with little prospect for permanent migration, although seasonal or temporary labor flows are somewhat more common. Financial resources raised from within a community are seen as a local resource, and intercommunity flows are limited by a "gap" system of credit allocation and the determination of leaders to use local funds for local investments. Under these conditions, substantial inequalities in factor rewards, especially personal incomes, might be expected between communities.

Evidence on the dispersion of personal incomes in China and the United States is presented in table 19.4. While urban incomes in China are distributed relatively evenly, the dispersion of rural incomes among provinces is markedly larger than the dispersion of average incomes across U.S. states. A similar pattern is evident for dispersion of average incomes among counties within individual provinces or among states. The level of TVP development is probably the primary determinant of rural per capita incomes in China; in 1985, the correlation between the value of rural industrial output per head and average income per head across China's provinces was 0.91.

Income inequality *within* Chinese counties, however, is usually much lower than inequalities between counties. For example, in Nanhai County the coefficient of variation of income per head among districts was only 7 percent in 1985.[8] And within districts and smaller administrative units, a range of measures, including compensating payments made to agriculture out of industrial profits, keeps income inequality within a fairly narrow range (as is shown also by the wage equations discussed below). China may thus be characterized as a "locally equal" society.

Table 19.4   Dispersion of Personal Income: Spatial Income Inequality in China and the United States, Selected Years

Area	Year	Percentage of mean		Coefficient of variation (%)[a]
		Highest	*Lowest*	
Provinces and states				
China urban[b]	1983	137	75	13
China rural[c]	1980	194	70	28
	1985	195	62	31
United States[d]	1981	134	72	14
	1986	140	70	17
Chinese counties				
Anhui urban[e]	1984	128	87	8
Jiangsu urban[e]	1985	127	85	10
Anhui rural[f]	1984	163	49	23
Jiangsu rural[g]	1985	164	62	23
U.S. states				
Michigan	1981	164	60	17
Mississippi	1981	163	65	16
Oregon	1981	137	81	12
South Dakota	1981	183	39	21

a. Standard deviation divided by mean.
b. Average per capita income of urban residents in the capital cities of each of the twenty-nine provinces, based on household surveys.
c. Average per capita income of rural residents in each province from household surveys.
d. Average per capita income by state.
e. Average wage per member of the urban work force.
f. Average per capita income for the rural population.
g. Average gross value of agricultural output (GVAO) per member of the rural population.
Source: State Statistical Bureau of China (1985, p. 62); (1986, p. 202); (1987, p. 204); U.S. Government (1983); *Washington Post* (August 21, 1987, p. C2); *Anhui Jingji Nianjian 1985*; *Jiangsu Jingji Nianjian 1986*.

Among the four sample counties, the degree of spatial inequality is striking (see table 19.5). Average per capita income in Nanhai county is 3.6 times that in Jieshou. The per capita wage bill of TVCEs in Wuxi is 28 times that in Jieshou. TVCE profits are even more unevenly distributed. These patterns point to the uneven pace of rural industrial development across China and the effect of low labor mobility.

An interesting question concerns the extent to which greater capital mobility could compensate for labor immobility. There are some examples of TVP firms relocating to poorer regions in response to lower labor costs, while balance sheet analysis confirms that rents in the TVP sector have indeed fallen with greater competition in product markets. However, such a process is likely to be slow, partly because of the importance of personal connections in establishing and operating businesses. In the meantime, the large rural inequalities, which appear to have widened with industrialization, are likely to continue. The degree of inequality may seem especially surprising given China's strong ideological commitment to equality and the powerful redistributional instruments available to the state. But whereas government can exert a strong influence over urban wages and incomes, it has no comparable instrument for equalizing rural incomes although, as noted below, some redistribution does take place through the fiscal system.

Table 19.5 Selected Economic Indicators in Four Countries, 1985
(yuan per capita of agricultural population)

Indicator	Wuxi	Nanhai	Jieshou	Shangrao	China
Average per capita income of rural population	754	1,029	285	322	398
Rural gross value of industrial output	4,656	2,313	244	49	207
Gross value of agricultural output	604	610	210	266	429
TVCE gross profits	512	208	9	4	24
TVCE wage bill	364	276	13	23	36

Note: TVCEs are town- and village-government-owned enterprises. For China as a whole, the figures are per member of the rural population. The agricultural population is an administratively defined category used at local levels, which includes people engaged in nonagricultural activities but not receiving grain rations or other subsidies.
Source: Information from fieldwork of World Bank / Institute of Economics of the Chinese Academy of Social Sciences research project; State Statistical Bureau of China (1986).

Incentives for Government Leaders

Without the deep involvement of community government leaders, China's TVP sector could not have grown nearly as rapidly as it has. The incentives for government leaders to establish and promote local industries are therefore crucial for an understanding of the characteristics of the sector. Following the approach of public choice theory, local governments and individual public decisionmakers are considered here as self-interested entities whose actions are geared toward maximizing their own benefits.[9] This involves analyzing the role of TVPs in their communities and the incentives for developing TVPs and using them to support other goals.

Fiscal linkages and discretionary powers. China's highly centralized pre-reform public finance system dated back to 1950. While even under this system certain extrabudgetary funds were mobilized and used by local governments, extrabudgetary funds in China as a whole in 1953 were equivalent to only 4 percent of the state budget. This proportion rose to over 35 percent by 1977, but it was not until 1980 that China began to decentralize actively and to offer more financial autonomy to local governments and state enterprises. By 1985 extra-budgetary funds were equivalent to 85 percent of the state budget.

In many rural communities, especially the more advanced, TVP industry has become the primary source of extrabudgetary funds, in the form of profit remit-tances and management fees paid by the firms to the local government. In Nanhai and Wuxi counties, industry provided 100 percent of these resources in the mid-1980s; even in Jieshou it provided 73 percent and in Shangrao 51 percent despite their low levels of industrial development.

For local governments, access to extrabudgetary funds is important. These funds represent their only substantial source of fiscal autonomy, since budgetary funds are mostly earmarked for specified expenses, notably salaries and administrative costs. In some respects, local governments in China resemble ministates because of their stable population bases. Yet they face important limitations on their powers. Deficit financing by any level of local government is not permitted, and they do not have the right to establish any new tax instruments or to set tax rates. Community governments therefore face a relatively "hard" budget constraint.

Typically, township governments now can retain for their own discretionary use a portion of above-quota tax revenues collected in their communities, which allows them to tap into part of the budgetary revenue generated by TVP development. Townships can retain 8-12 percent of above-quota tax collections in Wuxi, 20 percent in Nanhai, and 50-100 percent in Shangrao. The quotas themselves are increasingly being set according to a fixed percentage increase from some baseline level.

Typical financial flows among township firms and township and county institutions are shown in figure 19.1. Township firms pay direct and indirect taxes to the township. They pay management fees (actually a tax) to their supervisory agency, the township industrial corporation, which is best thought of as a commu-nity holding company under the direction of a township economic commission. Part of their after-tax profits is reinvested and part is turned over to the township industrial corporation. The township industrial corporation constitutes an impor-tant source of funding for government salaries and overhead, discretionary spending, and reinvestment in other township firms. It allocates these reinvested funds between firms (in our sample, investment by township governments accounted for more than 30 percent of start-up funds for township enterprises). The township investment corporation also assumes the debts of failing township firms and reallocates them to healthy firms to ensure their continued service.[10]

A tale of two townships. To illustrate the disparity in the degree of develop-ment among China's rural communities, comparative statistics for two townships

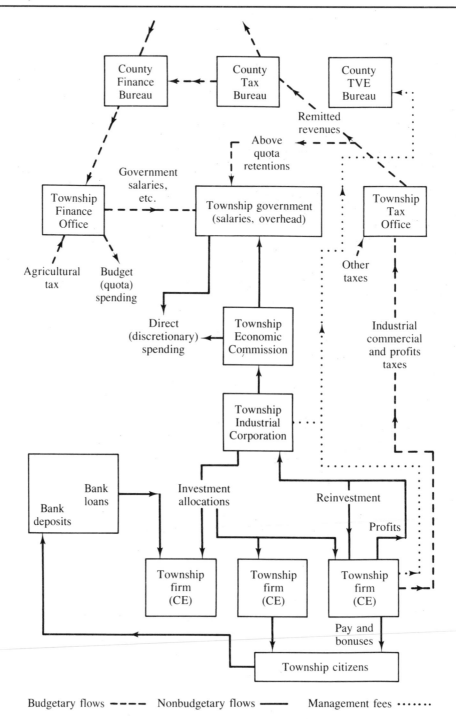

Figure 19.1 Township Revenue Flows and Community-Owned Firms in China

are presented in table 19.6. Township A is the most industrialized in Wuxi. Township B, in Shangrao Province, is one of the poorest townships visited during fieldwork; it has an average per capita income one-seventh that of Township A. Most of this disparity is due to differences in industrial output per head. The most astonishing differences are in local revenues and expenditures per head, which in Township A exceed those in Township B by a vast margin.

Table 19.6 Selected Economic Indicators for Two Townships in Wuxi and Shangrao Provinces, China
(in yuan)

Indicator	Township A (Wuxi, 1985)	Township B (Shangrao, 1986)	Ratio A / B
Population (number)	18,779	23,396	0.8
Average per capita income of rural population	907	131	6.9
Gross value of agricultural output per capita	399	197	2.0
Gross value of industrial output per capita	11,268	17	662.8
Sales income of township enterprises per capita	5,846[a]	14	418.0
Local revenue per capita[b]	1,268	9	417.6
Expenditure per capita	522	18	29.0

a. Industrial enterprises only.
b. Includes both budgetary and nonbudgetary revenues but not additional budgetary funds provided by the county for quota budget expenditures.
Source: Fieldwork of World Bank / Institute of Economics of the Chinese Academy of Social Sciences research project.

A breakdown of resource generation and use between the two townships is shown in table 19.7. In Township A, the vast bulk of tax revenues is remitted to the county, whereas very little is in poorer Township B, which receives a supplemental allocation from the county budget. Nevertheless, remittances from enterprises in Township A dwarf all budgetary allocations.[11] The differences between townships in government spending are also substantial (table 19.7). In Township A, almost 70 percent of expenditures are plowed back into industrial investment, whereas in Township B, 86 percent are used for services and administrative expenditures. Nevertheless, the amount spent on services and administration is greater in Township A, and its government is far more autonomous since almost all its resources are extrabudgetary. This ability to increase the autonomy of local government appears to be an important factor motivating them to promote TVPs.

**Table 19.7 Government Income and Expenditure in
Two Townships in Wuxi and Shangrao Provinces, China**

Income/ expenditures	Township A (Wuxi, 1985)		Township B (Shangrao, 1986)	
	Yuan (thousands)	Percent of total	Yuan (thousands)	Percent of total
Income				
Tax revenues	13,428	56.4	193.5	46.4
Less remitted to county	12,978	54.5	1.7	0.4
Retained	450	1.9	191.8	46.1
Refund from county	--	--	209.8	50.4
Remittances by township enterprises	10,390	43.6	13.2[a]	3.2
Less remitted to county	1,035	4.4	--	--
Total resources	9,805	100.0	414.8	100.0
Expenditures				
Investment in township enterprises	6,720	68.5	19.3[b]	4.6
Support to agriculture	900	9.2	26.0	6.3
Public and social services	1,050	10.7	285.7	68.9
Administrative expenditures	138	1.4	70.8	17.1
Unidentified (residual)[c]	1,097	11.2	13.0	3.1
Total expenditures[c]	9,805	100.0	414.8	100.0

-- not available.

a. Township B's enterprises had net losses totaling Y13,759 in 1986. These remittances were financed by additional bank borrowing and by drawing from depreciation allowances.

b. It is assumed that all budgetary expenditure "in support of production" other than items clearly specified as agricultural was for investment in township enterprises.

c. Total expenditures are assumed to be exactly equal to total township revenue resources, with the unidentified portion of expenditures derived as a residual.

Source: Fieldwork of World Bank / Institute of Economics of the Chinese Academy of Social Sciences research project.

Rewards to community government officials. The personal rewards and career prospects of community officials also depend greatly on income, employment, and revenue mobilization in their communities. These personal benefits can be divided into two types: pay, bonuses, and informal earnings, and prospects for promotion.

Pay, bonuses, and earnings of community leaders and factory directors in TVCEs vary significantly across communities with the average level of incomes and TVP development in their communities. This variation tends to be greater for villages and production teams than for townships. In contrast, socially acceptable limits to pay differentials appear to exist within communities, although these may be vague and change over time.

In Wuxi, the pay of a factory director is generally limited to twice the average pay of factory employees. Pay and supplements for village leaders are also about twice average pay levels in village factories. Workers' wages are linked to enterprise profits (as described below), so there is a relationship between enterprise profitability and the income of community leaders.

In Nanhai, leaders' pay is typically two to three times average income per worker at the town and village levels in their community. In one township, government leaders earned about yuan (Y) 2,500 a year, whereas incomes for village leaders ranged from Y2,000 to Y6,000 a year and appear to be linked directly to the profits of "their" enterprises. In some cases, such as in Xiqiao town, detailed incentive pay schemes have been promulgated for leaders of subordinate villages. With an annual base pay for a village leader of only Y660,[12] the possibility of earning up to Y1,100 for meeting various economic targets and Y10,000 or even more on the basis of enterprise profits created strong incentives for village leaders in Xiqiao to develop community enterprises and operate them profitably. The top pay of village leaders in Nanhai appeared to be about Y15,000 (some thirty times the typical wage in Shangrao), in a village where workers received about Y5,000 per year.

In Jieshou, owners of private firms (who are also managers) appear to be able to earn high salaries only by paying their workers much higher wages than warranted by local labor market conditions. In Shangrao there is also some linkage between local income levels and leaders' pay, but the incentive effects seem to be weaker because of the low general level of incomes and the consequently greater influence of state wage scales for officials down to the township level. Given the poor record of profitability of TVPs in Shangrao, there appears to be very little relationship between the performance of firms and rewards to their directors.

It is impossible to gauge the magnitude of informal incomes with any precision, but rewards of this type are typically an important part of total compensation. More common than outright bribery is consumption of community government or enterprise resources, from cigarettes to banquets to housing construction. Since more funds, especially more discretionary funds, are available in richer areas, leaders undoubtedly have an additional incentive for stimulating TVP development.

The interaction of national pay scales with sharp differences in local income levels causes *promotion and career incentives* to operate quite differently in different parts of China. In rich areas such as Wuxi and Nanhai, successful community leaders are generally unwilling to be promoted to higher levels because of the greater influence of the national wage scale at those levels and prohibitions against business involvement by township-level officials on their own account. In poor, backward areas, promotion incentives are far more potent. Not only is there little loss of income for promoted leaders, but the change in household residency status for those promoted to township or county level is of inestimable value.[13] In Jieshou and Shangrao, lower-level leaders actively strive for promotion. The criteria for promotion are undoubtedly subjective, but it is clear that at least since 1980 the economic performance of the community for which the leader is responsible has carried great weight.

Immediate financial incentives and career incentives therefore appear to complement each other, with financial incentives being more powerful in rich areas and career incentives more powerful in poor areas. Fieldwork indicates that, despite these differences in the mix of incentives, under almost any circumstances local leaders have had strong personal as well as bureaucratic incentives to develop a successful TVP sector of some kind. This is broadly true, even where TVP development has lagged or failed. Thus the main factors that determine the success of development must be sought in the patterns of constraints facing local leaders and the interaction of these constraints with the incentive structure.

The Dual Roles of Community Governments

Local governments play a dual role in industrial development, being both owners of firms and administrators of the local community. This can lead to tensions and inefficiencies in the operation of the TVCE sector, as well as bias against private enterprises. In certain cases, it can cause the linkages between enterprises and governments, described above as having favorable incentive effects, to operate perversely. In this situation, which is more likely in poorer areas, local governments can become an impediment to successful industrialization rather than a powerful force in its favor. This practice of excessive government exploitation of local firms can be termed "fiscal predation."

The household responsibility system radically altered the composition of property under the control of local governments. Agriculture, and the community population as a whole, became much less exposed to fiscal predation, leaving industry as the only major source of financing for extrabudgetary spending. Especially in the more advanced areas, governments underwent a successful transition from landlords to industrialists. But where enterprise development has not reached a self-sustaining stage, community governments have been tempted — in some cases even impelled by the inelasticity of basic services expected from local government — to extract funds from and through their enterprises to support their own consumption expenditures. Funds are levied from TVCEs regardless of their financial performance. Loss-making firms meet these requirements by transferring their depreciation funds (in effect "eating" their capital stock) or by additional borrowing, which means that local governments are indirectly using the banking system to finance their deficits. Such was the case in Shangrao, where enterprises made payments to local government (see table 19.7) despite very poor financial performance by firms.

Instances of "political" interference in the operation of community enterprises seem to be fairly widespread in rich areas. In Wuxi, for example, many enterprise directors admitted that their enterprises were overstaffed, occasionally by margins as high as 50 percent, and firms are often required to pay various expenses, including entertainment of guests, on behalf of the local government.[14] Nevertheless, the conflict between the two roles of community government is far more severe in poor areas, and this raises the issue of how rapidly the benefits of rural industrial development can be expected to diffuse under a policy of local self-reliance.

The independence of the banking system from local pressures in China and clear commitment to property rights (including accountability for losses) will be important in maintaining a tight budget constraint for local communities and holding the TVP sector to market-based behavior.[15] Although the problem of predation is most severe for poor areas that seek to use their enterprises to borrow from the banking system to fund current expenses, it could spread to more prosperous areas should China experience a major economic downturn.

Labor Markets and Incentives

Labor Markets for Rural Industry
Labor markets are still fragmented in China, with significant obstacles to both rural-urban and rural-rural migration. The extent to which the TVP sector is contributing to a loosening of the labor market and the extent to which rural firms face a reasonably competitive labor market are important issues in assessing the incentives for participation in the sector and the sector's place in economic reform.

Some indication of the mobility of labor in the four sample counties is provided by data on the original area of residence of employees in sampled enterprises (table 19.8). The most striking contrast is between the two advanced areas, Wuxi and Nanhai. In Wuxi, very few employees come from outside the towns or villages of their current employment; in Nanhai, almost half came from outside the community and 15 percent from other counties or provinces. This finding is especially striking since Wuxi County is considered to have a scarcity of labor, which is being reflected in an increasing capital intensity of production. The situation in the two less developed counties, Jieshou and Shangrao, lies somewhere between these two extremes.

Table 19.8 Original Residence of Employees in Sample
TVP Enterprises in China, by County
(percentage of total)

County	Same township/ village	Other township/ village in county	Other county	Other
Wuxi	94.0	3.0	1.6	1.4
Jieshou	79.7	12.7	4.8	2.8
Nanhai	50.9	33.8	14.2	1.1
Shangrao	80.9	14.8	2.1	2.2

Note: TVPs are firms owned by township or village governments or by private individuals or groups.
Source: Meng Xin (forthcoming).

This indication that Wuxi and Nanhai represent opposite points in the spectrum of rural labor markets is reinforced by other survey information. TVP industry in Wuxi relies almost entirely on workers who describe themselves as "permanent" whereas this category represents only 40 percent of employees in Nanhai, 76 percent in Jieshou, and 79 percent in Shangrao. Further, great shifts have taken place in the relative shares of permanent and casual workers in Nanhai, indicating major changes in the operation of the labor market. Permanent workers represented 92 percent of the total in 1980, 76 percent in 1983, and only 40 percent in 1985. Nanhai workers are more mobile than workers in Wuxi: 27 percent plan to leave their firm within three years and, probably because of this, there is far stronger pressure to distribute profits to the work force as opposed to reinvesting them. Indeed, as noted below, pay is higher in Nanhai TVP industry relative to Wuxi, essentially because the presence of a substantial private sector forces government industries to compete for labor.

Are workers allocated to their firms, or are they hired in a voluntary manner? Given the limits on choice because of population immobility, this distinction can be difficult to make very rigorously. A breakdown of recruitment according to various modes that correspond reasonably well to these concepts shows that voluntary hiring is most prevalent in Nanhai and Jieshou and lowest in Wuxi (table 19.9). Older employees are more likely to have been allocated to their firms, and so, interestingly, are the higher-paid workers.

Labor mobility and earnings distribution within local industry both appear to be heavily influenced by the presence of private enterprises. Few workers are allocated to private firms, and in booming, labor-short areas such as Nanhai, private enterprises provide a source of competition for government-owned TVCEs that is absent in the more tightly regulated Wuxi model. Thus, in 1985 average income in sample firms was higher in Nanhai than in Wuxi, and the dispersion of income was significantly greater. In a poor, labor-surplus county like Jieshou, however, the existence of an active labor market has much less effect in boosting workers' incomes.

With respect to labor dismissals, the survey found that most TVP employees have a fairly long time-horizon for employment with their firms: 75 percent plan to stay with their firms for at least five years and, possibly because the bulk of them are first-generation industrial workers, most appear to be basically content in their firms. As described below, TVP firms, whether public or private, appear to have some "communal" characteristics that distinguish them from most firms in advanced market economies. Nevertheless, enterprises whose directors claimed to have the power to dismiss employees accounted for 97 percent of all directors surveyed in Jieshou, 82 percent in Wuxi, 73 percent in Nanhai, and 68 percent in Shangrao. The actual number of employees dismissed for any reason was extremely small in all four counties, however, and it was clear, especially in Wuxi and Shangrao, that the power to dismiss employees was severely curtailed by local community governments. In labor-surplus Shangrao, such intervention in labor markets is more understandable than in labor-scarce Wuxi.

**Table 19.9   Recruitment of Workers in Sample TVP
Enterprises in China by Selected Categories**
(number of workers)

Category	Allocation	Voluntary	Total
By county			
Wuxi	270	191	461
Jieshou	84	209	293
Nanhai	99	154	253
Shangrao	78	66	144
Total	531	620	1,151
By age			
Under 20	40	114	153
20-29	233	320	554
30-39	168	117	258
40-49	71	57	128
50+	19	12	31
Total	531	620	1,151
By ownership			
Public	398	380	778
Private	33	111	144
Total	431	491	922
By pay (yuan per year)			
Less than 625	82	180	262
625-1,249	180	263	475
1,250-2,499	173	142	315
2,500-4,999	44	31	75
Total	531	620	1,151

Note: TVPs are firms owned by township or village governments or by private individuals or groups. Chi square = 73.4 for counties, 54.9 for age, 38.9 for ownership, and 51.5 for pay. All are significant at 0.1 percent.
Source: Fieldwork of World Bank / Institute of Economics of the Chinese Academy of Social Sciences research project.

Incentives and Pay Structures in TVPs

Pay systems differ considerably among TVPs, with those in the more advanced counties tending to be more complex. Surveys show that time rates are not the main method of payment for most workers. Piece rates are common, and bonuses are important for all but 19 percent of the sample. Whatever the specific form of payment, however, employees across all counties and types of firm perceive a clear relationship between their incomes and the profitability of their firms; only 10 percent see no such relationship while 71 percent consider it to be a strong one. There was also evidence of considerable willingness of employees to buy stock in their firms, should this become possible.

Despite the wide distribution of income levels reported by the sample, only 2 percent of respondents described their incomes as high relative to levels in their community and only 9 percent saw them as low. Furthermore, there was no systematic relationship between incomes and perceptions of relative level. This suggests that pay in TVPs tends to be set largely with reference to the general income levels in the community. TVPs thus have some of the characteristics of cooperative firms, although survey results indicate clearly that they are far from worker-managed.[16] There is surprisingly little difference between public and private firms in terms of reported pay, pay differentials, labor relations, and similar variables, except that private firms tend to be smaller and to have fewer technical or highly skilled workers.

The variables that determine pay may be considered in several classes. *County dummy* variables can be used to represent the stage of development of the area, and *ownership dummy* variables can represent ownership of the firm. If the firm is closely identified with a community, *firm dummy* variables can be used instead. Other firm characteristics are size (number of employees) and profitability (ratio of profits to sales). *Individual variables* include age (or experience), gender, number of workdays, occupation, and education.

A variety of statistical models was fitted to the data to explain log (pay) using the sample of 1,172 workers. County dummy variables alone account for 30 percent of pay variance, and introduction of a simple public-private ownership dummy adds little to this. Profitability of the firm enters significantly, and with the expected positive sign. Using firm dummy variables alone results in an R^2 adjusted for degrees of freedom of 0.57. Much of the observed dispersion of pay can therefore be accounted for by differences between firms. Moreover, non-parametric statistical tests suggest that average pay levels in firms rank positively with growth of the labor force, of output, and of output value per worker. They thus arise from the "pull" effect of labor productivity gains in the more dynamic firms in the presence of slowly responding labor markets.

Adding firm size, profitability, and individual variables to the model with firm dummy variables boosts the adjusted R^2 to 0.70. Women receive 14 percent lower pay than men, and apprentices receive 26 percent less than regular workers; group leaders and technical staff receive between 10 and 40 percent more. The effect of adding in an education variable is surprising, in that it indicates that employees with some college education receive *lower* pay than would be expected on the basis of other variables. In this connection, it is interesting to note that highly skilled employees are more likely to have been allocated to their firms and that the few college graduates in the sample are by far the most likely to want to leave their firms. This suggests that the market for human skills has not yet opened up for TVPs. Indeed, this is true of China as a whole, and examples encountered during fieldwork showed many ingenious ways in which firms sought to get around the problem of the missing markets for technological, management, and marketing knowhow.

Conclusions

Combining elements of public and private enterprise, China's dynamic TVP sector has become an important part of the country's rural economy as well as a major actor in industry. TVPs have been at the forefront of economic reforms. They are essentially market oriented on the output and material input sides, and they are outward oriented because of the tiny size of their home markets. TVPs represent an increasingly important source of competition for the state sector, while the potential for economically beneficial interactions between the two (for example subcontracting) is also great.

This review has highlighted some of the distinctive characteristics of TVPs, which are related primarily to their close ties to China's largely fixed-membership rural communities and to the local governments' relatively hard budget constraints. Almost irrespective of form of ownership, there is a close relationship between individual incomes and firm and community economic performance, and most individuals expect to stay in their firms for relatively long periods of time. In some ways, TVPs are akin to the so-called Z-firms, which follow Japanese models of labor relations and operate successfully in other market economies.[17]

The incentives for community governments to promote TVP development are extremely strong. Where the opportunities and resources have been present, the result has been an extraordinary burst of rural industrialization. In the more backward areas local government may have been an obstacle to rural development. Since the legitimization of private enterprise in the mid-1980s, some of the poorer areas have resorted to this option and achieved much more dynamic TVP growth than earlier.

The community orientation of TVPs also leads to certain problems, resulting from the fragmentation of markets for capital and labor and the multiple, sometimes conflicting roles of community governments. Even if resources are used relatively efficiently *within* rural communities, immobility of factors of production can lead to increasingly serious misallocations and inequalities *between* communities. A gradual opening up of capital and labor markets will be a priority task in the next stage of reform. A weakening of the involvement of community governments in managing rural industrialization is likely to be a gradual, long-term process. A strengthened legal framework within which TVCEs and private firms can securely operate will be needed.

National government policy toward the TVP sector has played an important, but essentially passive, role in stimulating TVP development. In the future, an important need will be to avoid government policies and practices that do major harm to TVPs; this is even more important than any positive measures (including allocation of public resources) to support the TVP sector. Discrimination against TVPs and, within the TVP sector, against private enterprise by government legal and regulatory apparatus should be minimized, with the elimination of differential treatment as a long-term goal.

Notes

1. Rural communities in China exist at three levels: the *township* (formerly the commune), which typically has 15,000-30,000 people; the *village* (formally the brigade), which typically has 1,000-2,000; and the *production team*, which has about 100-200. There are substantial variations in size and economic power among communities in different parts of the country.

2. The results of the project are detailed in Byrd and Lin (forthcoming).

3. In the course of the project, five qualitative and quantitative surveys and numerous interviews were carried out. Data were collected and analyzed on a sample of 122 rural industrial firms, 1,174 employees, and 67 rural townships to complement aggregate statistics at county, provincial, and national levels.

4. Despite rapid growth of private firms, by 1987 they still produced only one-seventh of the total industrial output of the TVP sector. Moreover, in most cases, the extent to which private firms could be established and could grow was still very much determined by the attitude of local government and its willingness to permit their use of land and other factors and to guarantee bank loans.

5. Strictly speaking, the right to use land rather than its ownership was assigned on an individual or household basis.

6. With interest rates held below market-clearing levels, China tends to experience excess demand for funds. Rural bank deposits are considered local resources, and communal governments exert a large influence on their use. Nevertheless, the more industrialized areas such as Wuxi have, for some years, been net borrowers from other areas.

7. TVPs have also benefited, relative to state enterprises, from more favorable tax treatment, although this advantage is being eliminated. The effect of mid-1989 policy changes, which apparently discriminate against TVPs in favor of state firms, remains to be seen.

8. Regional income inequality in the United States has fallen greatly over the past 50 years as a result of increased interregional mobility. For discussion of this topic, see Barro and Sala I Martin (1989). In rural China, by contrast, it has remained high because of limited mobility.

9. For reviews of public choice theory see Buchanan (1975) and Mueller (1976). This approach diverges from the more traditional view that government benevolently designs policies for society.

10. Local governments are slow to close loss-making firms partly because the debts of these firms represent a fixed cost.

11. Remittances in Township A are mostly out of enterprise profits. In Township B, enterprises actually made a loss but were still compelled to remit funds to the township government. This is characteristic of the "fiscal predation" practiced in some poor areas.

12. Village leadership positions are considered to be part-time jobs, which explains this low base pay.

13. Urban registration opens up access to cities for the official and his family and descendants and also carries with it a package of benefits.

14. A peculiar practice contributing to overstaffing is the compensation of farmers whose land is lost because of industrial development and those who have worked on construction without pay with lifetime jobs in the new firms. This was a particular problem in the hydro plants of Shangrao, where employees exceeded those necessary to operate the installations by large margins.

15. This is in sharp contrast, for example, to the self-managed enterprises in Yugoslavia, which have some similarities with the TVPs (especially TVCEs). The most important difference is in the nature of the local budget constraint. The self-managed enterprises

are larger and tend to control banks; social ownership of capital further weakens local accountability in Yugoslavia relative to China and contributes to the softening of local budget constraints. This has resulted in poor enterprise performance, deteriorated portfolios and a large deficit in the captive banking system.
16. Workers do elect their directors in some Shangrao firms; this innovation was introduced in an attempt to lessen the degree of political interference in management.
17. The term "Z-firm" was introduced by Ouchi (1982) to describe firms following Japanese patterns of labor relations sometimes referred to as "lifetime employment." In contrast, "Taylorist" firms follow a "hire-and fire" labor policy.

References

Balassa, B. 1987. "China's Economic Reforms in a Comparative Perspective." *Journal of Comparative Economics* 11: 410-26.

Barro, R., and X. Sala I Martin. 1989. "Economic Growth and Convergence Across the United States." Paper presented at the National Bureau of Economic Research Conference on Economic Growth, Cambridge, Mass., October 6-7.

Buchanan, J.M. 1975. "Public Finance and Public Choice." *National Tax Journal* 28 (December): 383-94.

Byrd, W., and Lin Qingsong, eds Forthcoming. *China's Rural Industry*. New York: Oxford University Press for the World Bank.

Johnson, D.G. 1986. "Economic Reforms in the Peoples Republic of China." Paper prepared for the Anniversary Conference of the Graduate Program in Economic Development, Vanderbilt University, Nashville, Tenn., October.

Lin, J.Y. 1986. "The Household Responsibility System in China's Agricultural Reform: A Theoretical and Empirical Study." Paper prepared for the Anniversary Conference of the Graduate Program in Economic Development, Vanderbilt University, Nashville, Tenn., October.

Meng Xin. Forthcoming. "The Rural Labor Market." In W. Byrd and Lin Qingsong, eds, *China's Rural Industry*. New York: Oxford University Press for the World Bank.

Mueller, D.C. 1976. "Public Choice: A Survey." *Journal of Economic Literature* 14 (June): 395-433.

Ouchi, W. 1982. *Theory Z: How American Business Can Meet the Japanese Challenge*. New York: Avon.

State Statistical Bureau of China. Various years. *Statistical Yearbooks of China*.

Svejnar, J. Forthcoming. "Productive Efficiency and Employment." In W. Byrd and Lin Qingsong, eds, *China's Rural Industry*. New York: Oxford University Press for the World Bank.

U.S. Government. 1983. *U.S. County and City Data Book, 1983*. Washington, D.C.: U.S. Government Printing Office.

20

Perestroika in the CMEA and the Challenge of the 1992 Program for a Single Western European Market

Marie Lavigne

Amid the whirlwind of dramatic reforms in Eastern Europe during 1989, the future of the Council for Mutual Economic Assistance (CMEA) was almost completely overlooked.[1] Not a single meeting of the organization was held in 1989, although January 1989 was CMEA's fortieth anniversary. The reforms in Eastern Europe together with CMEA's moribund condition point to CMEA's growing disintegration. Most of its Eastern European members are turning to the European Community (EC) for aid (Poland, Hungary) or for normalization of relations through trade and cooperation agreements. By the end of 1989, all countries but Romania had signed such agreements or were negotiating them; Hungary is openly seeking associated status with the EC. At the same time, new customs barriers are being erected internally to prevent export shopping by Eastern European tourists who, for the first time, are free to travel to neighboring countries searching for goods unavailable at home. Czechoslovakia was the first country to erect such barriers in the fall of 1988.

What are the likely consequences of these developments in view of the 1992 program for a single Western European market? Given the prospects for increased links between CMEA countries and the EC, is the CMEA likely to undertake sufficient reforms to offer its members a viable alternative to the lure of the West? The arguments presented in this paper suggest that, however dim the prospects of a perestroika for the CMEA, the member countries should not bury the organization too soon. If domestic reforms really evolve toward a market-type system, new opportunities might emerge in a reformed regional international market.

The End of the International Socialist Division of Labor

In the past, the CMEA has pursued two aims, which in the context of current reforms in Eastern Europe now seem incompatible. One has been a stimulus-response effort to strengthen socialist integration every time capitalist integration in Western European gained new momentum, through a dual process of imitation and differentiation. The second aim has been to adapt the CMEA to changes resulting from domestic reforms in member countries.

The Quest for Socialist Integration

CMEA's tendency to counter integration moves in Western Europe with moves of its own was evidenced in its adoption of a charter in 1959 — two years after the 1957 Treaty of Rome but *ten* years after creation of the CMEA. Similarly, the institutional strengthening of the CMEA in 1982 and adoption of the Basic Principles of the International Socialist Division of Labor, which were clearly supranational in intent, were steps taken in response to developments within the European Economic Community (EEC).

CMEA's efforts to adjust to domestic reforms in its member countries were exemplified by the Comprehensive Program of 1971, which defined socialist economic integration in a pragmatic way, to be achieved through a balance of "market" and "plan coordination" mechanisms. This move came in the wake of the socialist domestic reform wave of the mid-1960s, which sought to combine central planning and market principles. CMEA's program included limited liberalization of mutual trade (an increase in the share of traded goods without fixed quotas), improvements in the price-fixing system, introduction of limited internal convertibility of domestic currencies, and some coordination in planning to ensure growing cooperation and specialization in production.

During the 1980s, the contradictions inherent in these two tendencies became more apparent. The CMEA adopted the Comprehensive Program of Scientific and Technical Progress (the STP Program) in 1985, paralleling adoption of the Eureka research program that year in Western Europe. The STP Program for increased competitiveness in high technology areas was to be coordinated with the new wave of modernization in Eastern Europe following the investment freeze of the early 1980s. Thus the CMEA (or the Soviet Union as its driving force) was trying to achieve some of the efficiency of the EEC while maintaining its role as a mechanism for socialist integration. And while it was trying to adapt itself to the domestic reforms of its members, CMEA overlooked the widening diversity of these reforms.

The upshot of these various processes is that the old system of the international socialist division of labor has reached a stalemate, while a new type of "socialist market integration" seems almost impossible to imagine in the current context. While various explanations have been offered for this failure, all of them are implicitly or explicitly based on a definition of the nature of the CMEA in a political economy framework.

The Political Economy of the CMEA

Questions about the nature of the CMEA emerged as a by-product of what came to be called "the subsidy issue": was the Soviet Union subsidizing the Eastern European countries through the system of intrabloc prices, especially in the period 1973-83 when international oil prices were rising?

Marrese and Vanous (1983), who supported the subsidy thesis, applied standard opportunity cost theory to Soviet foreign trade data and concluded that the Soviet Union had been losing from differences in its terms of trade in intrabloc trade and trade with the West. In intrabloc trade, it had been selling (mainly oil) at less than world prices and buying (mainly machinery) at higher than world prices. Since there was no economic explanation for such behavior, the authors suggested that the Soviet Union received "unconventional gains" from this trade in terms of the political, ideological, and military allegiance of the Eastern European countries, while the latter received economic gains that compensated for their "unconventional [political] losses." This argument implies that what keeps the CMEA together is Soviet political domination, which the USSR maintains in exchange for preferential trade treatment of other CMEA members (Marrese 1989, 3).

While this argument may have been valid in the past, it does not explain the reversal of economic positions since 1986. One can hardly argue that the Soviet Union is now being "subsidized" by its partners in exchange for its loss in domination. Marrese and Wittenberg offer the more plausible argument that the USSR is now pursuing different political goals "of economic efficiency and viability in the international arena" (1989, 30). The desire to control the foreign policies of Eastern Europe no longer prevails over opportunity cost considerations, leading to a shift to increased trade with the West and a reduction in "implicit transfers."

An alternative view is provided by Holzman (1986) and Brada (1988), who argue that the subsidies and losses can be explained through the customs union theory. The formation of a customs union usually leads to trade creation among partners through the lowering of trade barriers, but it also leads to trade diversion at the expense of nonmember nations through tariff discrimination. Holzman argues that the standard theory can be modified to accommodate the specific features of centrally planned economies. For these economies, neither tariffs nor explicit quotas are necessary because the conduct of foreign trade is a state monopoly. Historically, says Holzman, the losses from trade diversion fell first on Eastern Europe and then (since the late 1950s) on the Soviet Union. In addition, the system leads to absolute trade destruction rather than trade creation, and all countries suffer from the resulting losses.

The political factor is evident in both these arguments. Both assume that the Soviet Union had strong political reasons for forming a polarized trade area with Eastern Europe after World War II and that its satellites had little choice but to agree. But what holds the CMEA countries together *now*?

Among those who have studied the specifics of socialist integration, two main interpretations have been proposed. Sobell (1984) distinguishes the "international protection system" of the CMEA, whose goal is to maximize stability whatever the efficiency cost, from market-oriented integration, which aims to maximize efficiency. But what then is the meaning of the numerous statements in the socialist literature criticizing CMEA precisely for its lack of efficiency in providing such stability? An alternative view is provided by van Brabant (1988), who argues that the centrally planned economies need, more than ever, to develop links with the West if they are to successfully implement their domestic reforms and sustain their modernization drive. But to do so, they need to be competitive in Western markets. How this can be achieved, however, remains an open question, although it seems probable that some more effective form of socialist economic integration will have to be the solution — at least for a transitional period.

Both Sobell and van Brabant assume that socialist integration is a reality, however imperfect it may be. Even if centrifugal forces build to the point where some countries wish to leave the organization, as Hungary threatened in 1988, to do so will not be easy. While the Soviet Union may no longer ensure the cohesion of the CMEA by imposing it on its European partners, the freedom of choice of CMEA countries remains circumscribed by their lack of competitiveness in Western markets.

Can the International Socialist Division of Labor Be Revamped?

The STP Program adopted in December 1985 was designed to increase the competitiveness of the socialist countries in high technology areas and to allow for a shift in growth strategy. It covered five areas: electronics, automation, nuclear energy, new materials, and biotechnologies. However, the Communique of the November 1986 CMEA session referred to the poor quality of cooperation and specialization, and it appears that the STP Program achieved almost no improvement in four years of implementation.[2] What went wrong?

All the CMEA countries realize that the socialist bloc is falling behind in competitive terms vis-à-vis the developed market economies and even some of the newly industrializing developing countries, which are increasingly taking EEC market shares away from CMEA countries. Efficiency gains require a shift from extensive to intensive growth, that is a shift from growth through the use of additional inputs to growth through rationalization of factor utilization, introduction of new technologies, and improvements in the quality of production.

The STP Program aimed at accelerating this shift through joint efforts, but changing the industrial structure of the Eastern European countries is a complex task. The structure has been shaped by a growth strategy favoring the energy- and raw materials-intensive industries that were developed to process raw materials imported from the USSR. Machinery industries were designed to meet the needs of the Soviet Union, and the poor quality of the production makes it impossible to sell these goods on Western markets. In addition, this pattern of production was powerfully protected by domestic heavy industry lobbies. This type of industrial structure both required and favored a centralized type of management, whereas efficiency considerations would have required more flexible mechanisms.

In addition, these economies suffer from a lack of hard currency, which limits purchases of modern equipment from the West. Although the most difficult period of adjustment — the early 1980s — is now past, these adjustments brought about a dramatic decrease in investment between 1981 and 1985 in almost all CMEA countries except the USSR.

The investment mechanisms of the 1970s have undergone radical changes (the Concerted Plan of Integrated Multilateral Measures) or simply disappeared (the Long-Term Target Cooperation Programs). What remain are a few costly joint investments in energy and raw materials, such as the Urengoi gas pipeline and some nuclear power stations. As for investments projected for 1986-90, no overall figures are available (see Belovich 1985 and Bogomolov 1986), but the burden of such operations is very heavy for participating countries.

The Concerted Plan, which was originally an instrument for coordinating five-year plans among CMEA countries, seems to have been integrated with the Collective Conception for 1991-2005 adopted by CMEA in 1988. The aim of the Collective Conception is to coordinate national plans on three levels: at the level of the central planning offices, as usual; at the level of economic ministries; and at the firm level. Coordination at the first level is bound to disappear with the abolition of central planning in most Eastern European countries. Coordination among economic ministries is difficult because of the ongoing changes in the number and competence of ministry staff in many countries, including the USSR. And finally, very little of the total trade between countries has ever been coordinated on the enterprise level — 7 to 10 percent, or even less in some bilateral relations (Krasnoglazov and Lavrov 1989, 4).

Several factors hamper the development of joint enterprises and direct-link arrangements. First, the present trade regime is based on price fixing, monetary settlement, and multiple shadow exchange rates, and CMEA trade is rigidly bilateral, based on trade agreements negotiated at an intergovernmental level and specifying the quantities or values of the goods to be exchanged. Second, enterprises lack real autonomy on the national level. It is now acknowledged that liberalization of intra-CMEA trade will be possible only after *domestic* enterprises receive free access to their own domestic markets, a change that has not yet occurred even in those countries in which enterprise reform has taken place.

The system of joint enterprises and joint links has failed to lead to any significant improvements under the STP Program. Of the 1,600 joint links and 28 joint enterprises established between partners in Eastern Europe during 1986-89, only in 5 percent of the cases do agreements even mention cooperation with respect to implementation of the STP Program (Cheklina 1989). Clearly, some form of market integration is essential if CMEA is to survive.

A Resurrection of Market Integration?

Mechanisms of Trade between CMEA Countries

The call for market unification voiced during the 1988 CMEA session was quite ambiguous, as had been most recent discussion of the topic up to that time. Economists were calling variously for some form of "free trade," "customs union," "free exchange zone," and even "common market," but none were clarifying what they meant by these terms (see, for example, Rusmich 1988). Even opponents felt compelled to pay lip service to the new ideas about markets, arguing rather tenuously that an international market could exist *without* domestic markets.

Even assuming that agreement is possible on a definition of what constitutes market unification, movement toward such a system will be, at best, a slow and difficult process. There is no free movement of factors of production within the CMEA. Capital flows do not exist, and the small exchange of investment goods occurs only within a strict framework of joint investment projects. There are some small movements of labor, particularly between border areas and from the less developed to the more developed countries, but all movements are decided on a case-by-case basis and tightly regulated through intergovernmental agreements.

The introduction of a "unified market" on even a very modest scale would also require liberalization of commodity flows. This would mean a dismantling of the bilateral system of intergovernment trade balancing through five-year agreements and yearly protocols. While in principle there is no objection to above-quota trade, in practice this trade constitutes, at most, about 7 to 10 percent of the total (Karavaev 1989, 37).

Yet far from decreasing, the obstacles to free trade seem to be increasing. Two examples, in particular, highlight this difficulty: the "trade fairs" in transferable rubles established by the Soviet Union, and the customs "war" between Czechoslovakia and its neighbors. In the first case "free" trade is strongly regulated; in the second, it is forbidden.

Trade fairs were established in the Soviet Union in an attempt to resolve problems that arose after individual enterprises were granted the right to trade on their own in 1987, bypassing the foreign trade organizations. Despite weak incentives and frequent violation of the rights of the enterprises by the bureaucracy, exporting enterprises managed to accumulate earnings both in hard currency and in transferable rubles. In principle, Soviet enterprises were entitled to use their transferable rubles for direct "shopping" in CMEA countries, but these countries refused to accept them for transactions which, by definition, were outside the bilateral intergovernment agreements. To solve this problem, the Soviet Union organized a trade fair, to bring together Soviet and Eastern European enterprises for direct trade in transferable rubles. What happened in fact, however, was that Soviet enterprises could buy goods from Eastern European firms only by including their "direct" transactions in an intergovernmental trade framework.

Transactions concluded during the first fair in Moscow in November 1988 accounted for only about 650 million transferable rubles of a total of about 2 billion (Karpich 1989 and Nekipelov 1989). During a second fair in Moscow in 1989, the amount traded reached 1,240 million transferable rubles, including transactions between Soviet enterprises, but only Polish and Bulgarian firms were ready to sell goods against transferable rubles (*Ekonomicheskaia Gazeta*, no. 46, 1989, p. 23). Enterprises from other countries agreed to supply their Soviet counterparts only on a barter basis. Under these conditions, not much could be expected from the next fair in July 1990 in Moscow.

The second case concerns the customs war between Czechoslovakia and some of its neighbors, which began at the end of 1988 when Soviet tourists, benefiting from relaxed travel rules for CMEA countries, flocked into Czechoslovakia with large amounts of rubles which they exchanged at the tourist rate and spent on goods in short supply in the USSR. According to intra-CMEA rules, the Czechoslovak foreign trade bank may convert such rubles into transferable rubles only at the noncommercial rate, which is less advantageous than the commercial rate. Because these transferable rubles were generated by commodity trade operations provided for in intergovernmental agreements, Czechoslovakia could not readily use them to purchase goods, even in the Soviet Union. The reaction of the Czechoslovak authorities was to prohibit tourist export of consumer goods altogether or to tax these exports at very high rates.

Although the measures were not directed specifically at the Soviet Union (they also affected Poland and, marginally, the German Democratic Republic and Hungary), their psychological impact was enormous as Soviet citizens discovered simultaneously the opportunities of liberalization and the limits of the intra-CMEA exchange mechanisms. A Hungarian participant in a round-table discussion on CMEA rightly described this type of customs war as a "state subsidies war," occurring as "a consequence of the noncoordination of prices for mass consumer goods within the CMEA and of shortages in the domestic markets" (Round Table 1989, 48).

As these two examples show, the prospects for a real customs union between the CMEA countries, entailing removal of internal barriers, are quite remote.

Price Setting

The question of the absolute level of intra-CMEA prices — the "subsidy issue" — is not discussed in the East European literature. In the West, however, the subsidy debate emerged in the early 1980s with publication of a study by Marrese and Vanous (1983) on Soviet subsidization of trade with Eastern Europe. Their interpretation was challenged, although the existence of the transfers has generally been acknowledged.[3] The few East Europeans who entered the discussion argued that the level of prices was not the central issue, but that the nature of the CMEA trade mechanism was, because it perpetuated obsolete production structures and isolated the CMEA countries from the world economy (Koves 1983). Intra-CMEA prices are widely criticized not because they are viewed as instruments of implicit transfers but because they are perceived to be irrational and to prevent efficient decisionmaking. These commentators view the problem as one of getting prices to approximate market-type prices more closely.

Proposals have been presented for a "concerted restructuring of domestic prices," which has meant essentially that *relative* prices in all CMEA countries should be nearer to *relative* world prices. Again, there was no agreement on the methods to be used: the Hungarian proposal was to use the exchange rate to link domestic prices more closely to world prices; the Soviet proposal was to increase the prices of raw materials and agricultural goods and to decrease the prices of manufactures. Should domestic prices indeed get closer in their structure, the old argument, discredited in the 1960s, for constructing prices from an "own basis" (deriving them from domestic prices) might be revived.

Domestic prices are, however, already the basis for fixing prices to be applied between enterprises that have direct-link agreements; they are also used to set foreign trade prices when a world price does not exist or cannot be easily calculated — for manufactured goods in particular. Only a few countries have experience with decentralized price-fixing, a fact that strongly impedes direct negotiations on prices between enterprises in intra-CMEA trade (Mitrofanova 1989).

The shortcomings of the current system are exemplified in the case of a Soviet-Bulgarian joint venture for manufacturing textile machinery. Domestic wholesale prices are much lower in the USSR than in Bulgaria; a given spinning machine is worth 30,240 rubles in the USSR and 67,000 leva (51,592 rubles at the official exchange rate of 1.3 leva per ruble) in Bulgaria. The contractual price has been set at 37,750 transferable rubles (Khakhina 1989). This is just one example of the inconsistencies deriving from a system of fixed exchange rates and nonconvertible currencies.

The Convertibility of Socialist Currencies

While few would argue that the collective monetary unit of the CMEA, the transferable ruble, is an adequate instrument of exchange, selecting an alternative system is complex. Convertibility includes such issues as which currencies should be made convertible (the transferable ruble? the Soviet ruble? the currencies of the smaller CMEA countries?) and to what they should be made convertible (other socialist currencies? capitalist currencies?).

Proposals for the convertibility of national currencies among CMEA members have emerged as one way of moving toward a unified market (Shelkov 1989). The first step was made in March 1988, when the Soviet Union and Czechoslovakia decided to settle all accounts arising from direct links and joint ventures between Soviet and Czechoslovakian enterprises in crowns or rubles, using a special rate of exchange that implied a slight devaluation of the crown relative to the official rate. Both countries reached a similar agreement with Bulgaria, and the USSR also concluded such arrangements with Poland and Mongolia. These arrangements are of little more than symbolic importance, however, since they cover so few transactions — less than 0.1 percent of bilateral trade flow (Sergeev 1989). In any case, it seemed by the end of 1989 that the new Czechoslovak leadership was ready to give up these new arrangements.

Other proposals have also surfaced, including some that had been proposed in earlier periods. These include establishment of a mechanism similar to that of the European Payments Union (which was dissolved in 1958 after successfully restoring the convertibility of the Western European currencies) and introduction of subregional convertibility between interested smaller East European countries (Shelkov 1989). But the prerequisites for such systems — a more active role for money in the domestic economies and a rapprochement in domestic relative prices — will be impossible to meet in the near future.

The rate of exchange remains a major stumbling block. While all proposals for convertibility assume that a "realistic" exchange rate can be found between a given domestic currency and foreign currencies, in fact a multitude of coefficients now link each socialist currency and other currencies, varying according to the products exchanged. Even in the cases in which there is a single commercial exchange rate (Hungary, Poland, and Romania), the ruble / dollar cross-rates are very divergent. There is no rational way of making them compatible since the divergences stem from the way these "commercial rates" are computed (average cost in domestic prices per unit of exports to a given country or area). The differences in relative prices, as well as in the commodity composition of exports, explain the differences in the cross-rates.

These differences are so significant that they provide some justification for temporarily retaining the current system of nonconvertibility while introducing various partial arrangements for facilitating trade. One such arrangement exists between Hungary and the USSR.[4] Hungary recently introduced a "currency market," on an experimental basis, for trade transactions beyond the quotas agreed upon in the intergovernment protocols. When a Hungarian enterprise sells to a Soviet enterprise in such transactions, it gets transferable rubles that it can exchange only on the new currency market (rather than at the National Bank, at the official exchange rate). When this market opened, the exchange rate was 27.5 forints per transferable ruble, but the rate has since settled at 15-16 forints, a logical consequence of Hungary's surplus position vis-à-vis the Soviet Union. In this context, decentralized Hungarian exports to the USSR should fall, and decentralized imports should increase (assuming that Hungarian enterprises will find something to buy in the USSR outside the bilateral quotas). The general expectation is that trade will decrease overall.[5]

Another solution might be the introduction of hard currency trade. Settlements on such terms already exist among some CMEA countries and may amount to 10-15 percent of total trade (Sergeev 1989). Many economists and some officials would contend that this would be a severe but efficient cure for the chronic diseases of the CMEA. Trade would certainly shrink (as countries could no longer "dump" on the CMEA market goods that could not be sold in the West), and productivity and competition would increase. But the remedy might be too radical if it cures the disease but kills the patient.

Yet another proposal is for the creation of a "special transferable ruble" (STR), convertible in hard currencies and issued by an International Socialist Monetary Fund (Shelkov 1989). This institution would be set up as a joint stock company, with its capital in hard currencies. While the idea is somewhat fanciful at this point, it might have merit if a similar operation — the introduction of a parallel convertible currency — is instituted on a national basis, as was discussed in 1989 for the Soviet Union (the "new chervonets" proposal).[6]

Currency convertibility and prices are related. As long as the currency used for settlements is nonconvertible, prices do not matter much. All that matters is the bilateral coordination of deliveries and quantities. Even lasting imbalances do not create substantial problems.[7] Prices play no role in the adjustment, and this would immediately change in the case of hard currency trade. Prices would then matter, and competition might develop between intra-CMEA trade and East-West trade, which would certainly harm intra-CMEA relations.

Thus CMEA efforts to move toward a "unified market" will be as difficult as were efforts to institute "coordination in planning." An integrated market can operate only when the constituent domestic economies are functioning in a market system and when their domestic structures are sufficiently close (as the experience of the EEC has demonstrated).

Domestic Reforms, Socialist Integration, and East-West Trade

All the Eastern European members of the CMEA are now engaged in domestic reforms. In the short term, the transition to a market economy is everywhere accompanied by disorganization of consumer and producer goods markets, hidden or open inflation, unemployment pressures, budget deficits, excess money in circulation, and balance of payments deficits. A stabilization program is obviously required. The new round of adjustments will be much more painful than the programs implemented in the early 1980s because the new governments must now take the opinion of the people into account and because the domestic economic situation has deteriorated considerably. Earlier, the task was mainly to restore the balance of payments equilibrium; now the task is to stabilize the entire economy — and to do so in a troubled political context.

The CMEA has had virtually no role in this process. The main coordinators have been the Western creditors — the International Monetary Fund, international assistance agencies, bilateral donors, and the task forces set up by Western banks or private institutions. Nor has the CMEA contributed a single useful economic policy concept during this process. One might well ask, then, whether any improvement of the CMEA will prove useful.

It was generally believed in the past that although the Eastern European countries openly or implicitly challenged the existence of the CMEA, the Soviet Union believed in its potential. This is no longer the case. Although this position is not yet officially expressed, Soviet scholars are very open in their criticism. B.A. Kheifets, an economist at the Institute of Economics of the World Socialist System, has strongly condemned the present model of the CMEA on three grounds: (1) it is no longer able to sustain traditional trade flows now that the energy-machinery trade pattern no longer fits, (2) it is incompatible with the technological requirements of a modern economy, and (3) it is in open contradiction to the domestic market-oriented reforms that are taking place, because its mechanisms are geared to the old planning system (Kheifets 1988, 90).

The same criticisms are expressed by Margarita Maximova, a researcher at the Institute of the World Economy and a well-known specialist on capitalist integration. Maximova particularly stresses the absence of microintegration at the firm level, arguing that it is precisely such integration that increases the transnationalization of the world economy (Maximova 1989, 67). Maximova has suggested that a new socialist European economic community could be established, comprising a group of interested countries that are at a relatively comparable level of domestic reform. When her proposal was described in 1989, its potential participants included Hungary, Poland, and the USSR. By the end of 1989, it seemed that the German Democratic Republic (GDR), Czechoslovakia, Bulgaria, and even Romania might meet the requirements for such a group. But is this a realistic proposal?

The CMEA countries look increasingly at the EEC and, as a result, are increasingly conscious of their weaknesses. They seek integration with the world economy even more than integration between themselves and dread the consequences for themselves of the evolution of the EEC toward a single Western European market. In 1989, Hungary openly expressed a desire to be more closely associated with the European Free Trade Association (EFTA) and the EEC — to the point of accession. While this may appear to be nothing but wishful thinking, a workable perestroika within the CMEA seems even less realistic. Depending on the nature of its association with West Germany, the GDR too is likely to move toward the EEC, while a more market-oriented Czechoslovakia would also seek a rapprochement of some kind. These three more industrialized and relatively sound economies would then emerge as a new solid economic core in Central Europe. Politically, such schemes will not be opposed by the USSR. The Soviet Foreign Ministry spokesman, Gennadi Gerasimov, has said that the Brezhnev doctrine of limited sovereignty is dead and has been replaced by the "Sinatra Doctrine," as expressed in the famous American singer's tune, "I Did It My Way" (*The New York Times*, 26 October 1989). But which way will that be?

If the CMEA were to disappear immediately — which would please most if not all its Eastern European members — no mechanism is ready to take its place in establishing a new pattern of trade among these countries and the Soviet Union. What seems likely to happen is that these countries will rush to trade with the West. Several signs point in this direction: the probable relaxation of CMEA rules and the lifting of EC import quotas applying only to Eastern Europe and their replacement with some form of preferences for Poland, Hungary, and perhaps Romania.

But how will trade relations among the Eastern European countries be managed in the future? Moreover, while Western experts (see, for example, Balassa 1989) and political leaders (Jacques Delors, in a French television interview in November 1989) point to the attractiveness of the huge Soviet market for the Eastern European countries should perestroika succeed, these countries themselves do not seem to be preparing for such an opportunity. Do they want to leave the Soviet market to the West, or are they convinced that perestroika will fail? Both hypotheses deserve further examination.

Afterword

Events have moved so fast since this paper was written at the end of 1989 that much of it must now be relegated to the annals of history. The forty-fifth session of the CMEA, finally held in January 1990, decided that the members of the organization should begin in 1991 to settle transactions in hard currencies and to trade at world prices. Already in 1990, intra-CMEA trade has begun to shrink, as predicted.

I have become increasingly convinced that some regional grouping is needed in what we may now already call the former-CMEA area of Europe. Such a structure is needed to deal with the legacies of the past and to assist with the restructuring of the domestic economies of the member countries. That the CMEA has failed does not doom all other attempts at regional organization in the area, although such an association must not be considered as a device to prevent the future integration of Central European countries with Western Europe. The road to such regional integration among the CMEA countries is not an easy one, and a managed transition will be required. An offer to assist in this effort at a new regional organization might usefully be put on the agenda of the European Commission, alongside the other East European reforms it is coordinating.

Notes

This piece draws extensively on material prepared for a paper presented at an international conference on "Socialist International Relations: Change and Continuity" organized by the Institute of Social Sciences, Seoul National University, August 24-26, 1988, and on more recent work of the author. Much of the work was done during a stay at the Bundesinstitut für ostwissenschaftliche und internationale Studien, Cologne, Federal Republic of Germany, funded by a fellowship from the Volkswagen Foundation. Along with the literature on the CMEA, the author relied on interviews with V. Sychev, the Secretary General of the CMEA (in 1986, 1988, and 1989); with academician O. Bogomolov, Director of the Institute for the Economy of the World Socialist System; and with I. Shiriaev, the Director of the International Institute on Economic Problems of the World Socialist System (in 1988 and in 1989, a few days before his death in November).

1. The CMEA includes ten countries, but this analysis is concerned only with the industrialized members of this community, that is the USSR and the six Eastern European countries — Bulgaria, Czechoslovakia, the German Democratic Republic (GDR), Hungary, Poland, and Romania; the three developing countries (Mongolia, Cuba, and Vietnam) are not included in the discussion.
2. The Program was published in *Ekonomicheskaia Gazeta*, December 1985, no. 52, along with the Communique of the 41st CMEA Session (17-18 December 1985). For a Western assessment, see Swiatkowski (1989).
3. See Brada 1985, Dietz 1986, Holzman 1986, Marer 1984 (one of the few authors to deny the existence of subsidies), Poznanski 1988, van Brabant 1985, C. Wolf 1985, and T. Wolf 1985.
4. During 1989, Hungary and the Soviet Union explored the possibility of conducting trade in hard currency, at world prices, beginning in 1991. Calculations by both countries showed, however, that if trade were to be conducted in dollars, Hungary, which has had surpluses in its transferable ruble trade with the USSR since 1985, would find itself with a deficit of more than 1 billion dollars, at least during the first years. This would result partly from a decrease in prices for Hungarian manufactures, which are currently sold to the USSR in transferable rubles and cannot be sold to the West because of their poor quality, and partly from a decrease in the volume of Soviet imports as the Soviet Union buys more from the West. For this reason, agreement on this point had not yet been reached by the end of 1989.

5. See Sobell (1989). I also discussed these issues with Ferenc Bartha, the chairman of the National Bank of Hungary, at a symposium on East-West Economic Relations organized by the Drager Foundation in October 1989.

6. The chervonets was a currency introduced in 1922 to restore the Soviet monetary system. Once this task was completed, the currency was withdrawn. For two years, two different currencies coexisted: the paper-money sovznak, which gradually succumbed to hyperinflation, and the chervonets, based on gold, quoted in dollars, and used for payments between enterprises and between enterprises and the State Bank. (This almost surrealistic episode in monetary history is related in M. Lavigne, 1977, "Scythian Gold and the Gold Standard: Soviet Attitudes to Gold and the International Monetary System," *Diogenes* 101-102: 26-49.) Proposals have been put forth recently for creating a similar system to reduce the "monetary overhang" in the USSR and begin a move toward convertibility.

7. It is true that the Soviet Union complained about being unable to import more from its partners when it had a surplus in transferable rubles (until 1987), and its partners began to complain when the Soviet Union developed a deficit in 1988. But the Soviet surplus seems to have been quickly absorbed in the black box of intra-CMEA settlements — perhaps through transactions for services in which the USSR is traditionally in deficit or simply through accounting devices. The Soviet trade deficit is bound to be eliminated by a cut in Eastern European exports.

References

Balassa, B. 1989. "Perestroyka and Its Implications for European Socialist Countries." Paper prepared for the Hungarian-U.S. Round Table held in Budapest, Hungary, November 22-25.

Bautina, N.V. 1986. "Plan i samostoiatelnost v khoziaistvennykh mekhanizmakh stranchlenov SEV" (Planning and Independence in the Economic Mechanisms of CMEA Member Countries). *Eko* no. 9: 157-74.

Belovich, A. 1985. "Koordinatsiia investitsii stran SEV" (The Coordination of Investments of CMEA Countries). *Voprosy Ekonomiki* no. 7: 113-22.

Bethkenhagen, J., and H. Machowski. 1986. "Oil Price Collapse Causes Problems for Soviet Foreign Trade." *Economic Bulletin* 23: 1-4.

Bogomolov, O., ed. 1986. *Soglasovanie ekonomicheskoi politiki stran SVE* (The Coordination of the Economic Policies of the CMEA Countries). Moscow: Nauka.

Brada, J.C. 1985. "Soviet Subsidization of Eastern Europe: The Primacy of Economics Over Politics?" *Journal of Comparative Economics* 9 (March): 80-92.

Brada, J.C. 1988. "Interpreting the Soviet Subsidization of Eastern Europe." *International Organization* 42, no. 4 (Autumn): 639-58.

Cheklina, T. 1989. "Direct Contacts: How To Use Them." *Foreign Trade* no. 9: 2-5. (English version of "Vneshniaia Torgovlia.")

Crane, K. 1986. *The Soviet Economic Dilemma of Eastern Europe*. Rand Publication Series R-3368-AF. Prepared for the U.S. Air Force. Santa Monica, Calif.: Rand Corporation.

Crane, K., and D. Skoller. 1989. "Specialization Agreements: An Effective CMEA Policy Tool?" In *Pressure for Reform in the East European Economies,* vol. 2. Prepared for the Joint Economic Committee, Congress of the United States. Washington, D.C.: Government Printing Office.

Csaba, L. 1988. "CMEA and the Challenge of the 1980s." *Soviet Studies* 40 (April): 266-89.

Desai, P. 1986. "Is the Soviet Union Subsidizing Eastern Europe?" *European Economic Review* 30: 107-16.

Dietz, R. 1986. "Advantages and Disadvantages in Soviet Trade with Eastern Europe: The Pricing Dimension." In *East European Economies: Slow Growth in the 1980s*, Vol. 2. Prepared for the Joint Economic Committee, Congress of the United States. Washington, D.C.: Government Printing Office.

Evstigneev, R.N. 1986. "Khoziaistvennye mekhanizmy stran SEV i integratsia" (Integration and the Economic Mechanisms of the CMEA Member Countries). *Voprosy Ekonomiki* no. 1: 138-45.

Holzman, F.D. 1985. "CMEA: A 'Trade-Destroying' Customs Union?" *Journal of Comparative Economics* 9 (December): 410-23.

Holzman, F.D. 1986. "The Significance of Soviet Subsidies to Eastern Europe." *Comparative Economic Studies* 28 (spring): 54-65.

Janosi, F. 1988. "Theoretical Possibility and Practical Necessity of the Establishment of a Democratic Common Market." Paper presented at the Conference on Alternative Models of Socialist Economic Systems, Gyor, Hungary, March 18-22.

Kamenski, A. 1989. "Foreign Workers in the USSR." *Foreign Trade* no. 8: 9-12.

Karavaev, V. 1989. "Integraciia i rynok" (Integration and the Market). *EkoSot* no. 9: 35-40.

Karpich, V. 1989. "Optovaia torgovlia sredstvami proizvodstva" (Wholesale Trade in Means of Production). *EkoSot* no. 4: 37-42.

Khakhina, L. 1989. "O meste i roli tseny" (The Place and Role of the Price). *EkoSot* no. 5: 27-29.

Kheifets, B.A. 1988. Technologicheskaia model integratsii stran-chlenov SEV" (The Technological Model of the Integration of the CMEA Member Countries). *Izvestiia Akademii Nauk SSR, seria tekhnologicheskaia* no. 6: 82-91.

Koves, A. 1983. "'Implicit Subsidies' and Some Issues of Economic Relations Within the CMEA (Remarks on the Analyses Made by Michael Marrese and Jan Vanous)." *Acta Oeconomica* 31: 125-36.

Krasnoglazov, B., and V. Lavrov. 1989. "O koordinatsii planov SSR s drugimi stranami-chlenami SEV" (The Coordination of Plans by the USSR with the Other CMEA Countries). *Planovoe Khozjajstvo* 3: 2-6.

Lavigne, M. 1983. "The Soviet Union inside Comecon." *Soviet Studies* 35 (April): 135-53.

Lavigne, M. 1985. *Economie internationale des pays socialistes.* Paris: Armand Colin. (Forthcoming in English, *International Political Economy and Socialism*, Cambridge: Cambridge University Press).

Lavigne, M. 1988. "The Evolution of CMEA Institutions and Policies and the Need for Structural Adjustment." In J. Brada, E. Hewett, and T. Wolf, eds, *Economic Adjustment and Reform in Eastern Europe and the Soviet Union.* Durham, North Carolina, and London: Duke University Press.

Linnik, A. 1989. "Konkurs idei, novye stimuly dlia KP NTP" (A Competition of Ideas: New Incentives for the STP Program). *Ekonomicheskaia Gazeta* no. 29 (July): 20.

Marer, P. 1984. "The Political Economy of Soviet Relations with Eastern Europe." In R. Laird and E. Hoffmann, eds, *Soviet Foreign Policy in a Changing World.* New York: Aldine.

Marrese, M. 1989. "Future Developments in the CMEA: Likely Winners and Losers." Northwestern University, Evanston, Ill.

Marrese, M., and J. Vanous. 1983. *Soviet Subsidization of Trade with Eastern Europe: A Soviet Perspective.* Berkeley: University of California, Institute of International Studies.

Marrese, M., and L. Wittenberg. 1989. "Implicit Trade Subsidies Within the CMEA: A Hungarian Perspective." Northwestern University, Evanston, Ill.

Maximova, M. 1989. "Razdumia o perestroike SEV" (Reflections on the Restructuring of the CMEA). *Mirovaia Ekonomika i Mezhdunarodnye Otnosheniia* 4: 67-77.

Mikulskii, K., ed. 1986. *SEV: novyi etap sotrughnichestva* (CMEA: A New Stage of Cooperation). A collection of essays by authors of socialist countries. Moscow: Ekonomika.

Mitrofanova, N. 1989. "Dogovornye tseny kak instrument vzaimodeistviia" (Contractual Prices as Means of Interaction). *EkoSot* no. 5: 20-26.

Nekipelov, A. 1989. "Some Problems of the Restructuring of the Mechanism of Socialist Economic Integration." *Foreign Trade* no. 5: 37-41.

Poznanski, K.Z. 1988. "Opportunity Cost in Soviet Trade with Eastern Europe: Discussion of Methodology and New Evidence." *Soviet Studies* 40, no. 2 (April): 290-307.

Round Table. 1989. "SEV — 40 let: otsenki, predlozheniia, prognozy" (The CMEA Is 40 Years Old: Assessment, Proposals, Prospects). *EkoSot* no. 5: 41-55.

Rusmich, L. 1988. "Tovarno-denezhnye aspekty perestroiki mekhanizma integratsii" (Commodity and Monetary Aspects in Restructuring the Mechanism of Integration). *Ekonomicheskoe Sotrudnichestvo Stran-Chlenov SEV* (The journal of the CMEA Secretariat). Quoted in *EkoSot* no. 3: 51-56.

Sergeev, B. 1989. "Skvoz valiutnye zavaly" (Through Currency Gluts). *Ekonomicheskaia Gazeta* no. 45: 23.

Shelkov, O. 1989. "K obedinennomu rynku: valiutnaia obratimost" (Toward the Unified Market: Currency Convertibility). *EkoSot* no. 6: 26-36.

Sobell, V. 1984. *The Red Market, Industrial Cooperation and Specialization in Comecon.* London: Aldershot, Gower.

Sobell, V. 1989. "Hungary's Push for Trade in Convertible Currency: A New CMEA on the Horizon?" Radio Free Europe Research. RAD Report No. 175.

Swiatkowski, L.U. 1989. "Perestroika of the Council of Mutual Economic Assistance: The New Science and Technology Policy." In *Pressure for Reform in the East European Economies,* vol. 2. Prepared for the Joint Economic Committee, Congress of the United States. Washington, D.C.: Government Printing Office.

Sychev, V. 1986. "Novye rubezhi nauchno-teknicheskogo progressa stran-chlenov SEV" (New Frontier for Scientific and Technical Progress in the CMEA Countries). *Planovoe Khozjajstvo* no. 4: 41-54.

Sychev, V. 1989. "40 let SEV: Itogi, poiski, perspektivy" (Forty Years of CMEA: Results, Quests, Perspectives). *Planovoe Khozjajstvo* no. 4: 3-11.

Terry, S.M., ed. 1984. *Soviet Policy in Eastern Europe.* New Haven and London: Yale University Press, for the Council on Foreign Relations.

United Nations, Department of International Economic and Social Affairs. 1989. "Economic Reform and Integration of Centrally Planned Economies." In *World Economic Survey, 1989.* New York.

Van Brabant, J.M. 1985. "The Relationship Between World and Socialist Trade Prices: Some Empirical Evidence." *Journal of Comparative Economics* 9, no. 3 (September): 233-51.

Van Brabant, J.M. 1988. *Adjustment, Structural Change, and Economic Efficiency: Aspects of Monetary Cooperation in Eastern Europe.* Cambridge: Cambridge University Press.

Wolf, C. 1985. "The Costs of the Soviet Empire." *Science* 230, no. 4729 (November): 997-1002.

Wolf, T.A. 1985. "Soviet-East European Foreign Trade: A Methodological Note." *Comparative Economic Studies* 27, no. 3 (Fall): 83-98.

Bibliography of Publications
by Béla Balassa

Publications by Béla Balassa

Books

Munkahelyi tajekoztato az epitoiparban [Workshop Administration in the Construction Industry]. 1955. (With I. Bakonyi.) Sztalinvaros.

Epitoipari onkoltsegvizsgalat [Cost Audit in the Construction Industry]. 1956. Sztalinvaros.

The Hungarian Experience in Economic Planning. 1959. New Haven: Yale University Press.

The Theory of Economic Integration. 1961. Homewood, Ill.: Richard D. Irwin; London: Allen & Irwin.

Trade Prospects for Developing Countries. 1964. Yale Economic Growth Center Series. Homewood, Ill.: Richard D. Irwin.

Changing Patterns in Foreign Trade and Payments. 1978. (Contributing editor.) New York: W.W. Norton. Revised and enlarged edition, 1970. Third edition, 1978.

Economic Development and Integration. 1965. Lectures delivered at the Centro de Estudios Monetarios Latinoamericanos (CEMLA). Mexico, D.F.

Trade Liberalization among Industrial Countries: Objectives and Alternatives. 1967. Council on Foreign Relations, Atlantic Policy Studies. New York: McGraw-Hill Book Co.

Studies in Trade Liberalization: Problems and Prospects for the Industrial Countries. 1967. (Contributing editor.) Baltimore, Md.: The Johns Hopkins University Press.

The Structure of Protection in Developing Countries. 1971. Baltimore, Md.: The Johns Hopkins University Press for the World Bank and the Inter-American Development Bank.

European Economic Integration. 1975. (Contributing editor.) Amsterdam: North-Holland.

Economic Progress, Private Values, and Public Policy: Essays in Honor of William Fellner. 1977. (Contributing editor, with Richard Nelson.) Amsterdam: North-Holland.

Policy Reform in Developing Countries. 1977. Oxford: Pergamon Press.

The Newly Industrializing Countries in the World Economy. 1981. New York: Pergamon Press.

The Balance of Payments Effects of External Shocks and of Policy Responses to these Shocks in non-OPEC Developing Countries. 1981. (With André Barsony and Anne Richards.) Paris: OECD Development Center.

Development Strategies in Semi-Industrial Economies. 1982. A World Bank Research Publication. Baltimore, Md.: The Johns Hopkins University Press.

Change and Challenge in the World Economy. 1985. London: Macmillan.

Economic Incentives. 1986. (Contributing editor, with Herbert Giersch.) London: Macmillan.

Toward Renewed Economic Growth in Latin America. 1986. (With Gerardo M. Bueno, Pedro-Pablo Kuczynski, and Mario Henrique Simonsen.) Mexico City: El Colegio de Mexico; Rio de Janeiro: Fundaçao Getulio Vargas; Washington, D.C.: Institute for International Economics.

Adjusting to Success: Balance-of-Payments Policy in the East Asian NICs. 1987. (With John Williamson.) Policy Analyses in International Economics No. 17. Washington, D.C.: Institute for International Economics.

Changing Trade Patterns in Manufactured Goods: An Econometric Investigation. 1988. (With Luc Bauwens.) Amsterdam: Elsevier-North-Holland.

Japan in the World Economy. 1988. (With Marcus Noland.) Washington, D.C.: Institute for International Economics.

New Directions in the World Economy. 1989. London: Macmillan.

Comparative Advantage, Trade Policy and Economic Development. 1989. New York: Harvester Wheatsheaf.

Articles and Communications (*since 1959*)

1959

"John Stuart Mill and the Law of Markets." *Quarterly Journal of Economics* (May): 263-74.

"Karl Marx and John Stuart Mill." *Weltwirtschaftliches Archiv* Band 83, Heft 2: 147-65.

"La théorie de la firme socialiste." *Economie Appliquée* (July-December): 535-70.

1960

"Collectivization in Hungarian Agriculture." *Journal of Farm Economics* (February): 35-51.

"Success Criteria for Economic Systems." *Yale Economic Essays* 1: 3-27.

1961

"Towards a Theory of Economic Integration." *Kyklos* 1: 1-17.

"Economies of Scale in the European Common Market." *Economia Internazionale* (May): 3-20.

"Patterns of Industrial Growth: Comment." *American Economic Review* (June): 394-97.

"Economias Externas Dinamicas e Demensao do Mercadeo." *Revista de Ciencias Economicas* (June): 3-17.

"The Factor-Price Equalization Controversy." *Weltwirtschaftliches Archiv* Band 87, Heft 1: 111-23.

"A New Look at Money and Credit." (With Henry C. Wallich.) *Harvard Business Review* (November-December): 70-78.

"Balance of Payments Disequilibrium and Elasticity Pessimism." *Kyklos* 4: 599-603.

1962

"European Integration and the Developing Countries." *Challenge* (May).

"Recent Developments in the Competitiveness of American Industry and Prospects for the Future." *Factors Affecting the United States Balance of Payments*. Washington, D.C.: U.S. Congress Joint Economic Committee.

1963

"Britain, the Commonwealth, and the European Common Market." *Banca Nazionale del Lavoro Quarterly Review* (March): 69-107.

"European Integration: Problems and Issues." *American Economic Review Papers and Proceedings* (May): 175-84.

"The Future of Common Market Imports." *Weltwirtschaftliches Archiv* Band 90, Heft 2: 292-316.

"An Empirical Demonstration of Classical Comparative Cost Theory." *Review of Economics and Statistics* (August): 231-38.

"Observations on Mr. Beckerman's Export-Propelled Growth Model." *Economic Journal* (December): 781-84.

"Trade Projections and Economic Model-Building." *The United States Balance of Payments*. Washington, D.C.: U.S. Congress Joint Economic Committee.

1964

"Tendances futures dans le commerce international." *Bulletin d'Information et de Documentation* (February): 1-13.

"The Capital Needs of the Developing Countries." *Kyklos* 2: 197-206.

"Observations on Mr. Beckerman's Export-Propelled Growth Model — A Rejoinder." *Economic Journal* (March): 240-42; "A Further Note." *Economic Journal* (September): 740-42.

"The Dynamic Efficiency of the Soviet Economy." *American Economic Review Papers and Proceedings* (May): 490-505.

"The Purchasing-Power Parity Doctrine: A Reappraisal." *Journal of Political Economy* (December): 584-96.

1965

"Trade Liberalization and 'Revealed' Comparative Advantage." *Manchester School* (May): 99-121.

"Whither French Planning?" *Quarterly Journal of Economics* (November): 537-54.

"Tariff Protection in Industrial Countries: An Evaluation." *Journal of Political Economy* (December): 573-94.

"Some Considerations on Trade Liberalization in the Atlantic Area." Brussels: Institut d'Etudes Européennes, Université Libre de Bruxelles.

"The Dynamic Effects of Economic Integration with Special Reference to the ECAFE Region." In United Nations, *The Asian Development Bank and Trade Liberalization*. New York.

"Payment Arrangements in Less Developed Countries with Special Attention to the ECAFE Region." In United Nations, *The Asian Development Bank and Trade Liberalization*. New York.

1966

"Les effets du Marché Commun sur les courants d'échanges internationaux." (With Alain Camu.) *Revue d'Economie Politique* 2: 201-27.

"Tariff Reductions and Trade in Manufactures among the Industrial Countries." *American Economic Review* (June): 466-73.

"American Direct Investments in the Common Market." *Banca Nazionale del Lavoro Quarterly Review* (June): 121-46.

"Planning in an Open Economy."
Kyklos 3: 383-410.

"Integraciòn regional y asignaciòn de recursos en America Latina." *Comercio Exterior* (September): 672-85.

"Die Entwicklungsänder in der Weltwirtschaft." In H. Besters and E. Boesch, eds, *Entwicklungspolitik*. Stuttgart: Kreuz Verlag.

"Aussenhandelstheorie." In C. D. Kernig, ed., *Sowjetsystem und Demokratische Gesellschaft*, Vol. I. Freiburg: Herder.

1967

"Trade Creation and Trade Diversion in the European Common Market." *Economic Journal* (March): 1-21.

"Trade Liberalization and the 'Kennedy Round': The Static Effects." (With M. E. Kreinin.) *Review of Economics and Statistics* (May): 125-37.

"American Attitudes towards Trade Liberalization in the Atlantic Area." *Moorgate and Wall Street Review* (Spring): 50-64.

"The Impact of the Industrial Countries' Tariff Structure on their Imports of Manufactures from Less Developed Areas." *Economica* (November): 372-83.

1968

"Effective Tariffs, the Domestic Cost of Foreign Exchange and the Equilibrium Exchange Rate." (With D. M. Schydlowsky.) *Journal of Political Economy* (May / June): 348-60.

"Tariff Protection in Industrial Nations and Its Effects on the Exports of Processed Goods from Developing Countries." *Canadian Journal of Economics* (August): 583-94.

"The First Half of the Development Decade: Growth, Trade and the Balance of Payments of the Developing Countries, 1960-65." *Banca Nazionale del Lavoro Quarterly Review* (December): 333-60.

"The Structure of Protection in Industrial Countries and its Effects on the Exports of Processed Goods from Developing Countries." In *The Kennedy Round: Estimated Effects on Tariff Barriers*. Geneva: UNCTAD.

1969

"Country Size and Trade Patterns: Comment." *American Economic Review* (March): 201-04.

"On the Comparison of Centralized and Decentralized Economies: Discussion." *American Economic Review Papers and Proceedings* (May): 33-37.

"Industrial Development in an Open Economy: The Case of Norway." *Oxford Economic Papers* (November): 344-59.

"Regional Monetary Integration of the Developing Countries: Comment." In R.A. Mundell and A.K. Swoboda, eds, *Monetary Problems of the International Economy*. Chicago: University of Chicago Press.

"Theorie und Praxis Wirtschaftlicher Integration." In C.D. Kernig, ed., *Sowjetsystem und Demokratische Gesellschaft*, Vol. III. Freiburg: Herder Verlag.

Statistical Indicators of Levels of Industrial Development. (With Helen Hughes.) World Bank Staff Working Paper No. 45. Washington, D.C.

1970

"The Economic Reform in Hungary." *Economica* (February): 1-22.

"Growth Strategies in Semi-Industrial Countries." *Quarterly Journal of Economics* (February): 24-47.

"Growth Performance of Eastern European Economies and Comparable Western European Countries." (With Trent Bertrand.) *American Economic Review Papers and Proceedings* (May): 314-20.

"The Impact of the Industrial Countries' Tariff Structure on their Imports of Manufactures from Less Developed Areas: A Reply." *Economica* (August): 316-20.

"The Effective Rates of Protection and the Question of Labor Protection in the United States: A Comment." (With S.F. Guisinger and D.M. Schydlowsky.) *Journal of Political Economy* (September / October): 1150-62.

"Tariffs, Intermediate Goods, and Domestic Protection — Comment and Rejoinder." *American Economic Review* (December): 959-63 and 968-69.

"La politica comercial de Mexico: analisis y proposiciones." *Comercio Exterior* (November): 922-30.

Industrial Protection in Developing Countries. World Bank Report No. EC-175.

1971

"Industrial Policies in Taiwan and Korea." *Weltwirtschaftliches Archiv* Band 105 Heft 1: 55-77.

"Trade Policies in Developing Countries." *American Economic Review Papers and Proceedings* (May): 178-87.

"The Theory of Planning: Discussion." *American Economic Review Papers and Proceedings* (May): 437-39.

"Regional Integration and Trade Liberalization in Latin America." *Journal of Common Market Studies* (September): 58-77.

"Effective Protection in Developing Countries." In J. Bhagwati, R. Jones, R.A. Mundell, and J. Vanek, eds, *Trade, Balance of Payments and Growth: Papers in International Economics in Honor of Charles P. Kindleberger*. Amsterdam: North-Holland.

"Effective Protection: A Summary Appraisal." In H.G. Grubel and H.G. Johnson, eds, *Effective Tariff Protection*. Geneva: General Agreement on Tariffs and Trade and Graduate Institute of International Studies.

"Prospects and Problems of British Entry into the Common Market." In A.K. Ho, ed., *Economic Policies in the 1970's*. Michigan Business Papers No. 57. Ann Arbor, Mich.: University of Michigan.

1972

"Domestic Resource Costs and Effective Protection Once Again." (With D.M. Schydlowsky.) *Journal of Political Economy* (January-February): 63-69.

"The Impact of Taxation on Capital Flows and the Balance of Payments in Canada" and "Capital Movements and Economic Growth in Developed Countries — Comment." In F. Machlup, W.S. Salant, and L. Tarshis, eds, *International Mobility and Movement of Capital*. New York: National Bureau of Economic Research.

"Uses of International Price and Output Data: Comment." In D.J. Daly, ed., *International Comparisons of Prices and Output*, Vol. 37 of *Studies in Income and Wealth*. New York: National Bureau of Economic Research.

"Economias Externas" and "Economia de Escala." In *Gran Enciclopedia Rialp*. Madrid: Proliber S.A.

"Der Neue Wirtschaftsmechanismus in Ungarn." In H.H. Höhmann, M.C. Kaser, and K.C. Thalheim, eds, *Die Wirtschaftsordnungen Osteuropas im Wandel — Ergebnisse und Probleme der Wirtschaftsreformen*, Vol. I. Freiburg: Rombach-Verlag.

"Trade Policy and Planning in Korea." In Sung-Hwan Jo and Seong-Ywang Park, eds, *Basic Documents and Selected Papers of Korea's Third Five-Year Economic Development Plan (1972-1976)*. Seoul.

"Proposal for a Reform of the Tariff, Export Subsidy, and Foreign Exchange System in Korea." In Sung-Hwan Jo and Seong-Ywang Park, eds, *Basic Documents and Selected Papers of Korea's Third Five-Year Economic Development Plan (1972-1976)*. Seoul.

"El Segundo Decenio Para El Desarrollo y la Integraciòn Economica Regional." *Revista de la Integracion* (November): 5-19.

1973

"Regional Policies and the Environment in the European Common Market." *Weltwirtschaftliches Archiv*, Band 109, Heft 3: 402-17.

"Planning and Programming in the European Common Market." *European Economic Review* (October): 217-33.

"Industrial Policy in the European Common Market." *Banca Nazionale del Lavoro Quarterly Review* (December): 311-27.

"Tariffs and Trade Policy in the Andean Common Market." *Journal of Common Market Studies* (December): 176-95.

"Just How Misleading Are Official Exchange Rate Conversions? A Comment." *Economic Journal* (December): 1258-67.

"The Firm in the New Economic Mechanism in Hungary." In M. Bornstein, ed., *Plan and Market: Economic Reform in Eastern Europe*. New Haven, Conn.: Yale University Press.

"The Economics of Fixed Exchange Rates," "Uncommon Arguments for Common Currencies — Comment," and "A Plan for European Currency — Comment." In H.G. Johnson and A.K. Swoboda, eds, *The Economics of Common Currencies*. London: Allen & Unwin.

"Monetary Integration in the European Common Market." In A.K. Swoboda, ed., *Europe and the Evolution of the International Monetary System*. Geneva: Institut Universitaire de Hautes Etudes Internationales.

"Regional Integration of Trade: Policies of Less Developed Countries." In P. Streeten, ed., *Trade Strategies for Development*. London: Macmillan.

"Implications for Integration of the World Economy: Comment." In L.B. Krause and W.S. Salant, eds, *European Monetary Unification and its Meaning for the United States*. Washington, D.C.: The Brookings Institution.

"Policy Issues in Adjustment Assistance: The United States." In H. Hughes, ed., *Prospects for Partnership: Industrialization and Trade Policies in the 1970s.* Baltimore, Md.: The Johns Hopkins University Press.

1974

"Trade Creation and Trade Diversion in the European Common Market: An Appraisal of the Evidence." *Manchester School* (June): 93-135.

"Estimating the Shadow Price of Foreign Exchange in Project Appraisal." *Oxford Economic Papers* (July): 147-68.

"New Approaches to the Estimation of the Shadow Exchange Rate: A Comment." *Oxford Economic Papers* (July): 208-11.

"The Rule of Four-Ninths: A Rejoinder." *Economic Journal* (September): 609-14.

"Monetary Integration and the Consistency of Policy Objectives in the European Common Market." (With Stephen Resnick.) *Weltwirtschaftliches Archiv* Band 110, Heft 4: 564-78.

"Purchasing Power Parity and Factor Price Equalization: Comment." *Kyklos* 4: 879-83.

"Project Appraisal in Developing Countries." In W. Sellekaerts, ed., *Economic Development and Planning: Essays in Honor of Jan Tinbergen.* London: Macmillan.

"Indicators of Protection and of Other Incentive Measures." (With D.M. Schydlowsky.) In N.D. Ruggles, ed., *The Role of the Computer in Economic and Social Research in Latin America.* New York: National Bureau for Economic Research.

"Tariffs." (With Trent Bertrand.) *Encyclopedia Britannica.*

"The Implications for the United States of the Expanded Common Market." *Joint Hearings before the Subcommittee on Europe and the Subcommittee on Foreign Economic Policy of the Committee on Foreign Affairs, House of Representatives, Ninety-Third Congress.* Washington, D.C.: U.S. Government Printing Office.

1975

"Reforming the System of Incentives in Developing Countries." *World Development* (June): 365-81.

"Latin American Trade Policies in the 1970s: A Comment." *Quarterly Journal of Economics* (August): 483-86.

"Economic Integration among Developing Countries." (With Ardy Stoutjesdijk.) *Journal of Common Market Studies* (September): 37-55.

"Trade, Protection, and Domestic Production: A Comment." In P.B. Kenen, ed., *International Trade and Finance: Frontiers for Research.* Cambridge: Cambridge University Press.

"Europe's Role in the World Economy" and "The Scope of A Common Regional Policy." In *Comments on "Economic Policy for the European Community: The Way Forward."* Kiel Discussion Papers 38 / 39. Kiel: Institut für Weltwirtschaft.

"The Korean Tariff Reform of 1971: An Evaluation." In *Collection of Papers on Korean Tariff Reform.* Research Material 75-2. Seoul: Korea Tariff Association.

"Korea's Development Strategy for the Fourth Five-Year Plan Period (1977-81)." In *Discussion Papers on the Guidelines for the Fourth Five Year Plan.* Seoul: Economic Planning Board.

1976

"The 'Effects Method' of Project Evaluation." *Oxford Bulletin of Economics and Statistics* (November): 219-32.

"Monetary Arrangements in the European Common Market." *Banca Nazionale del Lavoro Quarterly Review* (December): 291-308.

"Types of Economic Integration." In F. Machlup, ed., *Economic Integration, Worldwide, Regional Sectoral.* London: Macmillan.

Incentives for Economic Growth in Korea. In Korean. Seoul: Korean Trade Association.

"Definicion y naturaleza de un programa nacional de desarrollo economico." In *Programacion y Economia Mixta.* Mexico: D.F., Asociacion de Economistas Consultores.

1977

"European Monetary Arrangements: Problem Areas and Policy Options." *European Economic Review* (August): 265-81.

"The 'Effects Method' of Project Evaluation Once Again." *Bulletin of the Oxford University Institute of Statistics* (November): 345-53.

"'Revealed' Comparative Advantage Revisited: An Analysis of Relative Export Shares of the Industrial Countries, 1953-1971." *Manchester School* (December): 327-44.

"Export Subsidies in Developing Countries: Issues of Policy." (With Michael Sharpston.) *Commercial Policy Issues*, no 2: 13-50. Geneva.

"Réponse a Charles Prou." *Annales Economiques* 11: 104-6.

"The Income Distributional Parameter in Project Appraisal." In B. Balassa and R. Nelson, eds, *Economic Progress, Private Values, and Public Policy: Essays in Honor of William Fellner.* Amsterdam: North-Holland.

"Effects of Commercial Policy on International Trade, the Location of Production, and Factor Movements" and "Reply to Comments [by Tibor Scitovsky and Melwyn B. Krauss]." In B. Ohlin, P.O. Hesselborn, and P.M. Wijkman, eds, *The International Allocation of Economic Activity.* London: Macmillan.

"Korea's Place in the World Economy during the Fifteen-Year Plan Period." *Korea International Economic Institute Seminar Series* (November): 6-26.

"Industrial and Trade Policy in Portugal." In *Conferencia Internacional Sobre Economia Portuguesa*, Vol. 2. Lisbon: The German Marshall Fund of the United States and Fundacao Calouste Gulbenkian.

"Comments on A Balanca de Pagamentos Portuguesa" and "A Balanca de Pagamentos em Paises de Emigracao." In *Conferencia Internacional Sobre Economia Portuguesa*, Vol.1. Lisbon: The German Marshall Fund of the United States and Fundacao Calouste Gulbenkian.

1978

"Proposals for Economic Planning in Portugal." *Economia* (January): 117-24.

"Export Incentives and Export Performance in Developing Countries: A Comparative Analysis." *Weltwirtschaftliches Archiv* Band 114, Heft 1: 24-61.

"Exports and Economic Growth: Further Evidence." *Journal of Development Economics* (June): 181-89.

"The 'New Protectionism' and the International Economy." *Journal of World Trade Law* (September-October): 409-36.

"Resolving Policy Conflicts in the World Economy." *Banca Nazionale del Lavoro Quarterly Review* (September): 271-81.

"The Economic Reform in Hungary Ten Years After." *European Economic Review* (December): 245-268.

"La exportación de manufacturas en Mexico y la politica de promoción: Comentario." In *Politicas de Promocion de Exportaciones*. United Nations Economic Commission for Latin America.

"The Subsidy and Countervailing Duties Negotiations and the Developing Countries: Comment." In L.L. Perez, ed., *Multilateral Trade Negotiations and the Developing Countries: Possibilities for Special and Differential Treatment Measures*. Washington, D.C.: U.S. Agency for International Development.

"Comparative Advantage and Economic Integration in Western Africa." In *Cahiers Economiques et Sociaux* 2: 108-43. (Institut de Recherches Economiques et Sociales, Université Nationale de Zaire).

1979

"The Changing Pattern of Comparative Advantage in Manufactured Goods." *Review of Economics and Statistics* (May): 259-66.

"The Changing International Division of Labor in Manufactured Goods." *Banca Nazionale del Lavoro Quarterly Review* (September): 243-85.

"Accounting for Economic Growth: The Case of Norway." *Oxford Economic Papers* (November): 415-36.

"Export Composition and Export Performance in the Industrial Countries, 1953-71." *Review of Economics and Statistics* (November): 604-07.

"Incentive Policies in Brazil." *World Development* (November-December): 1023-47.

"Barriers to Development: Discussion." In E. Malinvaud, ed., *Economic Growth and Resources*. Vol. 1, *The Major Issues*. London: Macmillan.

"A 'Stages' Approach to Comparative Advantage." In E. Malinvaud, ed., *Economic Growth and Resources*. Vol. 1, *The Major Issues*. London: Macmillan.

"Intra-industry Trade and the Integration of Developing Countries in the World Economy." In H. Giersch, ed., *On the Economics of Intra-Industry Trade*. Tübingen: J.C.B. Mohr (Paul Siebeck).

1980

"The Tokyo Round and the Developing Countries." *Journal of World Trade Law* (March / April): 93-118.

"Prospects for Trade in Manufactured Goods between Industrial and Developing Countries, 1978-1990." *Journal of Policy Modeling* (September): 437-53.

The Process of Industrial Development and Alternative Development Strategies. Essays in International Finance No. 141. The Frank D. Graham Memorial Lecture held at Princeton University on April 17, 1980. Princeton, N.J.: International Finance Section, Department of Economics, Princeton University.

"Flexible Exchange Rates and International Trade." In J.S. Chipman and C.P. Kindleberger, eds, *Flexible Exchange Rates and the Balance of Payments: Essays in Memory of Egon Sohmen*. Amsterdam: North-Holland.

"Structural Change in Trade in Manufactured Goods between Industrial and Developing Countries." In J. Bognar, ed., *Szechenyi-Emleknapok*. Budapest: Magyarok Vilagszovetsege.

"Portugal in Face of the Common Market." In *2ª Conferencia Internacional sobre Economia Portuguesa*. Lisbon: The Gulbenkian Foundation and the German Marshall Fund.

"Growth Policies and the Exchange Rate in Turkey." In *The Role of the Exchange Rate Policy in Achieving the Outward Orientation of the Turkish Economy*. Istanbul: Meban Securities.

Economic Policies in France: Retrospect and Prospects. Johns Hopkins Working Papers in Economics No. 62. Baltimore, Md.: Johns Hopkins University Press.

Korea during the Fifth Five Year Plan Period (1982-86). Consultant Paper Series No. 10. Seoul: Korea Development Institute.

1981

"Trade in Manufactured Goods: Patterns of Change." *World Development* (March): 263-75.

"The Newly-Industrializing Developing Countries after the Oil Crisis." *Weltwirtschaftliches Archiv*, Band 117, Heft 1: 142-94.

"Policy Responses to External Shocks in Selected Latin American Countries." *Quarterly Review of Economics and Business* (Summer): 131-64.

"The French Economy under the Fifth Republic, 1958-1978." In W.G. Andrews and S. Hoffman eds, *The Fifth Republic at Twenty*. New York: State University of New York Press.

"Schlusswort." In H. Kramer and F. Butschek, eds, *Entindustrialisierung?* Stuttgart: Gustav Fischer.

"Shifting Patterns of World Trade and Competition." In *Growth and Entrepreneurship: Opportunities and Challenges in a Changing World*. Proceedings of the 27th Congress of the International Chamber of Commerce held in Manila in November 1981. Paris: International Chamber of Commerce.

"The Policy Experience of Newly Industrializing Economies After 1973 and the Case of Turkey." In *The Role of Exchange Rate Policy in Achieving the Outward Orientation of the Turkish Economy — II*. Proceedings of a Conference held in Istanbul, Turkey, in July 1981. Istanbul: Meban Securitries.

1982

"Structural Adjustment Policies in Developing Countries." *World Development* (January): 23-38.

"Economic Reform in China." *Banca Nazionale del Lavoro Quarterly Review* (September): 307-34.

The First Year of Socialist Government in France. American Enterprise Institute Studies in Economic Policy. Washington, D.C.: American Enterprise Institute.

"Disequilibrium Analysis in Developing Countries: An Overview." *World Development* (December): 1027-38.

"North-South Business Viewpoint — Financial: Comment." In *North-South: A Business Viewpoint*. New York: United States Council of International Business.

"The United States in the World Economy." In C. Stoffaës, ed., *The Political Economy of the United States*. Amsterdam: North-Holland.

1983

"Economic Policies in Portugal." *Economia* (January): 111-34.

"The Hungarian Economic Reform, 1968-82." *Banca Nazionale del Lavoro Quarterly Review* (June): 163-84.

"Reforming the New Economic Mechanism in Hungary." *Journal of Comparative Economics* (September): 253-76.

"Policy Responses to External Shocks in Sub-Saharan African Countries, 1973-78." *Journal of Policy Modeling* (June): 75-105.

"Outward- and Inward-Orientation Once Again." *The World Economy* (June): 215-18.

"Outward Orientation and Exchange Rate Policy in Developing Countries: The Turkish Experience." *The Middle East Journal* (Summer): 429-47.

"The End of a Liberal Era?" *SAIS Review* (Summer-Fall): 133-42.

"Trade Policy in Mexico." *World Development* (September): 795-812.

"Industrial Prospects and Policies in Developing Countries." In F. Machlup, G. Fels, and H. Muller-Groeling, eds, *Reflections on a Troubled World Economy: Essays in Honor of Herbert Giersch*. London: Trade Policy Research Center.

"The Adjustment Experience of Developing Economies After 1973." In J. Williamson, ed., *IMF Conditionality*. Washington, D.C.: Institute for International Economics.

"New Issues in Trade Policy in the 1980s: Comments." In W.R. Cline, ed., *Trade Policy in the 1980s*. Washington, D.C.: Institute for International Economics.

1984

The Economic Consequences of Social Policies in the Industrial Countries. Bernhard-Harms-Vorlesungen No. 11. Kiel: Institut für Weltwirtschaft.

"L'an III de la politique économique socialiste en France." *Commentaire* (Spring): 13-22.

"Industrial Protection in the Developed Countries." (With Carol Balassa.) *The World Economy* (June): 179-96.

"Adjustment Policies in Developing Countries: A Reassessment." *World Development* (September): 955-72.

"Trade and Trade Relations between Developed and Developing Countries in the Decade Ahead." *OECD Economic Studies* (Autumn): 7-25.

"Prices, Incentives, and Economic Growth." *Weltwirtschaftliches Archiv*, Band 120, Heft 4: 611-30.

"Medium-Term Economic Policies for Portugal." *Economia* (October): 543-67.

"External Shocks and Adjustment Policies in Twelve Less Developed Countries: 1974-76 and 1979-81." *Managing International Development* (November / December): 6-22.

"The Stages Approach to Comparative Advantage Revisited." *Prévision et Analyse Economique* (March): 29-54.

"Adjustment to External Shocks in Developing Countries." In B. Csikos-Nagy, D. Hague, and G. Hall, eds, *The Economics of Relative Prices.* London: Macmillan.

"The Policy Experience of Twelve Less Developed Countries, 1973-1978." In G. Ranis, R.L. West, M. Leiserson, and C. Morris, eds, *Comparative Development Perspectives: Essays in Honor of Lloyd G. Reynolds.* Boulder, Colo.: Westview Press.

"Adjustment Policies and Development Strategies in Sub-Saharan Africa, 1973-78." In M. Syrquin, L. Taylor, and L.E. Westphal, eds, *Economic Structure and Performance: Essays in Honor of Hollis B. Chenery.* New York: Academic Press.

"The Terms of Trade Controversy and the Evaluation of Soft Financing: Comment." In G.M. Meier and D. Seers, eds, *Pioneers in Development.* Washington, D.C.: World Bank.

"The Newly Industrializing Countries After the Oil Crisis: Reply." *Welwirtschaftliches Archiv* 3: 594.

1985

"French Industrial Policy under the Socialist Government." *American Economic Review Papers and Proceedings* (May): 315-19.

"Exports, Policy Choices and Economic Growth in Developing Countries After the 1973 Oil Shock." *Journal of Development Economics* (May-June): 23-36.

"Adjusting to External Shocks: The Newly-Industrializing Developing Economies in 1974-76 and 1979-81." *Weltwirtschaftliches Archiv* Band 121, Heft 1.

"La politique industrielle socialiste." *Commentaire* (Summer): 579-88.

"The Cambridge Group and the Developing Countries." *The World Economy* (September): 201-18.

"The 'New Growth Path' in Hungary." *Banca Nazionale del Lavoro Quarterly Review* (December): 347-72.

"Policy Responses to External Shocks in Hungary and Yugoslavia: 1974-76 and 1979-81." (With Laura Tyson.) In J.P. Hardt and R.F. Kaufman, eds, *East European Economies: Slow Growth in the 1980s*, Vol. 1, *Economic Performance and Policy.* Washington, D.C.: U.S. Congress Joint Economic Committee.

"Policy Experiments in Chile, 1973-83." In G.M. Walton, ed., *The National Economic Policies of Chile.* Greenwich, Conn.: JAI Press.

"The Role of Foreign Trade in the Economic Development of Korea." In W. Galenson, ed., *Foreign Trade and Investment: Economic Development in the Newly Industrializing Asian Countries.* Madison, Wis.: University of Wisconsin Press.

"Public Finance and Social Policy — Explanations of Trends and Developments: The Case of Developing Countries." In *Public Finance and Social Policy.* Detroit, Mich.: Wayne State University Press.

"The Problem of the Debt in Developing Countries." In *The International Monetary System and Economic Recovery.* Torino: Istituto Bancario Sao Paolo di Torino.

"Comparative Advantage in Manufactured Goods in a Multi-Country, Multi-Industry, and Multi-Factor Model." (With Luc Bauwens.) In T. Peeters, P. Praet, and P. Reding, eds, *International Trade and Exchange Rates in the Late Eighties.* Amsterdam: North-Holland.

"U.S. Direct Foreign Investment and Trade: Theories, Trends, and Public Policy Issues — Comment." In A. Erdilek, ed., *Multinationals as Mutual Invaders. Intra-industry Direct Foreign Investment*. London: Croom Helm.

1986

"Liberalizing Trade between Developed and Developing Countries." (With Constantine Michalopoulos.) *Journal of World Trade Law* (January-February): 3-28.

"Comparative Advantage in Manufactured Goods: A Re-Appraisal." *Review of Economics and Statistics* (May): 315-19.

"Intra-Industry Specialization: A Cross-Country Analysis." *European Economic Review* (February): 27-42.

"Policy Responses to Exogenous Shocks in Developing Countries." *American Economic Review Papers and Proceedings* (May): 75-78.

"Five Years of Socialist Economic Policy in France: A Balance Sheet." *The Tocqueville Review* (1985 / 86): 269-84.

"The Determinants of Intra-Industry Specialization in United States Trade." *Oxford Economic Papers* (1986): 220-33.

"Adjustment Policies in Socialist and Private Market Economies." *Journal of Comparative Economics* (June): 138-59.

"Japanese Trade Policies Towards Developing Countries." *Journal of International and Economic Integration* (Spring): 1-19.

"'Dependency' and Outward Orientation." *The World Economy* (September): 259-74.

"The Employment Effects of Trade in Manufactured Products Between Developed and Developing Countries." *Journal of Policy Modelling* (Fall): 371-90.

"Japan's Trade Policies." *Weltwirtschaftliches Archiv* 4: 745-90.

"Economic Development in Small Countries." *Acta Oeconomica* (3-4): 325-40.

"Intra-Industry Trade among Exporters of Manufactured Goods." In D. Greenway and P.K.M. Tharakan, eds, *Imperfect Competition and International Trade: The Policy Implications of Intra-Industry Trade*. Sussex: Wheatsheaf Books Ltd.

"Developing Country Debt: Policies and Prospects." In H. Giersch, ed., *The International Debt Problem — Lessons for the Future*. Proceedings of a conference held in Kiel, Germany in June 1985. Tübingen: J.C.B. Mohr (Paul Siebeck.)

"Selective vs General Economic Policy in Postwar France." In W.J. Adams and C. Stoffaes, eds, *French Industrial Policy*. Washington, D.C.: The Brookings Institution.

"North-South Trade Issues." In I. Frank, ed., *Trade Policy: Three Issues*. Washington, D.C.: Foreign Policy Institute, School of Advanced International Studies, The Johns Hopkins University.

"Mexico's Debt Problem and Policies for the Future." In R. Tremblay, ed., *Issues in North American Trade and Finance*. North American Economics and Finance Association.

"The Timing and Sequencing of a Trade Liberalization Policy: Comment." In A.M. Choksi and D. Papageorgiou, eds, *Economic Liberalization in Developing Countries*. Oxford: Basil Blackwell.

1987

"China's Economic Reforms in a Comparative Perspective." *Journal of Comparative Economics.* (September): 410-26.

"Intra-Industry Specialization in a Multi-Country and Multi-Industry Framework." (With Luc Bauwens.) *Economic Journal* (December): 923-39.

"The Importance of Trade for Developing Countries." *Banca Nazionale del Lavoro Quarterly Review* (December): 437-70.

"Effects of Exchange Rate Changes in Developing Countries." *The Indian Journal of Economics* (October): 203-22.

"French Economic Policy since March 1986." *The Tocqueville Review* (1986 / 1987): 311-24.

"A Primer in Culinary Economics, or How to Maximize the Culinary Utility of the Dollar in Paris." *The Tocqueville Review* (1986 / 1987): 377-415.

"The Extent and the Cost of Protection in Developed-Developing Country Trade." (With Constantine Michalopoulos.) In D. Salvatore, ed., *The New Protectionist Threat to World Welfare.* Amsterdam: North-Holland.

"Trends in International Trade in Manufactured Goods and Structural Change in the Industrial Countries." In L. Pasinetti and P. Lloyd, eds, *Structural Change, Economic Interdependence and World Development,* Vol. 3, *Structural Change and Adjustment in the World Economy.* London: Macmillan.

"Adjustment to External Shocks in Socialist and Private Market Economies" (With Laura Tyson.) In *Structural Change, Economic Interdependence and World Development,* Vol. 3, *Structural Change and Adjustment in the World Economy.* London: Macmillan.

"Economic Integration." In J. Eatwell, M. Milgate, and P. Newman, eds, *The New Palgrave Dictionary of Economics,* Vol 2. London, Macmillan.

"Market Access for Developing Countries." In J. Thesing, ed., *Church and Economy — Common Responsibility for the Future of the World Economy.* Proceedings of the Vatican Symposium on the World Economy, held in Rome, Italy, November. Rome: Mainz, v. Hase & Koehler Verlag.

1988

"The Interest of Developing Countries in the Uruguay Round." *The World Economy* (March): 39-54.

"The Lessons of East Asian Development: An Overview." *Economic Development and Cultural Change* (April): S273-S290.

"The Interaction of Factor and Product Market Distortions in Developing Countries." *World Development* (April): 449-63.

"Japan's Trade Policies in an International Perspective." *Harvard International Review* (April-May): 21-23.

"Inter-Industry and Intra-Industry Specialization in Manufactured Goods." (With Luc Bauwens.) *Weltwirtschaftliches Archiv* 1: 1-13.

"Policy Choices for Developing Countries." *Indian Economic Review* 23, no. 1 (January-June): 27-43.

"Agricultural Policies and International Resource Allocation." *Journal of Policy Modeling* (Summer): 249-64.

"The French Economy at the Outset of the New Septennat." *The Tocqueville Review* (1987 / 88).

"The Determinants of Intra-European Trade in Manufactured Goods." (With Luc Bauwens.) *European Economic Review* (September): 1421-37.

"The Debt Problem of Developing Countries and Proposed Solutions." In K.A. Elliott and J. Williamson, eds, *World Economic Problems*. Washington, D.C.: Institute for International Economics.

"International Trade and Factor Movements in Development Theory, Policy, and Experience: Comments." In G. Ranis and T.P. Schultz, eds, *The State of Development Economics: Progress and Perspectives*. Oxford: Basil Blackwell.

"Ouverture commerciale sur l'extérieur: Commentaires." In P. Guillaumont and S. Guillaumont, eds, *Stratégies de développement comparées: Zone franc et hors zone franc*. Paris: Economics.

Public Finance and Economic Development. PPR Working Paper No. 31. Washington, D.C.: Policy, Planning, and Research, World Bank.

1989

"The Adding Up Problem." *Banca Nazionale del Lavoro Quarterly Review* no. 168 (March): 47-72.

"Temporary Windfalls and Compensation Arrangements." *Weltwirtschaftliches Archiv* Band 125, Heft 1: 97-113.

"The Determinants of Export Supply and Export Demand in Two Developing Countries: Greece and Korea." *International Economic Journal* 3, no. 1 (Spring): 1-16

"Conditions for the Success of Perestroika." *Global Economic Policy* 1, no. 1 (May): 25-30. Journal of the Geonomics Institute for International Economic Advancement.

"Quantitative Assessment of Adjustment Lending." Background paper prepared for *Adjustment Lending: An Evaluation of Ten Years of Experience*. Policy and Research Report No. 1, Washington, D.C.: Country Economics Department, World Bank.

"A Conceptual Framework for Adjustment Policies." Background paper prepared for *Adjustment Lending: An Evaluation of Ten Years of Experience*. Policy and Research Report No. 1. Washington, D.C.: Country Economics Department, World Bank.

"My Life Philosophy." *The American Economist* (Summer).

"The Changing Comparative Advantage of Japan and the United States." (With Marcus Noland.) *Journal of Japanese and International Economies* 3: 174-188.

"France before Europe 1992." *The Tocqueville Review* (1988 / 89).

"Europe 1992 and Its Possible Implications for Nonmember Countries." In J.J. Schott, ed., *Free Trade Areas and U.S. Trade Policy*. Washington, D.C.: Institute for International Economics.

"Subsidies and Countervailing Measures: Economic Considerations." *Journal of World Trade* 23, no. 2 (April): 63-79.

"Outward Orientation." In H.B. Chenery and T.N. Srinivasan, eds, *Handbook for Development Economics*. Amsterdam: North-Holland.

"Introduction to Part III." In N. Islam, ed., *The Balance between Industry and Agriculture in Economic Development*, Vol. 5. London: Macmillan.

Incentive Policies and Export Performance in Sub-Saharan Africa. PPR Working Paper No. 77. Washington, D.C.: Policy, Planning, and Research, World Bank.

Financial Liberalization in Developing Countries. PPR Working Paper No. 55. Washington, D.C.: Policy, Planning, and Research, World Bank.

Adjustment Policies in East Asia. PPR Working Paper No. 280. Washington, D.C.: Policy Planning and Research, World Bank.

Tariff Policy and Taxation in Developing Countries. PPR Working Paper No. 281. Washington, D.C.: Policy Planning and Research, World Bank.

EMENA Manufactured Exports and EEC Trade Policy. PPR Working Paper No. 282. Washington, D.C.: Policy Planning and Research, World Bank.

"Public Enterprise in Developing Countries." Paper prepared for the 43rd Congress of the International Institute of Public Finance, held in Paris in August 1987. Published in German as "Öffentliche Unternehmungen in Entwicklungsländern: Probleme der Privatisierung." *Wirtschaftspolitische Blätter* 516 (1987): 699-713.

"'Revealed' Comparative Advantage in Japan and the United States." (With Marcus Noland.) *Journal of International Economic Integration*, forthcoming.

"Economic Incentives and Agricultural Exports in Developing Countries." Paper presented at the Eighth Congress of the International Economic Association, New Delhi, India, in December 1986.

"Economic Prospects and Policies in Mexico." Paper presented at the Conference on Industrial Organization, Trade and Investment in North America: United States, Canada and Mexico, held in Merida, Mexico, in December 1986.

"Next Steps in the Hungarian Economic Reform." Paper presented at the U.S.-Hungarian Roundtable held in Budapest in December 1986.

"The International Monetary System and Exchange Rate Policies in the Developing Countries." Paper prepared for a Workshop on IMS, EMS, ECU, and Plans for World Monetary Reform organized by the European University Institute and held in Florence, Italy, in April 1987.

"Reflections on Perestroyka and the Foreign Economic Ties of the USSR." (With Michael Claudon.) Paper presented at the Conference on Prospects and Implications of Greater East-West Cooperation, held in Middlebury College, Middlebury, Vermont on September 19-24, 1988.

"The Effects of Interest Rates on Savings in Developing Countries." Background paper prepared for World Bank, *World Development Report 1989*, New York: Oxford University Press.

"U.S. Trade Policy vis-a-vis Developing Countries." Paper prepared for the Symposium in honor of Isaiah Frank, held at the Johns Hopkins University School of Advanced International Studies in October 1988.

"Structural and Sectoral Adjustment Policies of the World Bank." Paper prepared for the Congress of the International Institute of Public Finance, held in Buenos Aires in August 1989.

"Changing Patterns of Specialization in East Asian Developing Countries." (With Marcus Noland.) Paper presented at the Fourth Biannual Conference on United States-Asia Economic Relations, held at Columbia University in New York City in June 1989.

"Policy Choices in the Newly Industrializing Countries." Paper prepared for the Conference, Attempts at Liberalization: Hungarian Economic Policy and International Experience held in Budapest in November 1989.

"International Trade in Services: The United States." PPR Working Paper, forthcoming. Policy, Planning, and Research, World Bank, Washington, D.C.

"Perestroyka and Its Implications for European Socialist Countries." PPR Working Paper, forthcoming. Policy, Planning, and Research, World Bank, Washington, D.C.

Index

Index